Stan Williams was born in 1941 in Toxteth, Liverpool. After graduating and qualifying as a teacher at Liverpool University in 1964, he left home and city to teach in Scotland.

On retiring from teaching in 2001, he was invited to write stories for the British Beatles Fan Club Magazine. This encouraged a return to his native roots and he began to shape these memoirs of a colourful, post-war Liverpool childhood. Besides writing and gardening, he spends too much of his time and energy anguishing over the fortunes of Liverpool FC.

PENNY LANE IS
IN MY EARS AND IN MY EYES

Stan Williams

PENNY LANE IS IN MY EARS AND IN MY EYES

MEMORIES OF
GROWING UP IN POST-WAR LIVERPOOL

Vanguard Press

VANGUARD PAPERBACK

A CIP catalogue record for this title is
available from the British Library.

ISBN: 978 184386 402 8

*Vanguard Press is an imprint of
Pegasus Elliot Mackenzie Publishers Ltd.*
www.pegasuspublishers.com

First Published in 2008

**Vanguard Press
Sheraton House Castle Park
Cambridge England**

Printed & Bound in Great Britain

To the memory of my mother's brother, Stan Thomas, who not
only rescued a family from poverty and restored its dignity,
but also saved my childhood.

Acknowledgements

In the beginning, when the only PC I was familiar with was *Dixon Of Dock Green*, it was Joan Whyte who did all my typing from an illegible longhand. I then bought my first computer, but lack of keyboard dexterity created the misspellings and slack punctuation of a chimpanzee, so I am eternally grateful to Susan McRobbie who, stoically, read all 165,000 words and gave me much needed moral support.

I must also thank my former colleagues at Fraserburgh Academy and the staff at my local newspaper, *The Fraserburgh Herald*, for their fortifying interest and help.

I am grateful to Anne Lomberg at my local bookshop, *John Trail Booksellers*, whose advice and honesty were much appreciated.

I am deeply indebted to Roger Hull, Researcher at the Liverpool Records Office, for providing me with some wonderful photographs of Sefton Park and other magical images from childhood.

During the editorial process, I benefited greatly from the scrutiny given by Chris Chamberlain and Mary Holmes at Pegasus Elliot Mackenzie. Likewise, I am indebted to Spencer Leigh for some vital words of wisdom; also to Kenny Sim for his advice and Mick O'Tool for giving my book a final check.

Needless to say, this three-year task could not have been completed without the constant support of my wife, Liz, and son-in-law, Andy, who, manfully, bore the burden of having to tell me how to use my new computer.

Last, but not least, there is the debt I owe to my brother-in-law, Davy Cardno and close friend, Dave Paterson, whose confidence in my ability to tell a story, finally persuaded me to put pen to paper.

CONTENTS

INTRODUCTION

I have never been able to use a diary like those who so effortlessly and efficiently seem able to map out and regulate their daily lives through the self-discipline of putting pen to paper. I prefer, haphazardly some would say, to burden myself with a minimum of organisational clues and signposts in committing most things to what Oscar Wilde called "the diary we all carry around with us", namely, the blessed memory. The engine room of my own retentive memory lies within a vividly and affectionately remembered childhood. As an only child brought up in a household comprising three generations, I was all eyes and ears; alert and sensitive to all that was going on around me, even if most of it was none of my business.

Within the home, I found a mystery in adult behaviour and conversation, which suggested they were activities well worth monitoring. Like most children of my generation who, when in the company of their elders were expected to be seen and not heard, I grasped the opportunity my supposed dumb ignorance gave me to watch and listen in to all that was going on. It was the same outside the home, either at school or at play, where I loved to observe the interactivity amongst my friends and take in the atmosphere of a place. I was socially involved and a part of it all, yet seemed to have a facility for standing back to get a better perspective on life's more interesting moments. Friends from childhood have declared that my inborn desire to chronicle events is aided by an access to playback, which they do not seem to possess.

For years friends have encouraged me to get down to writing about a Liverpool childhood, which was rich in social experience and inhabited by so many strong personalities. During a long teaching career in Scotland, and at some distance from those formative years of growing up in the Penny Lane/Smithdown Road district of Liverpool 15, I have, on more than one occasion, attempted to transfer my recall of people and events to the security of the printed page before they were lost in the mist of senility. The death of John Lennon in 1980 gave a new stirring to the simmering pot of memories. Yet, even such a strong stimulus failed to convince me that I could create something worthy of the past's strong influences on me.

The death of my father in 1977 and then that of my guardian Uncle Stan, a few years later, finally released me from a debilitating conflict of loyalty to the two dominant role models in my childhood. It was a burden which had persistently disabled me in my desperate search for a true understanding of the paradoxes of family life and relationships at No.52 Borrowdale Road. I still did not feel ready, however, to meet the challenge of being true to the memory of those I loved dearly and who so selflessly cared for me as a child, yet, in their hapless way had such a damaging influence on my emotional development.

In January 2000, *The Daily Mail* published a Dovedale Road School photo taken by notorious teacher Fred Bolt. It showed an eleven-year-old John Lennon, together with Jimmy Tarbuck and the BBC's Peter Sissons, enjoying themselves at an Isle of Man summer camp in 1952. The photo and a subsequent article by Peter Sissons in the *Mail on Sunday* encouraged me to contact Peter, who sat next to me in the A1 class of our Eleven Plus year in 1952-53. Together, we enjoyed the unsurpassed attention and sponsorship of a victorious post-war society, which clearly cherished its children, who were seen as the inheritors of a new age of peace and prosperity for all.

A common theme in our brief exchange of letters was a deep regret for the lost freedoms of childhood. It is a sad comment that, for all the alarming pace of technological and economic progress since 1945, our post-Second World War generation appears to have been uniquely advantaged and privileged compared to the children of today. Those post-war years were correctly described by Peter as being a time of total safety in play, whether in the narrow streets and back lanes of the Penny Lane/Smithdown Road purlieu, or in the country-field-fresh air of the majestic Calderstones and Sefton Parks.

The Fred Bolt photo hints at a gene-pool of exceptionally gifted pupils who attended Dovedale Road County Primary School in the late 1940s and early 1950s. In my letter to Peter Sissons I suggested that the Penny Lane neighbourhood might be due some renewed attention and programme investment from the BBC, not simply because of its eternal association with Lennon and McCartney, but also for its wider relevance to the social and cultural mores of a post-war generation of children who had "never had it so good".

Peter, in turn, asked me if I were the Stan "who used to keep the class enthralled with stories about Tom Thumb to give the teacher a break. They were brilliant." This simple, sweet remark proved to be the final trigger of encouragement I needed to unlock the door on my past and rediscover the childhood habit of being a storyteller. These stories are a fulfilment of a lifetime's desire to communicate the pleasure and the quality of a post-war childhood that, I fear, has been lost forever.

I hope that not-so-cleverly hidden away in these memories and observations, is the personal attempt to come to terms with the failure of my parents' marriage, and the untrustworthy nature of a father who undoubtedly loved me, but practised a cruel deceit on my mother whose subsequent death scarred me emotionally for the rest of my life. It is, I hope, a set of reflections not without humour, for that is the gracious gift which saves us in so many desperate situations of hardship and despair.

Above all, these memoirs are a testament to the unique goodness of my mother's only brother, Uncle Stan, who by intellect and moral courage rose high above his circumstances. Not only did he succeed in lifting his family with him out of dire poverty and an undignified existence, he also managed to heal its self-inflicted wounds and bind it together with his love and support. Without him I would never have been able to complete a lifelong journey to some sort of success, inner peace and self-awareness.

When Lot was told to find but one good man in the plains cities of Sodom and Gomorrah and God would save the people from destruction, he failed to find one redeeming soul. If Uncle Stan had been living down there, amongst that hopelessly lost and wicked society, then the story would have ended differently.

CHAPTER 1

GOING BACK TO No.52 BORROWDALE ROAD

It all began with the unexpected Millennium summer invitation to a special reunion of former pupils who had attended Dovedale Road County Primary in the school's golden years of late 1940s and early 1950s.

"You sat next to Peter Sissons in class. Perhaps you'll get the chance to meet him... and George Harrison."

"John won't be going that's for sure."

"He'll come back with a few of Jimmy Tarbuck's 'Ho, ho... Boom-boom' one-liners," said another family wag.

"Perhaps that's a good reason for not going," I replied.

I had left Liverpool in 1964 to begin a lifelong teaching career in Scotland and had not been back since the apocalyptically grim Thatcher years of the early 1980s. This was my chance to return in more optimistic times to my old neighbourhood of Liverpool 15 and to Penny Lane, that magical trysting place of a cherished Liverpool childhood. My close childhood friend, Ashley, who I had not seen for nearly forty years, had also received an invitation to the special Open Day at Dovedale and with none of the living luminaries able to attend, the organising committee had to make do with an influx of respectable, but socially obscure, post-war baby boomers. In spite of not quite fitting the bill, we were both curious and excited at the thought of a weekend of nostalgia in an old boys' world.

On a bustin' out Saturday morning in June, three buddies got off the bus from town at the Willow Bank pub on Smithdown Road. Ashley and I now had the pleasure of Brad's company after unearthing him from his bunker in Talton Road. Brad was not too fond of society. He was a loner: a difficult guy to pin down. Eventually, he surrendered to our annoying, persistent knocking at his front door. Press-ganged by the bond of friendship forged in the Smithdown Road district of post-war Liverpool 15, he joined us on our trip back to childhood.

The wonderful thing about a pub is that within the space of a short conversation it can create the atmosphere of a time machine. Seated comfortably in the Tardis-like snug of one of my granddad's favourite watering holes and with a pint of best bitter at the ready, we were more than happy to let our revered tribal historian navigate us safely back into the past with an hour or two of fruitful reminiscing. Another couple of pints in town, at the one and only Crack, followed by a nightcap back at our city hotel, was enough fuelling to restore a little of the enthusiasm of my youth. I slept away the next few hours in the deepest, disconnected peace and woke up, as keen as Tom Baker, to get the adventure going.

So, here I was, once more looking down Smithdown Road, and following the slow progress of a convoy of early-morning buses making their way to Penny Lane. I contemplated what surprises might be around the corner in the well-remembered streets, which a lifetime ago had circumscribed the world to me. A short walk took us to the corner of Gainsborough Road, where we turned to make our first port of call at the small, terraced house, which was Ashley's home until, at seventeen, he left for Oxford. One look at the front door and single bay-window of No.26 and I instantly recalled Ashley's unpredictable French mother, blessed with the stunning, fanciful name of Genevieve Alberte Margaritte Daufresne. What a deliciously, high-sounding mouthful to unload on nosy teachers, vicars and the like, who wished to delve into your pedigree. Having a string of exotic names, however, does not make someone a good mother and Ashley spent his happiest days down at No.59 Lidderdale Road, living with his Scots granny and kind-hearted Aunt Mary. That is, apart from the countless hours of playing with me, following a quick dash around the corner to No.52 Borrowdale Road.

Not a word was uttered; only a couple of silent prayers of thanks for our timely removal from such a sad, social decline. Brad could not share our feelings of deliverance, having been selected by an unkind providence to be the one to stay and suffer in the decay of Liverpool 15. Easily as clever as the rest of us at school, Brad enlightened my stuttering progress into maturity with his dry humour and creative intelligence. At fifteen, however, illness stopped his schooling in its tracks and he became a castaway, cut off from his right to a life of rich opportunity. Instead, he evolved, like a Sméagol, into one of the local eccentric personalities of the darkened environment into which he had been cast. Now a loner and a recluse in his own house, he suffered a diminishing sense of identity in the community he once knew and relied upon to sustain his humanity.

"What a fucking diabolical mess!" The three of us had taken a short cut into the next street, using one of the many narrow "jiggers", which had acted as the arteries of our travel and play as children. I did not need the incitement of Brad's colourful expletives to start me waxing lyrical about Thatcher, enemy of the people of Liverpool.

"So, there's no such thing as society, did I hear this bloody woman say, back in 1980? For what she did to communities like this, she should be hijacked from her retirement bunker and fucking well dragged up here by a vanload of scallys then forced to camp out in one of these infectious alleys for a few weeks."

I was glad to be out on the pavement of Gainsborough Road and breathing the comparatively fresh air of the traffic-filled streets. These narrow lanes, hardly wide enough for my granddad to have once pushed me along, seated on top of a wooden hand-cart and dressed up as a redskin chief, were now festering eyesores, littered with an accumulation of the filthy rubbish, which came spewing out from yards of the back-to-back houses.

We crossed at the top of Gainsborough Road, looking for one of the wider alleyways, which connected all the streets running parallel to Garmoyle Road. "Jesus!" said Brad. "The lane... it's all locked up like Walton jail." The lane was, indeed, fenced off like the entrance to a military camp. "What a fucking disgrace! I'm really sorry, lads... This is not nice, not nice at all. This is not what you came back to see, is it?" The poor guy was embarrassed for our sake about the Stalinisation of the old neighbourhood. With an involuntary leap away from the two us, he interrupted the slow progress of a sad-looking, middle-aged woman, trundling two plastic bags loaded with shopping. "Er... what's all this about, then missus?" Brad had little time for social etiquette with the people he now lived alongside, whom he was forced to regard suspiciously, rather than rely on as sympathetic neighbours and fellow sufferers. "What's goin' on 'ere in a free country, like?" The woman stopped, dumping her carrier bags down on the pavement to give her tired arms the rest they had been begging for, all the way from the shops on Smithdown Road.

Brad was lucky to have picked on such an obliging person, given that she had been bullied into a stalag mentality by years of fear and resignation. She had been won over to Brad's blunt line of questioning, rather less by his charm than by the fact he was referring to something which vexed her as clearly as it did him. "You won't get into these back lanes now, son... not without a set of keys." Ashley and I took great delight in the woman calling Brad "son". He had more than asked for the sarcasm by dyeing his cropped, greying hair a disastrous, alerting shade of tangerine. Although an acceptable match for his orange T-shirt, the hairdo clashed, alarmingly, with his fifty-eight-year-old face, giving him the look of a Jimmy Saville who'd just been Tango'd.

"It's the crime, son... burglary, vandalism, mugging, you name it. You can't leave your house for a minute without the fear that someone will get in. It's all been made secure. You can't get in and out of your own house now unless you're a member of the friggin' A-Team." These were changed times from the freedom of the 1940s, when we ran like the wind down these same, safe alleyways playing our games of Tick and Re-Alleyo. In those days, you could fall and graze an elbow without having to report to Sefton General Outpatients for an anti-tetanus jab. Parents had no alarm bells ringing about us falling on broken beer bottles or contaminated needles.

As we walked down Garmoyle Road towards Borrowdale Road, the neighbourhood took on a warmer, friendlier look. To my surprise and the uplifting of my spirit, the old street of attractive terraced houses, each with the luxury of double-bay windows, had defied the decay creeping into Liverpool 15 from the ruined, nineteenth century mansion houses of Upper Parliament Street.

Standing in front of No.52 Borrowdale once more affected me deeply. I was reminded of the Jesuit dictum, "Give me the child from nought to seven and I will give you the man." The bold statement of religious intent also tells the blunt truth about a family's role and influence over an infant, for good or ill.

This was the pit-stop of an energetic and excited child, where I would pull in like a little Juan Fangio – all fuel and energy, momentarily spent – to rest and be replenished for my next take-off into life: the place where my character and personality was shaped by the people and events of my earliest years. Here, I was Crown witness to the impact of adultery on a family; the deceitful unnerving behaviour of my dad and his mistress, Hilda, who stalked my mum through the last few, unhappy years of her life. Accompanying me into the emotional storm, which broke after my mother's death, was the reassuring presence of Uncle Stan.

From the pavement of Borrowdale Road I stared in at the left bay window of my old home, waiting for the Playschool presenter to transport me through into my Uncle Stan's study as it was, in the late 1940s. I used to stand mesmerised by the tall, glass-fronted bookcases containing such overpowering titles as *Kant's Metaphysics of Experience* and the foreboding *Concept of Dread,* by someone with the sinister name of Kierkegaard. As a seven-year-old, who still had a Mickey Mouse gas mask in his bedroom, I could be forgiven for believing that here was yet another dreaded German, whose war with me was not quite over. My favourite place to sit was at my uncle's heavy, oak desk, which he had planted near the window alcove. This was the sanctified seat from where his intelligence and spiritual strength flowed throughout the house. I would lock myself away in the room for hours; writing and drawing on the spacious surface, which my outstretched arms and fingers could never hope to span. I would try to decipher the ghostly hieroglyphics, patterned on the giant leather pad of blotting paper in a jumble of scattered letters, words, and disconnected sentences; the tiny, fragmented reminders of my uncle's unseen presence in the room.

The large, black telephone, sitting mightily on the desk was such a conspicuous item of middle-class dignification that it both impressed and intimidated me. Installed soon after my uncle returned from Oxford, this status symbol of the business and professional man was an essential requirement for Stan Thomas's busy social and sporting life. Pop claimed that the "monstrous new-fangled gadget" in the house was all the proof needed that he was now a man out of kilter, in an Orwellian world of impersonal communication; a dehumanised cipher. "That contraption is sinister Nellie. We'll soon all be at the mercy of a silent, secretive, bureaucracy, listening in to tap into our innermost thoughts."

When forced to answer the telephone, Pop got into the same diminished state of subjugation as he did when talking to Dr Smellie. I could not understand why my clever granddad tried to talk so properly to the good family doctor, and in doing so dropped more H's than the number of stutters George VI made in a speech to Parliament. Swilling around in Pop's exceptional intelligence was the residue of a working-class respect for people who had a status beyond his habit of being social with. Once in a while, Dr Smellie drove his posh, black Bentley car up to our front door to keep me from the dreaded diphtheria, or ease me through bouts of croup. Perhaps, part of Pop's problem was that, until my seventh birthday, he had been forced to pay his six shillings for medical attendance, while Aneurin Bevan had turned the tables on the newly created GP, making him come out to cure me for nothing!

Uncle Stan, the scholarship concession from the slums, had been top in a class of the city's brightest pupils, at the Liverpool Collegiate; Dr Smellie had been many places below him. That still seemed clever enough to let the man sound my chest. However, this knowledge made me ever more puzzled as to why Pop was unable to adjust his over-inflated social respect for this new servant of the State. Too much social history was involved to cure my granddad of his class conditioning. My respect for my uncle, meanwhile, had soared through the roof.

I was totally unaware of the burden my uncle had taken on, in providing for the family's needs. With his parents on a meagre pension, Mum unable to work and her absentee husband's contribution to my upkeep a minimal one, we were all fed and clothed from an overdrawn account with Martins Bank, at the bottom of the street. In 1937, out of a desire to bring some desperately needed income into the home, Stan Thomas left school half-way through his final year at the Liverpool Collegiate. He went to work for the GPO, but lasted only one day after being subjected to the swearing and blasphemy of the workmen he was sent out to supervise.

"For Christ's sake, Ernie!... You've severed the bleedin' cable again you brainless bastard. If I've told you fuckin' once, I've told you a fuckin' dozen times to be more bloody careful with those cutters, you silly twat."

My father would often tell me, "Your Uncle Stan is too good for this world." He was, no doubt, reflecting on the hurt others could, innocently at times, inflict on his brother-in-law's refined mind and pure heart. Personally, I cannot thank the men who came out with such disturbing profanities enough, for making my uncle beat a hasty retreat back to the classroom and pass his exams for university. I have always had a lenient attitude to the earthiness that swills around in the sweat and toil of working men, because it had guaranteed me such a quality of life as a child.

I looked down Borrowdale Road and realised that Ashley and Brad had disappeared into the next street. I should have joined them, but the memory of my old home and the towering presence of Uncle Stan placed me in front of one of the many mezuzahs, which had been firmly screwed into the doorposts of every room in the house.

"Why don't we take them off? The little metal boxes on the doors, I mean."

We were sitting in the back living room where Nan and Mum had encouraged a discussion about the need to decorate the hall and stairs. Before our arrival at No.52 a succession of devout, Orthodox Jewish families had sanctified the home with the small tokens of God's presence.

"No Mum. We must leave them as they are... To be saved from the bombing which destroyed our house in Fern Grove and then be given this wonderful home is an answer to prayer." Stan looked across at his mother. "They must stay in place, to remind us of God's leavening of family life, and as a blessing on our tenancy."

When Uncle Stan spoke like that no one wanted to argue with him. For starters, he had just played a heroic part in the war against Nazi anti-Semitism. More than that, he came into the world with a tolerance of others, which sprang from his belief that the love of God was poured down on all mankind. If I possessed but a fragment of his spiritual insight, it might explain why I wanted to touch the tiny relics as I passed by or, when I was alone, offer my silent respect before their sentinel presence.

One Saturday morning, with all the adults out of the house, my intense curiosity as to what seductive secret each little metal case might contain finally got the better of me. In the determined fashion of an incarcerated Count of Monte Cristo, I used one of Mum's hair-clips to carefully prise out the small piece of rolled up parchment without causing any damage. Like Indiana Jones having just

26

excavated the Ark of the Covenant, I opened it with great care. It contained a text made even more mysterious and alluring by being written in what looked to me like a forgotten language. Had I been able to translate the ancient Hebrew words from Deuteronomy 6: 4-9 I would have read:

"The Lord our God is the one Lord. And thou shalt love the Lord thy God with all thine heart, and with all thy soul, and with all thy might. And these words, which I command thee this day, shall be in thine heart. And thou shalt teach them diligently unto thy children, and shall talk of them when thou sittest in thine house, and when thou walkest by the way, and when thou liest down, and when thou risest up…"

The unfathomable text continued, but I did not need to read a single word of it to sense the holiness of the fragment of scripture. For all its insignificant size and appearance, the tiny casket contained words with the power and authority to command the mind of a Chosen People down the thousands of years since Moses first talked with God up in the mists of Mount Sinai. The ancient text, its eternal purpose unhidden from my child's sense of what was good and untarnished, was testimony to my dear uncle, living every day of his life in the fear and service of God. Curiosity had led me to discover something which, far from being a threat to my well-being, was a protector and guardian of the soul.

In a solemn mood I poked the sacred piece of paper back into its container. Gently, I placed a finger against it, before going out to meet up with my pals for yet another game of football.

"Hey, Stan… We're off!"

From the bottom of the street I could sense Ashley and Brad becoming impatient with my dilly-dallying. I breathed in deeply at the thought of my uncle's righteousness and remembered his unlimited forbearance of my impulsive, eccentric, childhood behaviour – especially after the death of my mother.

I ignored the shouts of my pressed for time friends. My memory was jipping-off again, back to a day in the late 1940s, when left to my own devices in my uncle's front room, I was determined to turn myself into a little librarian for the day. In 1950, apart from a beginner's Meccano set, my uncle's tiny, personalised stamp was the closest thing I could get my hands on to any form of technology. With the exaggerated sense of power felt only by the paper chasing bureaucrats of the new Welfare State, I merrily stamped "S H Thomas" for as long as a boring day's recuperation from chicken pox would allow.

Later that evening, after he had come home from school, Stan Thomas settled down in his study to decide which of his two latest book club purchases he would read first. "Umm, yes, I think I'll have a dip into Van der Post's *The Lost World of the Kalahari*. Enchanting stuff... Or should I make a start with the first few chapters of Thor Heyerdahl's *Kon Tiki Expedition*?"

"Hello... What on earth?" S H Thomas got up, went over to the nearest bookcase and took down a couple of his precious hardbacks. He quickly flicked through their pages. He took down a few more and then tried another shelf... and another. The virus had spread from bookcase to contaminated bookcase. "He's done the lot! They are all stamped... page after page... the whole blessed lot! Stanley! Where's little Stan, Nell?"

Like Bilbo Baggins, little Stan had completely vanished! Whisked away from punishment, I was once again standing in front of No.52 Borrowdale, having grown up long ago. I smiled in fond reflection of my uncle's forgiving and fair nature, remembering the cancellation of my *Beano* and *Radio Fun* for the next week. For a good thirty minutes I had remained in a trance, rooted to the pavement, trapped in the past.

"Come on Stan. We can't stay any longer. Not if we're going to get to Dovedale on time."

Dragging myself away, I joined my friends for the remainder of our slow walk to Penny Lane and the afternoon fete at Dovedale Road School. The school reunion left many memories for me to savour over the next few weeks. However, on the long train and bus journey home to my family in Aberdeenshire, it was the visit to Borrowdale Road which possessed my thoughts. Once back in Fraserburgh, I began to write about the childhood which had shaped me for better or worse.

CHAPTER 2

A GRIMM TALE OF CHILDHOOD ABDUCTION

On May 4 1945, in a tent on Luneburg Heath, "good old Monty" – for that's how people at the time seemed to refer to Field Marshall Montgomery – took the surrender of the German High Command and the war in Europe officially came to an end. I was nearly four-years-old and had begun to sneak an occasional freedom from under the skirts of Mum and Nan, out into Borrowdale Road with its impressive railway embankment at the top end of the street and the scary traffic of Smithdown Road at the other.

With tension evaporating like sweat on the brows of the eighteen Nazi war criminals awaiting trial at Nuremburg, I joined the older children as a curious onlooker to their games and victory celebrations. At one party in a house across the street, amidst all the excitement of the collective triumph over a very bad man with a nasty moustache and one hand held in the air as if asking to go to the toilet, I shit my pants which had me taken home before the jelly and ice cream were dished out.

"I go hide now… Here I am!" As I attempted to join in my first games of hide-and-seek, often locked away by some mean minded seven-year-old in the terrifying darkness of a brick air raid shelter which still stood in the street opposite my front door, I had no idea how much more dangerous a place the world had become in the summer of 1945 with the unleashing of the Atomic Bomb on Hiroshima and Nagasaki.

Oblivious to the fearful dawn of the nuclear age, my little Scouser's world was bent upon wakening to a day of peaceful play, within a community alive with friendly faces and warm, optimistic voices. Here, I was safe amongst liberated children who were being offered a security and freedom like no other generation before or since.

Now that the extreme dangers and deprivations of wartime were over, Mum and Nan became as obsessive about shopping with little or no money to spend as they were determined to go, twice a week at least, to the cinema and dream on about Robert Donat or Ronald Coleman. Dad and Uncle Stan were, doubtless, sitting somewhere twiddling their thumbs and waiting for their demob papers, when the two women began taking me on the No.46 tram to the shops in London Road.

London Road was a thriving thoroughfare; one of the main civic arteries, leading out from Lime Street and the city centre to the districts of Kensington and Wavertree. Many of its shops were more accommodating to the meagre purses of housewives in the years immediately after the war. The big T J Hughes store was so considerate of my mother's tight budget that any of my clothes not purchased from the Co-op, near Penny Lane, would be bought there.

My main entertainment in T J Hughes came from watching Mum pay for her items at one of the big counters. Before wrapping up a purchase with brown paper and string, the assistant would write out a sales-note, exercising the care in handwriting and the attention to detail of a Soviet Commissar sending someone to a labour camp for the next twenty years. After your pounds, shillings and pence were carefully enclosed within the bill, the screwed-up bundle was stuffed inside a tiny metal canister, which looked like Flash Gordon's space ship without its tail fins. It was then magically placed in a hole in the wall and blasted off along miles of pipes; up and across a galaxy of walls and ceilings to an office on the far-flung planet of Ming the Moneybags. Uncharacteristically merciful with the correct amount of change, Ming would send it, together with his Imperial stamped receipt, back down the same pneumatic shuttle as a sign of goodwill to all earthlings who cared to shop at T J Hughes.

Like a pair of moths drawn to the smell and textures of a wardrobe full of heavily scented old clothes, the two Nellie Ediths had the need, born out of a pre-war culture of poverty, to visit a certain second-hand clothes shop at the Crown Street end of London Road. It was no Owen Owen, or Bon Marché, that's for sure. Dusty, wooden floorboards strained and creaked under the weight of row upon row of overcoats, jackets, suits and dresses. Where they all came from only heaven and the Merseyside Society of Undertakers knew. On surrendering to Monty, had every German been forced to empty their wardrobes as reparation to the seriously underdressed ladies of war-devastated Liverpool? In a warehouse dedicated to the principle of "waste not, want not", mountain-high shelves of boots, shoes, hats, gloves and handbags lined the walls on the three or four floors of the war-damaged building which had, unlike the row of shops next door to it, survived the Luftwaffe's heavy bombing of the city.

My two ladies did not give a fig for the snobbery attached to the wearing of second-hand clothes. Many decent, poor people had to do the same thing. It is hard to ascribe an attitude of priggishness to a five-year-old, but I had my reservations about stepping into another person's clobber, especially items which might have been gracing a corpse only a few days earlier. That is why the shop appealed to me. It was more than a little spooky and I could imagine it as some great repository, where dead folk came to slip out of their unwanted togs before stepping out into an afterlife where the most expensive of brand new suits and dresses were handed out free.

Even in such hard times, those needy souls who were more than ready to adopt a second-hand jacket or skirt would draw the line at getting into someone else's underwear. Another hand-me-down item of clothing no one would ever contemplate bringing home was shoes. "If... when you're my age... you don't want to take a week to complete an afternoon's walk around Sefton Park then on no occasion must you wear second-hand shoes, Stanley." Pop was in the backyard, holding a hot shoemaker's iron. He broke away from applying a masterful black wax finish to the soles of his newly-repaired Sunday best to warn me. "You don't want to transfer the deformities of someone else's feet onto the elegant pair of trotters you have been blessed with, Stanley." He smiled and added, "Especially when it comes to football boots... or you might find yourself taking a corner when you run up to take a penalty."

While the women rummaged through the countless rows of skirts and blouses, I would slip away into a dense jungle of overcoats and military greatcoats, where the strong smell of mothballs made me feel pleasantly dizzy. To keep in touch with the progress of the two women, I occasionally peeled back the lapels of my naval officer's serge wigwam. Taking a gasp of air and a final peep through the buttonholes of an ex-Army or RAF greatcoat, I would slide down into one of my tailored caverns of darkness and safety.

If Ashley was taken along with me, the best part of an hour would quickly pass by without the women noticing what we were up to in our world of childhood fantasy. Leaving them to rake for a bargain, the two of us turned the countless racks of clothing into dark, dense forests inhabited by elves and dwarfs. There was no Darth Vader; none of Sauron's one-eyed trolls, deadly orcs and Ringwraiths to worry us in those days. Walt Disney had seen to it, however, that giants, sorcerers, witches and dragons were on the go; even the Big Bad Wolf and Wee Willie Winkie scared children to their beds in those days. We could conjure up our own monsters at the drop of a hat, as we battled our way to daylight and freedom past the assembled ranks of some evil queen's hand-me-down warriors.

Next to the clothes shop there was a large bombed building site, which had become the venue for those who liked the entertainment of the side-show. Here jobless extroverts attempted to prise some loose change from passing shoppers by trying their hand at juggling, sword-swallowing, fire-eating and even knife-throwing. My mother did not like to linger at so many temptations to tragedy and disaster, but I would beg her to stop and let me have a free peep at this imitation of the world of the travelling circus.

One day, my ring-side seat was lit up by the performance of a man who had just raised the spirit of Harry Houdini on his Ouija board. Unburdened by any patriotic obligation to consider himself part of Clement Atlee's plan for post-war economic recovery through hard work, but as desperate as Dan for a night's drinking money, the feckless fool had signed himself up to an unpredictable career as an escapologist. He was the stooge to a younger man who was doing all the talking, whilst holding a large sack in one hand and a fistful of dangling chains in the other.

The older man had stripped down to the waist. He combined the mummified features of Keith Richards with the knotty sinewy body of Mick Jagger or Iggy Pop. Indeed, he could have been the grandfather of any one of the Rolling Stones, save pretty boy Brian Jones. Who needs drugs and Rock'n'Roll when you have survived Belsen on a diet of workouts and circuit training? Thank God he was fit, because his survival would now depend on it.

The younger man went into a fanfare of baloney to arrest our attention. "My pal Hughsie here rehearsed his skills in a German prisoner-of-war camp, ladies and gentlemen. Once again he will defy the sack prison which I hold before you, just like he defied the Germans to lock him up for more than five minutes back in Colditz in 1942, 1943... and then twice in 1944!" He bound the older man from tip to toe in chains, making a great display of padlocking his wrists and feet. The would-be Houdini then stepped into the large sack, which was pulled up over his head and tied with a piece of rope. "To make an escape doubly difficult, I am now going to wind another chain around the sack... There we are, ladies and gentlemen... our Lazarus is now ready to burst forth from his tomb within three minutes as timed by this stopwatch."

At the age of five you are far from sure about many things and you certainly don't think, "Umm... three minutes. Have they practised this trick for a week at breakfast time, while they were waiting for the eggs to boil?" However, I guessed the man's chances of seeing the light of day again to be as slim as my Pop asking for a boiled egg at breakfast, in place of his customary morning fry-up. Well into the second minute of his hopeless struggle the sack fell over on to the ground, but still the writhing and grunting continued from within. Time and being tied up waits for no man and the crowd had begun the countdown. "Two minutes!" Three... four... five more minutes went by. "It's time to come out la. The pubs open in half-an-hour!" The last remark got to the man in the sack. His movements became more desperate and violent as he saw six pints of bitter flash by along with the rest of his life. The grunts, moans and cursing got louder and louder. Seven or eight minutes passed. "Hey, mate. The war's over. Hitler's dead. It's safe now. Come out, come out, wherever you..." Suddenly, the laughter and ribbing stopped as the body in the sack went "Aahh!"… before going limp and silent, like the crowd.

That was it as far as my mum was concerned. "Come on," she said to Nan, "We're getting Stanley away from this nonsense." I was promptly dragged from a scene of growing panic, like a terrier pulling on its lead, having sniffed out something compelling and irresistible in the backside of a passing cocker-spaniel. People rushed forward to grapple with the man's chains and open the sack, while I was led off to Woolworth's toy counter in a futile attempt to distract my mind. I think the man must have survived because there was no post-mortem later that evening as my mum looked, in vain, for the anticipated tragic headline on the front page of the *Liverpool Echo*. Haunted by the fate of the hapless Houdini of London Road, I could never imagine that I would soon be abducted, in broad daylight, off the street and placed in a sack of my own.

I was playing out in Borrowdale Road with another toddler. We were sitting on the edge of the pavement and drawing on the concrete slabs with small stones picked out of the gutter. My bad luck was to be in front of the house of a reclusive spinster, who lived a few doors down from No.52. The second piece of misfortune was to be playing with a five-year-old maniac from a tough family in the next street. Inexplicably, the boy picked up a piece of brick and threw it through one of the windows in the front door of the spinster's house. This was my first exposure to an act of vandalism. In stunned wonderment at the stellar-burst of splintering glass, I remained fixed to the spot while the little hooligan buggered off at high speed!

A rabid woman rushed out of her front door and onto the pavement. Trapped like a startled rabbit in the headlights of her rage I accepted my fate. I was grabbed by the collar, hauled inside her house and marched into the front parlour. The room had heavy, lace curtains on the windows; a perfect concealment for séances on a wet afternoon and for any other evil intention she might have towards me. I was locked in the room with a tick-tocking grandfather clock and a giant aspidistra, until the woman quickly returned with a sack like the one Mr Kenwright humped off his lorry and on to his back when he delivered our coal. "Oh… No!" I've seen this trick done in London Road and it did not quite work out for the man who was put in the sack! Is she going to tie me up in chains, too, before giving me three minutes to get out alive?"

The woman, who I guess must have been in her sixties, spread the neck of the sack open on the floor; she then lifted me up and plonked me down in it. I struggled and shouted for help, but at five you don't have much clout against an adult who wants to do you a mischief. Ask any infant, newly enrolled at school in 1946, and they would confirm the power and authority of a menopausal, bullying spinster placed in front of a class of fifty little kids. Before I knew it, she had the bloody thing pulled up to my neck and was about to tie it with a piece of cord. It was a script straight from the darkest pages of Hansel and Gretel. A nasty old witch had snatched me away. At that very moment she probably had the kitchen oven turned on at the regulo for roast pork. However, before she could over-excite herself at the thought of basting me with lard, on the kitchen table, there was a loud knock on the front door.

"Stanley... Are you there, Stanley?" The boy who threw the brick had redeemed himself by getting word to my house that a horrible old lady had dragged me off the street.

At the sound of my mother's voice the woman quickly let go. There was no command to "Keep your mouth shut if you know what is good for you!" I was simply delivered to the front doorstep as if nothing untoward had happened. "What on earth do you think you are doing taking my child into your house?" The woman tried to conjure up an argument by pointing to the broken glass lying inside her vestibule, but it was swept aside by my mother's outrage. "I don't give a damn about a broken window. When the police come to sort this out I'll be telling them about a kidnapping, while you can try to impress them with your tale of broken glass!"

I felt much safer hearing that the law would soon be summoned to sort the child-snatcher out. In those days, there was no better defence for an infant than the combination of an outraged mother and a policeman. When I got back home, I recounted my bizarre tale to Pop, who wondered whether reading *Grimm's Fairy Tales* to me had been a rash mistake. "Well, you see Nell, he's only five and without adult witnesses to back up what sounds like the outpourings of a very vivid imagination, who is going to take the story too seriously? He's safe and sound and that's all that matters."

There was a police constable who lived around the corner in Garmoyle Road and Mum was not finished with the matter. I wished that she had not pushed things any further, because the boy from Langdale Road had done me a big favour – the equivalent of ripping up my invitation to a Michael Jackson sleep-over at the Never Land ranch – and paid for it with a visit from two police officers! He had his comics stopped for weeks and in his house you could not have been given a worse punishment. I was just starting to be bought a weekly *Comic Cuts*. The lad had older brothers and between them they had purchased, swapped or stolen what I later realised had been a mighty selection of *Hotspur, Wizard, Rover* and *Adventure* comics, which lay stacked in great piles along the hall skirting boards. The current market value of that late 1940s treasure trove could have purchased every one of the ninety houses in Langdale Road back in 1946!

The policeman had stern words with my kidnapper, but that was all he could do when the main prosecution witness was barely out of nappies. It took me many months before I stopped quickening my step every time I passed No.42 Borrowdale Road. Habitually, I would take a sideways glance at the curtains of the front room for a sinister presence, waiting for the next innocent to cross her threshold.

I wondered whether there would still be an empty sack, kept at the ready for the next little child who took her fancy. I imagined the old crone sitting at her kitchen table and getting somewhat tearful over the small boy from up the street who got away. I had the disquieting notion that I continued to appeal to her discriminating appetite; served up on a platter and placed in the centre of her table presenting a done-to-a-turn, crackling countenance with a green Bramley jammed in my mouth! I loved all sport at school, but declined to enter the popular sack race at Lidderdale Road Infants, leaving it to those more comfortable with the feeling of being trussed up like a pig in a poke.

CHAPTER 3

MY GREAT ESCAPE FROM THE NURSERY IN SEFTON PARK

There was a wartime day-nursery in Sefton Park. It was at the end of Ibbotson's Lane, next to the Old Farm Field. In the early summer of 1945, with the war in Europe won and me not yet four until September, I was deposited there to let my mum take up a part-time job as an orderly at Sefton General Hospital. She was also trying to give Nan a few hours' break from looking after an over-active child, in between the self-inflicted drudgery of cleaning offices and scrubbing the floors of banks and shops on Smithdown Road.

The disastrous experiment to contain me lasted one day, which I celebrated by escaping from my prison in the park. I have always hated institutions of any kind and have never joined organisations happily, or for long. It is most likely that the people running the nursery were both competent and kind. They made the colossal error, however, of presenting me with a plate of mince for my dinner. "What... the... F... Farley's Rusks is this?" In all my four years of being reared on Cow and Gate and then my Nan's gourmet cooking, I had never seen such a doggie's mess served up as food. "This is about as attractive as a full nappy, and I know what I'm talking about." At this point a spoon was being lifted to my lips to tempt me to taste away my tantrum. My mouth and nose had repositioned themselves, Picasso style, on my face... "No! I won't eat it!" I banged the table and watched the dish rise like a flying-saucer from the Martian Ministry of Cleansing, taking the plateful of alien sewage to be dumped in deepest space.

After they had cleaned me up and wiped a few other children down as well, a perfect stranger, with whom I had no desire for intimacy, got very personal. "Come on little man. Let me take all these messy clothes off you. I think, perhaps, we'll leave on the natty pair of Co-op underpants and your woollen socks... Let's get you into bed like all the other girls and boys." The woman seemed to take an unnecessary pleasure in tucking me up like the toy teddy she, presumably, had been denied as an infant. No one had ever tried to put me down for a rest when the sun was so high in the sky, and certainly not in a room with a dozen or so comatose children. "Heinrich Himmler... It's only two in the afternoon! Everyone knows I have far too much nervous energy for catnaps! As a siren alert veteran of the Blitz, I refuse to lie down in the middle of the day!" Had the nursery possessed a giant gerbil wheel in the corner of the room, they might have succeeded better by placing me in it, with a Dairylea butty, and leaving me to tread my way to nowhere, whilst all the other world-weary babes slept their troubles away.

Curtained against the sunlight of the free world outside, and strapped down between the starch-stiff sheets alongside a bunch of weirdly compliant children, I made the first of many impulsive decisions in my life. Rejecting the eternity I had been given to contemplate my wrongful imprisonment, I was up and out of bed like a jackrabbit. I did not stop to dress. Indeed, I left one of my socks in the bed, like the Scarlet Pimpernel might leave his personal calling card for Citizen Robespierre to froth over, after legging it down a drainpipe from some French château. Luckily the window had been left open, at the bottom, to let in fresh air. It was a downstairs room with a short drop to the garden, and in less than a minute I had unlatched the gate to make my escape into the park. If only it could have been so easy for Nelson Mandela to walk away from Robin Island, Apartheid might have been overthrown a couple of decades earlier! I was free, but my striking resemblance to the Fairy soap baby, sporting only underpants and one trailing sock, made me extremely vulnerable to quick recapture. For those who question how the likes of John Mills, Leo Genn, Brian Forbes, Anthony Steel and Co. were able to escape from places like Colditz and walk hundreds of miles through German occupied territory, with neither the proper clothing nor a command of the language to avoid being captured, I am the living proof that J Arthur Rank was not making it up!

In the weeks following the liberation of Europe, I too, was free and walking home, unmolested, along a two mile stretch of Sefton Park. Uncle Stan was still busy mothballing his Swordfish in the Fleet Air Arm, so was it a case of navigator's blood in my veins? More likely, it was all down to an early knowledge of the park acquired through my toddler's walks with Pop. Like the tenacious tabby, taken on a family holiday and then left adrift in darkest Wales I had, miraculously, managed to pad my way back home. "Well, I've made it to the park entrance... Almost home... Just the local river of death, Smithdown Road, to negotiate and then a trot up to No.52, at the top of my street, over there."

I had overheard my mum telling a neighbour "The boy must have a Guardian Angel to get him out of the scrapes he finds himself in." Mum was right. Horace had turned up ahead of the script for *It's a Wonderful Life* to earn his first set of wings that day. Having followed me all the way through the park and to the brink of oblivion, he then whistled a black, Wolseley police car which drew-up, slowly, alongside us.

A serious-looking policeman wound down the driver's window and spoke to me as I was about to cross the road. "And where do you think you're going to, my fine fellow?" He could well have been Ernest the Policeman arrived in the nick of time from Toytown to prevent a senseless young lamb being served up as a cutlet on someone's dinner plate. "Over there," I said pointing, purposefully, with the same finger Moses used to carve a safe passage through the Red Sea. "I'm going to my house... Over there." Policemen never like you to give them the truth in such a disarming, matter-of-fact way. What they enjoy is a bit of evasiveness and a touch of the right-to-remain silent, so that they can work up a lather for some hard interrogation. My answer did nothing to impress the two officers inside the car. "I don't think so..." I am sure he wanted to add... "Larry, my little lamb," but decided that the law should maintain a strict and sombre attitude to the serious predicament of a lost child, found wandering all alone, in the buff, next to a main road. "I think that you should come for a nice little ride with us in the big car."

So that is how I came to spend my one and only day of pre-school nursery in jail. I was driven in style to Lawrence Road Police Station, where fingerprints were taken and a mug shot rushed to my mother at Sefton General Hospital. The café at the entrance to Sefton Park had an appealing notice in its window: "Our Sixpenny Special – A cup of tea, a biscuit, an Aspro, and our sympathy." Nellie Edith, no doubt, required something similar before she was able to gather enough of her muddled wits and claim her only child from police custody. She need not have worried about my welfare, however, for at that very moment I was being given a plate of sausages and beans, served up by the wife of the station sergeant. "Now why the hell couldn't the people at the bloody nursery have dished up something like this? If they had, I wouldn't be sitting here, like Baby-faced Nelson, in the local Nick!" I spent the next hour riding around the police station on a tricycle belonging to one of the policemen's children. "This is more like it! This is much better than lying down in a dark room and pretending to be dead after a plate of... There's a point... Should I let the police know about the attempted poisoning?"

My mother never worked again until I was well into my schooling at Lidderdale Road Infants. However, the men of the house would soon be home from the war. Perhaps the two of them would be able to harness my nervous energy and set me upon a more predictable path. Meanwhile, I had to be contained. Thank God, Mum found me Ashley! He saved me from the boredom of a home confinement with little scope for enterprise. The two of us were joined in our games by the irrepressible and extrovert Beth. Together, we rang the changes in our imaginative play and pushed back the constraining walls of No.52 Borrowdale.

CHAPTER 4

LIDDERDALE ROAD INFANT SCHOOL: TALES OF TORTURE, TERROR AND SEX

But now I am Six, I'm as clever as clever.

So I think I'll be six now for ever and ever.

Extract from "The End" by A A Milne

MY FIRST DAY AT SCHOOL

I was not one of the batch of post-war beginners who wanted to run, helter-skelter, towards the open gates of Lidderdale Infant School in the expectant, worrisome spring of 1946. Miss Leopold, the well-thought-of headmistress of the day, clearly knew more about my apprehensions than had been declared by an anxious, far from optimistic parent. In any conversation about my readiness for school, my mother would have been most circumspect, in order to have her uneasy, over-active child removed from the growing store of mischief available to him, in both home and street.

Mum had spent nearly fifteen minutes in Miss Leopold's office, getting me enrolled into what my granddad, imitating the inflection of W.C. Fields, had fancifully called "The lofty and noble cause of your necessary enlightenment." She had now departed, leaving my tiny hand in the firm grip of the extremely tall, upright spinster, who led me down a corridor to the Brave New World of the classroom, where learning was to be placed before all other desires and instincts. Suddenly, I felt very alone, unloved and unprotected against the resolute disposition of so many maiden-ladies, who looked as though they knew nothing, and cared even less, about the whims and fancies of little Stanley.

Miss Leopold knocked politely on the classroom door, and I entered behind her like a doomed Lord Carnarvon, about to violate the tomb of some ancient

Pharaoh. In all my forty years as a teacher, I cannot recall intruding upon such a noiseless, library-like world of busy children. I can remember but one colleague who demanded such industrious pre-occupation with silent activity, and he could only achieve this by gagging his pupils and nailing them to their desks with a claw-hammer! I looked about me at the forty-eight small faces, their rapt attention momentarily broken as all eyes were raised in my direction. Clearly, I was nothing special, for the little heads immediately went down again, in the manner of a Free Presbyterian congregation summoned to prayer, and dozens of tiny hands resumed their assortment of undemanding tasks.

A few of the less pre-occupied children, having drawn the short straw of a slate and stick of white chalk, were struggling to find any novelty in the Dickensian scribbling-pad. At one table, five brainwashed little boys were doggedly shunting sets of bright-coloured beads, backwards and forwards, along the rails of an abacus; arranging them into different patterns; trying to charm away their growing sense of disillusionment with the whole idea of this education malarkey. Two of the boys began to stare at me through the narrow metal bars of their counting-frames; infant felons longing for the freedom they knew I had just left behind in the world outside. Others were sat at tiny desks, working with large lumps of play dough. I was well past the stage of being enchanted with cheap packets of Woolworth's Plasticine, which we all had at home. This, however, was the real McCoy, only to be found in infant school classrooms. It was wonderfully pliable, vividly colourful material, and in such abundant supply that you felt rich in possession of the finger-pleasing stuff. The most promising activity was taking place around a large, freshly-filled sand-pit, where half-a-dozen children were happily re-creating the summer pleasures of a day out on New Brighton beach. It was just as well I hadn't brought along my bucket and spade, for we went sailing past what looked like the best way of being taught nothing, straight to the teacher's table at the front of the class.

"This is Stanley Williams. He should have been enrolled before Christmas, but his mother thought he was not quite ready to adjust to so many other children... He must be nearly five and a half by now." Miss Leopold was addressing a younger, concerned-looking woman in her mid-forties, who was seated behind a big desk festooned for a future festival of phonetics with a string of coloured cards, each depicting a letter of the alphabet. I was grateful for the emerald-green, hand-knitted cardigan she was wearing, as it brightened-up the stern expression she had fixed on me. The set of big, brown leather buttons, looking like a row of tiny soccer balls lined up for penalty practice down the front of her jumper, made me vainly hope that she might, soon, blow the whistle on all this nonsense and organise a game of football in the playground.

The gangling headmistress leaned forward to speak more discreetly into the ear of her colleague. "Apparently, he put up a terrible fuss about coming today." She paused at the beginning of a long passage of one-way conversation to gauge the level of my feigned inattentiveness. The beanpole bent as far forward as she could without snapping her whalebone corset. "His father is not living at home." Her voice lowered to a level of intimacy only used in my house when reference was being made to such hush-hush matters as illegitimacy, or my father's profligate behaviour with his mistress, Hilda. "There's another woman and they are living together..." She was longing to add the words, "in sin", but could not bring herself to utter such a godly condemnation in front of a classroom of infants. Instead, she settled for an address... "in Garmoyle Road just around the corner from his home!"

Miss Leopold returned her voice to a ground-floor level of discretion and continued to divulge the contents of a secret file on my pre-school history of social maladjustment. "It could explain why he's had trouble relating to other children in the street. Several little children have been... well... attacked!" Once more, she looked back over her shoulder. "I believe we have one of the little girls in this class, who had her pig-tails practically yanked out of her head. Another boy had his head banged against a wall, as well as having his glasses snatched off and dropped down a drain! I've been told that a few of the mothers in Borrowdale went to see Mrs Williams and asked her to keep the boy indoors until he goes to school." At this point I noted a grimace come over the face of the headmistress and wondered if any of the whalebones in her corset had become displaced? Whatever pain she may have been in, it did not stop her continuing with the tale of my malefaction. "Apparently his mother and grandmother take him everywhere with them ever since he burned down the vestibule curtains when left with his grandfather. He seems to spend an unhealthy amount of time in the cinema with the two women, watching too many Bette Davis movies. I think you will need to watch him very carefully for a few weeks."

Throughout this trawling of my struggle to adjust to infant life, my ears had been pricked back like a thoroughbred colt, its head poking over the stable door to get wind of what the punters were making of his chances for the coming season. "I say!... That can't be me they're talking about, can it? Surely not? Me, the angelic little fellow whose tinted studio portrait, dressed in satin shirt with Fauntleroy collar, beams down charm from the marble mantelpiece into every corner of my mum's front room? You just watch it mate! My mother will have a fit – and then see a lawyer – when she hears about all this bad-mouthing of my blessed name!" Miss Leopold straightened up into her skyscraper of a body. I looked up to her face, reflecting the morning sunlight on the ninety-sixth floor, then across at the drained-looking expression of my teacher. I was now certain that I was dealing with very different women to my doting mum and soft-hearted Nan. I was being loaned out to some seriously non-maternal, quantifiably unfeminine ladies, who liked to flatter themselves with the deceitful, sexually-active title of "Miss".

With such women, there was none of the friendly, indulgent attention I was guaranteed at home as the "Little Emperor" within an extended family. "Hello my fine fellow. How best can the three generations within this household suit your particular humour – nay, act on your every whim and fancy – today?" The new custodian of my life from 8.30am until 3.00pm, each Monday to Friday and possibly forever, said nothing in response to Miss Leopold's disturbing, yet challenging, character reference. She left me at her desk and walked with the headmistress to the classroom door, where a few more whispered words of sinew-stiffening advice were given. Miss Aitked returned and without wasting breath on any hint of a welcome, handed me an abacus. I was pointed in the direction of a table with the one remaining empty place in class, where five small boys were sitting behind abacus bars in an open-plan prison. It was the seat which had been awaiting the arrival of my uneducated little bottom for the past four months.

BARRY JONES IS TAKEN BY THE GESTAPO

"Someone has made a most dreadful smell! Come on, come on! Quickly now!... Who is it?" Not one of the infants moved a muscle. I was well into my first year at Lidderdale and here was exciting drama at last. "I will not ask you again." There was still no response, but I noticed that a few noses were beginning to twitch. "It is, surely, a disgustingly naughty little boy. We all know that much, don't we girls?" The woman was perfectly correct to flatter the girls, who seemed to have an unnatural control over their bodily functions. You didn't have to be the manager of a sewerage works to know that it was Barry Jones who had done it in his pants. The core of the meltdown was being vigorously signalled by Barry's wilting desk mate, who had a couple of fingers pegging a set of unfortunately-wide nostrils against the unmistakable smell. Filling your pants in the classroom was the ultimate weapon of the infant terrorist. It was Hiroshima and Nagasaki rolled into one. It devastated the lesson with fallout guaranteed to destroy all mental faculties for many long, contaminated minutes of nauseous disruption and disorder. The infrastructure of classroom government was blown away in the panic and mass hysteria created, especially amongst the girls, by the thought of death by shit fumes.

Barry was, by several inches and a few pounds, the biggest boy in the class. He, therefore, had the potential for a bowel movement of seismic proportions. In desperation, Miss Aitked removed the small handkerchief, which she had been holding to her pursed lips. Her menopausal voice ascended to the acute pitch of a Mother Superior, who had just found a used condom under a novice's bed. "Now before I am forced to smack each and every one of you with my slipper... For the very last time of asking! Will the boy responsible for the dreadful smell stand up at once?" It was one of those ill-thought-out utterances, which desperate teachers often make and immediately regret. She knew that a very serious error of judgement had been made.

The atmosphere in the classroom had ripened to the point where even the most tranquillised and properly brought-up of the white-knuckled girls could take no more. A dozen fingers pointed in Barry's direction and he stood up to ruin his mother's fastidiously arranged woollen socks – the ones with the proud, green cub-flashes – in his own "bob a job". Miss Aitked finally cracked. She flew back to her desk, opened a drawer, pulled out a large block of yellow scrubbing soap, and pointed it angrily at Barry, as if it were a primed grenade ready to be hurled into his stinking trench. Holding her secret weapon of torture aloft in one hand, the panic-stricken woman rushed over and dragged the mortified boy from our midst. He was about to be handed a lesson in Victorian cleanliness, which for the rest of his life would rank it a vaulted heaven above godliness, as the virtue he hated most!

For a matter of some ten excruciatingly long minutes, the class sat in petrified silence listening to the mixed sounds of running tap-water, the teacher's continual gasping for breath and, most disturbing of all, Barry's wailing cloakroom aria, delivered in a bel-canto of spitting and spluttering. When Miss Aitked led Barry back into the classroom, to be presented to us as the most affective cure for any remaining loose bowels amongst her pupils, he looked as if he had been through 007's decontamination process in Dr No, but with Odd Job for company, rather than the welcome distraction of a naked Ursula Andress. His socks were missing; his shirt and grey-worsted trousers were soaked through. Indeed, I suspected that all his clothes had been removed, scrubbed, wrung-out, then pulled back on like a wet suit. The most alarming thing was the sight of all that foam, bubbling-out between a Wallace-like elasticated mouth and clenched tombstone teeth, from his enforced chewing and swallowing of the foul-tasting, antiseptic soap. After the brief, Maoist, public display of rectification, he was led back out to the cloakroom toilets for a merciful mouth rinse and, hopefully, a more thorough towelling down.

Miss Aitked, believe it or not, was a kind and decent woman. However, in spite of nearly six years of national struggle against Nazism, she was still unable to break free from the pre-war methods of institutional control, which would not have been out of place at a Gestapo headquarters. Poor Barry! He was a more robust and resilient lad than most of us. He needed to be! He had been delivered from the tyranny of Adolf Hitler, who might have turned us all into blocks of soap, only to be subjected to an SS-style forced-feeding on a ghastly bar of Sunlight's bitterest carbolic. Today, it is the pupils who, if they so choose, pull on the jackboots of authority to lord it over the classroom. Sponsored by a civil liberties-obsessed, legally-prescribed system, they are able to defy the democratic rights of their fellow pupils, and even threaten teachers with some dangerously extravagant and perverted interpretations of freedom.

PINOCCHIO COMES TO LIFE

Going to the toilet was a big issue at Lidderdale Infant school. Whether it was a piddling number one or a kamikaze-kid diving on a full breakfast, loaded up with deadly number two, it was boys who were the problem. Conveniently built by nature to ignore the signs and notices for any public convenience, they possessed the pliant, elasticated pieces of plumbing, together with the wide-legged short trousers, to relieve themselves whenever, wherever, they wanted. I hated going to the boys' toilets in the main school building, because it meant interrupting playground activity. Often, I would take the risk of having a criminal, but strangely satisfying, pee in a dark corner of one of the unlocked air-raid shelters, which still stood in the schoolyard. On this occasion, I was spied upon by two six-year-old future Presidents of the Women's Institute, who thought it their moral duty to report me for desecrating a monument to the people's wartime struggle. I was given a punishment thought fitting for such sacrilegious and puerile behaviour.

After interval, I was sent down to the nursery class, where I was made to join in their senseless cavorting on the "Fairy Carpet". The fancifully-named piece of equipment, surely, conjures up a delightful image of nymphs and cherubs dancing to the Beethoven *Pastoral* on a swath of dell grasses. However, it was nothing more than a green tarpaulin, rolled out every day for clumsy, flat feet to stamp upon in the great cause of BBC Radio's *Music and Movement for Schools*. My humiliation trailed behind me into Miss Aitked's afternoon lesson, where I was made to stand in a corner of the classroom for the rest of the day in the unwholesome company of Pinocchio. He, or should I say, "It", was a beautifully made, authentically clothed, spookily lifelike, carbon copy of the Walt Disney character, which wanted to goggle at you, no matter where you happened to be sitting in the classroom. Complete with strings, the brilliant replica did nothing to reassure some fifty impressionable five-year-olds that the addition to the class of something even more wooden-headed than themselves was no more than a harmless, inanimate, toy.

A sudden darkening of the sky outside, accompanied by the rumble of thunder, made me shrink back into the gloomy prison corner, which I had been forced to share with the propped-up puppet. I couldn't help but take this well-dressed piece of voodoo seriously. It had one arm resting carelessly on a stack of nursery books, as if telling me that it had just read the lot of them while we were out at break. Its legs dangled over the corner of a work-table, as it stared down, mockingly, at my worsening predicament. The overhead storm and a blackened room had become the puppet's busy accomplices, ratcheting up the fear in my head. Only a week earlier I had been taken to the Plaza on Allerton Road, where I had marvelled at, but also been somewhat disturbed by, Disney's story of the little wooden boy who had come to life! Now, at each thunderclap's introductory flash of lightning, like some inert Frankenstein creation, the doll seemed to be inviting life-giving power from the kinetic elements outside.

I had always been one of those infants afflicted with the imagination to put monstrous, creeping flesh onto the bones of many an expurgated fairy-tale. As I stared into the painted wooden face of the limp, expectant thing seated there next to me, I knew the curse had struck again. "Oh, no, not another lightning flash! I'll swear the damn doll just winked one of his staring, lidless, white-lacquered eyeballs at me!... Surely, Miss Aitked won't be so cruel as to leave me here with this malevolent marionette when, in half an hour's time, the rest of the class run off home to play." I began to imagine the highly-animated, tea-time conversation Beth would soon be having with her mum. "Stanley was naughty. He peed in one of the air raid shelters at playtime. So the teacher put him in a corner with Pinocchio for the whole afternoon during the terrible thunderstorm... He's still there... left in the classroom all alone with the big, scary doll. What if Pinocchio gets down from a shelf and drags Stanley off into the bushes in Sefton Park?" I was eventually allowed home to tell a tale so bizarre they took away my big jigsaw puzzle. It depicted a donkey-eared, long and leafy-nosed Pinocchio, walking along the bottom of the blue ocean, amongst the swirling shoals of multi-coloured fishes looking for Monstro the whale. The doll could walk under water, as well as on it!

It is one thing to have been the victim of an over-excited imagination. What a relief, however, to grow up in a time of moral and public propriety and be spared the bullying into a premature imitation of corrupting adult behaviour. In those far off days, children were not robbed of their childhood innocence by a twenty-first century society, which encourages seven-to-eleven-year-olds to skip puberty and plunge headlong into the murky waters of teenage culture. However, the downside of such innocence was a foolish ignorance about sex. There was neither any family conversation, nor was there any mention, at school, of this taboo subject. Parents and teachers alike were programmed to quell all forms of inquiry, lest it should arouse the sexual appetite.

Thank heaven, therefore, for the Wendy House at Lidderdale Road Infants! Without it, our ignorance would have been total and our natural instinct for discovering about ourselves, smothered. Best of all, this supplement to the school curriculum enabled us to play our games of discovery without any sense of wrong-doing, or feelings of guilt. The Wendy House stood near Miss Leopold's office at the end of the long main corridor. Its introduction into the life of the school was either an act of sublime naivety, or proof that behind the public repression of sex there was some sound intuition about children's natural behaviour. This was not one of your cheap, modern, plastic affairs with Scooby Doo, or Pooh Bear pictures stamped onto frail, shifting walls. Our escape from the tedium of writing and sums was an impressive wooden structure. What is more, it had a stout front door; not the flimsy, modern door-flap, which any spook might enter at will. We were the tenants of a substantial piece of property, capable of placing any huffing, puffing wolf on a ventilator before a single windowpane could be rattled loose, or a wooden roof tile need replacing. Inside the tiny seven-by-six feet single room with its curtained windows, there was a small table and two chairs. The table was laid out with miniature teacups, side-plates and a set of toy cutlery, so that we could imitate the simplest and most satisfying routines of domesticity.

It was a friendly, social idea; the pairing of boys and girls in the top infant class at break time and then sending them down the corridor together, in a state of matrimonial bliss. There they would suck milk through one another's straws in a Never Land home. Off we would toddle, clutching our half-pint bottles of Hanson's full cream milk, a health-giving bonus of the newly created Welfare State. This left a set of fingers free to endure the vice-like grip of an over-enthusiastic little spouse-for-the-day. The ritual was a much anticipated delight, especially if there was a chance of your partner being a bosom pal, like Beth, or one of the class beauties, such as the divine Pat Kendal.

"Stanley Williams and Brenda Mulloch... You will go together to the Wendy House at playtime today." A trip to the Wendy House with Brenda Mulloch was something very special. It was a guarantee of startling enlightenment, to whet the appetite of any small boy for the idea of, one day, growing up! Even at the tender age of seven, Brenda knew how to provoke goggle-eyed attention from the boys with brazen flashes of crotch. I would be toiling-away, head down; the tip of my tongue squeezing itself through my front teeth as added impetus to my wavering concentration. "Hey! Stan... Look at this!" The soft, secretive whisper from the row of desks behind my right shoulder was as compelling as it was familiar. It could only be Brenda. The urgency in her repeated call for attention was a sure-fire guarantee that I was going to get a rich reward for plodding through the long morning's struggle with tiresome sums.

Brenda's behaviour was as reckless as it was inviting. Once I had checked out the teacher's whereabouts, to make absolutely certain that I could not be implicated in the imminent rationing of softer-than-soft porn, I was free to turn my head and give Brenda the concentrated, eager, one-eyed look, which Lord Nelson must have given Lady Hamilton when he arrived home from six months at sea. Brenda would swivel in her chair, switch on a Cheshire cat face, and then give me a startling flash of what lay behind the stretch-to-bust, elasticated, left-leg of her navy blue knickers. Anyone going to the Wendy House with Brenda came back with a grin on his face that lasted a fortnight.

It was Liverpool City Council policy, in those days, to abandon co-education once our infant schooling was over. Lidderdale was, therefore, my sad farewell to having girls for company in the classroom. I missed them as a hard-working encouragement to my own progress and struggle for maturity. Girls were often inexplicable, contrary, tantalizing little tittle-tattlers. In essence, however, they were the most sympathetic and desirable of companions. I think I must have also sensed that beyond my sister-less, infant fascination with the mystery of gender, something far more pleasurable and satisfying lay in store, with or without the grin of a Cheshire cat.

CHAPTER 5

FLY ME TO THE MOON

"It's getting dark… We'll have to go in soon." It was mid-October and one of those frustratingly short-measured playtimes after tea, when autumn's cooling friendship with a Capricorn-bound sun still allowed us to turn a blind eye to the wintry warning of the evenings drawing in. Over the last few weeks, darkness had begun to fall much too quickly for two little boys who never seemed to tire of playing together. Ahead of us lay the big winter freeze of 1947-48 and all the talk amongst the women in the street was about the forthcoming marriage of Princess Elizabeth to the handsome Philip Mountbatten. My more immediate concern was how best we could pass away the next ten minutes, before the call came from our front doorsteps to come in for bed. "Hey, Ash… Look at the size of the moon up there."

Ashley and I were in the lane running along the railway line at the top end of Lidderdale Road. We were sitting with our backs to the wall of Tommy Hill's garage. Tommy's lights were on as he worked into the evening, mending the latest breakdown in a succession of clapped-out bangers to be towed to the doors of his small repair shop. I was looking up at an impressive full moon. It was newly suspended above the gathering darkness in nearby Wavertree Playground, only a dangerous scramble away across the high railway embankment, guarded by a wall of sandstone blocks, which rose like a castle's defences at our feet.

"I know… I'll take you to the moon." Ashley's eyes lit up in the reflected light of earth's pizza-pie, hanging brightly above us in the looming night sky. "Superman can do it in seconds… So can Mighty Mouse. We can't be away for long." Ashley was no fool and proved it, later, by gaining an Open Scholarship to Oxford. At six, however, I had the one-year edge, as the over-imaginative director of our play who was about to push my little pal's faith in me to the very limits. The friendship we enjoyed was that of close brothers. We had been playing together since our mothers first collided with their prams at the corner of Borrowdale Road in all the excitement of VE Day. Before the age of ten we had each lost a parent. Ashley was left with a mother whose personal agenda relegated any desire she may have had to look after him properly. He turned to Uncle Stan as a surrogate parent and was never away from our house. Always ravenous, he took his meals at No.52 Borrowdale Road and often came on holiday with us to keep me occupied. Falling prey to the exaggerated claims of his enterprising mentor proved to be a regular indulgence of my clever little playmate.

Of much greater influence on my fertile imagination than any first steps towards an education at Lidderdale Road Infants were my late 1940s trips to the Grand Cinema on Smithdown Road. Even before the war was over and the men were back home to check an excess of film going for a four-year-old, I was being taken to the pictures at least twice a week with Mum and Nan, as the only way the two women could overcome the problem of a baby-sitter. My resourcefulness in play was fuelled by what I saw from my propped-up seat at the Grand. What your average child made of the great MGM and Twentieth Century Fox black and white melodramas, it would be hard to guess. The experience certainly stirred my brain into some highly unusual activity, besides putting me off Bette Davis for the rest of my life.

A Mighty Mouse cartoon often came on before the big film and he was the cat's whiskers as far as Ashley and I were concerned. This tiny, barrel-chested rodent had muscles where cats didn't even have places. He was the ultimate super-hero for two toddlers who had only just mastered the art of sitting on the toilet. Far mightier than Mickey, he generated much greater respect than the constantly terrorised and on-the-run Jerry. He lived on the moon and sat about, eating cheese, until summoned to earth by the bended knee supplication of desperate mice, whose lives were being seriously oppressed by evil-looking, gangster-like tomcats. To Ashley and me he, not Captain Marvel, was the "Big Cheese".

My *Film Night 46* background and an obsession with Mighty Mouse may explain why I made the outrageous promise to take Ashley to the moon and back before we were dragged into our beds.

"How are we goin' to get there?" Ashley asked.

"You can hang on to me and I'll fly you there," I boldly asserted.

"But... you can't fly," Ashley replied, cautiously.

The credulous tone in his voice, however, suggested that now I had begun attending infant school I might... just might... be able to do things he could only dream about. This gave me some hope that, in the next fifteen minutes, I might raise his expectations to the heavens.

Ashley sat knees-up with his chin cupped in his hands. He thought hard before attacking my ludicrous idea. "You can't fly. If you could you wouldn't walk to school everyday. You would fly there and fly back home, but you don't... And you don't fly to Sunday school either. Only Jesus can do that. You walk there… with me!" That's the bloody trouble with five-year-olds who are going to end up at Oxford – they enjoy an intellectual argument.

"I'll prove it to you… that I can really fly. Sit here and don't move. I'll sneak back home for a few seconds and get my magic cape… It's hidden in the coal shed."

I ran down the back lane and returned a minute later with a home-made Mighty Mouse cape, which was nothing more than a piece of blue flannelette bed-sheet Nan had ripped up for me to fly around in. "Now, I can't do this if you're standin' next to me. I need some space… Come down the lane a bit and you'll get a better view."

I led Ashley down the jigger to my back door and told him to watch out for me in a few minutes' time at the top of the lane. Leaving the little fellow non-plussed, I raced down to the bottom of the lane and then around the corner into Lidderdale Road. I sped all the way back up to Tommy Hill's garage. Peeping out from behind the garage door I was pleased to see Ashley still standing where I had left him; transfixed and staring up at the blackening sky above the railway line wall.

Allowing myself a long run-up and shouting "Here I come… Up, up and away!" I dashed across the twelve-foot gap at the top of the lane. Two steps from the Borrowdale Road side I made the biggest and most exaggerated leap I could conjure up. With arms outstretched and fists clenched, I punched my body skywards. The timing was perfect and the trajectory of my leap could not have been better executed had I taken off from a trampoline. The way Ashley saw things, I had simply continued ever upwards, behind the high wall at the other side of the lane! I hared all the way down Borrowdale Road and back up the lane to Ashley, chuffed to death with what I hoped was the perfect illusion. It was like the Bob Beaman take-off at the 1968 Olympics in Mexico; a once-in-a-lifetime fluke with no illegal wind assistance and not a hint of Black Power to help me on my way.

"You've come back down. You flew. You really flew. Up and up… I saw you!" Ashley marvelled at my feat for weeks and asked me to do an encore. Magicians are foolish, however, to repeat a trick to a discerning child, no matter how much he wants to believe in nonsense. Over the next couple of weeks I declined, several times, to give another demonstration of my superpowers, knowing that the fast-approaching winter nights would put an end to our playing out in the streets until next April. By then, it would be all forgotten. We would have moved on from Mighty Mouse to Robin Hood, a much more down-to-earth character in his feathered hat, laced tunic and Lincoln green tights!

On that night of the big yellow moon, in late October 1947, I still had to handle the rash promise I had made to my best buddy. "Are you goin'to fly us to the moon, then?" Ashley was far more serious and hopeful about a quick trip now that he had seen me defy gravity. "Er... I think I saw your Aunt Mary out lookin' for you as I ran up Lidderdale Road just now. We'll have to leave goin' to the moon for another night... Ta ra, see you temorra!"

CHAPTER 6

SEFTON PARK: PARADISE ON MY DOORSTEP

Back in the summer of 1945, with victory won but my dad and uncle not yet home from the war, it fell upon my grandfather to take me on my first walks around Sefton Park, which he described as, "The countryside at the bottom of our street." By the following spring he had drawn up an itinerary of places to visit in a regular cycle of unhurried, mind-awakening strolls around one of Northern England's finest examples of Victorian municipal benevolence. Being taken around the park by my Pop was like going on a voyage of discovery with an old sea dog, who could teach me fresh tricks and show me new wonders on each trip.

Down Borrowdale Road I would trot, occasionally doubling my three-year-old's step, in order to keep alongside my fit-as-a-fiddle grandfather. Every one of his healthy strides was taking us away from the red-bricked terraced houses, harsh pavements and gravelled streets of Liverpool 15, to a paradise beyond the fumes and noisy traffic of Smithdown Road. Here lay a parallel world of soft horizons with unresisting, grassy fields framed by tall sycamores, lime and horse chestnut trees. A mere ten minutes' walk from my front door and I was in a landscape of inviting woodlets, lakes and gardens, bowling greens and tennis courts. It was a kid's wonderland of duck ponds, boating lakes, swing playgrounds and the children's open air theatre, as well as being the venue for the Bertram Mills Circus and the big, Collins summer fairground. Adults could lay claim to the bowling green, tennis courts, or a seat at the cricket ground. Those seeking peace found sanctuary within the shining beauty of the Palm House, or from taking blissful, evening walks in the magical Fairy Glen.

On our travels together, Pop said little in the way of baby talk. He preferred to humour himself by teasing me with puzzles, or educating me about the natural environment of a place that was to become my second home. Slowly, I opened like one of the park's flowering plants, allowed to flourish a little longer away from the stress-and-strain world of being grown up. I especially loved going to visit the Palm House. Here my natural over-excitement with people and things was given a friendly Scouser's "Calm down! Calm down!" In the drowsy, sub-tropical atmosphere, I could wander off amongst a jungle of exotic plants, where the wonderful confusion of species, so rich in their bamboozling variety of names, would make me ponder the size and scale of the earth I had been placed upon.

I could not leave the Palm House without paying my respects to the statues outside the building. Set on encircling plinths, in front of the countless reflective panes of glass, they had been placed to honour great naturalists and explorers, such as Charles Darwin and Captain Cook. There was always a strange, spiritual calm about the place, reflected in the harmony of the glass palace with its surrounding, quiet pathways and concealing hedges. Mum would bring a book to this oasis of peace within the park. While she sat reading on one of the comfortable benches, Ashley, Beth and I would play in and out of the bushes, under the watchful eye of our stone guardians, whose hint at a brighter future in a better world we were about to fulfil with lives open to rich opportunity.

Occasionally, in an attempt to tire me out, Pop would walk down to the children's swings in Aigburth Vale. After half an hour of pushing me higher and higher up into the sky, he would drop in to see family friends, the Pidgeons, who owned a big public house nearby. Here, Edward Thomas, a man saddled with a demon-drink reputation, displayed great self-discipline in the presence of his little grandson. Refraining from an under-the-counter pint of strong beer, he would content himself with half an hour of mild conversation and a couple of dangerous Woodbines, before accepting the novel suggestion of a cup of tea with a salmon paste sandwich.

"How many beans make five?" Pop would ask. "Oh dear, is there an answer I can give without looking like I'm five-year-old Jack, barking up the wrong beanstalk?" I would pause, on the pathway alongside Sefton Cricket Club, to consider the limited options presented by an uncertain number of fingers. "Umm... Four, plus one? Too easy. Three, plus two? Possibly. Two, plus two, plus... Hey! Where is this senseless sum taking me?" I would look up into my granddad's smiling face and tell him that I hoped to make a more intelligent guess after a large plate of beans on toast for my tea. I didn't have to wait long for some enlightenment. "The answer Stanley is a bean, half a bean, a bean, a bean and a half and a bean!" It was my first lesson in fractions, which progressed to the value of the copper coins in his pocket. The test of any real understanding came when he asked me how many farthing sweeties I could buy if he gave me a penny!

"If there's one duck behind a duck, one duck in front of a duck and a duck in the middle, how many ducks are there?" When Pop opened his box of conundrums to amuse himself at my bafflement, we could only be on our way to feed the ducks at the Big Lake. A writer of songs for the old music hall, he loved to tease me with riddles and verbal nonsense, which were merely a pretext for trying to widen a small boy's knowledge of the world. "Now here's a weighty problem for you, my young man... Which is the heavier, a ton of lead, or, a ton of feathers?" The first time he asked me that question I would have paused for a good minute, while I imagined Sylvester the cat being hit on the head; first by a feather, and then a big piece of lead pipe dropped from the top of a skyscraper window by Tweety Pie! That I came up with the wrong answer both amused and pleased my clever Pop, as it allowed him to inform me that appearances can be deceptive. He would explain about gravity; that things have weight and can be measured; that being obsessed with accuracy is what makes science different to imagination. "You see, Stanley, imagination has no limits... Science without imagination takes us nowhere." In that pre-school year before I went to Lidderdale Road Infants, we played our post-war version of Trivial Pursuit. It was so much more rewarding and useful than being given a Werther's Original by some pretentious old fart in an Arran sweater.

When I was a little older and allowed to venture into the park on my own, I still had a hankering to feed the ducks. They did well not to rely on any Dr Doolittle sense of moral responsibility I may have felt for the welfare of our feathered friends. In spite of being well-nourished, I was forever hungry and unable to resist dipping into the bag of stale buns and cakes, which Nan always placed in my hands before I left the house for the park. I had been given a stomach-full of Christian instruction concerning the symbolism of bread. No one in the family, including my irreligious father and agnostic Pop, would allow me to waste a scrap of food, whether at the meal table, or elsewhere.

Habitually, I would walk to the ducks at the Big Lake weighed down with a heavy conscience about all the appetising leftovers which were soon to be thrown their way. Perched on my shoulder, a first cousin of Jiminy Cricket raised his top hat to me and began to prattle. "I've looked in the bag, pal... Cor! Two Sayers cakes, an iced bun and two cobs of bread... With a little more effort on your part, Stanley boy, you could have scoffed this lot off at home. Mind you, it's still possible to finish the job, right now. So what, if your dad is right about your eyes being three times as big as your belly... Doesn't the Bible say that animals are a good bit below man in the natural pecking-order? Go on... We all appreciate you're a greedy little bugger. The ducks can wait another day to be fed." I was certainly an insatiably hungry child. The type you would want to keep for a week rather than a fortnight. The upshot of my ravenous appetite was that every time I arrived at the lake, all the ducks' food was gone. I swear on Daffy Duck's cleft palate that I always set out with the best of intentions, only to be overwhelmed by a craving similar to Ben Gunn's *Treasure Island* passion for a piece of cheese, no matter how stale.

Long before I arrived at the lake, the bread would have been stuffed down my throat, leaving one empty bag to be held to my mouth, blown up, and then burst to smithereens. Standing there, looking at the dozens of happy, quacking ducks feeding on the kindness of others, made me feel even guiltier of moral ineptitude. I began to fear that some of the older drakes recognised me as the tormenting little sod who, week after week, promised so much, but delivered duck-all. Breaking away from the feeding frenzy, they paddled in to the water's edge and stared at me, disconcertingly, down their fluted, whispering beaks. One of them spoke in a Donald Duck sort of voice: "We know you mate. Where's the bread then, eh la? What, none again... Lord, love-a-duck. It's just hit me. You've scoffed the bloody lot... You sad, greedy, little bastard! I hope the next one of your Nan's stale rock-buns chokes you!"

If Pop was not taking me to feed the ducks, then it was to see the birds at the aviary, set back in a crescent of shrubbery off the main footpath leading to the central café. "Do you know what it means to be as proud as a peacock?" Pop asked. "You don't? Well then... I'll just have to introduce you to someone who does." The small aviary boasted only a limited collection of birds, but who needs a cast of thousands to impress when a mature peacock is around to strut his stuff? This feather-brained David Dickenson was a truly magnificent specimen, who swaggered about the confines of his living quarters, while a dowdy, disinterested spouse sat in glum resignation, looking so much like a Hilda Ogden to his Richard E Grant's Scarlet Pimpernel.

The great thespian show-off would wait until a sizeable crowd had gathered in front of his cage. After a quick, beady-eyed check on the passage of the sun to make sure the hourly spectacular was on time, he would begin his swank towards the gathering audience. The arrogant sod would look us all up and down and then, satisfied that we were a collection of humans worthy of a matinee performance, he would switch on the Blackpool illuminations in his fanned tail. Within the herringbone arc of feathers, dozens of startling eyes peeped out at me from a frail curtain of psychedelic blues, greens and indigos. If only this peacock could sing. Forget *Dr Doolittle* and *The Lion King* – this fellow was meant to play the lead in *Joseph and The Amazing Technicolor Dreamcoat!*

On each visit to the Big Lake, I was allowed to stop and pay homage to Peter Pan. I had a lot in common with the boy who did not want to grow up. He stood perched on top of a rock of bronze, which on close examination revealed peeping pixies, fairies and other tiny, woodland creatures from his kingdom beyond the first star of the morning. Peter was one of our childhood talismen, helping us escape into a world of fantasy, whether it be at war with Hook and his pirates, robbing the rich who dared travel through Sherwood Forest, or saving the stage coach from a marauding band of Apaches. Behind the statue and within a railed section of grass there was a Wendy House on permanent loan from Never Land. Made of roughly hewn branches, knitted together with small twigs, it boasted a thatched-roof with a large top hat for a chimneypot. On the front door, irresistibly defying the public notice telling children not to be sorely tempted, was nailed a big, black boot. Every disobedient kid, with the lawless confidence of the flying boy himself, was prepared to chance the park keeper's watchful eye and put it to proper use as a knocker!

The most magical of the J M Barry set pieces, however, was a fifteen foot model of Captain Hook's galleon, *The Jolly Roger*. Complete with masts and sails, the floating headquarters of Pan's nemesis had defied all the Luftwaffe's wartime attempts to sink it. Throughout my childhood world of make-believe, it weathered the gales, ice and snow of winter. Unlike many of the season's ill-fated ducklings, it also managed to repel the constant attacks and gnawing by plundering, pirate water rats. Sadly, it did not survive the dawning of the age of the vandal and a bunch of mindless teenagers succeeded where nature and the nasty Nazis had failed!

In the winter months, dozens of acres of the park's playing fields surrendered to the hoards of footballers, who battled it out on iron-hard earth or muddy quagmires, to stick a sappy, suet pudding of a ball between a couple of hastily erected goal posts. As a young teenager, when not playing myself, I loved to walk through the park on a Saturday afternoon in winter and wander about the patchwork of busy soccer pitches. Each was an open-air theatre, Shakespearean in the players' enactment of a comedy of errors and foul murderous intent; treachery and betrayal by linesmen and referees as base-hearted as their Blackshirts uniform. It might simply have been my fancy for the colour of a team's strip, or a sharp whistle blown for the drama of a penalty, which tempted me to a touchline. I would linger for ten minutes or so, before moving on to the next mud-spattered contest being played out, across the acres of open field. Along the narrow miles of white-washed touchline, like rows of hardy crows balanced on taut telegraph wires, hundreds of spectators braved the elements to crudely shout their encouragement and precious pieces of technical advice. "You just sort him out Kev! If that little sod ever tries to nutmeg you again like that, just you chop the bugger's legs from under him!" Many tried to keep warm with brisk, distracted conversation about football, family and life in general. The thin columns of warm breath rising in the freezing air looked like tiny smoke signals being sent out to a pack of shin-hacked, cartilage-worn soccer braves, on the warpath, and about to take a few scalps.

Despite all the tut-tutting and much nodding of heads from perplexed wives and pals on their way to the citadels of Anfield or Goodison Park, you had to admire these football-crazy fools. Undaunted by the hostile weather, they rubbed their hands and stamped their feet in a constant battle against the penetrating cold. Dispiriting in its intent, it seeped through the leather soles of shoes unsuited to hours of standing on the chilly, soggy, grass. On a filthy, cold day in late January, many wives braved such sentiments at the Saturday dinner table. "You need your head feeling. What sort of clot wants to venture out against wind, rain and snow to watch grown men… some of them old enough to have to take all their teeth out before a match… wallowing in a mud bath?" Yet support their ragtag and bobtail teams, in all weathers and changes of season, they did. Such stubborn, half-frozen fanatics seemed to prefer a contest on that borderland of sporting competence, where technique was absent and play often dirtier than the weather; when brawn and insensibility to pain met mindless aggression on the raw edge of winter's breath.

Accompanying my thoughts on the journey home were the echoing notes of referee's whistles.

"I can understand where the lads who think they're Billy Liddell, or Wally Fielding are coming from, but why in heaven's name does anyone want to be a referee?"

"Yea… and they have to pass exams as well just so they can blow a silly, bloody whistle in someone's ear-hole at the weekend."

"Hey, even if they pass, they can't enjoy a single kick of the ball, let alone join in the excitement of scoring a goal."

"Perhaps, they're all rejects from the police force… ex-prison wardens, failed park keepers… snidey buggers who enjoy keeping others in their place."

"Too bloody right. Who else would love to run around, in the pissing rain, being so seriously hated and abused every Saturday?"

There always seemed to be one, lonely fanatic attached to every team. Useless and rejected as a player he became a camp follower, hanging on to his place on the fringe of the fraternity by surrendering his life in the cause of those more capable of lacing up their boots on a Saturday. He would be the first to arrive and the last to leave the wooden dressing rooms, set back among the trees. It was he who carried the goal posts, Calvary fashion, out to some far distant pitch, where his team's dire lack of talent would, all too often, mean a 6-0 crucifixion. Drubbing after drubbing, it was he who was left to haul the posts back into the smell of sweat and camphor, where the mood was as desolate as on any dark, Good Friday.

Unrewarded in this sporting life, but faithful-unto-death in the service of his team, he could be seen before every home game, marking out the pitch with whitewash. A generation of players later, he would still be self-employed in the same thankless task, whilst trying to ignore the chants of young boys familiar with the television trials of Yosser Hughes. "Gizza job. I can do that… I can paint the lines straight… Go on… Gizzit!" Enveloped in one of the recurring winter smogs of late 1940s Merseyside, bandy-legged, sightless wingers needed all the help he could give them to run in a straight line along shrouded touchlines. What else could prevent them scoring a goal or two for another team in the same red and white stripes, playing on a pitch at the far end of the park?

The damp, redundant feel of the park in late and misty autumn appealed to the melancholic side of my nature. There were cheerful days in early December, when the polished mirror of a sun, low in the sky over Aigburth Vale, dazzled through the glass of the Palm House turning it into a chandelier of celestial brilliance. Even in the bleakness of January, with fields, groves and pathways empty of life, there was a latent optimism in the power and inevitability of nature. When I kicked out at a drift of long-dead horse-chestnut leaves, as if shooting at goal, or looked back at my lone trapper's tracks, imprinted across a clearing of virgin snow, it was always with a feeling of elation and hope. I knew that this was merely a required period of rest for the park and come spring, life and vigour would return.

How blessed we were to have such rural peace in the heart of busy, Liverpool 15. Only the suburban rich, in their prime-site bungalows out at Woolton, could afford to gaze from sun-sheltered gardens onto a tree-lined golf course beckoning beyond. For the fortunate children from the terraced streets off Smithdown Road, living next to Sefton Park was like having a National Park as an extension to your street. Scallywags from the wartime dereliction of Toxteth and the Dingle stood, open-mouthed, to take in their first visit to this Garden of Eden. Sefton was in a different class to the flat, functional ordinariness of Princes Park, which was Toxteth's nearest expanse of playing field. Here the grass had been worn into baldy, iron-hard runways, which served Granby Street boys well when I had to face their bodyline bowling on the most dangerous cricket pitches in the civilised world! The smaller, more ornate Calderstones Park, out in posh Menlove Avenue, would win all the prizes for its well-tended flowerbeds and rose-gardens. Sefton was the best, however, not simply because it was the biggest of Liverpool's parks. Entering it was like being given free admission into the grounds of a country estate. It was my passport to continuous adventure and pleasure. Spending my childhood playing in its parkland was heaven on earth.

I was sitting down on Sefton's Old Farm Field with Uncle Stan. We were joined by most of the neighbourhood's tribe of eleven-to-fifteen-year-old boys, who were taking a rest during one of our eternal series of England versus Australia Test matches. It was the beginning of the 1952 school summer holidays. Given a decent run of weather, a fair wager could be made over our permanent occupation of the Old Farm Field pitch, for the next six weeks of our happy, young lives. We were laughing at the antics of a bunch of Toxteth toughs, not more than a hundred yards away from us across the field. Without an Uncle Stan and his bag of cricketing paraphernalia, they were making an arse of trying to play the game of gentlemen. A small, makeshift bat, along with an orange box stood on its end for an improvised set of wickets, had refashioned the English middle-class summer obsession into something more fitting for these street-wise boys from Liverpool 8. As we sprinkled the tiny blue sachets of salt into our packets of Smiths crisps and swigged back the bottles of lemonade Uncle Stan had bought from the café at the entrance to the park, we joked and made remarks which would have got us thumped, for sure, had the Toxteth boys heard one single word of our piss-taking.

Our wicked banter was too much for Stan Thomas, listening in with his usual moral concern for any excess in our youthful, deregulated conversation. "You see those boys over there... The ones you evidently think are so worthy of your cynical wit." All mockery ceased and some twenty or more young lads went as quiet as church mice, waiting for their hero to utter his "Thought for the Day". We hung on every word of this pint-sized Hercules with the giant moral authority. I hope you appreciate that while this is back-yard activity to you lot, those boys have come from Grafton Street and Warwick Street... not too far away, Stanley, from where we used to live in the 1920s."

At this point he paused, possibly getting a flashback to the basement tenement in the shadow of Liverpool Cathedral, which had been his squalid home as a child. He would never forget the abject poverty his parents had fallen into by the early years of the twentieth century; the TB and rickets, which put him in a Wirral sanatorium for three years of lost schooling. He remembered the bitter cold and damp of the cellar rooms in winter; the lack of medicine which caused his saintly brother, George, to die of pneumonia when he was nine years old.

His words, perhaps, caused him to reflect on the rescue of his family to our new life at No.52 Borrowdale Road. How far his brains and moral courage had allowed him to travel, since the days when his mother, my Nan, took in washing or scrubbed the houses of the rich to contend with her husband's years of self-induced idleness, and heavy drinking.

There was always some deep thinking going on in Uncle Stan's head. Even when he was relaxing, you sensed there were moments when unwelcome ghosts from the past had crept up on him. Here we were playing cricket, but he had been given a reminder of the unpleasant reality of life for all too many, who were still forced to live in the areas of post-war decay around Myrtle Street, Upper Parliament Street and much of Liverpool 8. Such an environment was no longer a threat to me, thanks to Uncle Stan, who had begun his escape in the spring of 1930, on a heaven-blessed day when his persistence with a broken bicycle chain allowed him to arrive late at the Liverpool Collegiate examination hall. He needed a clean-up but, eventually, sat down at a desk to gain the City Scholarship which rescued his family and changed many lives for the better. In 1948, with my uncle at Oxford, Mum and Nan took me with them to see *How Green Was My Valley*, when it made a return to the Grand Cinema on Smithdown Road. It was clear from the conversation, afterwards, that my mother saw her brother's success, and the family's salvation, reflected in the story of the clever Welsh schoolboy scribbling his way to Oxford; saved from a life of soul-destroying drudgery down the pits and into one of self-fulfilment.

Standing back from his past, on the great expanse of the Old Farm Field and watching the Toxteth lads revel in their day of cricket, my uncle's thoughts were interrupted by a marvellously uneducated stroke to leg, which sent a fielder racing towards us for the ball. Having applauded the length and accuracy of the return throw to the wicket, Uncle Stan resumed the short homily he was so keen to deliver:

"There's some likely looking lads in that bunch, I'll grant you. They have cycled up to Sefton Park... two on a bike, by the look of it... with little more than the desire to get some fresh air and have some fun playing cricket. Well, let's call it cricket, but from where I'm standing, a ball and a makeshift bat seem to be only items of cricketing equipment they possess. They may know nothing of W G Grace, and Jack Hobbs but, by heck, they know that this is their only chance of a summer holiday, away from the backstreets and bombed building sites of the some of the poorest areas in the city."

That was part of the deal we all accepted in wanting to be with Uncle Stan. No one would call it a downside, but there was always a moral responsibility he called upon in all who had dealings with him. He was right, of course, and we knew it. For these scallys from the inner city, this outing to the park with a couple of empty lemonade bottles filled with water and a bag of jam butties would more than make do for my fortnight's holiday in Colwyn Bay, Ashley's trip up to Edinburgh to see his Scots relatives or the fortnight in Scarborough, where the Barclay brothers were off to next week.

Before we resumed our game, I watched this wild bunch of alternative cricketers run like hares across the field to the iron fountain, where they splashed their faces with its refreshing water and refilled their empty bottles. Thanks to Uncle Stan, I had taken in the fact that they had left the backstreets of some of Liverpool's worst slums behind them in a noble pretence at getting a day out in the countryside. For most of them, this would be as good as it got.

The bottles of water we guzzled down from the fountain at the Old Farm Field were as prized as purchases of Dandelion and Burdock from the café at the Ullet Road entrance to the park. We preferred to drink gallons of the superior, unflavoured tap water, piped all the way through the cool earth from Liverpool's reservoir at Lake Vernwy in Wales. It was the best tap water in the country at the time and for many years after. Like professional boozers who knew all the best pubs to frequent, we had our favourite drinking places. By far the coolest, best-tasting water came from the big cast-iron fountain, thoughtfully placed in the shade of trees at the bottom of Greenbank Drive. It had a domed top, like a Saxon helmet, and underneath its rim, a lion's mouth spouted out the most soul-refreshing stuff at the twist of a large ornamental knob.

When the sun-filled, blast-furnace of a day had, finally, seen a great contest decided, I would deny myself a last fill-up at the fountain, determined to prolong my thirst with a further ten-minute walk back to my house. When in this mood for self-inflicted torture, I would ignore the rest of the gang as they chatted on the winding down way home. My mind was locked into a secret plan of survival, set against the dry barren wastes of the Sahara or Kalahari. More than once, I heard the voice of Frankie Laine echoing in my head:

> *Keep a movin' Dan*
>
> *Don't you listen to him Dan,*
>
> *He's a devil not a man,*
>
> *And he spreads the burning sands*
>
> *With water.*

And then, the echoing bastard of a chorus. "Water... Water... "

I tried not to talk; not to think of how dry my mouth was getting, as I pressed on past the railings and allotments along Greenbank Drive. I steeled myself against an involuntary, sideways glance at a spade-weary old gardener, mopping his brow and slaking his parched throat, with his back to the sun in the middle of a bed of cabbages:

> *Old Dan and I*
>
> *Our throats burned dry*
>
> *And hearts that cry*
>
> *For water*
>
> *Cool... clear... water.*

The smash hit of the summer of 1955 was weakening my will. I dismissed the look of pleasure on the faces of children as they walked past with mouth-watering bottles of pop, raised to wet and eager lips. I gritted my teeth against the cruel sucking; the deliberate, over-the-top enjoyment of their dripping iced-lollies. I was determined to hold out in this mental dust-bowl, and let my ever-growing desire for a cup of Nan's tap water build up to the craving of a lost Legionnaire, crawling from one dried-up well to another.

At last, no more mirages, when the night, the stars and I were all reduced to shimmering pools of water. I was across dangerous Smithdown Road and into the final 100 yards sprint up Borrowdale Road. I dashed through the front door, and shot down the hall like a Raj Colonel's wife who had just eaten her first plate of over-seasoned Madras curry. I made straight for the kitchen sink and the great consummation, when I poured the first of many cups of delicious tap water down my withered throat. I held the cup to my lips, and then closed my eyes, before gobbling down mouthful after restorative mouthful. At ten, this quenching was as close as I could get to ultimate satisfaction. That is, until girls began to unlock my other juices.

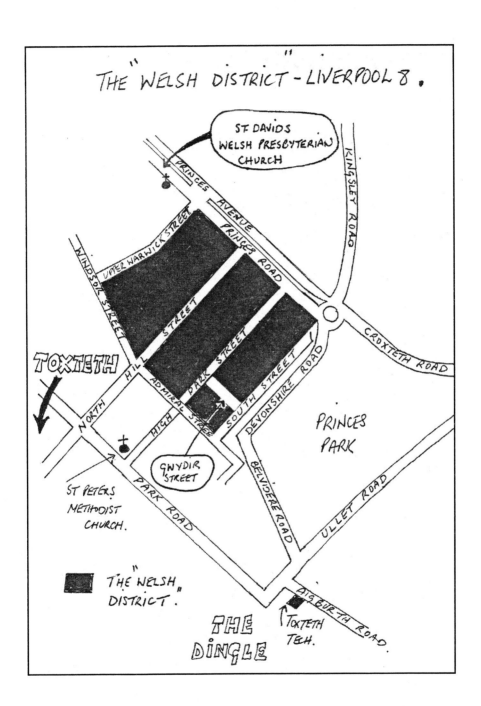

THE "WELSH" DISTRICT - LIVERPOOL 8.

CHAPTER 7

THE DARK SIDE OF EDWARD THOMAS

Having now passed the pre-pension age venerated by the Beatles, and feeling in a similar fine fettle to Paul McCartney's seaside postcard-of-a-ditty, I can so much better relate to how my granddad – a much fitter man than I – was facing up to old age, back in 1945. My silver-headed Pop was not that close to the grave as my infant's mind might have imagined. Perhaps the decades of being a slacker had done him no harm at all.

"Your Pop had an overwhelming desire to avoid work at all cost."

I was eight or nine, before I began asking my father about the history of Edward Thomas. He, of course, enjoyed the opportunity to make an unfavourable comparison with his own virtues of sobriety and industry.

By the time I started asking such questions, instinct told me to have respect for a man who seemed to be much more than the ceremonial head of the family. I seriously doubted the royal prerogative was a dead letter, sensing that his authority could be activated if the situation demanded it, and a taste of the old days brought back. Pop seemed happy, however, to defer most matters to my uncle, who had defied all the heavy odds his father had stacked against him.

"Nan said that there was no work for people before the War… that you and Pop couldn't get a job even though you tried."

My father had been so determined to find work in the 1930s that he took a leaf out of mad dog Norman Tebbit's manual for the unemployed, got on his bike and rode off into darkest Lancashire.

"No one could get work, that's true. I had a go at everything I could if it came along, or was advertised in the papers. I even tried to sell from a suitcase, door-to-door, in places like Preston and Blackburn, but no one had money to buy things."

"Did Pop go with you?" Dad started to laugh.

"Pop went no further than the pubs off Lodge Lane. He made a profession out of being unemployed, son… years and years of it. What annoyed me was that your granddad was highly literate and educated beyond the rest of his classmates, when he left school in the early 1890s. He was certainly qualified enough to have been one of the first in the queue for a decent job. He was a brilliant copperplate writer."

"Copperplate. What does that mean?" I asked.

"It's an old-fashioned, elaborate style of handwriting. Pop was as good as you could get."

"I've seen it. His songs are in the box of papers on the top shelf in the kitchen cupboard... They're all written like that."

"That's his hurried hand, mind. His proper writing was so elegant, and he was such a good copier that, before the war, the police lifted him... twice... for questioning in forgery cases. That's the truth... Straight up."

Forgery? The thought of Pop being a forger excited me. What a story to tell all the Dick Barton fans at school.

"Was Pop a criminal?"

"A criminal?"... Arthur Williams smiled at the thought of it. "I don't think so. Mind you, some of his old music hall songs were... No. Pop's pen work was so skilful that the police included him in their interviews of people they thought were clever enough to forge bank notes."

Edward Thomas was the youngest child and only son of John Thomas. What a name! However, it could have been worse. He could have been christened John William, or worse still, John William Richard. Whether having a father with a name like that gave Pop – when sober that is – his prudish hang-up about sex, I don't know. It certainly did not stop him, under the influence of ten pints of draught Bass, from behaving like a dick in nature as well as name.

Pop's grandfather, Thomas Thomas, was a labourer in the stone quarries near Old Colwyn in North Wales, before he migrated into Liverpool in the 1860s. His three sons all went into the building trade and Pop's father, John, was the most successful of the artisans, building streets of houses in the Princes Park district, as well as the Welsh Presbyterian Church on Princes Road, known locally as the Toxteth Cathedral.

As a child, there would come the point in every No.86 tram or bus journey into town, when Nan would remind me, as we passed St Luke's at the corner of Leece Street that over there was the church where Pop's father and mother, Hannah Hughes, had married in 1878. I had no need of the constant repetition of family history to rivet my attention to the wondrous desolation and devastating beauty of this symbolic war ruin.

In 1881 my grandfather was born in Gwydir Street in the Welsh enclave of Liverpool 8. Hannah Hughes, her two girls and young Teddy were enjoying the home comforts provided by their prospering master builder of a father, until drink undermined his health as well as his business, leading to an early death, aged fifty-six, in 1903. The slide into poverty forced my grandfather to leave school at twelve, and abandon the family's plans for him to stay on as a Dickensian-type of student teacher. At sixteen he was clerking, playing a lot of football and courting my Nan. He was clearly as skilled at sex as he was at soccer, because it took him five years to get Nellie Dawkin pregnant. The family rallied round the young couple and made sure they were respectably married in 1902 at St Peter's Church near their home in Princes Park.

How Edward Thomas and Nellie Edith Mansell Dawkin, both from relatively comfortable home backgrounds, drifted into the dire poverty which beset them for the next couple of decades, I do not know. Had his father's fondness for alcohol enabled drink to take a similar grip on my teenage grandfather? No one ever wanted to talk about the past. I had to wheedle information out of people, like drawing blood from a stone. Nan's sister, Peg, was one of the few members of the family to break ranks, thinking that her teenage great-nephew should be given a more balanced view of his family background.

"Your Nan had to get married. You know that don't you?" Well, no... I didn't. That's the last thing I would ever have been told.

"Such behaviour means nothing now, but then... with both coming from good families... Well it caused a stir. After courting for five years, suddenly, there was wedding at St Peter's Methodist Church in High Park Street. The baby, your mum, was born a few months later in 1902. These were desperate, poverty-stricken times for Ted and Nellie. It was more than ten years and several miscarriages later that Uncle Stan's brother, George, was born in 1913. This was when they were living in one of the cellar homes in the terraced slums off Frederick Street."

My mind attempted to fashion a meaning out of the human degradation, suffered by those who struggled with such a bleak existence beneath the rising gothic tower of Liverpool's new Anglican cathedral. Given the squalid lives of the thousands of people living under its shadow, such a monument to holiness was a desecration; a visible sign of the hollowness of man's pretentious expression of belief in a loving, caring God.

"With your Pop back from the Great War, and your Nan nearly forty, Stan arrived in September 1919." Once more, I got this vision of the great cathedral rising, ever-upwards to heaven, in celebration of my saintly uncle's birth.

I have often wondered at the miracle of how so many poor families stayed together, given the lack of hope during those decades of unemployment and slum squalor, in early twentieth century Liverpool. Nan was the main reason why our family stayed intact. Gentle in spirit, but with the immense physical strength and stoicism of the peasant-class from which her sister and brother believed she came, she submitted to her lot. She tried to make good her husband's idleness by taking in washing and busying her powerful arms to scrub the houses of the rich in Myrtle Street and Abercrombie Square. Nellie Edith seemed born to cope with hardship and the abuse, which Pop handed out in his worst moments of drunkenness and brutality.

Pop's laziness became the stuff of family folklore. He loved his bed so much that in the Blitz, when half of Fern Grove had been blown away he would not lift his head off the pillow, even though the air raid warnings were sounding. Nan's brother, Bert, had become a new and useful source for my collection of tit-bits about the rarity that was Edward Thomas.

Some ten years younger than his eldest sister, Bert was an odd character who found himself a job of sorts in and around Williamson Square in the late 1940s and early '50s. In spite of a bad speech impediment and a pronounced limp, he could fairly blow a whistle to summon taxis for the theatre-goers. He claimed that Pop gave him his gammy leg and articulated jaw when, as a baby, the sixteen-year-old show-off had thrown him high into the air and then forgot to catch him on the way down! Bert used to stay over at Fern Grove, when the bombing got bad. That is, until a blast ripped the door off the Anderson shelter in the back garden. He was fascinated by Pop's ability to sleep away any thoughts of being the next target of the Luftwaffe.

"They came for him during the First World War, you know. Ask your Nan. Yea, they came for the bugger twice."

"Who came for him?"

"The Military Police."

"Who are they?"

"They're the army soldiers who come for you if you don't turn up from leave or if you have run away... deserted." He could tell by the look on my face that he had started something he did not know how to finish. "You'd better ask your Nan or Dad. They know more about it than me."

I carried this line of questioning on to my father who, in his shirt sleeves and with the sun beating down on his bare arms and resolute expression, was manfully applying himself to the task of rowing me up and down Greenbank Park

Lake. Dad used to come round to Borrowdale Road once a week and take me into town to see the cartoons at the Tatler News Theatre. Sometimes it would be an evening visit to the cinema, or even a day out to New Brighton. On this occasion, he must have felt energetic enough for a little light exercise before his lunch. I was sitting on the long wooden seat at the stern of the boat, watching him do all the work, and hoping that I would be given a shot at manning the oars. It gave me plenty of time to ask questions.

"Uncle Bert said that the Military Police came for Pop... twice!"

Dad didn't reply at first. He was well into a bit of showing-off, skilfully manoeuvring both oars in a counter-action to swiftly make the boat do an about-turn at the far end of the lake. Pleased with his little demonstration of oarsmanship and satisfied that we were now travelling smoothly in the right direction back down the lake, Arthur Williams was ready to spill a few beans.

"Well... the second time was very serious, because the South Lancashire Regiment were embarking for Europe. He was brought before a court-martial."

"A court-marshall. What's that?"

"It's when they put you on trial in a military court. During the war, if they found you guilty they could shoot you."

"Was Pop shot?"

"Well if he was, I'd like to know who was repairing your shoes out in the backyard this morning... you soft head!"

"What I mean is... What did they do to him?"

"He defended himself and somehow got off with it. He's a very clever man, your Pop. Plus, he's got the vocabulary to disarm a High Court Judge."

Many years later, after having suffered from depression whilst at university and then as a teacher, I began to wonder whether a faulty Thomas gene had been passed down to me. Could a depressive disposition explain the idle nature of this a highly intelligent, creative man who so readily avoided work, slept like a log while the neighbouring houses were blown to smithereens, and faced a court-martial for not joining up with his regiment on time? Was Pop's drink problem, like his father before him, anxiety driven? No Prozac then, mate. Not in a society where mental illness came out of the same box of tricks as the madness of Bedlam.

The drink-inspired tyranny at home was very hard to cope with. Tough, resilient and obedient to her duty as a wife and mother, Nan would not give up hope that the finer side of Edward Thomas might, one day, prevail. She clung to the attributes her husband displayed in his days of sobriety and good humour, when the man settled himself to be content with clerking and scribing for others. She would acquiesce in the false hopes he had for his songwriting and resign herself to a week when no wages would be put on the table; the wasted days, when he and his music partner spent their time hawking the latest efforts from publisher to publisher.

These were also the great days of working-class football on Merseyside, when he took his son, my uncle, to the park; days when soccer truly belonged to the masses. How many suicides were prevented by the jerseys-for-goalposts legions of the poor and unemployed, who organised a daily routine of self-survival on the hand-made pitches of Sefton Park, Princes Park and Wavertree Playground? Later, as a student, when I walked across these vast playing fields, I caught occasional glimpses of the ghostly figures of discarded men, still playing their endless games with an abandonment and passion which, for a few hours, had pushed despair beyond the touchlines to gaze on as envious spectators.

My father and mother were married in 1933. They were soon forced by the economic depression to live with the Thomases in Fern Grove. Pop was now into his fifties, yet still able to play for Earl, or Marine in the Lancashire Combination. Soccer was his passion and he could have made a great career for himself, but for the drinking and the casual use of his talent.

"Dad... Nan told me that Pop played football all the time, rather than work. Is that true?"

"Not quite. When he wasn't playing footy he was in the pub celebrating himself with a few rounds of Bass."

"Was he any good?"

"At knocking down draught Bass?... He was the world's best. I'm just teasing. I never saw the great 'Bogie' Thomas when he was at his footballing best."

"Bogie?"

"You know what a bogie, is don't you?"

Had it been the season for colds and sneezes I would have promptly picked a big crust from out of my nose and contemplated chewing it. However, it was a lovely day in late spring and with the catarrhs of winter well and truly past, I could only shake my head.

"It's the undercarriage of a locomotive, son. Your Pop could glide past defenders like a well-greased truck on a railway line as if he was on wheels. He was on Everton's books, but the drinking finished any chance of a successful professional career. His great days were over by the time I married your mum. The reputation lived on though, and he still liked to remind his pals in the pubs about the glory days, when he was the Golden Vision with his flaxen head, twinkle-toes, and shimmy of the hips."

"But Nan told me that he played for money?"

"So he did… and that's why he never needed to be out of work. Before the First World War and into the 1920s there were many big dockland companies like Bibbys, Bryant and May and the big tobacco and sugar firms. They competed in their own leagues with very good teams and big crowds turning out to watch them. Pop had no problem in getting a job, but the lazy sod chose to play when he needed the money. His preference was for lying in bed every morning and then spending the rest of the day writing his songs… or drinking his time away in the pub."

"Was he as good as Uncle Stan?"

I had given my dad the chance to put his only male rival for top-spot in my affections clearly in his place, but Arthur Williams did not need to think about it.

"Pop was very good son, so a lot of people told me, but Uncle Stan should have played for England. I used to watch him play for Liverpool City boys, when he tore the opposition to shreds with his dribbling. If the war had not claimed his attention, he would have signed for Major Buckley at Wolves in 1939 and been a star of that I am certain."

In the years before the war, when they all lived together in Fern Grove, Arthur Williams and Pop got on well, until the small matter of his son-in-law's adultery undermined their relationship. The presence of my father in the house at Fern Grove was a blessing to my Nan who, for the first time in her married life, had protection from her husband's violence when he came back home drunk from the pub.

"It's well past closing time. He should be here any… That's him in the hall. Oh dear, Nell, I hope he's not going to be violent." My dad had heard the alarm bells ringing and came in from the back kitchen to give some moral support to Nan and Mum, not long home from working late as a waitress in town. He took a chair from under the table and sat down next to Nan, who was on the edge of the settee and in a state of fear. Uncle Stan, now sixteen and still at the Liverpool Collegiate, had sensed trouble and was studying upstairs. The back living room door was pushed open and Pop stumbled in, full of drink and aggression.

"What's this, eh?… A welcoming party? A firing squad?"

"You've not been in since three o'clock Ted. Your dinner's ruined and I was hoping for the dole money."

"Well you can damn well hope in vain. I've been having a drink with Billy Hughes. We've been reminiscing about football... They know. You don't. Just how damn good I was."

Pop had fallen in with cronies who liked to ply him with stories and compliments about the days of his pomp, for which they were generously rewarded with drink from money he had, often, not earned. My grandfather was a great Liberal Party supporter. There were many sober reasons why a working-class man of intellect and social conscience would wish to vote for the party of Campbell-Bannerman and Asquith. Pop's political hero was the one-time Chancellor Lloyd George. This radical provider of the new social insurance schemes had blessed the unemployed with a few shillings, which Pop was then well pleased to stuff into his pocket for booze money.

"Ted... you promised me and Nell that you would stop the drink. Not while Stan was still at school anyway. It's cruel of you Ted."

Pop launched himself across the room at his wife, and went to strike her. My dad, who was a good four inches taller and considerably heavier than the flyweight Bogie Thomas, leapt from his chair and intercepted the blow. He grabbed Pop from behind and threw him against the pegs of heavy coats hanging on the door into the kitchen. Arthur Williams was not only twenty years younger than his father-in-law, but could handle himself when he had good reason. He gripped Pop by the neck and pressing his head against the door, whispered not-so-sweet nothings into his ear.

"If you lay one finger on Nellie again while I'm in this house, I'll swing for you... Do you hear me you bullying bastard!"

That was it. Nan now had a champion and more than thirty years of domestic abuse stopped that night. An appreciation of my father's protection, as well as her unresentful nature, might explain why she found it possible to cope with her son-in-law throughout the years of his adulterous behaviour with Hilda. When my dad's second marriage to Hilda turned into a tortured, savage existence, Nan could figure out where the violence came from. She knew that for all his faults, Arthur Williams could never lay a finger on a woman – not even a woman who deserved a bloody good hiding.

It was only as a teenager that I began to appreciate the Jekyll and Hyde effect which alcohol had on my grandfather's personality. Nan's sister told me the worst story of the lot.

"Nellie began taking little Stan to sleep with her on the nights when Pop went out drinking, in the hope that his presence in the bed would... well... protect her from unwanted sex. It didn't stop your Pop, though." My uncle saw and heard things which his heavenly little soul could not cope with, as much as he tried to bury such experiences deep in the darkest recesses of his psyche.

In suffocating his own sexuality, my uncle passed on some terrible hang-ups about sex. It took his death, some forty years later, to shake off the remaining constraints and conditioning of my childhood. I can remember, when I was little more than ten, being called into his study one evening after tea. Mum had been dead for less than a year and, no doubt, he felt his responsibility towards me more than ever. He was a loving, paternal man who would not wish to create anxiety for a child who was showing all the symptoms of emotional trauma. However, he was totally unaware of how intimidating he became, when sat behind his big desk surrounded by all his books and papers.

"Have you anything you want to ask me, now that you are beginning to grow up?"

"No."

"Are you sure that there is nothing you are being taught at school which is troubling you. Questions you might want to ask. Questions about the way you are made... about the differences between boys and girls... between men and women."

"Oh, oh..." I said to myself. "There's no way I'm going to let you talk to me about sex. I'd rather follow the diagrams and writing on the lavatory walls at school than listen to your Sophocles version of the birds and the bees. Anyway, I've got Beth to keep me right."

"You're not saying much, Stanley... are you?"

"No."

"There are important changes about to take place in your body... and I don't want you to worry about these things. Is there still nothing you wish to talk to me about?"

"No."

I left Uncle Stan's study, my imagination fired up with alarming thoughts about the unspecified changes, which were about to wreak havoc with my metabolism. Suddenly, I had this vision of myself behind Uncle Stan's desk, slugging back a hideous, green concoction made with the help of a junior chemistry set... I clutch at my throat; my writhing body falls to the floor behind the desk. I get glimpses of it rising and then falling again; I utter the most agonising, unearthly noises. My *Classics Illustrated* assures me, however, that such antics are totally consistent with and essential to the painful metamorphosis... Slowly, the hairy hand of Edward Hyde comes creeping over the edge of Uncle Stan's desk.

In sharing family life with his brother-in-law, my father was able to watch the many girlfriends come and go. In the late 1940s I, too, became fascinated by the number of young women who were brought home, only to quickly vanish from the scene. With his sexual intent firmly bottled up and laid away for a frothy, vintage uncorking when the time for consummation would be blessed by the Almighty, Stan Thomas seemed to frighten the ladies off with an intimidating intellectual intensity and an over-idealistic, romantic approach to relationships. When, finally, he married in 1954, it was to someone who came from a very respectable, middle-class background, appreciated propriety and was impressed by his culture and intelligence. My Aunt Margaret was thirty-four years of age when she married Uncle Stan. She, too, might well have sensed the danger of being left on the shelf.

My uncle's puritanical inhibition was an inherent part of his ascetic, self-denying nature. Parents cannot, however, escape responsibility for helping to make their children what they are. As an infant he had witnessed behaviour within the home, which shook him to the core of his being. His own childhood was a no-go area of conversation. These were dark avenues of the past, down which I was forbidden to walk, let alone explore.

Yes sir, Pop had a lot to answer for. However, back in that summer of 1945, he was simply my silver-haired granddad, who could still take the in-swinging corner kicks for my uncle to head firmly past me between the jackets, set down on the lush grass of Sefton Park. His was the hand I took as I made my first steps away from the company of the overprotective women in my life. Uncle Stan's goodness refused to condemn his father, who he defended with the silence of the grave. He could never betray him by casting up the past, clinging to the Fifth Commandment which told him:

"Honour your father and mother, so that your days may be long upon the land which the Lord your God giveth you."

Rather, he wanted to encourage the rehabilitation of this clever and unfulfilled man, whose own life had been diminished by the inner demons, which only alcohol could keep sedated. Throughout my childhood at Borrowdale Road, Pop turned himself into a fair imitation of the complete man of intelligence, self-education, and acquired breeding.

My dad took a more humorous and cynical view about the transformation of Edward Thomas. "Look at your Pop, son," he would say as we watched him walk down Borrowdale Road for his morning constitutional in Sefton Park. "Look at the old bugger. Who does he think he is... The man who broke the bank at Monte Carlo?"

Arthur Williams smiled, wryly, as the born-again Edward Thomas made his way down the street, tipping his trilby at the ladies on his way to a daily walk around the manor estate. Kitted out by Uncle Stan with a couple of elegant suits to complement the erudition beaming from his fine-featured face, now that it was stone cold sober, Pop looked the part of the sophisticated Edwardian gentleman he had always desired to become. It was a role that came late in life, but it suited him; a lovely little cameo, which an unhappy association with Mr Booze had prevented him from successfully auditioning for in the wild, beer swilling pre-war years.

"If only those women, who seem to treat him like he was a member of the Royal Family knew about the years of drinking, ale-house brawling, and especially the way he treated your Nan... He wouldn't be able to charm the knickers off them, then!"

CHAPTER 8

ON HOLIDAY IN ANGLESEY 1947

Before she became a hospital orderly at Sefton General, my mum cleaned the houses of posh people off Allerton Road and Menlove Avenue. Nan scrubbed out shops and offices in Smithdown Road. After rent, gas and electricity were paid it would leave only small change for a couple of cinema tickets and some sweets so that a romantically-inclined mother and daughter could indulge themselves, twice a week, at the Grand near Penny Lane. It certainly did not pay for the first-class way I was clothed and fed in those years of post-war austerity. By 1948 both my grandparents were beneficiaries of the Attlee Government's Pension Plan, but Pop's subscription to the family budget was as minimal as it had ever been. His input was quietly cerebral. After a compulsory breakfast of fried bacon and egg, he would make his first foray into the pages of the morning newspapers and then go for a walk around Sefton Park. After lunch, he might read a few more chapters of his library book, before a final scrutiny of the political and sports pages led him in suitably relaxed mood to the most demanding task of his day, namely the completion of the *News Chronicle* and *Manchester Guardian* crosswords.

After his demob, my father quickly got a job, but was never with us for long enough to make a fitting contribution to my upkeep. One week he seemed to be at home and the next he was gone to be with Hilda. I assumed that he was still on wartime manoeuvres – and in a funny sort of way he was! All through my years of toddling off to infant and then primary school, Mum received little money from a man who judged his tram driver's wages would best be spent keeping Hilda sweet. My dad stayed at home while we were off to Anglesey. Any holiday plans he may have had did not include his wife and son.

I can remember watching the classic, 1935 MGM version of *Great Expectations* with my mum, at the Grand Cinema. I readily identified with the secret sponsorship young Pip was receiving from his unknown benefactor, Magwich. I knew who was keeping me in school uniforms and providing birthday and Christmas presents; finding the extra money for a new pair of swimming trunks, a cricket bat and football boots; producing tickets from his pocket for the circus, or a half a crown to spend at the fairground in Sefton Park. It was the same generous patronage which now provided the first of our annual family holidays to North Wales.

In the sweltering heat of August 1947 Uncle Stan booked his parents, sister and me into a working farm on Anglesey. This was my earliest experience of a holiday away from the busy streets, smoking chimneys and the bombed building sites of Liverpool. When, in 1946, I ran back home from Lidderdale Infants to show my first reading book to my mum, I believed the countryside tale of "Old Lob" and his collection of farmyard animal friends to be a fairy-tale invention. My world outside the home was made up of the Pier Head with a river full of big ships, docks and giant cranes; a city centre bulging with shops, cinemas, theatres, and roads full of traffic; busy neighbourhoods with their narrow streets echoing to the noisy play of children. Now, I was going to get a glimpse of the rural life most Welsh Scousers had run away from a little more than a century ago. I was going to stay for two weeks with Old Lob – or at least a close relative of his!

It was a dream holiday for a six-year-old boy growing up in the war-damaged Liverpool of 1947. One morning I would be exploring the darkest corners of the massive ruins of Caernarfon Castle; in the afternoon, I was back across the Menai Bridge and dodging jellyfish in the warmest sea I ever splashed about in. Another day saw the family taking a bus trip to picnic at Betws-y-Coed, with Snowdon looking down on us for much of the time. I had never been so aware of the taste of home cooking or appreciated the quality of fresh eggs, milk and butter than at the dining table in that farm kitchen in Anglesey.

In spite of my concern for the welfare of my stomach, the most abiding of all the happy memories parcelled up in that magical holiday was not of my legs racing an empty stomach back to the tea table each day. Neither was it running around the ramparts of a great medieval castle, nor the day out to the beach and funfair at Rhyl. Not even the visit to a real haunted house in Conway could top a romantic interlude which corrected my young boy's ambivalent attitude to the girls I played with. It was an experience that stretched my expectations of what tender possibilities might lay ahead, once I knew more about these alluring, older females. There was something so captivating and emotionally satisfying about this very special moment that I kept its poetic imagery vivid and secure for the rest of my life. As a young man, hopelessly seeking the girl of my dreams, I would reflect upon the illusory picture it created of what being in love must be like.

One evening, after tea, there was yet another glorious sunset and the whole family went outside to enjoy it. We left the farmhouse to take a short walk before turning in for the night. Suddenly, there she was… the eighteen-year-old girl from the farm, running across fields of corn against the backcloth of a fire-glow Turner sunset, flooding in from across the Irish Sea. On and on she ran, free from her toils at last and eager for the young man who was coming to meet her from another farm on the far hill.

My early trips to the cinema with my mum had got me well-used to the clichéd, Hollywood last-reel climax. At six, I was a budding Parkinson and no sucker for the choreographed, windy-hill embrace which encouraged Mum and Nan always to have their handkerchiefs at the ready. This was different. It was not the creation of a film studio's dream-machine. This was not an entertainment to send us to bed happy and contented about the false state of the world. It was for real and happening in front of my eyes.

In her joy and excitement, the girl was oblivious to any audience; her arms were extended and already welcoming an embrace as she ran and ran, fuelled with a passion for the love of her life. As the young sweethearts met, she was swept off her feet and then swirled around, her hair dancing in a golden diffusion of sunlight before the little ballet was sealed with a long, burning kiss. To the lovers we did not exist; nothing else mattered but their moment of sublime togetherness. Behind them and across the late-evening sky, as guarantor of yet another glorious day to come, the sun was spilling out a soft, flame-red blanket of colour over the edges of the western horizon's darkening clouds. My mother and Nan were women whose lives, like millions of other un-liberated working-class nursemaids and skivvies, lacked most of the tenderness and certainly all the romance of such a *Gone with the Wind* setting. In the months to come, the two of them would search together through the countless romantic novels, on the shelves of Bassnett's book shop, to replicate its impact on their raw emotions.

CHAPTER 9

WALKING THE WALK

It was little wonder I had such a confused and divided set of loyalties towards my on-and-off father and constant, guardian uncle. My dad's main priority was Hilda. Any money left over from pandering to her whims and fancies he preferred not to add to Nan's slim housekeeping budget, but spend on our weekly outings together. On these occasions he would give me a sample of his tastes in food and entertainment. This was his chance to give me the benefit of some sharp observations on human behaviour and always there would be a throwaway remark about the lenient way I was being brought up. Not that my dad ever uttered a bad word about his wife's family. Given the attitude of most people then towards adultery as blatant and persistent as his own, he would have had a hard neck to throw any stones from the large glasshouse he had chosen to live in.

To my father's credit, it was not in his nature to undermine my elevated view of the Thomas family, whom he knew I loved dearly. What he felt compelled to do, however, was to get me out from underneath the protective skirts of women and wean me off the infatuation I had for every word uttered, every move made, by my uncle. Dad felt that his brother-in-law was not the best person to teach me about the real world. "Lovely man that he is, son, his mind is too much focussed on higher things." My father wanted my ideas to be more firmly rooted in the practical realities of life.

Arthur was a maverick as well as an adulterer. No sooner was he home from the war, in the spring of 1946, than he resumed his role as the itinerant member of the family. One minute he was AWOL, living with Hilda; the next he was part and parcel of my life at Borrowdale Road, sleeping in my mother's bed, cooking for the household and having another shot at being the family man. I liked him being at home, even though the discipline he imposed made a lawless enjoyment of life more difficult for a restless, inquisitive child. What I did not look forward to was him giving me a bath with such vigour that my skin radiated like a terminal, fluorescent kid, force-fed on thousands of packets of *Ready Brek*. After one of his scrubbings my arms gave off such an unnatural glow, I could read my comics under the bed sheets without the aid of a torch! However, as unexpectedly as he would, suddenly, re-appear to sit with us at the kitchen table, my Scarlet Pimpernel of a father was gone again; back to Hilda's flat around the corner, to set the street tongues wagging in his wake. His style of absentee parenting left

Uncle Stan with the real job of bringing me up. It was hardly surprising, therefore, that his impressionable little nephew began to display mannerisms which had clearly not been handed down through the paternal genes.

"Why, may I ask, are you walking like that, Stanley?" My natural reaction was to think, "Walking like what? There's nothing funny about the way I walk, mate… all great sportsmen and heroes walk like this." The two of us were making our way down Borrowdale Road to get a tram into town, when my dad took sudden exception to the way I was putting one seven-year-old foot in front of the other. What he did not care for was my subconscious attempt to copy the bandy-legged, pigeon-toed walk of his great scheming, inside-forward of a brother-in-law. Stan Thomas was the ultimate role-model for a boy growing up in the years immediately following the Second World War. Fleet Air Arm war hero and Oxford Blue; local sporting legend with Tranmere Rovers, and FA Amateur Cup Winners Pegasus; opening bat for Birkenhead Park and Sefton Park cricket clubs. As a consequence, the boys in the neighbourhood followed him like the Pied Piper, any time there was the chance of a game in the park with any kind of ball.

The legacy of rickets was turned to advantage, as he employed his bandy legs to dazzle and deceive defenders with his amazing dribbling skills. Soon, the diminutive forward, whom the Goodison crowd had dubbed the "Little Jew", was skipping past tackles to the roars of the fifty thousand, who regularly turned out to cheer on Liverpool City boys, in the depression years of the mid-1930s.

Dad knew he could never present me with a CV like that. However, the lack of any such glowing reference from the Supreme Council of the planet Krypton did not prevent Arthur Williams from wanting to see much more evidence of himself in me than the bow-legged Corinthian Casual, who could waltz in and out of the massed ranks of mesmerised defenders as if the soccer ball had been glued to his feet.

Such thoughts must have been passing through my father's mind when, halfway down Borrowdale Road, he stopped and turned me round to face him. "Look at me, son." He bent his knees and lowered himself down to stare directly into my face and so stress the serious nature of his leading question. "Have you been wearing Uncle Stan's old football boots to play football in?" The pint-sized forward had tiny feet for sure, but he would have needed to be in a forward line alongside four Oompa-lumpas, for me to be able to step into his Prenton Park cast-offs. My dad was the last person I would tell even the whitest of white lies to. It would be a fatal miscalculation of his tolerance for a little boy's moments of moral indecision. I, therefore, quickly corrected myself. "No… Well, I did try his boots on, but even when they were laced up tight they fell off." Dad smiled and straightened himself up. "We can't have you walking like that. The next thing is you'll be pecking the ground for birdseed... Watch me... I'll show you how to walk properly." He stood me alongside him, facing down the street, and proceeded to demonstrate his RAF parade-ground technique.

Thankfully, after a dozen or so paces, he stopped and allowed me to catch up. "The placing of the feet is very important. Your toes should be pointed outwards... like this...and not at each other!" I was now galloping alongside a man whose highly polished toecaps were set at an angle only Nijinsky would have contemplated before leaping six feet into the air! My father's body had gone as straight as a broom handle; his arms began to swing rigidly back and forwards, giving him such momentum, I was afraid the wind might lift him into town ahead of me. Our journey to the tram stop was delayed a good five minutes, while I took instruction then gave a small demonstration to convince my dad that, one day, I might become the dream child of an over-zealous warrant officer. I showed Ashley the new way of walking. He laughed so compulsively, it cured me of ever having the notion to walk like anybody other than myself.

It was the same with the way I parted my hair, tied my shoelaces and ate my food. Every time Dad took me out for the day he was handed a ton of evidence that he was not the main player he wanted to be in the daily nurturing of his son. For all this, he proved to be a powerful influence on me. The older I get, the more I find myself displaying peculiar traits of character, which my wife and children tell me have their genus in the mind and personality of my old man. Beyond this, he offered me a more secular, practical alternative to the demanding, pilgrim-path trodden by my idealistic, self-sacrificing uncle.

As a child it was always a constant struggle to balance the shifting weight of my feelings between a dependable guardian uncle and an errant, but very likeable father. One thing I did know for sure; my father had certainly won a few battles to impress me with his many genuine qualities, but had lost his war to turn me into the man he wanted me to be.

CHAPTER 10

WINTER WONDERLAND AT THE BIG LAKE

Sunday in the park was very much a highlight of the post-war family's weekend routine in Liverpool 15:

> *Six days shalt thou labour and do thy work*
>
> *But the seventh day is the Sabbath of the Lord thy God:*
>
> *In it thou shalt not do any work,*
>
> *Thou nor thy son, nor thy daughter*
>
> *Thy manservant, nor thy maidservant,*
>
> *Nor thy cattle*
>
> *Nor the stranger that is within thy gates*
>
> *And on the seventh day thou shalt rest.*

This is what the Ten Commandments have to say about Sunday. Well, that is what they sounded like, back in 1945. Not just the Bible, but the Government also believed it was everyone's God-given right to take a well-earned rest from hard work on a Sunday. The Seventh Day was a Holy Day, set apart from the weekly norm of business and entertainment; a time for quiet family activity, if not churchgoing. No street games were allowed and only the heathen played football or cricket in the park.

Sunday evening saw hundreds of people out walking in the Fairy Glen, or venturing further across the park to the band concerts at the Big Lake. The adults sat and talked on the grassy knoll, next to the bandstand, giving the children free rein to run up and down the steep slope. Below us, polished brass instruments competed on every note to catch the last rays of the dipping sun. We played hide-and-seek while our parents, shelving all thoughts of the week ahead, threw back their faces to enjoy the last few hours of the long day's warmth and light. The mellow tones of trumpets, cornets and trombones flowed over their heads, up the hill and over the trees into the wide-open spaces of the park. Who needed tranquillisers when people could begin the new week with a little space to breathe in deeply, before facing up to the troubles of tomorrow? The evening drew to its close with families making the slow walk back home along the allotment-lined pathways of the park. For all the advances in communication and personal liberties since the 1960s, people have been robbed of the ability to seek happiness in simple, inexpensive pleasures.

The sun did not always set on warm, summer evenings of music and play by the Big Lake. Winter came to take its inhospitable grip on the landscape of the park and keep me away for weeks on end. Not so, in the coldest winter I can remember, during the Narnia freeze-over of 1947, which transformed shivering Britain into an arctic province of the Baltic and Liverpool into the new seaport of Latvia! This was the winter when Sefton's Big Lake froze to a polar depth, turning the surface of the ice into a giant open-air rink. The Dickensian Christmas-card scenes, displayed on the mantelpieces at No.52 Borrowdale, suddenly came to life. It was as if the ruler of this transient kingdom of numbing cold and icy chills had relented in his trespassing acts of meanness and cruelty to all living things. In a brief, careless mood of sentimentality for the beauty he had created, the wild blizzards were silenced, as life and fun were allowed back into the park.

One bright, cold morning, Pop took me down to see this Winter Wonderland of skaters performing their ballet. I stood mesmerised, as they traced their patterns on the lake's frozen surface, manoeuvring and gliding past one another with the ease of the birds, testing the thin air overhead. Most were merely enthusiastic novices pleased with a few, imperfect steps. One or two, however, were brave and confident enough to contemplate a leap. Some wore long winter coats, buttoned from neck to boots. Others sported head and neck scarves, encouraged to trail behind them as they raced to dodge the bite of the wind. They seemed to take no notice of the cold, which I felt keenly but dared not report to my Pop for fear he would have me taken home, too soon, for a plate of Nan's home-made ham and lentil soup. Several braziers had been placed along the lakeside and their glowing heat drew us in to share the warmth with other chapped-faced spectators. "Here you are, son. Try these, but wait a minute before you put one in your mouth… they're straight out of the fire." The smiling woman handed me a couple of roasted chestnuts, which I let dance about in my palms until I was sure the heat was out of them. She then handed out mugs, half-full of a hot, beefy drink, which was the beginning of my childhood addiction to Bovril. Slowly, I felt my body heat being restored. I was pleased that the piercing cold could no longer undermine my will to stand a little longer and watch the softening of uncaring winter's face.

In friendlier seasons there was a lot of activity at the Big Lake. There were always long queues of people waiting to take out one of the many large rowing boats, which plied up and down during the months of summer. It was a place for picnicking and watching small boys, bent double over the water's edge trying to launch their sailing boats; somewhere to take a net and a jam jar to catch tiddlers, in one of the stagnant ponds nearby; a stretch of inviting water on which to cast, hopelessly, with a piece of string and bent safety pin.

The Aigburth Drive end of the lake was used by the BBC to film the *Boys From The Black Stuff* sequence when Yosser Hughes tried to drown himself. Having already punched one policeman on the nose, Yosser broke away from a police car and ran into the park. He would, no doubt, have enjoyed being with me in the early 1950s when, gob-smacked, I watched a young Teddy Boy head-butt one policeman, and punch another smartly on the chin. Having thrown all caution to the wind, he then threw off his drape jacket and brothel-creepers to take a sprinter's dive into the startled ducks on the lake. The lad could certainly swim. Johnny Weissmuller, racing home for a 4.00pm jungle jump with Jane, could have gone no faster! As the two policemen blew their whistles and ran around the lake to try and head him off at the far bank, he continued to power his way through the water. Reaching the other side minutes ahead of his out-of-breath pursuers, he sprang onto the gravel path and legged it through the trees towards Aigburth Drive. All I needed to complete my entertainment was the Tarzan jungle call to echo across the park, as he disappeared through the undergrowth still in his sopping socks.

In 1949 the lake was drained for reasons as murky as the mud on its bottom. "Excuse me, Mrs... Williams, isn't it?" The policeman looked down his checklist of the residents of Borrowdale Road. Do you mind if I ask a few questions relating to the murder at the Cameo Cinema last night?" The spooky thing for me was that Mum and Nan had planned to go to the Cameo on the night of the infamous gunning down of the manager and his assistant. I do not believe for one minute that the insignificant matter of an A certificate, indicating the film's unsuitable subject-matter for an eight-year-old boy, would have cautioned them against taking me along.

I had followed my mum to the front door because I was a nosey little bugger, who had been spying out of the front room window on the unexpected police activity in our street. I was hoping the officer would ask me a question, so I could tell him that all this costly police work could have been prevented. "I should have been there, officer. They were going to take me... screen censorship laws not withstanding... and then I could have changed into my Superman outfit and sorted it all out." The murder was the biggest piece of headline news in the Liverpool of the late 1940s. A man called Kelly was eventually caught and hanged for the killing at the Cameo, a small picture-house in one of the streets off the top end of Smithdown Road. Edgar Wallace himself would have raised a glass to the fatal night scenario of a flea pit like the Cameo showing a film so suited to

Kelly's murderous intent. Thanks to my mum's shopping spree into town that day, I missed seeing "The Blue Lamp", in which a certain PC 49, played by Jack Warner, was gunned down by the next screen heart-throb, Dirk Bogarde.

"Did anyone in the house go to the pictures last night?" "Has anyone seen or heard anything unusual in the street, or the back lane? Have you been out to the backyard and checked the shed and outside toilet since yesterday?"... It was my Nan he should have been asking all these questions to. After a lifetime of social deprivation, she still preferred the chilled excitement of sitting on an outside loo to the unaccustomed splendour of the inside toilet of our new Hotel Babylon, with its slide-across-your-bum sheets of Izal toilet paper. This hardened peasant preferred wiping her arse with the torn up pieces of last Sunday's *News of the World* and leaving the front-page headline, "I was the Lord Chancellor's Call Girl", boldly tattooed on her buttocks for the rest of the day. If Nan said she had nothing to report, other than the fact that the senna pods had worked wonders on her constipation, if not her piles, they could all go back to the police station for a cup of tea.

As I stood staring up into the earnest face of the man in blue, I could not tell him what we all were destined to know a few months later. "You will find the murder weapon, officer. It's a gun with enough fingerprints on it to get Kelly convicted and executed. First of all, though, you'll have to drain the Big Lake in Sefton Park. Come on... I'll show you, if you'll give me the reward money to buy a Dick Tracy two-way wrist radio from Bassnett's shop."

The police did not need me to solve their crime. Someone gave them the tip-off to dredge the Big Lake. It must have seemed like looking for a needle in a haystack, but they found the murder weapon on the lake's slimy floor. The success of the investigation gave me an early, serious respect for the long arm of the law. As I stood gazing at the ugly crater and a mountain of debris which had, temporarily, ruined the beauty of this popular part of the park, I remember asking myself "Where do all the ducks, geese and swans go to when their world is sucked up, overnight?" Not to the aviary that's for sure. Sir Percy the peacock would not tolerate the competition!

CHAPTER 11

WATCHING THE CRICKET IN SEFTON PARK

In those jam-packed summers of childhood, where memory of the weather remains un-blighted by the misery of global warming, my mind's eye has me basking in warm sunshine under the bluest of skies. Back then, it seemed to be a fact of life that when not actually playing cricket, we were watching it at Sefton Cricket Club's beautiful ground, a mere five minute stroll from my front door. All I had to do, for three or four hours of free Saturday afternoon entertainment was cross busy Smithdown Road and walk along the impressive Greenbank Drive entrance to Sefton Park, where an avenue of huge, Victorian mansion houses provided a welcome of wealth and leafy privacy.

As a toddler, it was a regular routine of summer to be taken down with Beth and Ashley to the grassy, south-facing embankment that marked the perimeter of Sefton's carefully manicured pitch. Here, whole families gathered in their thousands for a long afternoon of picnicking and chatter. The men tended to dump their bicycles and group together on the narrow southern perimeter for more serious conversation about the strategies of a contest my Pop claimed was the best sporting mirror of a game of chess.

The impressive club pavilion was set against a backcloth of trees and shrubs. To the right of the clubhouse there was a ticket enclosure, which had defied the wartime requisitioning of much of the city's metal railings. It boasted a set of terraces facing the afternoon sun, which were decorated with comfortably shaped, slatted, wooden benches, painted an enhancing colour of bottle green. Those who were getting a little stiff in the joints joined the wealthier and more snobbishly discerning of spectators to view the proceeding, as much in the spirit of open-air theatre as of sporting spectacle. There were always plenty of Panama hats, canes, walking sticks and sun brollies on view: items of class paraphernalia which never graced the hallstand at No.52. Here sat the regimental blazer and old-school-tie brigade, prominently separated from the ranks of the common herd sprawled out on the grass next to the pitch.

I once asked Pop what he was doing as he sat with a newspaper on his lap, staring away into the fire. "I am cogitating Stanley." He seemed to like the word so much he said it twice… "Cogitating." Well, he wasn't the only one in the family who liked to get to the bottom of things. In the years following my mother's death, I always seemed to have something on my mind, especially when my body was taking a rest. Sitting on the sloping grass, absorbing the slow, hypnotic pace of a game, I would distract myself by looking across and wondering about the fenced-in posh people, who did not like to be ringside with me amongst the masses, but were prepared to squander sixpence on a ticket allowing them quarantine from the mob.

The genteel-looking ladies in that select section of the crowd fascinated me; so finely turned out, in contrast to my harassed, hard-working mum and Nan. From lowered sunglasses peeping out beneath wide-brimmed straw hats, they would check their programmes for the name of the handsome, athletic-looking third-wicket-down now striding out to the crease. No orgy of communal feasting on the grass for them. They had brought along their thermos flasks of tea and thinly sliced mustard and cress sandwiches; some took care to drink from cups far too fragile for use outside the small dining rooms of their neat little semis off Mather Avenue. A whisky flask raised to a gentleman's lips, its polished metal picked out by the sunlight, would occasionally flash in celebration of a high-rising six into the cabbages and carrots of the nearby allotments.

The festival atmosphere around the ground meant more to a seven-year-old than any game of cricket, which from Pop's description seemed to require the patience of Job combined with the mental concentration of the Mekon. The best thing about the occasion for me was when the picnic tablecloth was laid out with its assortment of paste sandwiches, Eccles cakes and cream buns, alongside essential bottles of cream soda and dandelion and burdock.

With the sun high in the sky, I sat filling my face and looked contentedly about me at the large crowd of people still pleased to celebrate the end of wartime rationing. A comforting religious feeling, akin to the Galilean Feeding of the Five Thousand, would come over me as I wondered how many of Uncle Stan's cricket bags could be filled with the scraps left behind when this lot finally went home! Our mothers would settle on coats or small, tartan blankets to gossip, while Beth and I, easily bored by the stodgy rules and strategies of the often slow-moving spectacle, broke away to play a serialised game of Robin Hood in the nearby bushes and shrubbery. As king of the outlaws, I did not seek permission to take my Maid Marion and escape the attention of our parents for half an hour of make-believe, under the camouflage of the park's dark and leafy Greenwood. The regular reward for our good behaviour was a three-penny piece to go and buy a cone, or wafer, from one of the many ice cream vendors who patrolled the fringes of the crowd. This was not a day of relaxation for anyone alive to the chance of making money while the sun shone so brightly on their enterprise. Not if they were prepared to shed a few pounds in weight and pedal a bicycle adapted to carry refrigerated drums of the real McCoy, back and forth from the shops and cafés on Smithdown Road. Once all the fresh milk ices had been gobbled up, I had to settle for a block of Walls in its greaseproof wrapping and, perhaps, ask for a couple of wafers if I wanted to make more of a meal out of it.

For a few years, in the late 1940s, Uncle Stan left teaching to try his hand at management at Lever Brothers, Port Sunlight, the home of a trillion soap-suds and Billy Walls. The fact that I thought I heard the words "whale oil" mentioned in one of my uncle's conversations did not put me off wanting to devour something which looked like a bar of carbolic soap. Insider knowledge of the exotic nature of the ice cream's contents only made its purchase more desirable by giving me a mental picture of epic voyages into the frozen Polar seas. Captains as mad as Ahab braving it to bring me back slabs of frozen blubber, which were then magically given the Willie Wonka treatment and turned into something the mind, if not the taste buds, found a lot more palatable. Whether in jest or not, Uncle Stan told the family that the formula for Stork margarine was not much different from the recipe for the ice cream, which was made in another part of the giant, factory complex. Whatever alchemy may have turned Nan's slab of deadly baking fat into ice cream, watching cricket at Sefton meant eating a Walls. To this day, I still pick up an occasional tub from the supermarket because the sixty-year-old recipe of unidentified oils and vanilla transports my taste buds back to Sefton Park and midsummer days of cricket, in that sweet springtime of my life.

My uncle was such a legend in his own backyard that when he turned out for Sefton the entire neighbourhood went down to watch him opening the batting. At 5' 4" he was some sight to behold. Out to the wicket he strode, a diminutive, One-Day warrior, laden down with cricket pads the size of a Roman infantryman's soccum shield. The courageous wee fellow would then heroically set out to subdue the fiery pace of the early bowling, striking out for the boundary as often as he could. I have one special memory of him trying to please his loyal support of young boys with a whirlwind knock. For the first few deliveries the portents were not encouraging. He sneaked a single with his second ball, and then his batting partner could only manage two runs to keep the fan club waiting for the bowling to change ends. However, our expectations of the amazing, wee man came up to scratch in the next over when, in quick-fire succession, Stan Thomas hit two fours, a six, another four and then another massive six into the regularly-bombed cabbages beyond the path down to the Big Lake. The last ball had the evening crowd of thousands expecting thirty runs in one over, but he was clean bowled. What a reception he got on his walk back to the pavilion. The fact Bootle had beaten Sefton that day did not matter. I had to wait for Botham to see Uncle Stan's imitation of Dennis Compton surpassed.

"Now, Stanley, stand still... Don't flinch! Just stand and watch the bowler run in. Pay careful attention to the flight of the ball as it moves through the air."

Once I had swallowed the last piece of Nan's home-made jam sponge and gulped down a glass of milk, Uncle Stan was up from the tea table and ready to take me down to the practice nets at Sefton to face my nemesis... "The unnecessary fear you seem to have, Stanley, of a small leather ball." He was not a man for profanity; otherwise he might more honestly have prefixed the words "bastard of a..." to his benign description of what I regarded as a primed grenade. As much as I trusted my uncle, on this occasion I doubted the experience would be of any benefit as, in my head, there was a little umpire in a long white coat, telling me to run to the hills at the first sign of intimidating bowling.

The truth is that I had never recovered from seeing my uncle come home from an afternoon's work as opening batsman for Birkenhead Park with his nose split, broken in two places, and stuffed with blood-soaked cotton wool. He had a distinctly Jewish set of features to start with. Now he looked like a Yiddish Mr Punch! I also had inherited the sizeable family schnozzle and did not want to ruin my chances of, one day, bagging a decent-looking girlfriend because some senseless bugger had thrown a small incendiary device between my eyes:

> *And the Lord said unto Moses*
>
> *All Jews shall have round noses,*
>
> *Except for Brother Aaron*
>
> *And he shall have a square-un!*

So ran the stanza of the unknown Dovedale playground poet, who had sussed-out that Aaron, in spite of his excellent, priestly credentials for leading the Israelites down into the Promised Land, was also a failed opening batsman for the Canaan Second Eleven!

Some of the lads I played with clearly saw bowling as an alternative form of capital punishment. There were boys in Toxteth and the Dingle who believed they could kill you with the right execution of a full toss. What if the playing surface wasn't the level, razor-cut billiard table I believed all the wickets in heaven to be? With nightmarish thoughts of hospitalisation running through my head, I was far from confident about the protection afforded by the uncomfortably low screen of mesh netting, somewhat treacherously anchored by a few angled poles roped and pegged into the soft, green turf on the boundary of Sefton's pitch.

"This is it, Stanley. It's a long run-up... a very long run-up. Here's a real fast one coming down... Let's see how the batsman deals with it." The man tearing towards us looked more than ready to deal with anyone skittle-brained enough to stand, like me, at the end of a long, narrow alley with walls of string. "Here he comes. Don't move away! Don't flinch... Keep your eyes on his arm and especially on the ball." I felt my uncle's hand pressing firmly into my shoulder, as if he was trying to massage some courage into me.

"This bloody ball is going to hit me smack in the face. I know it!" I sensed from the runway run-up that the bowler had sniffed out my fear; just like the fiend-of-an-Alsatian on Garmoyle Road knew I was scared stiff, as it stood there snarling and chortling away to itself, watching every step of my wide detour to the other side of the street. I was doomed and about to be served up as a sacrifice to the unknown god of broken noses and cracked skulls.

"Don't worry. Don't be intimidated. We have the net to protect us... There's absolutely no danger in this type of bowling, Stanley, if you watch the ball all the way. You're..." I was about to hear the empty words, "...completely safe", when the delivery skimmed the net, travelled another twelve feet, or so, and hit me smack in the middle of my forehead.

If the giant Goliath could be taken out with a small stone, then a game of cricket against the Philistines might have saved King Saul the mobilisation of the Israelite army. It took a few anxious seconds to convince my uncle that I was not dead. How many fingers did he and his twin brother have on their amazing collection of hands? I hadn't a clue. I was a good five minutes lying flat out on the grass, before I could be gently raised to my feet and led back home. Later that evening, as I passed the kitchen door on my way to bed, I overheard Uncle Stan telling Pop that the best tonic for my unfortunate syndrome would be to promptly take me back for a few more encouraging knocks on the head! As I made my way up stairs, I heard the voice of comedian, Arthur Askey, on the kitchen wireless, signing off with... "I thank you... and goodnight!"

Uncle Stan was now the only active sportsman in the family. Pop was in his seventies and my dad well into his forties. The only real exercise Arthur Williams now gave himself was to climb in and out of his cab as a city council bus driver. Arthur, however, did not approve of his brother-in-law basking in all the glory as the ultimate sporting hero in the family. Although he was past running like a headless chicken around a football pitch, the odd game of cricket in Sefton Park was too much of a challenge for him to resist.

On a typically roasting summer's afternoon in the school holidays Dad arrived, unexpectedly, at the Old Farm Field to find us well into yet another test match series. He signalled he was opting to join the fielding side, with the hope he would soon get the chance to show us that he still had a little of Fiery Fred Truman left in him. He liked to call his odd style of delivery "bowling", but used an arm action so uneducated and savage that had it been witnessed by a visiting member of the MCC Rules Committee, there would have been an immediate phone call to London, followed by a prosecution for bringing the game into disrepute! Whereas Stan Thomas preferred to tease the batsman with well-flighted slow spinners, which seemed to hang about in the air before looping in to take your off stump clean out of the ground, my dad hurled the ball at you in the style of a Yankee pitcher. Every delivery was aimed at either your head or your chest. Arthur Williams made no concessions to cowards, pregnant women, small children or nancy boys. He treated batsmen as if their heads were on perches at a fairground coconut shy and he was out to win a prize by knocking a few blocks off!

He had barely laid down his jacket when a masterly stroke by Tony Brooker sent him chasing to fine leg. To his credit, he caught up with the ball, but misjudged his footing, trod on the rolling piece of red leather and catapulted himself into mid-air! The game was suspended for about ten minutes, to allow the writhing and groaning to subside to a level which would not interfere with the state of play. Arthur Williams needed time to compose himself, so that he could ask for his jacket in the manner of a man who had publicly declared John Wayne to be a draft-dodging poof! Slowly and painfully, Dad limped away as the game resumed. Far from being a callous reaction to my father's predicament, it was the best means of keeping my gaze off the crippling figure who, with the support of some conveniently placed allotment railings, was inching his sorry way home.

My father was off his work for many weeks with torn ankle ligaments. I saw him a few days after his tumble on the Old Farm Field. He was sporting a set of crutches Robert Newton would have been proud to hop around Treasure Island on. Not knowing how to commiserate with a man whose lack of nimble footwork had caused his ego to deflate faster than the ballooning of an elephant-like left ankle, I turned quickly on my heels and vanished up the nearest jigger, before he could set his pained expression on me.

CHAPTER 12

ARTHUR THE TERMINATOR

My father was no sporting hero. This fault, however, did not prevent him from making a strong physical impression on me. Only my granddad, performing under the influence of the IOC banned stimulant, draught Bass, could attempt to match the natural, instinctive aggression which manifested itself whenever Arthur Williams felt threatened.

"Don't go near a cornered rat!" Pop barked the order at Uncle Stan who, home from Oxford for Easter 1948 and armed only with his practice cricket bat, was about to try to glance the terrifying creature into the sink at silly mid-off. The fear on the faces of my mother and Nan panicked me as much as the thought of this relentless coloniser of drains and plague-ridden sewers making its last stand in our kitchen. Rats give me the creeps. They always have done, and always will. I blame the Pied Piper of Hamelin for lifting the lid on my subconscious loathing of the venomous rat; playing his evil, hypnotic tune to lure innocents, like me, into a dance of death. Tom Thumb, one of my favourite characters in the *Beano*, only made things worse. There he was, tiny mite, in made-to-measure tights and feathered hat, fighting for his life against a giant rat, with nothing bigger than a large sewing needle to pierce its black, malignant heart. Pop put the icing on the cake of my rat revulsion, when he read me passages from the M R James ghost story *Lost Hearts* in which Parkes, the butler, recalled hearing, "tales from the men in the shipyards about the rat that could speak." Ughh! The presence of the repulsive, dangerously trapped creature in front of us demanded some super-hero intervention. It was my dad, however, who took charge of the proceedings.

Without adding one wasted word to heighten the anxiety of the situation, he squeezed past Mum and Nan, cowering at the kitchen doorway and went straight over to the crunching gnawer of raw flesh and bone. As the rat arched its back, priming itself for a fight to the death, Dad kicked it against the back door. Taking the split-second chance which the stunning blow had given him, he snatched it up by the end of its long, bootlace of a tail and banged it several times against the kitchen wall, streaking the bottle green paint with the filthy rodent's foul, red blood. The rat was so dead, I felt safe enough to creep forward and take a closer look at its loathsome, lifeless body. It was, then, ceremoniously carried out to the dustbin by my Nan, who had emerged, greatly unburdened, from her hiding place in the pantry.

The manner in which my father had despatched the rat confirmed him as a person who would not want any son of his to take his hat off to an assailant. "Thank you so much for that unwarranted, totally unexpected punch in the face. Please do it again as I found the experience so brutally, refreshingly honest!" Arthur Williams had observed that my upbringing, under the supervision of his Christian brother-in-law, discouraged any form of aggression outside the context of sport. During the times my father chose to live with us he would turn the early evening, after tea, into a training session, falling to his knees on the polished linoleum in the back living room, to bring his head and chest within range of as many blows as I could land on him. Temporarily released from the straitjacket of "turn the other cheek" behaviour, I would attempt to give him a hiding, as he showed me how to protect my body and face, before encouraging a salvo of fairy-cake punches. Within a few weeks of such coaching, he obviously hoped I would be too much for the Bugsy Malone hoodlums whom he imagined to be out there, waiting to halt my first steps on the mean streets of Liverpool 15.

"Arthur, you shouldn't be showing him how to hit other little children like that. It's the same with you wanting to take him to the wrestling. He's only just started Lidderdale Infants. Fancy showing a six-year-old all those horrible. What do you call them?... 'Holds', that's it... and all the other terrible things that wrestlers do to one another. He's been trying arm-locks on his Nan. It's a good job she's as strong as an ox. It doesn't help him grow up to be a considerate person, Arthur." It was another two years before Dad managed to wring out of my mother her grudging consent to let me go with him to the Liverpool Stadium. I would return home ignorant of the fact that my entrance ticket had been issued to me by his mistress, the horrible Hilda, but filled with dramatic tales of lawless ring behaviour.

"Then Jack Pye picked up the tin bucket in his corner and cracked it over the other wrestler's head... The referee tried to stop Jack Pye hitting his opponent back, but that just made Jack Pye even madder and he threw the referee across the ring... The other wrestler then got to his feet and hit Jack Pye over the head with a wooden stool." Mum would wince at every blow, my detailed eyewitness account of proceedings confirming all her worst fears about the barbaric tastes of her husband. Pop, however, hid his amused approval of my honest appraisal of such a sham sport behind the gently shaking pages of his *Echo*.

"I saw Masambula tonight, Mum... Dad says he is so black that he floods the ring with a tinge of the Congo at midnight. What's a tinge, Mum?... He bent the other wrestler's body over his knees and the man's back made a horrible creaking sound like Nan's clothes pulley in the kitchen, when she hoists it up with all the wet washing on. He was carried away on a stretcher, moaning with all his bones broken...and everyone was cheering." They stopped me from going to see Jack Pye and others like Count Bartelli for months after that vividly colourful and embellished piece of tabloid reporting. My mother added it to her dossier of twenty good reasons why Arthur should continue to have only a limited and prescribed access to her impressionable little son.

It was just as well that Mum did not hear some of my father's finest mortal combat tips, given casually on our days out together. Dad rationed them out in the sincere belief that my submissive nature needed to be considerably toughened up.

"Look, son...if you are threatened and it's one-to-one up some dark alley, or behind the air-raid shelters in the school playground, don't bother to ask anyone for permission to do what I'm telling you now. First, kick the boy hard in the shins, very hard... as if you were taking a penalty or a goal kick. He'll double-up. That's when you punch him in the guts again. I mean as hard as possible, in the pit of his stomach... right here."

At this point he opened his jacket and placed my hand on his solar plexus. He had tensed his muscles for dramatic effect, and it felt like a brick wall. Was this meant as an encouragement for me to break my fist on some tough boy's iron chin? My eager corner man sensed I was losing this fight on points and built me up for a last round knockout.

"His head will come right down... Hey! Hey! Listen to me. Don't back away! Now's your big chance to either punch him in the jaw, or butt him in the forehead. Either way, that should settle matters."

"Either way?"... Umm? That didn't sound too good to me. This script from a James Cagney movie had one obvious flaw in it, which I felt compelled to point out.

"What if it doesn't settle matters, Dad? What if the boy I hit... say a bigger, harder boy than you first imagine, just grins like Little John did when he roared with laughter at Robin Hood's attempt to crack his head open with a long staff. Whack! And it just snapped on Little John's head... Remember, the film Dad?" My father laughed at the thought of a draft-dodger like the great Errol Flynn dumped into the river by the massive Alan Hale Jnr. "Well if that's the case, son, you'd better get your skates on and move faster than you have ever done in your life."

Over the next couple of months, in the best of my all-action dreams, I found myself going through variations on this Hollywood tough guy routine. Once, or twice, I think I can remember it working to plan – like a dream you might say. Most times, however, I woke up, either running for my life, or having just skinned my knuckles on the wall next to my bed!

As a teenager, I came back home very late one night. My grandparents were in bed, and having no key, I was forced to think about breaking in through a back window. From my seat at the Grand I had seen enough of Louis Hayward as the Saint, manoeuvring his way into the most burglar-proof buildings, to be confident of being able to gently unpick any friendly window catch. I began prowling around in the back yard looking for the best option, not realising that my father was inside the house making one of his rare visits to check on Nan, now that Pop was so ill upstairs. His radar had picked up unwelcome signs of life at the back of the house. Suddenly, a light was switched on in the back kitchen. Next, I heard the ominous click of the lock in the kitchen door being turned, followed by the heavy bolt being drawn. Then, nothing… Absolute silence! There was not a sound for fully two or three minutes.

I tried imagining that I was an extra coat of white distemper on the wall of the washhouse, which was proving to be such a poor choice of backcloth for my attempt at invisibility. I was praying that the living room lights would not be switched on and the curtains pulled back, to expose me trying to evade the camp searchlights in Stalag 17. I could hold my breath no longer and had decided to break the tomblike stillness with a gulp of fresh air, when a hand came round the corner of the washhouse and grabbed me by the throat. I had a split second to scream out. "It's only me!"… before getting the living daylights thumped out of me a few hours ahead of sunrise.

Perhaps, the synchronised maiden sisters, who lived in the house opposite, found themselves jolted wide awake, in tandem, as a disembodied voice screeched into the darkness of their separate back bedrooms, "It's only me!" When they got up the next day their debilitating and embarrassing hot flushes would be a thing of the past! Never again did I risk breaking in after hours, in case the family Terminator had beamed himself down into No.52 for the night!

I do not know where my father's reaction to sudden threat came from. It was an aberration of his normally pleasant personality and unassuming manner; an accessible monster, ready to be unleashed from its padlocked cellar, if and when the situation merited. This was the case, one night, in the late 1930s, when he was a conductor on the Ribble buses, and three drunken soldiers attacked him on a last journey back into Liverpool. The men were after his leather bag of copper and silver coins, together with the tin box of one pound and ten-bob notes, which he kept under the stairs, until he got the chance to hand it over at the end of his shift. He saved all the cash that night, and gave the three squaddies such a thrashing it made their landing on the beaches of Normandy, a few years later, feel like a relaxing date out at the seaside. Pop told me that two of the men ended up in hospital; one had a broken jaw, another with enough stitches in his face to permanently remind him of having been given too close a shave with the spike of my dad's conductor's ticket-punch.

This violent little episode took place in the days when protecting yourself, not to mention your passengers, and the bus company's money, was deemed powerful mitigation in a successful plea of self-defence. My father escaped jail sentence, but went unrewarded with a swift promotion to the lofty rank of Ticket Inspector... "That's for people whose faces fit," he once told me. While he worked for Ribble buses, more significant than flirting with a criminal record, was Arthur's meeting a busty clippie called Hilda, who was about to start fondling his loose change, before handing out the first of many free rides.

My dad was no better and no worse than the countless numbers of men who have walked away from the constraints of marriage and reneged on their responsibilities to a family. In my father's case, it was for a slow poisoning of his passion for the woman, who so finely whetted his shackled sexual appetite. The most frustrating thing about him was how he made it so bloody obvious that his behaviour was as muddled as it was perverse. He was aided in all his lying and cheating by an adoring, forgiving wife, who continued to allow his body, if not his surrendered soul, to return to her bed at Borrowdale Road.

The dereliction left in my mother's life made it impossible for a grown-up son to find a true reconciliation with his father. I loved him, but the affection and trust he so obviously wanted from me was beyond my capacity to give. In the midst of all the insecurity and confusion, which his deceit and selfishness visited upon my childhood, he did manage, however, to make a difference to my life. I was blessed by the fact that my dad received an unfathomed depth of tolerance and compassion from Uncle Stan, whose Christian spirit was active in moderating the hurt and family anger towards him. It was this God-inspired generosity which, in turn, enabled me to be given occasional glimpses of the goodness hidden within Arthur Williams. What a struggle the light of his virtue had, in trying to break through the dark camouflage of secrecy and evasiveness. He was, I believe, truly desperate to find some peace and happiness in this world, as he had no faith in the next. Sadly, the dual existence he had created for himself turned him into his own persecutor.

CHAPTER 13

THE THOUGHT OF HILDA

The thought of Hilda sent shivers down my spine. Throughout my primary school years she frightened me more than any other person I knew. My big worry was that she might not be a person at all. When Mum fell ill with the headaches that would eventually kill her, my constant fear, if the worst ever happened, was of being taken by my father to live with the woman Ashley claimed was a real, live witch. He reckoned her to be the genuine article; as bona fide as the crone on a broomstick, who plagued little Dorothy all the way along the Yellow Brick Road. Although many of Ashley's seven-year-old concerns related to making sure he got a square meal each day, as a future recipient of an Open Scholarship to Oxford, his word was to be taken seriously. He warned that Hilda might agree to look after me, only to feed me up before shoving me, head first, into her electric oven.

Mum was extremely vigilant in keeping me out of Hilda's sight as, since the early summer of 1948, her arch rival had come to live only a few streets away from our house. One day, however, whilst hidden in a shop doorway, and with my mind full of Ashley's fanciful notions about the true intentions of my dad's mistress, I got the chance to take a good look at her, as she was peering into the window of a shop on Smithdown Road. Hilda's heavily lipsticked mouth and painted face confirmed the worst fears that here was a cruel, calculating woman, who planned to get my mother out of the way for good. Ashley had created a nightmare scenario of the wicked stepmother. I could see it all clearly; Hilda would concede to my father's wish to have me live with them, so that she could control and diminish me. She would then put an end to me and reign supreme in the affections of my father.

Such was the background to a faint tapping sound at the front door. It was already dark outside and getting close to bedtime for an eight-year-old. I was about to take my first, reluctant steps upstairs when the persistent rapping, odd for any time of the evening, alerted me to the unexpected visitor. The hall light was out and the vestibule door half closed, so whoever it was did not see me coming. "Bela Lugosi! It's the unmistakable form of Hilda, crouched down like a creature of the night... and come rat-tat-tatting at the glass above the letterbox." So desperate was her desire to get a message to my father, she was prepared to risk a humiliating confrontation with a family only too willing to be her judge, jury, and

High Executioner. Suddenly, Hilda became aware of someone in the vestibule and darted away into the shadows, across the street. I feared the woman so much, but hated her even more. The sudden advantage of having her on the run emboldened me to open the front door and pursue my tormentor into the night.

I was out on the pavement in a flash, but Hilda had vanished into thin air! She possessed no Ring of Power, however, and I sensed a lurking presence. I knew she was still about the place, if only I could look hard enough. The enemy was now on my territory and within my grasp, in the land of my imagination. "I am Hawkeye, chief scout and Indian fighter… She, a traitorous Iroquois intruder into the family encampment." I lifted my nostrils to the get the scent of her sickly perfume before fixing my stare on the front garden of Simone Cohen's house opposite, where I guessed Hilda could not hold such a bent position, behind the hedge, for much longer. I approached her hiding place with all the stealth of a buckskinned backwoodsman; taking a deep breath I crouched down so that our eyes met through the leafless, lower branches of the privet.

"Hello," I said, making a deliberate effort to sound as cool and casual as Davy Crocket, surrounded by a dozen of Santa Anna's Mexican cut-throats, even though my little heart was beating like a drum inside my woollen jumper. "If you're looking for my mum, she's in the house waiting for my dad to come home from work." I got the mouthful out without gulping, and then turned away before I got the shock of a reply. I had done myself proud and said all that was necessary. I went back into No.52 to report to my mother, Pop and Nan, who were seated around the fireplace in the back living room.

Uncle Stan had been out while all this was going on. Without his restraining presence the three other Thomases were galvanised into an over-hasty reaction and ran out into the street to confront the family's bête noire, but she had legged it. "What a hard neck! What a damned, brazen act of cowardice," Pop shouted after the phantom who had melted away into the night. The street lamp picked out something fluttering about on the pavement, and Mum bent down to pick up Hilda's undelivered, pencilled note. Slowly, she translated the few scribbled lines, of bad grammar and spelling, which desperation had forced the woman to risk putting down on paper:

"I must see you quickly, Arthur. You must come round to the flat as soon as you get in. You are very cruel to leave me for days in suspense, without even a word. I am very upset. You are not a man of your word. You are a liar and a deceiver. You must come and see me tonight."

That is as near as my memory can get to the exact words Mum read out, with Pop interrupting to berate Hilda's "appalling unfamiliarity with the English language." Back inside, seated at the warmth of the kitchen fire, the note was passed around the grown-ups once more as its content was silently digested. It was then folded and placed in a drawer of the kitchen sideboard for Uncle Stan to examine when he got home. There were lots of angry words spoken later that night, when my dad came home to a hot reception, sidelining his cold supper to the waste bin.

I had been packed off to bed in anticipation of a serious confrontation. When the inevitable rowing started, I crept down to a half-way point on the stairs and took up the best position for monitoring any conversation which might squeeze out through the unclosed door of the back living room. Everyone was so busy apportioning blame and heaping burning coals of condemnation on my father's head, that they remained oblivious to my presence on the dark staircase in the hall. For once, I don't think they cared if I heard some home truths being told.

Pop, incensed with anger, led the attack on his adulterous son-in-law. It was the first time I had ever heard my grandfather swear. "You're a devious, thoughtless bastard, Arthur, to think you can use this girl of mine and this home to suit your own selfish ends." Uncle Stan had arrived back. I could hear him, pleading that calm and reason should prevail… "For Nellie and the boy's sake, Dad, let us handle this matter with as much understanding of one another as we can." My dad was having none of Pop's moralising. He could not discount what he knew of the dark times before the First World War: Nan's painful recounting of her husband's drunkenness and the near wrecking of their home life. Then there were the years of the 1920s and '30s; two decades of idleness, much of it self-created, when my young father had been Nan's only protection against a Bass-swilling little bully who, head full of rage at his own unfulfilled dreams, would pick a pub fight with anyone before coming home, skint, to intimidate his children and violate his wife.

No thank you! Arthur Williams was not taking any of that sanctimonious crap from the born again, Edwardian gentleman, Teddy Thomas. "You're a bloody hypocrite, Pop. What a hell of a long time it has taken you to see the light!" Fists were raised. Pop had his sleeves rolled up for action. He growled an impossible challenge at my father. "How do you want it, Arthur? Rough… or smooth?" The door of the kitchen opened on what had first sounded like groundbreaking radio drama. Now I had the bonus of a balcony cinema seat to see that Pop had adopted the street fighter's stance. With fists clenched and head well tucked in between the shoulders, his flyweight's body seemed to be constantly shifting its balance in the bobbing, weaving style of a little street slugger, who triumphed by perpetual motion. It was Errol Flynn, Douglas Fairbanks Jnr. and James Cagney, all rolled into one Hollywood-style entertainment, right there in my own home!

Uncle Stan intervened in time to prevent a free-for-all. His calming voice restored order as the cries and tears of the two women subsided. Suddenly, someone became aware that the door had opened on an escalating drama whose uncertain ending I should not be allowed to catch the drift of and it was, once more, banged shut. The conversation lowered and I could hear little else to educate me about how my father's passion for another woman had got us all into such a state.

I left my listening post and went back to bed. I had heard enough, however, to guess that my dad would not stay in the house beyond the time it took to pack all his belongings into one small suitcase. He did come to my bedroom door to look in before he went back to Hilda. I pretended to be fast asleep as he stood in the doorway for a few seconds, and then he was gone. I lay for some time thinking about things, before I drifted off, satisfied that all the whispering ghosts of the past few years had, at last, developed a set of clear and lively tongues. Those family skeletons I had heard people speak about, which seemed to live a hush-hush existence, shut up in airless cupboards, had finally put on some unhealthy flesh and stepped out onto the light. Perhaps my young mind could now get the chance to make head, if not tail, of it all. I woke up next morning to be told that Dad had left home; this time I knew it was for good.

CHAPTER 14

STRANGE GOINGS ON IN THE ATTIC

Apart from a small gas fire in my uncle's study, all the main downstairs rooms were heated by coal fires. The only extra heat came from the wafts escaping from the back kitchen, as meals were cooked or when the steam from Nan's washing filled the air. During the winter months, the temperature in the bedrooms was a powerful discouragement for me to play upstairs and children got no help from central heating to encourage them to sit up reading in bed.

I made do by pulling the sheets and eiderdown over my head, using my body heat to slowly bring the air temperature around me up to the more satisfactory level of a lightly-grilled piece of toast. Possessing nothing more than a small torch, I managed to extend my enjoyment of the day well past "lights out."

Once the *Eagle* had made its first appearance in April 1953, I would lie on my stomach with the comic propped up against my pillow and spread open at its centre pages. This allowed me to give half an hour's full attention to the da Vinci-inspired *How it Works* section, with its amazing cross-sectional colour diagrams of modern wonders, such as *The World's First Jet Plane*, or *The World's First Atomic Submarine*. If this advanced course in engineering had over-stimulated my brain, I could then turn to the more sleep-inducing entertainment offered by PC 49 and super-slueth Harris Tweed.

My last port of call would be in the company of that dirty old sea-dog, Captain Pugwash, or should I say dirty old bastard, John Ryan, the art master from Harrow who drew him. Edited by Methodist minister, Marcus Morris, the *Eagle* professed a high moral tone, so heartily approved of by Uncle Stan. Like millions of other monitoring parents, he was blissfully unaware that among Pugwash's motley crew of pirates were the fifth columnists of licentious, late twentieth-century *Viz* humour, with names like Master Bates, Seaman Staines and Roger, the cabin boy! Pugwash was the only speck of smut to get through the comic's filth filter.

In my bedroom, however, there was one serious obstacle to a good night's sleep. I could have done with hiring a top class destroyer of demons, like Van Helsing, to climb into the attic above my head and sprinkle his magic water on to its rafters and floor. In winter, the greatest calamity that could befall our house was the freezing up of the tank in the cockloft. Dutifully, Pop would climb up into the rafters and place two, tiny, slow-burning candles in small saucers near the water pipes.

"Why are you doing that, Pop?" My granddad had come into my room with a ladder and proceeded to climb into the attic to protect the precious pipes from a late-night December freeze.

"Well, Stanley, the difference between a temperature of one degree above and one degree below freezing point spells tragedy for everyone in this house. These two trifling flickers of flame provide enough heat in the coldest hours of the night to keep the air temperature under the slates above freezing point."

The attic was a den for our gang of seven and eight-year-olds. Here I sat with Ashley, Beth and Margaret Jones, uncomfortably balanced between the broad joists, in order to imitate the closed society of a depleted version of the Secret Seven. Our most privileged discovery was a small opening in the attic wall, linking Nos.50 and 52 Borrowdale, which enabled us to make amazing progress into several other houses down one side of the street.

"Hey... look, Stan. There's a crack between the plaster and the floorboards. You can peep down into one of next door's bedrooms below."

"Gizza look, Ashley... Blimey! I can see Mr Hughes taking off his shirt and vest in front of the wardrobe."

"Shhh! Let me see again... Cor... He's just taken off his hair and put it on a chair!"

Nearly a half-century before Scully and Mulder investigated such phenomenon, this was as frightening and surreal a moment as I can remember. We carried the burden of this classified information around with us until a boy at school told me that he had an uncle who wore a wig! We were too young to know what irony meant, but months later we found out, from reports in the *Liverpool Echo*, that our X-Files neighbour, a plumber by trade, had lingered a little too long whilst mending the water tanks above the nurses' showers at Sefton General Hospital. He had been caught spying down on the soapy nakedness of three young nurses, to make the type of Peeping Tom headlines which fairly dented the confidence of his lady customers ever to call him out again to lag their pipes for the winter!

After 1948, when my mum's health began to fail and with the shadow of Hilda looming over my life, the attic became a hidey-hole where all my fears and insecurities could skulk about. As I lay in my bed, head on a soft pillow and face turned towards the open door of the loft, I could see the two, tiny optimistic specks of candlelight as if they were struggling to shine for Jesus in one of Hell's dark corners. My real torment was not the prospect of an Arctic freeze-over, but the fact that Jack Frost was not alone up there! I waited for sleep to end the ordeal where far less accommodating creatures than mischievous Jack, would gather to look down at me from the open Alice doorway, high up on the wall across from my bed.

I could only stare back, hypnotised, at the unguarded gateway to imaginings as black as a witch's heart. By day the cock-loft was merely an out-of-bounds temptation into adventurous play, but at night I would lie there and watch the shadows begin to lengthen across the room, fearful that if sleep did not come quickly then bright moonlight would begin to play nasty tricks at the latch of the small door, slowly re-opening an inky portal to more tormented dreams. This would have meant Uncle Stan rising from his bed, in the room next door, to give me a moment of calming reassurance.

CHAPTER 15

MY AMAZING BSA

Say boys, say girls

Do you know who is who?

I'm the great broncobuster

Rodeo Hugh

I've chased wild beasts

All over the show,

Got them in such a bungle

Frightened them so,

That they'd nowhere to go

Poor things, they ran back to the jungle!

Awful... ain't it! That is why I've let you off with just the first verse of one of Pop's songs written for the old music hall. There were dozens of them – comic, romantic, and First World War lyrics – lying in his box of private papers, tucked away at the top of the tall cupboard in the back living room. Once more, I had scaled the highest shelf and taken down the box of tricks to amuse myself re-reading my favourite, which appealed to a small boy's obsession with cowboys. It was called *Rodeo Hugh* and its artless doggerel mesmerised me. It was so bad it was good – if you see what I mean.

It was during the summer holidays of 1949 and I was filling in time waiting for Pop, who was getting ready to take me on a tram to collect my new BSA. I had first seen the dream machine over a year ago, in the window of a bicycle shop opposite the bombed remains of St Luke's Church at the top of Renshaw Street. I wanted that bike so badly and pestered my mum for the rest of the year to buy it.

"What a beezer!" I told Ashley. "It's got the latest American streamlined design, with a curved crossbar and handlebars like a motor bike. I've never seen anything like it... I'm going to ask to get it for Christmas!"

Well I didn't get it, did I. It was far too expensive an item to be bought on short notice and clearly took Mum saving for the best part of a year, plus a generous chip in from Uncle Stan, for me to be told the good news that, at long last, the bike was mine and waiting to be collected at the shop.

I had given up all hope of ever getting that bike, so my excitement in taking the No.86 tramcar into town with Pop was only exceeded by the rate at which I had outgrown it in the past year. The singular model was made for a seven-year-old and I was nearly eight when I first began to goggle at it, through the shop window, in the summer of 1948. I could see it getting smaller and smaller with every trip into town. Now that I was, finally, about to get my hands on it, I was nearly nine! My mum had clearly not allowed for nature, plus Nan's cooking, to have raised my legs and seat another inch or more off the ground. Pop and I got off the tram at St Luke's Church and within minutes I was wheeling my prize possession out of the shop and on to the pavement for the long journey home.

"The bike looks a little small to me, Stanley... Hang on a minute... we're going back into the shop."

Pop spent some time with the bicycle man, who pointed out that there were no bigger bikes in that model.

"Oh, please Pop... Let me have the bike. I'm not that tall. You can raise the seat for me in a few months time, if I need it."

"I'll adjust the seat and the handle bars for him right now," said the bicycle man. He's not ridiculously big for the bike... and at his age boys grow so fast that these bikes don't last more than a year or two anyway."

So that was that. I was on my way home with the brand new BSA, which was already too small for me. Fate, however, had me destined to own a prototype of a Raleigh Chopper thirty years ahead of its time.

Pop let me ride the bike all the way home, avoiding the most dangerous city tram routes. He kept pace with me all the way up George Street, into Upper Parliament Street and then onto Princes Avenue. From here, it was a wonderful downhill run to Smithdown Road, along tree-lined Ullet Road. The three-mile cycle ride was an odyssey and one of the most memorable things I ever did as a child. My grandfather's high level of fitness made it such a doddle for him but, less than ten years later, the forty Wild Woodbines he had smoked, each day, since he was sixteen took its toll, and all the athleticism of his youth surrendered to lung cancer.

Once we had crossed Smithdown Road into the bottom of Borrowdale Road, Pop allowed me to race on to impress my pals, who I could see playing out at the top of the street. As they came running down to meet me I went into a fit of exhibitionism, whirling the small pedals for all I was worth. The trailing corner of my Pack a Mac, thrown on during a rain shower in Ullet Road, suddenly got caught in the front wheel. The plastic raincoat was sucked off my back and into the spokes, forcing me to practise the remarkable emergency stop which I was to execute, later in life, during a driving test in Galashiels. My delayed reaction nearly threw the examiner through the front windscreen. This was even better! I took off over the handlebars and hit the tarred gravel on the street like an infected corpse being catapulted over the battlements of a besieged medieval castle.

When my pals got to me I was sprawled out with a split lip and chin which required stitches at Sefton General. The showroom bike was badly scratched and damaged. It needed new spokes on the front wheel, plus a new front mudguard and bell, but no amount of polish and remorse could remove the damage to its maroon lacquer and dazzling transfers.

"That will teach him to think he's in the Manx TT with Geoff Duke" was my dad's only comment." Arthur Williams had not paid anything towards its purchase, so he probably congratulated himself on money well saved.

Coming under such fire on the first day of its commission, bestowed my bike with a mantle of indestructibility. Normally, I took great care of my possessions, but not my less-than-a-day-old, war-scarred BSA. It had been painfully baptised as an enduring piece of hardware, which I took onto the streets confident that no amount of "Look... no hands" and "Look... I'm standing on the seat" trick riding, would distress it. In our chasing games through the local streets and parks, it endowed me with a recklessness which allowed me to leap on to the backs of the hunted enemy, leaving my bike to fend for itself – Herbie style – against railings, trees, lampposts and the sandstone blocks of railway walls.

When the call of the Wild West got to me, I saddled up to become the Scarlet Horseman, scourge of all bad men in Arizona and hero of the Saturday matinee serial at The Grand. This caped cowboy crusader was something of a misnomer, as the serial was filmed in black and white, so his scarlet cloak looked more like one of my Nan's old, white bed sheets. "Hey... There's an idea, now..." Nevertheless, this man in the grey mask and flapping cloak went one better than mild-mannered Clark Kent, by passing himself off as a cripple. That was until the Scarlet Horseman was called for, whereupon he leapt up as if he had been miraculously blessed at a faith healing. When people asked him how he got to be so crippled I was waiting for him to say that, as a nipper, he had owned a BSA bike... and once, whilst showing off to a bunch of prairie kids, had got the end of his cloak caught in the spokes of the front wheel.

CHAPTER 16

GOING TO THE GRAND TO SEE BETTE DAVIS

Mum and Nan were never out of each other's company; doing all the housework in tandem and shopping like a pair of inseparable twins on Smithdown Road. I suppose that going to the pictures together was merely an extension of the domestic life they shared. Such constant companionship must have been to the detriment of my parents' marriage, in which my father claimed to be an outsider for my mother's attention, if not her affection. Arthur Williams' obsession with Hilda suggested the man had a serious axe to grind.

Once the tide of war had turned and the bombing ceased, the two women were free to indulge in a mutual passion for going to the cinema. With the men of the house not yet demobbed and unable to question the wisdom of exposing a four-year-old to the scary, goo-goo eyes of Bette Davis, I was taken with them. In the Liverpool 15 of the late 1940s they had the pick of half a dozen cinemas, within a mile radius of our home. The Grand Cinema, near Penny Lane was, however, the nearest and cheapest passport to a world of make-believe. The two Nellie Ediths had claimed the small picture house as their own, personal, theatre of dreams.

Today's multi-screen complexes have taken us back to the intimacy of the original nickelodeons. By the standards of the 1930s and 1940s, when some thirty million people in Britain went to the cinema every week and there were places like the Roxy, in New York, which could accommodate over six thousand people, the Grand was a small theatre, seating less than five hundred. It was privately owned and run by Max Heilbron, husband of Rose Heilbron, the first woman in England to become a judge. Not belonging to any of the big cinema chains, it tended to repeat all the Gainsborough, Rank, and Hollywood box office successes of the Thirties and war years.

For good or ill I went to the Grand with Mum and Nan twice a week as the programmes rotated through a two-day change of schedule. We never went on Sunday. Only witches, warlocks and other sons of Satan went on the Lord's Day. Such people waited for the church services to be over and the streets cleared of good living folk before slinking along to watch films, whose foyer posters attracted my lurid curiosity with their graphic illustrations of a world of wickedness, where murder, prostitution and gangland violence were the norm.

Comfortably seated in the stalls, I was plonked down next to my mum with her coat acting as the necessary cushion and my legs hardly able to stretch beyond the edge of the red moquette seat. This inventiveness gave me enough elevation for a glimpse of the screen, between the heads of the people in the packed rows in front. From this little throne I was treated to the great Chaplin silent screen gems of *The Gold Rush* and *Modern Times* as the two women submitted, with tear-soaked handkerchiefs, to the appalling pathos and sentimentality of his *City Lights*. I could only peep through fingers at the terrifying slapstick of Harold Lloyd, desperately holding on to window cleaner's planks, ropes and buckets, suspended against skyscraper buildings, hundreds of feet above the pavements of New York. Weaned on the majestic films of Alexander Korda, I made friends with a giant genie and flew on a magic carpet with Sabu, in *The Thief of Baghdad*. I marched through the hills of the Northwest Frontier to the skirl of the pipes, in *The Drum*. I fought fist and sabre with Douglas Fairbanks Jnr., Victor McLaglen and Cary Grant, to keep the Union Jack flying over the Khyber Pass in *Gunga Din*.

Thankfully, I have never smoked. I managed to shun the habit, which for many decades of my life was promoted as the fashionable thing to do. I may, yet, have to join the queue of litigatious passive smokers demanding retribution from tobacco companies who encouraged them to puff away to their heart's content in thousands of cinemas like the Grand. From the age of four until my mid-teens, I must have gone through a bonded warehouse of Senior Service as I sat in the warm, friendly darkness, where chain smokers seemed to have inherited the earth. Back then, people seemed not to notice breath which hit you like an ashtray full of stale fag-ends. No one commented on clothing and hair reeking of nicotine and tar. I suppose people coped the same way as Elizabethans learned to live with the smell of rotten teeth, sweaty armpits, and sex-soaked crotches. Of course, no one in those childhood days knew the medical truth about the glamorous addiction; for all it was still an age of social and moral propriety, we had not yet been visited by the thought police of late twentieth century political correctness. Smoking was the coolest thing to do, especially if you and your big date wanted to look at each other as if you were Clark Gable and Marlene Dietrich. I was happy to be surrounded by smoke when I went to the cinema because it added a tangible ingredient to the "wondrous strange" atmosphere of the place.

Every now and again, I would look up into the rolling stream of dust particles and eddies of cigarette smoke, which came flooding down in a narrow beam of light from a place of unearthly mystery, high above the balcony. What a deadly cocktail of Woodbine, Craven A, and Capstan Full Strength was being mixed together in the stale air to pleasure the audience's senses! Oblivious to the hidden dangers within the swirling, addictive confection, I marvelled at the hypnotic effect of myriad dancing specks of dust, as they magically performed in the shaft of bright, white light above my head. Once, or twice, I had the notion I could see deep into the incandescence and pick out legendary faces in the passing clouds of celluloid; the gods and goddesses from MGM, Warner Brothers and Twentieth Century Fox, transmogrifying down to the screen from their Olympus in that tiny room high above the gallery.

When I was six, Cary Grant became my first screen hero. He was someone President George W Bush could have sent to Iraq to stiffen the sinews of his troops with utterances like, "'Ow can I get a nice little war going?" He could then have been dispatched into the mountains of Afghanistan to look for Osama bin Laden. Just as he had interrupted a temple full of Kali worshippers in *Gunga Din*, Cary would have swaggered into one of Al Qaida's mountain hideouts singing, "Maybe it's because I'm a Londoner… that I'm going to pay you bastards back for the Edgware tube and bus bombs of 2005!"

In spite of the Grand not being a first-run theatre, for the price of a child's threepenny ticket I was treated to all the classics, such as *How Green Was My Valley, Mrs Miniver, Rebecca, Goodbye Mr. Chips, Citizen Kane* and *Casablanca*. I knew who Henry the Eighth was, well before I knew what History was about. He was the magnificent Charles Laughton; a big, beheading bully to some, but to me just a grumpy old sod, with a heart of gold, who balked at the thought of getting into bed with someone as scary-looking as Elsa Lanchester's Anne of Cleves.

I helped Robert Donat escape from the train on the Forth Bridge in *The Thirty Nine Steps*. I re-ran the amazing duel between Ronald Colman and Douglas Fairbanks Jnr. in *The Prisoner of Zenda*, so that Ashley and I could fence like fuck with wooden swords, up the stairs, along the landing, and into every bedroom of No.52 Borrowdale Road. I felt such pity for the limping Charles Laughton, as Quasimodo. Acting with one eye transferred halfway down his cheek and a hump on his back the size of a sack of Kenwright's coal he sat, love-struck, staring at the unattainable beauty of Esmeralda. For months afterwards I was compelled to stick a cushion up my jumper and lurch from room to room, lamenting, "I'm as ugly as the man in the moon". When Laughton swung down from his perch, high up on Notre Dame Cathedral and snatched up Maureen O'Hara to the safety of the great bell tower, with the crowds below chanting "Sanctuary!… Sanctuary!" I wanted to jump up in my seat and cheer, as if Liverpool had just scored the winning goal in the FA Cup Final at Wembley!

"You're not going to take him to see *Wuthering Heights*, are you Nell? Heavens, if the film is anything like Bronte's book the ending will scare the lad to death!" Pop's words of caution went unheeded. The lure of Olivier and the fragile beauty of Merle Oberon were too much of an enticing flame for my star-struck moth of a mum. The film did scare the bollocks off me, but I am so glad I saw it in those early post-war years of big screen, black and white magic. It was a much edited *Wuthering Heights* without Yorkshire accents and the soul-satisfying back-cloth of the real Yorkshire Moors. Nevertheless, the film was so full of atmosphere that it had an impact on me as a child as overwhelming as *Great Expectations* and *Oliver Twist*.

Seeing *Oliver Twist* was the only time I can remember being taken to the cinema by my mother and father, who was once again living with Hilda. Conscious of the attempt my parents were making to reconcile their marriage, I paid extra-special attention to their body language that night, looking for any small gesture on the part of my dad, which might betray a sign of affection towards my mother. He gave away as little as mean old Fagin!

Once I was a little older, Dad began to take me to the cinema but never to the Grand. In his mind it clearly failed to live up to its pretentious name. He always took me to the privately owned Mayfair in Aigburth, where Hilda worked at the ticket booth and provided him with free passes. I did not like going to the Mayfair. It was too posh, expansive and lavishly furnished for me. If the main purpose of a film was to have you sitting on the edge of your seat, then what did it matter how comfortable and elegant the seat was? Besides, the Mayfair short-changed you by showing only one big film and you were out onto the pavement again far too quickly for my liking. I liked the claustrophobic atmosphere of the Grand, where a lack of ostentation made you appreciate the value and magic of the action taking place on the silver screen.

After washing the tea dishes and making themselves look smart, Mum and Nan would leave to catch the last show at 7.30pm, making sure they arrived to get their full money's worth out of the nine-pence, rear-stalls seat. They would want to be comfortably settled for the first short, which was often a film commissioned by the Government, as a means of educating the British taxpayer into the workings of one of the newly nationalised industries like coalmining and shipbuilding.

There was always a cartoon, no matter what film was being shown. That fact says much about the indiscriminate nature of audiences in the 1940s who relied mainly on the cinema to bring humour into their lives. After the definitive brilliance of *Snow White*, in 1937, Walt Disney was king. His mouse, however, did nothing for me; neither did the duck in the sailor-boy suit. Mickey was too well mannered and urbane for my taste. I preferred Tex Avery's Looney Tune characters, where all the nonsensical violence and eccentric, off-the-wall humour was uncensored, mocking the demand made upon children to behave normally at all times. Whilst the Thomases were totally unmoved by the "Er... What's up Doc?" wisecracking of the "wascally wabbit," my dad would laugh until the tears ran down his face at Bugs Bunny or Tweety Pie and Sylvester. I loved the warm secure feeling I got from being in a packed cinema, with everyone creased up at the same stupid things which a seven-year-old thought hilarious.

As someone who would end up teaching politics, I suppose it was natural that the newsreel should fascinate me. At the Grand we got *Pathe Pictorial*, with its rousing symbol of a lively looking cockerel, crowing to awaken a war-weary world. I can remember seeing the last few months of the war in Europe from my seat in the Grand. I have a disturbing memory of someone important hanging upside down from a lamppost.

"Mussolini was shown on the Pathe News tonight, Pop. He was strung from a lamppost together with his mistress... At least, I think it was them."

"Well, if it wasn't, then it should have been," was Pop's quick reply.

One night, a packed cinema audience rose from their seats to applaud a stout, old man in a trilby hat. He was defiantly sporting a fat cigar, as he used a stick to pick his way through the bricks and rubble of a bombed street, in London. The clapping and cheering lasted for many minutes and left me feeling elated without quite knowing why this granddad figure was, clearly, more popular than Johnny Weissmuller. I would soon learn all about the great Winston Churchill, whose garrulous radio voice had sustained the nation throughout the war and who, mercifully, stopped Hitler turning me into a bar of soap!

The 'B' movie followed the newsreel. A sinister-looking man called Edgar Lustgarten, who looked like he could have murdered someone for the price of a packet of fags, introduced stories based on true crimes. The Edgar Wallace murder mystery was another of the typical, stock-in-trade filler. The most exciting moment of an Edgar Wallace film was when the grim-looking bust of the great crime writer revolved slowly on a badly lit plinth, during the opening credits. "I'm watching you Stanley Williams. I know just where you are sitting! I know what you were up to this afternoon, behind Uncle Stan's back!" Whenever I go into an art gallery or museum and see an alabaster bust of some famous, dead person, I expect it to turn and tell me Edgar Wallace was asking for me!

After an interval for a Walls ice cream, popcorn, or a soft drink, the lights dimmed for the main feature film, which usually lasted a few hours. All in all, it was unwise to promise anyone that you would be home for your mug of cocoa before 11.15pm. It was far too long to leave Pop with an overactive four-year-old, who could not keep quiet for long enough to let him listen to his favourite radio shows like *Radio Newsreel*.

A plentiful supply of sweets, plus the promise of a choc ice was, however, never enough to shut me up especially if it were a Tarzan film I had been taken to for the second time for peace in the house. "This is the bit where Tarzan is injured and the rhino charges and tries to kill him... the big ape and Cheetah try to protect Tarzan... but the rhino keeps charging and the ape gets trampled on and killed... then Cheetah runs to get... " A woman in the seat behind leaned over my head to address my mum. "If you don't mind... We don't need a running commentary. We've paid to see a film, not to listen to the Grand National on the radio."

The woman trying to silence my chatter was not to know that my mum's two miscarriages, followed by the death of two baby girls and then my unexpected arrival when she was forty, gave me a dispensation greater than any Pope could bestow. "And how old are you?" my mum asked, turning her head just enough, so as not to miss how my story ended on the screen. "Would I be wrong in thinking that this is a film for children, as well as adults?" She spoke ever so quietly from the side of her mouth, while still tracking the progress of a screeching Cheetah, in his clumsy, jungle floor journey to get help from Jane. "For goodness sake, the boy's only six and I'm not familiar with the jungle... He's only trying to let me know what is going on."

Mum and Nan were obviously transported somewhere else when they took their seats in the Grand. Like Ronald Colman's Sydney Carton, in a *Tale of Two Cities*, they were waiting to be taken to "a far, far better place", well removed from the dull monotony of the uneventful existence they both shared. If there was a Gainsborough film showing, bringing some eighteenth or nineteenth-century melodrama into their drab lives, then they would be an extra five minutes early to be glued to the screen for Margaret Lockwood's *Wicked Lady*. Miss Lockwood was no Sharon Stone, but the heat coming off the celluloid in those clinches with James Mason was enough to melt Nan's sixpenny second-hand bargain of a pair of Bassnett's specs. Slowly, the ill-fitting purchase would persist in sliding down the bridge of a nose that Prime Minister Golda Meir could have swapped her for without a single member of the Israeli cabinet noticing!

Mum was entranced by Bette Davis and would not miss any of her films. The greatest of the Hollywood man-eaters, however, always made me think of the dreaded Hilda. Even the friendly, orchestrated background of an incessant unwrapping of caramel toffees and the rustling after pear drops as they were continually sacrificed up into gob-smacked mouths could not remove the tension I felt whenever Bette Davis lit up the screen. In full, dramatic flow she seemed to spit out her lines of grand passion like a deadly serpent. I was taken to see The *Little Foxes*, which I remember best for the scene where she watched her husband die whilst registering every expression known to man. I can remember my mum saying to Nan on the way home from the Grand that night, "You don't know what that woman's face is going to do next." The type of woman she played seemed to hit an inner-chord of admiration with my gentle-spirited, loving mother. Secretly, she must have approved of the hard-bitten personality, who dished out as good as she got from the men in her life.

Uncle Stan expressed a calm concern to his sister that I had seen more marriages destroyed by Bette Davis and Joan Crawford than the number of German planes shot down in five years of war! He stopped Mum and Nan taking me with them to see the film *Jezebel*. Luckily, the movie returned the following year to entice the pair of them back for a second helping. With Uncle Stan away at Oxford, I got the chance to stare, mesmerised, up into the face of a woman who seemed to run the show. I had heard Mum and Pop make references to "that scheming woman". However, I had not yet made the connection between the shenanigans of Bette Davis as a spoilt Southern girl, trying all sorts of wicked tricks to get her fiancé back from another woman, and the secret life of my dad with Hilda, the real life husband stealer.

Brad stands outside one of the fenced-off back lanes which are now, sadly, a feature of the present-day landscape in my old neighbourhood.

No.52 Borrowdale Road, taken in the Millennium summer when I returned to Liverpool for a reunion of pupils at Dovedale Road School. The once polished red brick walls have been tarted up with flaking paint, but the house looks remarkably unchanged since it was my childhood home throughout the 1940s and 50s. Even the hedge looks the way I last cut it, back in the summer of 1960.

The front parlour of Beth's house at No. 73 Lidderdale Road. It was here that John and Pete's teenage hanky-panky went on - as recorded in Albert Goldman's book, "The Lives of John Lennon."

"A four of fish and finger pies.
In summer, meanwhile back..."
...The shop is still frying.

A photo of my mum taken in 1931. She was 29 and had just met my dad who was only 22. The thought of being left on-the-shelf had persuaded her to tell him that she was 25. Hilda, my stepmother, was also five years older than Arthur Williams. "I was a sucker for older women, son."

Dressed in his 835 Naval Squadron flying kit, Uncle Stan is ready to climb into a Swordfish and go hunting for German submarines.

My uncle with the ball at his feet in a 1942 photograph of 835 Naval Squadron football team. He played for Liverpool Schoolboys and was about to sign for Wolves when the war ended any thoughts of a professional career. After the war, he played for Oxford, Pegasus and then Tranmere Rovers where the tackling, in the old Third Division North, was the most barbaric he suffered in all the yeas he played football.

On the dodgems at Southport funfair in 1949. Was it my mum's driving which had me looking so nervous and unhappy, or was it, perhaps, the presence of the two grown men in the dodgems behind us? If an adult tried to do that today he would quickly find himself on the Sex Offenders Register.

"And though she feels as if she's in a play
She is anyway."
Beth and her best friend Margaret Jones dressed for their "Soldier, soldier, won't you marry me," duet at a St Columba's Church concert in the early 1950s.

My Spartan uncle and I take a testicle-numbing seat in a Highland stream near Ullapool in the spring of 1952.

Something ex-President Gerald Ford could not do - toss and catch a tennis ball whilst walking and smiling for the camera. This happy photo of me as an eleven-year-old, striding alongside Uncle Stan and his wife-to-be Margaret, was taken at Otterspool Prom in 1953.

I receive the South Liverpool Baseball Championship Cup for Dovedale from Leonard C Jones, Chairman of the Liverpool Schoolmasters Sports Committee, as a curious George Harrison looks on.

Uncle Stan's wedding, August 1954. A few weeks before my thirteenth birthday, I pose in my first pair of Terylene long trousers next to my Nan and Pop. Well into their seventies, both look mighty uncomfortable at being so dressed up.

My dad recuperates at Hilda's flat, following an operation in the early 1950s. The double hernia was the end of his spell driving and lifting for Speedy Parcel Deliveries. He soon went back to his old job behind the wheel of a bus, and the certainty of swapping a regular rupture for a fine dose of piles.

CHAPTER 17

BASSNETTS SHOP: AN ALADDIN'S CAVE

All the fun and excitement of a night at the Grand Cinema on Smithdown Road was given the glacé finishing touch with a compulsory pop-in to Bassnetts open-all-hours shop, which stood a few yards from the cinema's entrance. In this Aladdin's cave of exotic delights, every imaginable type of boiled and chewy sweet glittered down from large, glass bottles lining the rows of shelves. Below, at a child's eye-level, and within easy reach of their eager fingers, lay multiple arrangements of chocolate bars, sherbets, liquorice toy sweets, and other penny delights. The shop was also a readers' bazaar with an eclectic range of British and American comics, dime paperbacks and second-hand romantic novels for borrowing. Its selection of comics was second to none on the whole two-mile stretch of Smithdown Road, making the shop a magnet for all boys in the neighbourhood. At Bassnetts you could buy comics dedicated to the matinee idols of countless B cowboy movies, such as Bill Boyd, Rod Cameron and Rocky Lane. The crown jewels on display were Action Comics' flagship characters, Superman and Batman. However, to boggle your judgement about the best sixpenny read you could also choose from: *Tarzan, Captain America, Green Lantern, Mad, Classics Illustrated, Tales from the Crypt* and its shock cover companion, *Weird Tales*. Dozens of amazing titles were laid out like an Adelphi Hotel wedding feast; an endless gourmet selection to set before the drooling lips of little boys.

My favourite was the new superhero on the block, Captain Marvel. He did not need to run into a gent's toilet, or force his way past a queue of people waiting to get into a telephone kiosk, when he refashioned himself into his alter-ego. He simply said the word "SHAZAM", and a flash of lightning changed him from kid reporter, Billy Batson, into a crimson-clad muscleman blessed with what every Alpha Male would like to find in his Christmas stocking – the wisdom of Solomon, the strength of Hercules, the stamina of Atlas, the power of Zeus, the courage of Achilles and the speed of Mercury! The comic was such a big hit in the 1940s that Superman got scared and sued his rival's publisher, Fawcett. Sadly, DC's lawyers did to Captain Marvel what all the evil in the universe had failed to do, namely, liquidate him, along with all his extended Marvel family members, including a flying dog! I sorely missed the kindred faces of this friendly posse of superheroes, who in the pages of *Whiz* sustained me through weeks of chicken pox misery in the winter of 1950-51.

All these degenerate gems of American literature were banned reading by order of Uncle Stan. Nevertheless, I smuggled in what a limited amount of pocket money allowed and engaged in a thriving swap system at Dovedale Road School. My granddad was always ready with a few proverbial words of wisdom. "Never look a gift horse in the mouth", was one of his favourites. One day I got the opportunity to practise what he had been preaching. I was sitting on the near-empty top deck of a bus coming back from town, when I saw a half-crown piece, shining up at me from the dusty floor. "Now Stanley, that's not yours to keep, is it? Someone has dropped their hard-earned money out of a sacred purse, or pocket. Be a good lad and hand it over to the conductor on your way down the stairs." The high moral tone of the phantom whisper suggested that it was the voice of Uncle Stan, speaking to me in one ear. Fortunately, my dad was also chipping in with his more worldly advice in the other, more receptive, lug. "Do you know the person who has lost that money? No you don't and neither does anyone else on this bus.... Now listen, Stanley... If you hand that money over to the conductor, I know what'll happen. I work with the buggers and they're not all like your dad and Uncle Stan. He'll simply put it in his own pocket and buy himself a couple of packets of cigarettes, in the staff canteen, at the end of his shift." I picked up the piece of pirated treasure and stayed on the bus well past my home stop to the door of Bassnetts, where I leapt straight into my Aladdin's Cave. I purchased five of the most desirable DC Comics and secreted them into my bedtime bunker for a week of under-the-cover bliss.

The two Nellie Thomases could never pass Bassnetts on their way to the Grand Cinema.

"Oh Nell, I'll need to pick myself another pair of specs."

"Mum. You must have half-a-dozen at home."

Yes, but the print in the books is never the same size... and the lenses often fall out."

My Nan had a ritual of making for the large tray of second-hand spectacles on the main counter. She took a good few minutes rummaging around; picking up, putting on; squinting at labels on the bottles of sweets to select the correct magnification. Finally, satisfied with her lucky dip, she would go into the shop's side room, where the tables and shelves were loaded up with hundreds of books for lending. There she would begin her race through the pages of as many novels as possible, before the last house at the Grand started.

Nan also had a system for choosing the right read in a hurry. She made for the shelves of romantic novels and proceeded to look for the gilt letters of a title that grabbed her by the throat. She needed a headline which would garnish any tasteful romance with the hint of a generous helping of fleshly lust. A more exotic title, flaunting a little *Eastern Promise*, would clearly tempt her to turn a few more pages. *Desire in the Desert* might have an Arab Sheik riding in to offer her more than a bite of his Turkish delight. *Splendour in the Grass* might employ an itinerant Spanish gardener, who would get to work on Lady Fotheringham's herbaceous border and create enough heat and passion to make her compost self-combust. Nan would always consult the synopsis to confirm or dispel any optimism created by a book's title. "Envied by other women... lusted after by men," sounded tasty enough. "Married to a wealthy landowner, who treated her as his property, Tess was also a slave to the passions aroused by Jethro, her husband's dark and mysterious new overseer." That sort of nonsense would do her nicely, thank you.

The pages of Chapter 1 would then be scanned for evidence of the heroine's worthiness of her further attention. It was better if she was poor, but intelligent; of humble stock, but with the hint that an apparent lack of pedigree might not make her quite the mongrel people at first thought. A quick dash to the middle had to sustain the story's prospects with enough words of desire, pain and torment to spur her on. Finally, the last couple of pages would be scrutinised for a sentence, which might betray the fairy-tale ending, which her own real life circumstances seemed unlikely to conjure up. All had to end well. Mr D'Arcy was not a bounder after all. Mandalay could burn for weeks but Rebecca was not a sacrificial offering. Nellie Thomas required to know such things if she were to feel comfortable with her fireside adventure.

"These two will do me, Nell." This was my signal to end my flicking through the flashy artwork of a Dick Tracey comic and move to the shop entrance, where I would be a few steps nearer seeing Stewart Granger and Vivien Leigh in Hollywood's highly Technicolor version of Bernard Shaw's *Caesar and Cleopatra*. Uncle Stan would be better pleased with me trying to digest this film's somewhat adult story line, than being made to ponder upon the moral dilemmas faced, next week, by Johnny Weissmuller, when he swung Jane up into his tree top home in *Tarzan and his Mate*.

129

CHAPTER 18

THE CHILDREN'S SATURDAY MATINEE AT THE GRAND

The Saturday afternoon pilgrimage to the children's matinee at the Grand was the Mecca of entertainment for neighbourhood kids, where a threepenny-piece provided a rich menu of cartoons, a slapstick comedy, and a main feature film, usually a Western. There was always a nail-biting serial like *Jungle Jim*, which boasted Johnny Weissmuller as its star. He was, alas, no longer the tree-top swinger, but now a middle-aged white hunter. He had swapped the sweaty loincloth for a baggy, air-conditioned set of tropical khaki trousers. These failed to disguise a midriff bulge substantial enough to keep him afloat for weeks, should he fall into any jungle river. That is, if he wasn't first eaten by the crocodile, which could remember the hammering he had given it in MGM's *Tarzan Escapes*, some seventeen years and six trouser sizes ago.

In the years immediately following the war, the children's matinee was often preceded by a talent show, organised by the owner of the Grand, Max Heilbron. On these special occasions he played an organ, which appeared from the bowels of the pit in front of the stage. I have a memory of one of his family – perhaps a daughter or granddaughter – singing to us on the narrow stage in front of the screen, as unruly boys on the back seats sucked all the juice out of their lollies before hurling exploding sticks of ice over our heads and down the necks of the short-sighted, sitting in the front rows. My constant companion, Beth, could never be constrained in her seat for long and was more than ready to have a bash at imitating the songs of Shirley Temple and Judy Garland.

Like all boys under the age of twelve, I lapped up anything to do with the myth of the American Wild West. In our childhood games of imitating the generous choice of Hollywood cowboy stars, we were a time-warp journey away from today's computer-generated, epic fantasies like *Lord of the Rings*. Play was very much dictated by our own imagination and in the late 1940s we, happily, settled for cowboys as our living legends. Redskin headdresses, tepees and tomahawks were popular birthday and Christmas gifts for kids. On a Saturday we would all troop into the Grand to take part in a feeding frenzy on the staple diet of B westerns; hopefully, we would pick up a few new tips needed to continue the struggle between 'goodies' and 'baddies' into the next week of street and playground games.

When Pop talked about cowboys, I listened attentively, knowing that here was someone who, as a boy, had been taken to Buffalo Bill's "Wild West Show", when it toured Britain in the 1890s. My granddad delved into the mythology of his own childhood to stir-up my imagination with the exploits of his favourite silent screen hero, Tom Mix. "Now there's a real, rootin' tootin' tough guy. Do you know that he was a former deputy sheriff and rodeo star before he went into films? He wouldn't let other people do the stunts for him like your, so-called, cowboys of today... 'Singing Cowboys' people like to call them now... They couldn't win a singing contest with a coyote!" I was so impressed with old Tom's CV that, at school, I ended up defending the reputation of a guy who had died without ever speaking a word on the screen! To prove to my pals that he ever existed, I was forced to cut out his picture from a film book, showing the hawk-faced legend wearing a Stetson hat big enough for a wagon-load of settlers to get protection from prairie sun-stroke under its brim. "What does he need a hat that size for?" I asked Pop. "Well, without the hat, Tom would have nowhere to carry the bales of straw for his wonder horse, Tony."

In the late 1940s kids were forbidden to explore their sexuality. Parents and teachers, alike, instructed us in a manner which suggested that sex did not exist. The cinema was our main experience of culture outside the home and schoolroom, and here we were encouraged to adopt the weird, asexual personas of our American cowboy film heroes. When we galloped along to watch the latest Hopalong Cassidy movie, we did not realise the burden of celibacy we were taking home with us, from our edge-of-the-seat enthrallment. Hollywood was sending us out across life's lone prairie, with pack horses loaded-down with repression, as we sought to imitate these all-action men, who had no apparent interest in, let alone passion for, the opposite sex.

If sex was the unmentionable fact of life, then the heroes we cheered and stamped our feet to at the Grand were the High Priests of abstinence as they tried to tame the Wild West. These paragons of virtue couldn't allow themselves to be caught in some two-bit, hotel-saloon bedroom, with a gun-belt still strapped on and their trousers in a knot around their boots. Role-models for millions of kids, our gunslinging heroes must have carried saddlebags full of bromide pills to suppress any unhealthy urges, and keep them as celibate as Cliff Richard. The mere touch of a woman's blouse, or a brush against a bare forearm before riding off into a Wyoming sunset, was enough to keep a fella from having unnatural thoughts about his horse for a whole cattle-drive.

The big Saturday matinee favourite was Hopalong Cassidy, alias William Boyd who, while I was glued to my seat in the Grand, had been riding out of the Bar T Ranch for the past thirteen years. He must now have been well into his fifties when we were asking him to bend bullets like Beckham. Unlike England's blond soccer god, "Hoppy" had the silver, wispy hair that made David Gower such a turn-on for Jonathan Ross in the TV quiz show *They Think It's All Over*. Perhaps, he wanted a head to match the colour of his milk-white stallion, Topper. His startling appearance was made all the more glaringly odd by his preference for an all-black outfit to hide his acres of middle-age spread.

In another snub to human nature, not one of these guardians of the law and ladies' knickers ever seemed to need the toilet. Perhaps, being born without an arsehole helped them ride so tall in the saddle. Certainly, John Wayne walked as if he was about to fill his six-gallon hat with the relaxing, untroubled shit he'd been dying to have since his breakthrough cowboy role in *Stagecoach*, way back in 1939. Roy Rogers, Gene Autry, and Tex Ritter all carried two sets of fancy six-guns and engaged in well-choreographed fistfights, but both were most successful when they sang the baddies to sleep, before slipping on a pair of handcuffs.

At the end of each film, there was always time set aside for a tedious homily from the hero.

"I don't want to see any of your pesky faces around these here parts, ever again... d'ye hear?"

The voice of sidekick Gabby Hayes would then chip in:

"Yep... That's right, Roy... Just you tell 'em good now!"

Big, ugly gunmen would be chastised and warned never again try to rob the bullion stage, unless they had first shaved Bluto's ten o'clock shadow from their identikit faces, so as not to cause palpitations among the female passengers and other travelling shrinking violets like timorous librarians, or bookkeepers. Five hundred nine-to-eleven-year-old boys would then gallop home knowing that the world was in a safe pair of gun slinging hands.

I could not live without my Saturday afternoon fix at the Grand. It was, therefore, with a rising feeling of anxiety that, late one Saturday morning in the winter of 1948/49, I kept returning to the front room window to look out in total disbelief and utter dismay. Someone up there had drawn the curtains on my life for the day. "That's it, then!" My early morning school football match at Penny Lane had been called off. It was now 1pm and I seemed doomed to be held prisoner in my own home and so miss the afternoon matinee. Dressed against the wall of weather in scarf, gloves and my long gaberdine raincoat, I was ready to scarper out of the front door, when I heard Pop in the hall, talking to Nan. "No, he's not going anywhere, Nellie. It's no use pleading for him... He's not venturing out into that pea soup of fog and soot!" I kept out of sight in the front room, returning to the window every few minutes, believing that I could take a leaf out of Superman's book and stare the porridge outside into smiling, summer blue skies. Suddenly, like Yosser Hughes, I could handle the persecution no longer. I took the impulsively foolish decision to get out of the house before anyone could stop me, regardless of the consequences.

No sooner had my feet negotiated the front doorstep and turned down the street, I was lost! I could only direct myself by holding on to the large privet hedges which fronted the small gardens of Borrowdale Road's line of terraced houses. Stubbornly, I edged my way down the pavement, imagining I was Victor Mature as Samson. With eyes burnt out by the heat of a Philistine poker, I was feeling my way over to the main supporting pillars of the Temple of Baal, so that I could heave them over and destroy the enemies of Jehovah. Stumbling from the collapsing blocks of stone I progressed from street to shrouded street.

I began to talk to myself like a lost hill walker, missing on the third day of aimless wandering in the thick mists of craggy mountains. Oh, how I regretted straying into a land where I could not see further than the nose on my face! In desperation, I got down on my hands and knees and peered at the black letters of a street sign, standing out like God-sent Braille. Al..ver..ston Road! "Holy Moley!"... Where has the railway bridge and road junction at the bottom of Nicander Road gone to?" I struggled on for another half an hour, before lurching into a familiar set of school railings. I had made the monumental error of navigation, which would have seen Sir Walter Raleigh bring back a shipload of Patagonian penguins to the court of Elizabeth I instead of a reeking hold of Golden Virginia. I had drifted south, across the most notorious accident black-spot on Smithdown Road, and all the way to Dovedale Road School!

Completely knackered and fearful about my chances of getting home before Parliament passed the Clean Chimneys Act, I sat down on the chilly pavement in front of the school playground. The smog had wrapped me in a clinging, damp blanket and my arse was getting as numb as my brain. I heard Uncle Stan's voice repeating his invitation of a few days ago. "I'll take you to the pictures and you'll see something to make you get stuck in on the football field, Stanley! I'm going to take you to see Walt Disney's *Scott of the Antarctic*."

Two hours of raging blizzards, snow and ice were the stars of a film that fairly put me off camping with the scouts ever again. I sat staring into a wall of mist and got the vision of Captain Oates rising from his squat, frozen position on the permafrost within Scott's gale-blasted, ice-tomb of a tent. He, too, was cut off from the life-support of a friendly hot water bottle placed, snugly, in his bed, together with a clean set of pyjamas, warmed in the redundant oven of the kitchen fireplace, at No.52. "I'm going outside. I may be gone for sometime." I thought to myself, "You're even sillier than I am... At least I had the excuse of wanting to see Roy Rogers in *My Pal Trigger*.."

Suddenly, the front headlamps of a large, black van pierced through the fog like Flash Gordon's spaceship cutting through the murky atmosphere of the planet Mungo, and picked me out slumped against the playground wall. Within seconds I was in a warm cab, rescued from the desolate, icy death feigned by John Mills and staring ahead into the thick smog which had threatened to swallow me.

For some insane reason, the driver was making an emergency journey to a house in Ullet Road and said he would drop me off at Borrowdale. After fifteen minutes of fraught, snail's-pace driving, my adventure was over and I found myself, like the children's TV cartoon character Mr Benn, once more at the bottom of my street of familiar, terraced houses. My spirits lightened as I realised that the smog had begun to lift. It was now moving south across the city, bringing an equality of discomfort to the middle-class golfers out at Woolton, whose handicap competition would soon have to be abandoned.

By the next Saturday, I had fully recovered from my ordeal along with the verbal chastisement that followed. Once my lunch had been scoffed down, I was haring down Garmoyle Road to the same Smithdown Road junction I had moon-walked only a week ago. There seemed to be hundreds ahead of me in the long queue, which stretched around the walls of the Grand. I was preparing myself for the disappointment of being turned away from locked cinema doors, when my dad's unlikely appearance made it an afternoon to remember.

"He has made his bed, so now he can go and lie down on it." I presumed my granddad must have been referring to his son-in-law's preference for stretching himself out with the horrible Hilda, an activity which had exiled him from our home. I had not seen Dad for many weeks, but here he was, making a deliciously rare and rewarding intrusion into my life.

I was about to sprint the last few hundred yards to wait in the lengthening cinema queue, when an oncoming tramcar applied its screeching brakes, bringing it clanking to a halt on its rails, in between one of the official passenger stops. My dad jumped down from his controls and ran towards me, dodging the confused traffic on the busy road. With the attention of his passengers now fully alerted to an interlude of drama, sent to lighten their dull progress into town, he lifted me clean off the pavement in a huge bear hug. Digging deep into one of the great pockets of his navy, tram driver's overcoat, he came up with a half-crown piece, which he placed into my grateful palm, closing my fingers over it to impress upon me the intimate nature, as well as the value, of the gift. He wished me an afternoon of fun at the pictures and darted back to his controls. The electric-powered engine started up and he was on his way. A packed tramcar of amused passengers waved me encouragement as I dashed to keep my appointment with *"Old Mother Riley Detective"*.

The incident was unremarkable by today's liberal standards in the work place. However, in the late 1940s, it was an eccentric departure from adherence to the rules and strict routine of work, especially for employees of the city council. It was not merely the spontaneous act of recognition and affection, which I remember so well. There was also the sad, accompanying image of a man who had made a desperate choice in his life. He had given up his family for another woman. When I reported the episode back to my mum, she regarded the impressive gesture as a shallow and easy one to make for a father who no longer had to look after his son from day to day.

I prefer to have another perspective on my likeable, charming, but deceitful father. I see him climbing back into his driving seat, plagued by conscience and a regret his day could well have done without. In his own way, my dad loved me as much as he could. He was desperate for my love and attention, but he wanted Hilda more than anything. He knew it. I knew it. He knew that I knew it. All the way to the Pier Head terminus, his concentration would be interrupted by a conflict of emotions welling up within him. This very unsentimental man, who had a real problem handling affection and conveying his feelings, was struggling hard to keep me interested in him as a father.

In the mid-1980s, while on holiday from Scotland, I revisited my old childhood haunts in Liverpool 15 to find that the Grand had gone. It had been demolished to make way for a petrol station. The open courtyard of petrol pumps, free air machines and the like, which once had contained a packed and expectant audience, now looked such a tiny, inconsequential triangle of unoccupied space. I stood and pondered on the sorcery of how, all those years ago, when seated within the cosy darkness of the little cinema's darkened auditorium, the place would transform itself into an expansive galaxy of countless stars. I quietly thanked the Grand for sprinkling me with the magic of the Golden Age of films and film stars. Included in my memory of so many unforgettable performances is my father's touching little cameo on the day when he stopped the traffic to give his small son the rarely surrendered token of his affection – a lasting, heartfelt hug!

CHAPTER 19

LISTENING TO THE WIRELESS

I developed a love of radio – or the wireless, as we preferred to call it – in the years of fireside family togetherness, immediately after the war. By the age of six, I had acquired an appreciation of the interesting snippets of information which could be gleaned from paying unobtrusive attention to the adult conversation at No.52 Borrowdale Road. Suddenly, listening to grown-ups on the radio became a meaningful pastime. With the exception of my cultured, Oxford-educated Uncle Stan, we were not a middle-class family which went in for singing around the piano and playing charades in the drawing room. Apart from reading, doing jigsaw puzzles and occasionally turning the house upside down in my play with Ashley, the radio was the only form of home amusement. To me, it was as wondrously impressive a piece of technology as broadband digital wizardry is today.

Tuning into a radio programme was a highly technical procedure, only permitted to women and children if a man wasn't around to tortuously twiddle the knobs until the required station was located. Human nature has not changed over the past fifty years. Whilst retaining none of the mystery of a plastic dial, the modern, hi-tech remote remains firmly in the possession of the dominant silverback, whose trigger-happy fingers flit, seeking out the most likely button to deny women their slug of *Coronation Street* or *East Enders*.

My post-war childhood was located in the Golden Age of Radio, when its intimately accessible stars were as mega as those of the Silver Screen. At primary school, we swapped cigarette cards with pictures depicting radio favourites, or flicked them, to get your card nearest to the air raid shelter wall and win all the cards being thrown. Some boys built up collections which, today, would fetch thousands of pounds at auction. As soon as Lidderdale Infants taught me to read, I eagerly looked forward to my weekly fix of *Radio Fun*, with its cartoon adventures of a host of radio stars, such as Arthur Askey, Tommy Handley, Jimmy Jewel and Ben Warriss, Wilfred Pickles and Derek Roy. Issy Bonn's "Funklefeffer Family" fascinated me, as the stories contained the Jewish sense of humour which so richly warmed the conversation in Simone Cohen's house across the street, making it such a welcoming place to be.

Pop staked first claim to the wireless by earmarking the big armchair next to the Bakelite Philips set, as the best seat for listening in comfort. We had no electric sockets in the house, so the brown Hovis of a receiver worked off a two-way adaptor in the ceiling light of the back living room. I used to sit and imagine the unending flow of voices and notes of music travelling up on the airwaves from London, as in a Merry Melodies cartoon. Marshalling themselves in the gateway of the light socket, they would babble down the twisted cloth cable and magically sort themselves into meaningful conversation or recognisable tunes.

My grandfather commandeered the radio for programmes like *Radio Newsreel*, the thought provoking *The Brains Trust*, and *Any Questions*. The latter provided regional interest by moving about Britain from week to week, with broadcasting's first great question master, Freddie Grisewood, giving any young David Dimbleby listening an early lesson in how to make sense of the diverse opinions of a celebrity panel of experts. The whole family gathered for the nation's favourite parlour game *Twenty Questions*, with radio's most popular panellist, the monumental Richard Dimbleby, whose presence you could sense patiently waiting for his chance to ask, "Is it animal, vegetable or mineral?" This was the probing first question in a race to name "The Mystery Object", which had been ever so discreetly announced to hushed millions by the cryptic voice of Norman Hackforth.

Hackforth was as scary as the pitch darkness; a speaking shadow, chained up in some dungeon, deep in the bowels of Broadcasting House. Employing the strict confidentiality of the town's most trusted undertaker and in a manner which detached you from all others in the room, he would reverentially reveal. "And the next object is... A bassoon... A bassoon." He may well have chosen the word "baboon", or "balloon," for both would have served the game's purpose equally well. A first impression might be that his was a minimal contribution, but without the Mystery Voice *Twenty Questions* would have lost its soul.

Another man from the sepulchre was Valentine Dyall, who had clearly stolen the voice of the Grim Reaper... "This is your story teller, The Man in Black, bringing you another *"Appointment with Fear."* He scared listeners far more than siren alerts and the drone of approaching German bombers. This programme ran from 1943 to 1948 and I can remember being up late one evening and getting a message from the grave which put me off sleep for days. Episodes like "The Bodysnatchers" and "The Pit and the Pendulum" made him Britain's answer to Vincent Price.

The character and quality of a voice was the X-factor in deciding whether a person was going to be a success on radio, then, as it still is today. I must have fallen into an infant slumber dozens of times under the spell of Alvar Lidell's trustworthy, wartime baritone. As I entered primary school, other unique voices became part and parcel of my family life. I was encouraged to tune in to conversations beyond my ken by the gruff, honest tones of Gilbert Harding. Listening to cricket meant being bowled over by the rolling, rustic resonance of John Arlott. "So it's Tyson to Miller now from the pavilion end... Here comes the familiar long run in bowling for the middle stump again, I'll wager... Oh! It's a sizz-ill-er!" Also, much appreciated in the home of an ex-Keeble College man was John Snagge's rhythmic, "In... Out... In... Out..." as the quintessential accompaniment to the Oxford and Cambridge Boat Race.

My father was, by the width of the Atlantic Ocean, the most modern member of the family. His enthusiasm for the American-inspired consumer revolution about to transform our lives challenged the serious, bookish attitudes of Pop and Uncle Stan. Just around the corner from our house, in the Garmoyle Road flat where my dad lived with Hilda, there was no prejudice towards the invasion of transatlantic razzmatazz into our British way of life. The dial on their radio had a mind of its own and both were suckers for the new, lowbrow culture frowned upon by my uncle and grandfather.

Wantonly turning to the dark side, they tuned-in to the American forces stations and 208 meters medium wave, where a new form of low-life called disc jockeys played a continuous effluent, thought too fruity for the BBC. My irreligious father risked a mighty conversion by one of the many hell-fire preachers on Voice of America to listen to what he referred to as "a better choice of music". I never went around to his flat, but in our times out together he would let me know how clued up he was about the latest Top Twenty, which was broadcast on Radio Luxembourg every Sunday from 11pm until midnight. The idea of Arthur Williams, with an unwelcome morning shift on the buses ahead of him, wanting to sit into the early hours listening to Frankie Laine and Johnnie Ray (whom Pop described as "tone deaf because he's stone deaf") gave him great street cred with my pals.

One of his favourite programmes was *Jack Jackson's Record Round Up*. When it was moved to a Sunday evening slot in 1950 Pop called it "A deliberate piece of programming to compete with going to church." He wanted someone to provide him with better evidence of the degeneration of the BBC. Although my granddad seemed earnestly unwilling to attend worship he was, nevertheless, mightily inclined to back God up over the need for a bit of peace and quiet on a Sunday. He clearly thought, "No wonder Arthur likes that man Jackson... They're both up to no good!" As a fan of the Marx Brothers, Danny Kaye, Tex Avery and Looney Tunes, what made Jack Jackson compulsive listening for my dad was his zany American style with a fast-moving line up of gags, new record releases, and dialogue pieced together on tape with music snipped from recordings. It was cool, up-to-the-minute, and... fucking great! Jack Jackson was middle-aged, but as an ex-trumpeter and dance-band leader, he knew his stuff. He also had the mental outlook of a sixteen-year-old rock'n'roller.

"This is the BBC Light Programme. It is 6.45pm... *Dick Barton, Special Agent!*" And then the unforgettable, galloping signature tune; a cross between the Lone Ranger's *William Tell Overture* and a *Z Cars* chase through the streets of Liverpool. "Come on... Come on... Hurry up! It's starting!" Pop's concern for me not to miss one second of the opening minute of frantic music meant that he would already be seated and rattling the tin-plate surround of the kitchen fireplace, until the thin sheet of enamelled metal vibrated throughout the house to the *Riverdance* of his slippered feet.

Another great signature tune was the one that stopped all household traffic, every Saturday just before teatime. "It's five o'clock and time for... *Sports Report.*" Synonymous with the programme's status and popularity was the enunciated reading out the classified football results while Pop sat, pencil and paper at the ready, hunched over the Littlewoods pools coupon on his lap. I especially loved listening to the Scottish results, which included some of the most gloriously exotic Caledonian names I had ever heard in my young footballing life... "Alloa Athletic 2, Stranraer 2... Cowdenbeath 3, Stenhousemuir 2..." and the verse-mongering result I begged to happen, just that once, but it never did... "East Fife 4, Forfar 5."

On Sunday afternoons, after the weekly family banquet of a roast dinner, we gave ourselves a two-hour feast of radio entertainment. *The Billy Cotton Band Show* was always on as we were finishing our meal. The fast-moving programme of musical comedy featured Alan Breeze, who sounded so Jewish he turned every song he sang into a number from *Fiddler on the Roof*. He would have been completely at home singing *My Yiddishe Mama*, at one of the Cohen's parties, across the street!

The big Sunday treat was *ITMA*, which stood for 'It's That Man Again', a wartime, newspaper catchphrase used to describe the dastardly goings on of a certain Adolf Hitler. The whole family was hooked on the most popular radio comedy show ever, with a post-war listening audience of thirty million! Its Scouser star, Tommy Handley, was probably the greatest radio comedian of all time. The series I remember best was set in place called Tomtopia.

"What does Tomtopia mean?" I asked Pop.

"It's a pun, Stanley... a play on words." I still did not get the message.

"It's another name for Utopia," explained my granddad.

"What does that mean?" I asked again, still as baffled.

"Don't you worry your little head about it, Stanley. It will never happen."

I went about for some time thinking, "What is never going to happen?" After forty years of teaching and nearly sixty-five years of hoping for a better world I now know what Pop meant!

By the 1930s, variety had taken over from the music hall which Pop had written songs for. Once the war was over, a demob-happy bunch of new comedians came on the radio, honing their skills into a microphone instead of having to tour the old theatres, year after year, working their way up from the bottom of the bill. *Variety Bandbox* was one of the most popular shows for parading the talents of new funny men like Charlie Chester, Max Bygraves and Frankie Howerd, whose style of comedy Pop thought far too crude. He needed to see Billy Connolly – crude to a fault, but one of the funniest men alive!

These were the days when all radio scripts had to be sanitised by BBC producers wearing sterile underwear. The great variety star, Max Miller – probably the top British stand-up comedian of the 1930s to the 1950s – was on the radio regularly, but not as often as his fans would have liked. Once banned by the BBC for five years, this hugely popular performer was forced to keep the stream of double entendres and blue jokes for his stage routine. It suited neither him nor my dad's favourite, Max Wall, to have their comic instincts suppressed by the antiseptic scrutiny of the Governors of the BBC.

I can remember my dad coming home from a Max Wall concert, at the Empire Theatre in Lime Street.

"That man is the funniest comic in Britain, Stanley. I laughed so much I could hardly drive my tram straight the next day."

"But a tram runs on rails."

He laughed out loud. "That's how funny the man is, son… that's how funny he is in the wig, the black tights and pointed boots. When he walks across the stage with his knees bent, his backside is chiselled enough to chop your Nan a pile of sticks." Pop was unable to contain a response.

"The physical stuff… the slapstick… that's all right, Arthur, but the man's jokes are beyond being crude. He's offensive."

"I know you're not very keen on modern stuff, Pop, but there were women in the audience peeing themselves with laughter… and then Max began his funny walks… the St John's Ambulance men had to be brought in to people collapsing with tears steaming down their faces screaming for him to stop."

Pop was unimpressed. The thought of a woman surrendering all sense of propriety in the fight to control her bladder was too much for him. Max became my favourite, too, but his filthy tongue got the better of him once too often.

"When roses are red they are ready for plucking. When girls are sixteen they're ready for…" Wall had to apologise for one such risqué joke on the radio in 1954. It was accepted, but that kind of near the knuckle routine, together with aspects of his private life, made him unpopular with some at the BBC. Not with my dad, however, who would continue to wink at me whenever the name of the great Professor Wallofski was slandered in our house.

The script for *Educating Archie* was as squeaky-clean as the wooden dummy's detachable head. Bizarrely, this was the most popular radio programme of the early 1950s. With a total lack of talent, and hidden away in a BBC recording studio from any public scrutiny of a mouth with a mind of its own, the world's worst ventriloquist, Peter Brough, did not need to be any good when he had the likes of Julie Andrews, Hattie Jacques, Tony Hancock, Beryl Reid, Harry Seccombe, Bruce Forsyth and Max Bygraves to support him. Eric Sykes co-wrote the script, which won *Educating Archie* many top entertainment awards in the early 1950s, so he may well be responsible for the Bygraves' song, which epitomised what the show was all about:

You take the legs from some old table

You take the arms from some old chair

You take the neck off an old bottle

And from a horse you take some hair.

You take the hands and face from off the clock

And, Archie, when I'm through

I know I'll get more yummy

From that dumb, dumb, dummy

Than Brough ever got from you.

Ventriloquists like Peter Brough were just one of the absurdly successful acts created by woodenhead producers at the BBC. "How good a ventriloquist is Peter Brough?" I asked my dad the next time I saw him. At the easily tricked age of nine it had, nevertheless, crossed my mind that such an unlikely act might be based on one of the great con-tricks of radio broadcasting.

"Do you know who Albert Pierrepoint is, son?" I knew all right, because of my sneaked reading of *The News of The World*. Also, being a hangman was a profession many of the boys at school ranked second only to that of being a train driver!

"Yes. He's the man who hangs people when they are found guilty of murder."

Dad smiled in anticipation of what he was going to say next.

"Well, son, do you know he's got a bag which he puts over people's heads before he hangs them?"

I said "No" and was tempted to ask him "Why?" However, I chose to save the possibility of a deliciously macabre answer for another time. My dad was now trying his best not to ruin his punchline by laughing.

"I'll guarantee that if someone put a bag over Peter Brough's head and then sat you and me up in the back row of the balcony at the Empire, we would still be able to see that man's lips move."

I now had enough rope to hang the charlatan with in the Dovedale playground.

If radio ventriloquism was not surreal enough for your taste then you could try the wireless wizardry of Sirdani "The Knot-ical Magician", with his catchphrase "Don't be fright!" Here was a man with the nerve to try and teach me conjuring tricks on the radio! If this did not convince Stalin that the British were a far scarier proposition than all of America's nuclear weapons put together, then he had only to tune in to *Variety Bandbox* on a Sunday night. The show's presenter, Derek Roy, would announce, "Ladies and gentlemen... the next act is one you've all been waiting for all evening. We now present a truly amazing juggler from the East German State Circus..." I would sit staring into the ether, imagining it tumbling out of the radio's small speaker, and waiting for the sound of half a dozen clubs to hit the kitchen floor. "He's a marvellous juggler, isn't he? He's been at it for three minutes now and hasn't dropped a fucking club yet!"

I was at an age to be greatly impressed by Leslie Welch the Memory Man. I had already seen one cocksure memory man shot dead, whilst on stage, in Hitchcock's film *The Thirty Nine Steps*. It gave me the early impression that clever people could sometimes know a little too much for their own good. "I think I'm right in saying," was the way this Mekon-brain of sporting trivia liked to display the incredible warehouse of facts stored inside his small, yet accommodating head.

"That man is really clever, isn't he Pop?"

"Clever?... Not clever enough, I'm afraid, Stanley."

"What do you mean?"

"Well... ask him who scored the goal?"

"What goal?"

"Let him work it out, my boy. He's the clever clogs, who knows everything about football."

Leslie Welch made me wonder how such a walking encyclopaedia managed to crank his cranium off the pillow each morning to face up to the task of soaking up all the new day's information.

At Dovedale Road Primary School, the radio was used to encourage us to sing and take an interest in all types of music, from folk songs to Beethoven symphonies. The BBC's *Singing Together* programme was relayed, holiday camp fashion, from the headmaster's office through a Tannoy system, to a speaker on the stage in the main hall. We would sit, cross-legged, on the polished wooden floor and wait for the radio presenter to ask us all to stand and sing from the pages of our BBC handbook. With voices celebrating the return of circulation to our legs and feet, we would race through the endless verses of *Dashing Away with the Smoothing Iron*, or put heart and soul into the unbelievably litigious *Johnny Come Down to Hilo*:

> *I nebber see de like since I'd been born,*
>
> *When a big buck nigger wid his sea-boots on,*
>
> *Says "Johnny come down to Hilo,*
>
> *Poor old man."*

Before Darcus Howe gets his black satin undies in a twist, those were the lyrics as printed on the pages of our BBC song booklet. They were words which had little or no relevance to our young lives; we sang away totally disconnected from the rights and feelings of unseen peoples an ocean-span apart from us.

Learning from the radio at school meant concentration on what someone else was saying, which today's pupils find an impossible thing to do. It helped us create our own satisfying images of people and places. In History lessons I was magically transported like the *Beano's* "Jimmy and his Magic Patch" back to Ancient Greece, where knowledge was spiced up with Herculanean dollops of myth. I can vividly recall Pheidippides staggering into the school hall to collapse and die, but not before he spat out his news that the Greeks had triumphed at the battle of Marathon. Agamemnon sent us across the Aegean Sea to capture Troy and bring back the gorgeous Helen. I could then sit and try to imagine the beauty of the face that launched a thousand ships and rank it alongside that of Hedy Lamarr, Yvonne de Carlo and the unrivalled Ava Gardner.

Another term and we were battling deck-high radio waves around the Cape of Good Hope with Vasco de Gama, as he opened up the trade routes to India. I remember the disappointment of being told that he died on Christmas Day. What a bummer! Being born on Christmas Day was altogether a different matter, but the frustration of dying just as you were about to eat your Christmas pudding was too much to contemplate! I stormed the Heights of Abraham with General James Wolfe and almost took the bullet that did for him. Unfortunately, I failed to stop Lord Nelson meeting a similar fate on the deck of his flagship, *Victory*, at the Battle of Trafalgar.

A few years later, I can remember being taken to The Walker Art Gallery, where the tour of great paintings found our school party standing in front of a huge canvass entitled *The Death of Nelson*. The teacher was memorably sad and respectful "There he is, poor fellow, lying mortally wounded… propped up and breathing his last to dear old Hardy." Right enough, it was an impressively sombre and sorrowful sight. Officers surrounded him with fraught looks on their faces and all around lay the prostrate bodies of dead or dying sailors. My pal John P edged closer and whispered, "It should be called "Who farted?""

After school, when I was not engaged in sport, I came straight home to listen to *Children's Hour*. Over the years, I grew attached to the distinctive voice of a presenter called David as I progressed from *Toytown*, through *Just William*, *Norman and Henry Bones the Boy Detectives*, *Jennings at School* and then on to the fuller-flavoured aperitif of *The Adventures of Sherlock Holmes*, with Carlton Hobbs staking an early claim to be my definitive Great Detective. I usually had the back living room to myself for my late afternoon treat. Sat in Pop's chair next to the radio, with a glass of juice and a jam biscuit to keep my stomach company, I entered the world of Arthur Conan Doyle for an hour before tea. My mind paced alongside Holmes, up and down his apartment at 22b Baker Street. I would follow him and the indomitable Watson onto the busy London streets crammed with horses, carts and carriages from the BBC's sound department. I hurried to catch up as they passed down cobbled alleys echoing to the footsteps of low-life criminals and evil masterminds like Professor Moriarty. One week they would be at the Thames, amongst the noises of the quaysides and wharves of London's sprawling docklands. The next adventure would have me trailing them through the swirling mists of Dartmoor and feeling the cold chill up on the tors as they looked for the hellhound, which was both the curse and destroyer of the Baskervilles.

The encouragement to think inventively was part of the immense contribution which radio made to the education of a whole post-war generation of children. We knew how to listen back then when there was no television, bent on serving-up programmes of stodge to set the brain on autopilot. Our reward was a free passage into a vast, uncharted ocean of knowledge on a high-rigged, three-masted vessel of the imagination. Radio unlocked the creative intelligence within children; acting like a small pebble, it stirred the mind with rippling waves of creative thought.

By the time I went to secondary school, I had *The Goon Show* to give me a proper perspective on life and help me through the worst Cold War years of the 1950s, when the constant threat of nuclear Armageddon scared the pants off a generation of teenagers who wanted to live forever. The Goons came on the radio in the spring of 1952. It was the year of the first British A-Bomb tests, and this most unlikely of BBC initiatives – along with radio ventriloquists – may have been part of an intelligence attempt to convince the Soviets to abandon their plans to sweep across Western Europe and occupy these Islands.

Any subsequent 1984-style brainwashing of the British would have been a useless task. A nation which would, religiously, tune-in to *The Goon Show* every week was, clearly, barren soil for any humourless ideology to take root.

"Are you Ah Pong?" asked Neddy Seagoon to a Chinese shopkeeper in the Street of a Thousand Aaa... So's.

"Yes... We Ah Pong until eleven o'clock at night!"

Spike Milligan's surreal scripts and the cartoon quality of the daft voices (none dafter than Eccles and Bluebottle) had us believing that the old farts who governed the BBC had let something wonderful slip through the micromesh of their conservatism and strict censorship.

On that dark day in 1961 when *Radio Fun* was taken off my newsagent's shelf, the wireless I knew and loved as a child rode off into the sunset, slumped in the saddle like Alan Ladd's Shane; mortally wounded by the deadly six-guns of television. In September 1967, the Home Service became Radios 4 and 2, and the Light and Third programmes were reorganised into Radios 1 and 3. All my old programmes were gone. I was sixteen, but the new streamlined, modern radio made me feel much, much older.

The radio programmes I listened to in the 1940s and 50s marked a great watershed of social and cultural change. No other radio performer epitomised that sea change more than a certain G H Elliot, otherwise known by his stage name of *The Chocolate Coloured Coon*. Hanging on to a name like that into the 1960s would have got his old, charcoaled face kicked in at the BBC Manchester stage-door, and then seen him arrested for inciting a night of racial violence in Moss Side.

Listening to G H Elliot, panting out his signature tune of *Lily of Laguna*, was a very confusing experience for a seven-year-old:

> *She's my lady love,*
>
> *She is my dove, my baby love,*

It seemed that no sooner had he finished bleating away, this relic from the old music hall was having praise heaped upon him by Uncle Stan and Pop for his poetry, novels and plays. My ears pricked up every time I thought I heard the distinctive surname. The prefix T S, or the manlier sounding George, didn't fool me for one minute. *Palace of Varieties* would come on, and the thin vocalisation of *Lily of Laguna* would draw me into the kitchen thinking, "Here's that old bugger Elliot, again! He's some turn, him... Black's up a treat, too, for an intellectual. Not only can he tap-dance his eighty-year-old clogs off, he's more than capable of dashing off *The Mill on the Floss*, and *Murder in the Cathedral*, while he's waiting in the wings!"

Political correctness was something we were not familiar with in my childhood and, to be honest, it was a happier one without it. The hundredth show of *The Kentucky Minstrels*. was broadcast in December 1948. It included a cast of black artists, who did not seem at all put out in having to call themselves names like "Pussyfoot", "Bones", and, the one my dad liked best, Ike "Yousah" Hatch. You should repeat that middle name slowly to yourself, whilst opening your eyes as wide as you can and rolling your eyeballs around in their sockets, clockwise fashion. Following that, turn yourself in to the nearest office of the Commission for Racial Equality.

As I sat in the kitchen of No.52 enjoying such unlikely entertainment, the 1960s were a long way off, never mind the galactic journey to a far too politically correct twenty-first century Britain. If, today, we want to stand above hypocrisy on the true moral high ground, in a well-meaning, well-adjusted, multi-cultural society then we will have to lighten up.

Since the death of my old wireless half a century ago, I have taught thousands of pupils about the denial of human rights, freedom and dignity to countless millions of this planet's citizens. All those years ago in the innocence of childhood I was as empty of prejudice as I am today. Encouraged by the far-from-thoughtless souls in charge of the BBC, I now rejoice in the politically incorrect radio programmes of the post-war years and the humour of facing up to how others sometimes see us. They were part of the real Radio Fun, and when they were over I picked up my *Beano* again. On the top of the front page, leaning against the first letter of the comic's bold title was the character of "Little Black Sambo" sucking away at his water melon; not giving a hoot what you were thinking and, seemingly, offended by no one.

CHAPTER 20

THEY DON'T MAKE NEIGHBOURS LIKE THEY USED TO

"Ah, there you are Stan… On the scrounge again, I'm afraid, old boy." Uninvited, Gerald Dunn had popped his head around the door of Uncle Stan's study, ushering in enough of the overpowering smell of shaving lotion to justify my father's sceptical view of the man's true gender. Secretly, I was happy with the interruption to a one-way game of blow-football with my uncle, which was giving me the face of Elmer Fud trying to get a note out of a bunged-up bugle.

I was only eight, but had already taken exception to this poncing imitation of a Romeo, who regularly let himself into our house to borrow anything he could get his hands on. My uncle's sheet music disappeared, along with books, magazines, records and tennis rackets. He once borrowed a cricket blazer and tie, probably to pass himself off as a club captain with all the impressionable young things at the training college dances. "If that mamby pamby asks your Nan for one more ounce of butter, I'll bloody swing for him!" My dad could not contain himself as he watched Gerald making off after yet another successful raid on our larder. Over the years, he removed a mountain of tea and sugar, unconcerned about returning items so precious in a time of post-war rationing. All were taken with a sailor's promise and never returned. Then he made the fatal mistake of trying to keep one of Uncle Stan's best cricket bats, at the start of the new 1948 season when he was opening batsman for Birkenhead Park. This was seen as theft, rather than borrowing on the never-never. Was that a tear I noticed welling up in the eyes of Gerald Dunn? I'll swear the fresh carnation in his buttonhole visibly wilted under a two-minute, spell-binding over of condemnation from the only real cricketer in the street.

I was pleased to see my calm and controlled uncle get mad once in a while, especially with someone who, in dad's words, "Flounced in and out of our house like a J Arthur Rank leading man… all deodorant and hair oil!" My dad had a loathing of limp-wristed British film stars with the notable exceptions of Stewart Granger and James Mason, who had both passed the testosterone test and graduated to Hollywood. Dad saw Gerald Dunn in the same upper-class, theatrical, ladies-man mould as Anthony Steel, who he would have liked to get in a dark room without his hairdresser and make-up girl to protect him. The unmarried thirty-something lecher from up the street would glide past the gang of us kids as we sat on the pavement, totally unaware of our sniggering. My dad's comments were always the best. "Well, I ask you... Just look at that, Pop. Cricketing blazer, open necked shirt, cable sweater, flannels and flimsy shoes... the cane and colourful silk cravat. For heaven's sake! It's the middle of November, with not a drop of sun for the next six months! Where does he think he think he is... St Tropez?"

Beth had him sized up, though, nudging me to observe this Casanova of the college campus, preening himself in any window where the garden hedge was low enough to give him a satisfactory view of his matinée idol appearance. As soon as Margaret Jones was into the fourth year at Aigburth Vale High he began a spell of regularly meeting her on her way home from school to talk about classical music. He even invited her across the street to listen to his record collection; no doubt in the secret wish to test the strings on her finely tuned, as yet untried Stradivarius. All the younger boys had desires for Margaret but, besides being a decent girl, she was that one year older and beyond our reach. I wanted to kick his leathery balls in, as he dallied on his front door step to check that the silk scarf was properly adjusted on his slim, powdered neck. What a hard neck, too!

Fuzzy-Wuzzy was a bear

Fuzzy-Wuzzy had no hair

Fuzzy-Wuzzy wasn't fuzzy...

Wuzzy?

Fuzzy Wuzzy was, clearly, not all there. We knew that, but as children we made no allowances. In those days, the care of people with mental disability was a private, secretive function of hush-hush institutions; hidden away from prying eyes, behind a comforting barrier of tall trees and acres of lawns. Such was the ignorance of society to mental illness that Rainhill, situated a few miles beyond Huyton, had the undeserved notoriety of a place only one step removed from Bedlam. To the children of the neighbourhood, Fuzzy Wuzzy was someone who had managed to tunnel his way out of such a prison. Good for him! He could now throw off the shackles of home confinement, to indulge in glorious self-expression.

Fuzzy did not help us think any better of him by hurtling around the streets on his sister's bike, with a wicker basket attached to the front handlebars. The basket was a cockpit of sorts, for a large teddy bear, dressed in leather flying helmet, jacket and knitted scarf. Up and down the streets he whizzed, taking both hands off the steering, whilst ringing a large chrome bell, attached to the handlebars. We always stopped to cheer him as be sped past, but having a fan club never persuaded Fuzzy to get off his bike to speak to us. To do so would have meant having to surrender the mystery of who he was. We were pleased to have him remain an untouchable character; someone who made our world a more interesting, entertaining, place.

His party trick was to race down the edge of the pavement and make for the narrow gap between the row of stone lampposts and the curb. It was a circus trick, perfected for our attention and although routine, it stopped our games in the way a newly lit fuse grabs attention on Bonfire Night. One day, the firework finally blew up in his face when he accelerated his bike and seriously misjudged the distance. He was very lucky not to go straight through the large plate glass window of next door's front room, as he cleared the privet hedge with plenty to spare. "Fuzzy" was out of action for many weeks and the popular chant that went up whenever he appeared was, temporarily, silenced.

All children need fairy tales and monsters, so desperate are they to be scared to the very brink and then, in the nick of time, hauled back to safety. Once past infancy, the trust we place in adults carries a latent suspicion, if not fear, of human intentions. We were wonderfully provided with a most satisfying real-life fright figure to stir up a mixture of the worst feelings within us.

There was an old man, who used to sit on a low, sandstone wall at the end of the street. I guess he might have been sixty, but to us he looked as old as Methuselah. Gaunt and unshaven, he was so alarmingly dishevelled and uncommunicative that, with a battered trilby pulled down over his ears, he could have been mistaken for the grandfather of Freddie Kruger. Every day the bony fingers of our bogeyman would rattle the sliding bolt of the back-door entrance to his lair, before he emerged to shuffle down the cobbled lane in his long, soldier's trench coat. Often, our hair-raiser would have to run a gauntlet of taunts about his scruffy, weird appearance, as he trailed a pair of untied shoelaces behind him through dust and puddles of rain. In our ignorance and to our shame, we relied on this pathetically sad figure to amuse, or scare us as the mood of our play dictated.

Sitting in his reserved sun-trap on the wall, he would appear to be asleep. This was our signal to edge slowly towards him, daring one another to disregard the sudden, involuntary fits of shaking that his body often went into. The game was to fix your concentration on the old man's closed eyes, while trying to be the bravest and the first to touch his ragged coat; only then could you run away, justified. His role was to foil you with a sudden jerking of the head, bolt upright! With eyes still raging against the Great War, which had destroyed him, he would spring up. "Arrgh!...Arrgh!... He would growl, waving his stick in the air, his mind momentarily ordering a frail body into one final attack on the enemy. The poor old codger was such an important feature of our daily routine; such an elemental part of our thoughtless play.

"The sad old man who you were taunting and having such fun with. Do you know what made him like that?" Uncle Stan had appeared to stop our wicked fun. The set of our glum faces was as good as a "No... but, please don't tell us."

"Do you know that he was once a big, tall healthy young army corporal? That is, until he was gassed and shell-shocked in the mud of Flanders."

We were given a brief pavement history lesson about the Somme and the horrors of trench warfare. It was a very sobering moment and never again did any of us try to have fun at his expense. Schooling, in those days, did nothing to educate us away from the stereotyping of disability and abnormal behaviour in others. As children, we were experts in the business of creating Boo figures, in an age long before the computer-generated images made them far less believable because they did not have to make the tortuous journey from the womb of our own imagination.

The neighbours in Borrowdale Road were extremely friendly. Five years of war had silenced the noisy play of children in Liverpool's streets, and adults welcomed their return as proof that life was back to normal. Mr Banks, so suitably named for a person whose job it was to manage the accounts and overdrafts of his customers, lived two doors up from our house and drove a wonderful, maroon Riley. Even more fascinating to me were his two great passions for model railways and astronomy. Having such special hobbies made him my equal: someone as childlike as the rest of the kids in the street. Mr Bank's house had as many tracks, carrying locomotives, carriages and trucks through it, as did Crewe Railway Junction. The only downstairs room without a branch-line was the front bedroom where his sick wife often lay resting. I think we all knew what was making her ill! What she needed was to get the next three-thirty train, which came past her door, and bugger off to recover somewhere else.

For all the talk of him neglecting his wife, Mr Banks was very pleasant to us youngsters. He impressed Uncle Stan by being a Fellow of the Royal Astronomical Society. More important than the high-sounding letters after his name was his possession of a ten-inch reflecting telescope, which I would marvel at peeping out from his attic window. On special nights, when the sky was particularly clear and black, and a stage-struck moon paraded herself in front of a chorus line of stars, I knew where the lonely, childless, Mrs Banks could find the husband, whose eyes were never so longingly focused on her unheavenly body. Occasionally, Mr Banks would be kind enough to bring his precious apparatus down from his roof.

"The wireless says that the sky will be very clear tonight. So would you like me to dismantle my telescope and set it up down here in the street, then you can all have a good look at the craters on the moon… Would you like that?"

For me, a closer look at the heavens and the chance to see a flying saucer eclipsed the spectacle, of November the Fifth!

Ashley, Beth, Margaret Jones and I, would queue up with the other kids, waiting for our turn to climb on a kitchen chair and take a two-handed grip of the telescope's brass eyepiece. Mr Banks would re-adjust the focus and direction of the lens for each child until, bathed in the mystery of reflected sunlight, the barren, grey landscape and the clearly defined craters of the moon came into view!

"Mr Banks… could you point the telescope down the street for me, please… at the red star in the sky over Sefton Park."

"Of course… but it's not a star, you know, it's a planet."

The untwinkling object was Mars, our next door neighbour in the solar system and the planet which, because of an Orson Wells radio play, had predisposed most earthlings to have a real fear of little green men from outer space. By the time I was eleven, I had read and seen the film version of H G Well's *War of the Worlds*. The hair-raising experience of the Technicolor screen adaptation forced me and Ashley into making plans about where to hide on the fast-approaching day when bug-eyed Martians, having had time to develop their vaccine against the common cold, decided upon a return visit to complete their conquest of Earth.

It was an education living in a street with Jewish neighbours. I loved being invited over to Simone Cohen's house, across the street. Simone's father was one of the many Jewish shopkeepers on Smithdown Road, whose fingers played a fine tune every time he rang open the till. "Oh, Mrs Williams! The boy can read like a dream already and he's only three… If he can count up to a hundred by next year he can do the books for my husband." Of course, I would not be telling Mrs Cohen that I could not read yet, but made a bloody good job of making up the story to go with the pictures on each page of her daughter's first books. I liked playing in Simone's house and being allowed to attend a couple of their family parties. The singing, hand clapping and dancing of the adults was a revelation to the little Gentile boy from the far more reserved atmosphere of his home, at No.52. The conversation was littered with wit and comic improvisation. As a result, I grew up to love the Jewish sense of humour. The disarming self-deprecation, central to their very funny parodies on family life and relationships in general, belongs to a people totally comfortable about who they really are.

If being a Patriarch meant ruling the roost at the family table, then Pop Thomas found himself completely put in the shade, by old grandfather Cohen, who I watched from my mum's bedroom, taking his meals, in the front room of No.51. Not only was the Father of the Tribe served first and foremost at the table, but he wore the crowning authority of his trilby at breakfast, dinner and teatime. Raised in a home where social and moral principles placed good table manners among the defining features of civilised living, I guessed my Pop would be more than a little envious of the status, which enabled a Jew to be so disrespectful to the rest of the family at the meal table.

Peeping out from behind the bedroom curtains on the occasion of old grandpa Cohen's funeral provided me with an indelible memory of the cultural differences with our Jewish neighbours. It made much more of an impression on my senses than their preference for cooking in olive oil, rather than the white lard, which we liked to block up our arteries with. My Nan's frequent cry of, "I can smell the Jews frying fish!" was as funny and acceptable then as it would be politically incorrect today. The old man's coffin was carried from the house, as three female, professional mourners, wearing black dresses, and with their heads covered in black shawls, gesticulated and wailed the family's grief at the world from the front doorstep. I had never much cared for the thought of being dead, mainly because you had to spend eternity with no guarantee of ever getting a game of football. I now had three more good reasons for not wanting to be dead and Jewish at the same time!

It makes you wonder where children today, sharing in a middle-class conformity of parental incomes, family interests and materialistic aspirations, can find the substantial neighbourhood characters, who offer a real life challenge to the cardboard celebrities of the *Big Brother*, *Love Island* brand of television. I had plenty of interesting people to fascinate me as I grew up in post-war Liverpool 15. Thank God, I had my childhood before the destruction of the true urban, working-class communities and did not have to surrender to modern, over-the-top, PC values. Such dangerously authoritarian political correctness would have prevented me getting such a comprehensive education from observing the things which make people so fascinatingly different.

CHAPTER 21

BETH OF LIDDERDALE ROAD

Only the narrow top lane running along the railway line into Borrowdale Road, prevented Lidderdale Road from enjoying the prestige of a small, secluded cul-de-sac. Today, the same neat set of streets which run between Wavertree Playground and Smithdown Road, seem diminished since I played in them as a child; shrunk, perhaps, by fifty years of generous Lancashire rainfall. However, back then when a square-mile of neighbourhood was the known world to you, your street became a kingdom in its own right, its significance magnified by the expansive play of its children; the coming and going of foreign emissaries such as milkmen, postmen and coal merchants; not forgetting an occasional, exotic visit from a dangerous-looking rag and bone man.

"Stanley Williams… What on earth are you up to? I'll cut your whistle off… you little Errol Flynn you!" Beth's mum had raised her melodious voice an octave to part the leaves of the privet, behind which I was crouched with my four-year-old playmate. Mrs Davidson was just in time to stop me taking a good hard look at what lay concealed within Beth's navy blue knickers.

In the austere decade following the Second World War, society was still clinging on to many of the old Edwardian attitudes and sex was a subject denied a place in any conversation with children. The respectable working-class families of Wavertree were as careful as the sober residents of the new suburban villas out in Crosby and Woolton to mind their P's and Q's on this hush-hush subject. Most of us were totally ignorant on matters of sex and my family made sure that I remained top of the class in innocence and bafflement. I was an only child with a totally unsatisfactory knowledge of what little girls were made of. My Victorian granddad and repressed Uncle Stan had a calling to impose strict censorship on the most oblique references to sex. As a small boy, I can remember being hurried away from the sight of a heavily pregnant woman, who had made an unexpected visit to our house. The bomb disposal squad at No.52 was hell-bent on rushing me out of harm's way of the UXB-of-a-stomach being given emergency treatment in Pop's easy chair. Meanwhile, I was plonked down in the bunker of the front room with my *Dandy*, and left to ponder the sort of mortal danger I might be in. Wasn't the war over, and with it all fears about getting blown to smithereens? The lack of explanation for the air-raid dash to safety only fuelled my desire to further investigate the precarious state of health of so many women in the neighbourhood. What mischief lay behind the alarming appearance and such obvious discomfort? This I had to do for myself, rather than turn to someone as intellectual and unworldly as my dear uncle who, with reference to a set of Leonardo da Vinci anatomical drawings, would have given me an indigestible account of the workings of both the male and female body!

"Off you skedaddle my lad ! If I catch you it will be a proper waste of time trying to look down any more girls' knickers when you grow up!" The moment Beth's mum had exposed me as a little Casanova, I was off like a rocket around the top corner of the street and down the jigger to the back door of my house. Of course, the very next day I was back on the front doorstep of No.71 Lidderdale Road.

"Hello Mrs Davidson. Can I come in and play with Beth?"

"Well now… That depends on the mood you are in. So long as it is nice play and you don't still think you are Errol Flynn."

Errol Flynn? It's that man again. For years I did not know who or what she meant. That is, until my dad irreverently brought *The News of the World* into the home on a Sunday.

Restored to the comfort of Mrs Davidson's front room, I was content to let Beth boss me into a vague idea of table manners before she felt comfortable about sitting me down to a tea party with a couple of her most favoured dolls. On the other hand, she might want to dress both of us with the contents of a big box of old hats, scarves and enormous shoes. The kind and wise Mrs Davidson had clearly dismissed my previous day's ungallant behaviour as an involuntary surge of toddler testosterone.

My mind still draws back the lace curtains on the bay-window of that cosy front room. I remember the tiny alcove being rigged with a couple of big tablecloths, behind which flimsy veil on our world of make-believe the two of us would get ready to entertain our respective families. The adults sat chatting, some with wry smiles on their faces, drinking cups of tea and dunking their biscuits as they waited for the show to begin. It was a scene of simple-minded family fun, in rude contrast to the Fifties tale of teenage shenanigans, as recorded in Albert Goldman's *The Lives of John Lennon*.

Beth and her boy friend Pete Shotton, together with Pete's pal John Lennon and his girlfriend had come back to Lidderdale Road. They quickly retired to the front parlour, where they settled down to some serious hanky, if not quite the full panky. Beth's unsuspecting mum had taken a tray of tea and cakes into the front room. Unwisely, she did not think to knock before entering; worse still, as far as the two horny lads were concerned, she had appeared a couple of minutes ahead

155

of schedule. It wasn't just the meringues which were on show and noted for their remarkable stiffness! These were parlour games far removed from our infant days of innocence, when Mrs Davidson's tray of refreshments would interrupt nothing more illicit than a tea party, which Beth had neatly set out on the floor. No hanky-panky, then... Not even Andy Pandy! Just me and Beth, together with a few well-dressed dolls and a teddy bear addicted to rich tea biscuits.

At twelve, I knew as little about copulation as I did about calculus. I would have needed a time machine to discover that cunnilingus was neither the Irish airline, nor the billowing cloud formation you saw before a thunderstorm, during the cricket in Sefton Park! Ashley and I both needed Beth to lead us through a continent of pubescent ignorance concerning carnal matters.

"You want buy filthy postcard, Mister? Much too mucky for missus to look at, but plenty good for you... Yes?" No... It was not a back street behind a bazaar in Cairo, but the school toilets at Toxteth Tech. The little Jewish wizard of exchange and barter, who showed me a photo too dirty even for the notorious reputation of the dilapidated bogs at the far end of the school yard, now probably owns a porn empire stretching from Liverpool to Vladivostok.

"Where did you get that from?"

"Can't say... It's from Germany and there are nine more of them."

"Jees, if I were caught with photos like that I would be doused with holy water before being handed over to the police."

"You were talking yesterday about your uncle's Second World War leather flying jacket. You said that it was hanging up in his bedroom wardrobe and that he's getting married. Well, he won't miss it, will he? Unless, he's going to take his wife up for a spin in a Spitfire. I'll swap you all the photos for it... What d'yer say?"

A couple of days later, the boy made a special after-school visit to the back door of my house. Here, to my lasting shame, I traded a war hero's fleece-lined, leather flying jacket for a set of photos so obscene they would readily burn any set of pawing fingers. Hermann Goering and all the other Nazi perverts my Uncle Stan had risked his life to save me from would have climaxed on the irony of it all. I took my first good look at the hair-raising images alone in my bedroom with a chair wedged against the door! I wanted absolution and then to be rid of the contamination as quickly as possible... but not before, first, showing them to Beth.

Ashley and I stood with Beth under a lamppost, in the jigger down from Tommy Hill's garage. We began to wilt under her erudite explanation of what was actually going on in the ten graphic pictures of sex acts, which had lain grilling away on the springs under my mattress for too many dangerous days. They were images of mind-boggling complexity. The men and women in them could have been modelling for one of the Cubists, so little clues did they give about what was going into where, and by whom.

"They look like they're in a Zorro movie. They've all got masks on."

"That's not masks… it's a blackout over all the eyes."

"What's that for?"

"That's so the police can't identify them."

"Blimey!… With cocks like that the police would just need to make them take their pants off!" Ashley was right enough. They all had todgers like Sir Lancelot – big enough for Queen Guinevere to marvel at through his heavy suit of jousting armour!

We took the photos up to Tommy Hill's garage at the top of the lane and showed them to him. He had a good look, gave a broader smile with each photo he stared at… and then decided to have another, even better, goggle at before advising me to get rid of them as quickly as I could. The next day I shoved the lot down a gutter drain in Sefton Park. For weeks I was waiting for the City Cleansing Department to arrive with a couple of park keepers and a policeman to cart me off to borstal.

Tommy's garage was still there in the summer of 2000, when I returned for a reunion of Dovedale Road pupils. The small garage, now run by Tommy's son, was closed for business that Saturday. Still thinking of Beth, I walked from the garage down the cobbled lane until I stood underneath the two adjacent back bedroom windows which had, fifty years earlier, welcomed the bleary light of morning into a new day of shared excitement and fun. In the warm, brighter evenings of spring and summer we liked to pull up the windows and chat ourselves into a more receptive attitude to the intrusion of sleep into busy young lives. We would have talked the moon across the black night sky, if it had not been for Mrs Davidson coming out into the back yard to call last orders on all conversation for the day!

One evening, as dusk accompanied me through the preamble of getting ready for bed, Beth caught my lecherous eye in the yellow light of her uncurtained bedroom. She did not notice me, being totally preoccupied in her frustrated attempts to squash some flying thing against the wall above her bed. In an increasingly careless state of anxiety Beth chased the ill-fated insect all over the room. Finally, she cornered it at the window and drew me into a voyeur's paradise by gathering up the hem of her nightdress for one great effort to crush the moonlighting moth. My anticipation stretched with her across the windowpane in this last, desperate, fingertip chase to corner the fluttering fleck. Agonisingly, Beth's nightie climbed higher and higher up the, seemingly, endless pair of legs until my mounting excitement was, suddenly, squashed against the cold glass! Only then did she look across and see me. Annoyed at my enjoyment of the free peepshow, she swiftly closed the curtains against the night, leaving me with the tantalising image of her silhouette moving slowly out of sight.

Ashley was spending the night at No.52, and we were determined to resist the creeping tiredness which seems to beset and corrupt the world of grown-ups.

"Hey, Ash! Can you see something trying to get in at Beth's window?"

"Yeah… It's big and black. It's got six… no, eight legs and two heads with gamma-rays coming out of a Cyclops eye in each head!"

"Lois is in trouble. This looks like a job for Superman."

Once more it was time to don the home-made Superman suit, kept hidden under my bed for emergency transformations into the Man of Steel.

"Get into bed with the sheets over you. Stuff my pillow next to you, and then if anyone does look in they'll think we're both in bed."

"Where are you going?"

"Out of the window. I'm off to rescue Lois Lane… Up, Up and Away!"

I pulled up the window and, faster than a speeding bullet, negotiated the outhouse roof, a couple of garden walls, another shed roof and one more drain-pipe, to touch down on Beth's window sill. Some fifty years later, Ashley swore blind that I had leaped the width of the back lane in getting to Beth's window. Mind you, our conversation that day was fuelled by many pints of beer and the same stickler for the truth also claimed that when we were five, he saw me fly over a house!

Taking all talk of superpowers with a pinch of salt, I made it to Beth's window cursing my father Jor-el for despatching me to a planet without a tailor familiar with the bizarre fashions of my doomed planet Krypton. In negotiating Beth's backyard wall, the piece of red curtain I used for a cape had fallen from my neck. The wrinkled pair of Nan's stockings stitched to my maroon swimming trunks had twisted into an unaccommodating shape. The discomfort was like having a lump of kryptonite stuck up my arse and did little to help me establish a foothold on the narrow ledge.

I tapped firmly, on Beth's window. My weakening grip on the surrounding brickwork demanded someone please come as quickly as possible.

"Who's that out there?"… It was not the voice I wanted to hear. Beth's mum had pulled back the curtains so quickly, I struggled to stay upright.

"It's only me, Mrs Davidson. Can I come in please? I can't keep my feet on the ledge." She did not seem to hear me as she tried to focus into the darkness outside.

"Is it a bird or a plane? Is it Quasimodo's little brother, claiming sanctuary from the other hair-raisers in the belfry?"

Desperate to keep my balance, I spread myself across the window like the Lurpak butter man under a hot table knife. One side of my face became super-glued to the glass, the freeze-frame expression pressed into a monstrous, one-eyed stare so intense it could have set fire to the eiderdown on Beth's bed. Mrs Davidson lowered her head; pressing her face to the glass she looked straight into mine.

"Oh! Dear God! What is…? Is that you Stanley Williams? You strange silly boy. Get down at once and go back to bed! I'll be seeing your uncle tomorrow!"

I had Beth and Ashley to thank for fuelling my childhood imagination and turning me into a junior Walter Mitty. In my senior years at secondary school I had fanciful ideas of becoming an actor. Instead, I went for a Geography degree at Liverpool University. Going for the "safer option" was a decision I regretted for many years. Had I really wanted to be the next Albert Finney, I would have paid no heed to Uncle Stan's warnings about a failed career and penurious existence. His argument was that the safe and sensible thing to do would be to gain qualification into the no less theatrical profession of teaching. Here, in that quaint era of firm discipline and respect for authority, he assumed I could be as thespian as I wanted, with a captive audience of subservient pupils who would have to suffer in silence.

Likewise, I would have dismissed my father's tuppence-worth of working-class paranoia, about arseholes being damaged beyond repair by the predatory packs of poofters who scavenged mercilessly at every stage door in the land. So I fell in with the brigade who the cynics will tell you, "Don't do, but go and teach." I decided to fall back on Yosser's great one-liner of an excuse for unfulfilled dreams. "I could have been a footballer… but I had a paper round!"

CHAPTER 22

ST COLUMBA'S CHURCH: BETH STEALS THE SHOW

Outside the family at No.52 Borrowdale Road there was the extended family of St Columba's Church. In the unpampered post-war years of self-denial and gratitude to God for victory over Hitler's Third Reich, attending church was both a personal obedience and an integral part of community life. It was a matter of routine, as well as conscience, for most working-class families to send their children to Sunday school every week. Once he was home from the war, Uncle Stan took up a new commission from God to supervise my first steps on a clearly sign-posted path to a righteous life.

By religious conviction and social conscience, Stan Thomas was a Methodist. My mother's adherence to all her brother said and did saw to it that I, too, was baptised a little Methodist at St Peter's Church High Park Street. It also predicted that, just before my fifth birthday, I would be taken by the hand and walked the long mile down Garmoyle Road to the nearest Methodist Sunday School in Wellington Avenue.

This devout Christian was taking his promise to be my spiritual guardian and guide on peril of his soul, as he sat down beside the group of five-year-olds in the circle of kindergarten seats at Wellington Avenue. Even his pocket frame would not allow him to squeeze into one of the tiny, spindle-backed armchairs and so come down to my level. He made do by plonking himself on the floor, from where he sang the infant hymns – about being one of God's precious jewels and a sunbeam for Jesus – with the enthusiasm you could only find, today, at an Evangelical meeting. He clapped and did all the coolest arm movements that a five-year-old will try to impress you with.

Later, I realised that this highly intellectual and cultured man was the living embodiment of the gospel story, where Jesus placed a child in front of a crowd and then said something like. "Unless you have the same simple approach to God with the same simple faith and pure trust as little children... emptying your mind and heart of all the adult claptrap about being intellectually superior... then you cannot hope to enter the Kingdom of Heaven."

I would often think back to that tiny room of chairs in Wellington Avenue, when the Lilliputian scale of the furniture only served to magnify the innocence and humility of the man, who was beginning to take the place of my absentee father.

By my sixth birthday, Uncle Stan had become a regular worshipper at St Columba's Welsh Presbyterian Church, which stood at the Greenbank Drive entrance to Sefton Park. A switch in denominations meant little to my uncle, other than manifesting a belief in the scripture: "In my house there are many mansions." At six, the proximity of St Columba's to our house better suited my unpredictable bowel movements which, on the long walk home from Wellington Avenue every Sunday, had found me caught short on more than one alarming occasion.

"The little fellow has filled his pants again, Stan. What a mess he was in when he got home from the Sunday school. You would think someone at the church would be making sure the children went to the toilet."

"The teachers can't do much, Pop, if Stanley won't tell them that he needs to go."

"Well, that's the third time it has happened. Nellie had to leap out of the bath again and throw him in the soapy water for a good cleansing." I can well remember the shock of seeing all that black pubic hair on a grey-headed old woman. It made me even more curious about adult genitalia, which refused to age with the rest of the body.

My uncle's lack of worldliness sometimes rendered him utterly clueless about how dodgy people can be. He saw goodness in everyone. I really feared for the souls of those he, occasionally, expressed his doubts about. I had visions of such people having millstones tied around their necks and being thrown into the depths of the ocean.

"I know that he's only a little boy, Pop, but why can't he knock at someone's door on the way home and politely ask to use their toilet." I was at my listening post at the foot of the hall stairs and marvelled at the level of expectation my uncle had of me:

"Excuse me, Madam, for ringing your doorbell just as you were thinking about draining your Brussels sprouts, but there's a turmoil going on down in my bowels... Could I, possibly, make an urgent visit to your toilet before I do a very childish thing in my pants?" Anyone passing might be put off their stride by the hideous facial expression I had conjured up, in trying to imitate the gargoyle features of my father's hero, Max Wall.

What was Uncle Stan thinking about? Who knows the sort of a reception a six-year-old might get from knocking on the door of a complete stranger to ask if

161

they could come in and take down their trousers for an out-of-the-blue number two? What if there was a paedophile sitting in the parlour, or a pervert in the pantry, rubbing his buttery hands together with glee? It was certainly safer for little children in those days, when close-knit communities kept an eye out for one another. However, that fact did nothing to lessen my reluctance to show trust in someone I did not know from Adam.

"I don't want you to think I don't admire and respect Uncle Stan, son... He's a lovely man, but he's so naïve. I wonder sometimes if his Fleet Air Arm experience numbed the part of his brain which reacts to fear. Your uncle has a fear of God, but has no fear of man... People just aren't what he gives them credit for."

Deep down, I was like my father. I could never trust that all people worked for the good of others. On those Sunday mornings, when an hour of soul-enrichment had loosened my bowels to the point of surrender, it was a much safer bet to shit myself, but arrive home safely.

Most respectable working-class families despatched their children, like clockwork, to Sunday school each week. The Sabbath was a day like no other. Liverpool 15, indeed the whole city, went as still as Toxteth Park Cemetery. Cinemas, theatres, cafés – all shut their doors. Lorries shunned the roads and public transport ran to skeletal schedules. Forbidden to play with Ashley, I was expected to sit quietly in the front room dressed up in my best clothes and read a book or an acceptable comic. Nan and Mum would be slaving away preparing the Sunday roast in the kitchen, whilst Pop sat buried in the newspapers, without a solitary religious thought daring to enter his intelligent head. Uncle Stan would be upstairs, shaving and singing his head off, getting himself ready for church. He was the only one in the house who went to church, and I got the feeling that the rest of the family believed he had enough clout with the Almighty to keep us all in His good books.

I looked to Sunday school to provide me with a boost for a long day of no social activity. Along with Beth and Ashley, I went for an hour of hymn singing, Bible study and the unspoken joy of being in classes with girls, a treat denied by the Liverpool Education Committee's policy of segregation beyond the years of infant school. The older girls were in a flowering of their sex and created pleasurable thoughts and expectations, which lasted me throughout the week.

Scholarship was an important a part of Sunday school, as it was at day school. There was none of the secularised programme of learning which, today, parades as Christian education. The twenty-first century seeker after religion would have to go to a synagogue – better still, a mosque – for a proper indoctrination into a faith. In the late 1940s, Sunday school took its educational responsibilities most seriously. Whilst not wanting to make little mullahs out of us, we were expected to prove our knowledge and understanding of the Bible under the duress of an annual two-hour, written exam. The papers were rigorously set by the National Sunday School Union in conjunction with the Lancashire and Cheshire Presbytery of Wales. They included questions for eleven-year-olds on the life and teaching of Jesus which, today, would only be asked in a seminary.

"In the Sermon on the Mount, what did Jesus mean when he talked about the Kingdom of God? You may refer to Matthew Chapter 8, and any parables in the gospels to illustrate your answer."

There were no gift-wrapped, multiple-choice questions designed by modern crackpots, who regard the possession of knowledge as the privilege of an elitist few.

God is… tick the one you think is correct:

(a) An old man with a long white beard.   (c) The father of Santa Claus.

(b) The maker of Heaven and earth.   (d) Robbie Fowler.

Little wonder that, along with hundreds of other Merseyside prize-winners, we were proud to attend the presentation of beautifully ornate certificates – classified from pass upward to honours – at the Methodist Central Hall in Renshaw Street. What a break it was from scholarship when a youth club was started up in 1951.

"What a serve! Twelve-seven. Oh, Oh… I'll get it." It was a St Columba's Youth Club night. Ashley and I were having a game of table tennis. We watched as the ball rolled across the floor of the church hall and then underneath one of the big cupboards which lined the walls.

"Hang on a minute. I can just about squeeze my shoulders in… Can't quite reach in far enough. There seems to be some sort of a dummy stuffed away against the wall."

There had been a concert a week earlier to give the Minister, the Rev. W Johns, a fond farewell before his family left for their new life in Canada. Two members of the congregation had put on a comic ventriloquist act with one of them dressed in a suit and dog-collar, sitting on the other person's knee. As I stretched out an arm to search for the table tennis ball, a most bizarre thought entered my head.

"It looks like the dummy of the Minister from the concert. I'll have to pull it out to get at the ball."

As I tugged at the coat, the bundle of clothes turned its scary face on me and stretched out a large, dirty finger to press a… "Shhh!" against my open lips. Had I been Pip, alone in that bleak, windswept graveyard when the criminal form of Magwich reared up from behind one of the gravestones, it would have shaken me no less rigid. I ran for a club leader and brought him to the cupboard, hoping that my vivid imagination had been overdosing on thirty minutes of *Journey into Space*.

It was an old tramp, who must have sneaked into the church hall when it was first opened. Somehow, he had managed to squeeze himself into the narrow space behind the biggest storage cupboard where, for the next three hours, his body was subjected to the tortures of a Vietcong prisoner cage. Only when we had all gone did he intend to emerge for an Adelphi night of luxury on one of the stage sofas, warmly wrapped up in a spare curtain and comforted by a bottle of the hard stuff.

After reviving the sad old bugger with a cup of tea, one of the leaders took him off to the nearest hostel. Pulled from his hidey-hole, I'll bet he was not one bit hallelujah-happy at being cast into the open arms of the Sally Army. With his half-bottle of Bells confiscated, what terrified him most was the prospect of a carbolic scrubbing, which would tear every hair from his well-weathered testicles.

St Columba's was always putting on plays and concerts. It was Beth who tried to encourage me to engage in the carnival life of the Welsh church.

"Stan… I've got a big part in the Sunday school play. I'm a Dutch girl in the story of the little boy who saved Holland from drowning by keeping his finger in a crack in the dyke… The boy is very important. You could play him if you ask."

"Oh, Yeah… and I'll stand poking my finger into a hole in the scenery for an hour. No thanks."

"Well then, you and Ashley can be the Dutch boys who go for help."

"Do we get to eat any Dutch chocolate?"

It was Easter 1950 and Uncle Stan had just come back from a soccer tour of Holland with Pegasus, the most famous amateur football team in England. In spite of Dutch football being amateur, such was the post-war interest in soccer he had just played against Ajax in front of a 50,000 crowd. Best of all, he had brought me back a dozen, luscious, Dutch Easter eggs and a real pair of wooden clogs. The play, therefore, was a God-sent opportunity to wear them without the fear of getting laughed at in the street, so I turned up for rehearsals and got a small part.

On the first night of the play, an eager audience settled on the hard, wooden seats in the church hall to let the curtains draw back on a small crowd of children gathered in the village square. Beth had the prestigious task of saying both the opening and closing lines. Confidence was no stranger to Beth. She boldly stepped forward from the other children, smiled at the audience, curtseyed and then made such a powerful and convincing job of saying the play's last line that she cued all the other kids into the grand finale of a singing chorus.

Beth had short-circuited the entire show. The whole cast appeared, like Pavlov's dogs, to take their final bow. Perplexed little faces looked about the stage for a Cecil B. DeMille to yell "Cut!" The curtains were drawn in panic and then promptly re-opened again! Every child had the bloody nerve to either curtsey or bow for having done bugger all!

A ripple of laughter was followed by loud and sympathetic applause, which turned into an abandonment of wild clapping normally associated with a successful first night in the West End. The curtains were pulled shut, once more, and the cast given a few minutes to compose themselves before the play started again, this time without a hitch. When it was over, the audience went home believing they had been part of a richly entertaining theatrical experience. All the children were seen as budding little stars, but Beth's performance was the main talking point for weeks. By accident – or design – she had stolen the show!

CHAPTER 23

SAILING ON THE NORFOLK BROADS

It was the summer of 1950. Ashley and I were standing outside a gift shop on the main street in Great Yarmouth with Uncle Stan and his close friend, Albert Lilley. It was typical of my uncle's kindness that he helped pay for Ashley to keep me company on our fortnight's holiday to the Norfolk Broads. Albert had hired an eight-berth yacht for the two men and five women from the Lilley family, plus an extra cargo of two small boys who said they would, willingly, squash into the hold in the prow of the boat.

"So… What are you going to buy from the shop with all those half-crowns Uncle Stan gave you this morning? Apart from more ice creams, that is?"

I pointed to the big, rotating stand of picture postcards, on the pavement outside the shop.

"I'd like to send a postcard home to Mum, Nan and Pop" I looked, warily, across at Uncle Stan. "I think I'll also send one to my dad." Given the current flamboyant nature of the man's adultery, my uncle gave nothing away.

I was tempted to get my father the saucy, seaside card depicting a puny, bald-headed man in a vest, getting shade from the sun under the shadow of his wife's enormous breasts, but I knew that I would be refused a stamp to post it anywhere. Reluctantly, I picked out two identical, smut-free views of the beach at Great Yarmouth. Uncle Stan addressed my dad's card to the flat around the corner in Garmoyle Road, where he lived with Hilda in outrageous proximity to the Thomases at Borrowdale Road.

"You'll have plenty of money left, then, if that's all you're going to spend," said one of the women. "Don't lose it… It's a lot for a little boy to be carrying around all day in his trouser pockets." She looked across at my uncle in a disapproving manner. No doubt, Uncle Stan believed that he was educating me into a sense of responsibility for handling money. It certainly was a lot of cash – a whole pound in the real currency we used to handle before metrication made foreigners of the British. By putting me in charge of the purse strings for the rest of the holiday, it was hoped that I would evenly ration out the pocket money between my pal and me.

The woman's prudent questioning of the lack of common sense, in allowing a nine-year-old boy take charge of so much money, caused me to dig deep into the pockets of my short trousers. Nothing… both empty! All the money to keep Ashley and me happy for the rest of the holiday – gone!

Well that was it. My life was over… ruined for the next two weeks, anyway. Someone ring up Albert Pierrepoint and tell him to get the noose looked out and ready. "I've lost all my half-crowns. I must have left them on the beach, where we built the two big sand castles."

Early that morning, we had come into Great Yarmouth by bus from nearby Ormsby Broad and gone straight to the beach, where we stayed until the afternoon. The women had plonked themselves down on deckchairs to read and sunbathe, while Ashley and I played football on the sands with Uncle Stan and Albert. We cooled off with bouts of swimming in a sea mercifully free of the jellyfish, which seemed to ruin every family holiday we took on the coast of North Wales at Llandudno or Colwyn Bay. The last hour was spent making two giant sandcastles, which we hoped would withstand the first surges of an incoming tide.

I could remember taking the shiny pieces-of-eight out of my pocket, to stop them annoying my bollocks every time I knelt down to do some serious architectural work on the walls of my castle. I had dumped the silver into the soft sand and was too engrossed in my labour to notice it sinking slowly out of sight. My dad would have had a fit. I could hear his voice.

"Your uncle has about as much common sense as the bank manager who loaned a monkey £100 to set up a market stall selling bananas. His stupidity has been well rewarded!"

My distress at the thought of losing all our spending money persuaded three of the adults to take Ashley with me back to the sands. "Look… our castles are still there. The tide has not washed them away, forever." I had remembered building them near the Wellington Pier and their ornately decorated walls of gleaming shells were a signpost, guiding us back to the spot marked X. We picked the most likely places to dig with our tin spades and then began to excavate the site with the care and attention of two archaeologists painfully exposing the bog remains of an Iron Age warrior. Unbelievably, I unearthed six of the pieces, but as deep and as wide as I dug, I could not complete the set. However, with most of the pieces recovered, the fairground treat was back on the agenda.

As Pop, in the twang of W C Fields, would have put it, "Rescued from bankruptcy, my dear boy, rescued from bankruptcy!" My equilibrium restored, I went on to enjoy one of the best holidays of my life. We were safe as houses in that hammock, strung up in the small hold below the foredeck. Once the hatch was lowered on us, in the late evening, we lay head-to-toe in the Third Class steerage with eyes shut and lugs pinned back. The comforting flow of adult conversation, filtering through the wooden walls from the cabin above our heads, removed all fear of the dark and suffocation. This was the real thing compared to sailing the seas of my mum's front room in a galleon fashioned from pieces of re-arranged furniture. Kept under lock and key like two rebellious cabin boys, we imagined ourselves stowed away in the hold of a high masted schooner, as we talked ourselves into a drowsy passage of rewarding dreams; two young sons of Sinbad, combing the Seven Seas for an adventure Douglas Fairbanks Jnr. would be proud to sign up to.

The yacht had a small rowboat in tow. When Albert decided to take a break from the tiller for a few hours and drop anchor on a quiet stretch of water, Ashley and I were allowed to jump overboard and swim around the boat, or row off into a nearby island of reeds, where we could play at river pirates. I was aware of the mute swans. On reflection, the birds did seem a little too curious about our presence, and were clearly not so dumb that they found us an unwelcome transgression into their territory.

"I'm not too sure of those swans. There are so many of them on The Broads. They seem to operate in packs and the way they look at you, especially when you are eating. It fair sends a cold shiver up my spine." I was listening in, once more, to the conversation coming from the cabin above our heads.

"Well it's not as friendly as feeding the ducks at Sefton Park Lake, that's for sure, but they won't harm you," said Uncle Stan.

"Haven't you read about the attack on some people fishing a few days ago? It was reported in the local paper."

For all his learning, Uncle Stan never seemed to bother with newspapers when he was on holiday. It was as if his mind needed a break from the tensions of world affairs, as reported in the columns of his *Manchester Guardian* and *News Chronicle*. He had the invasion of South Korea by the Communists of the North to make him wonder if, all too soon, he would be climbing back into the cockpit of a decrepit, World War Two aeroplane. He anguished about the United States of America testing its new 'H' Bomb amidst the isolated, untouched beauty of the Pacific atolls. Then there was the sinister American politics of Senator Eugene McCarthy and his Senate Witch-Hunts to make him shudder at the thought that this "One nation under God" was now the self-proclaimed leader of the free world.

Much worse for this soccer man than all the fears created by the Cold War, was England's humiliating 1-0 World Cup defeat – by the USA of all countries! Such ignominy for a team which contained the illustrious names of Matthews, Finney and Mortenson... It was more than he could bear!

"Where did you get that story from? I've never heard of swans attacking people," said Uncle Stan.

"The newspaper is in the cabin somewhere. I brought one back, yesterday." We could hear the woman scrabbling around looking for her paper. "Here it is. It's at the bottom of the second page." As if for my benefit, someone began to read bits of the report out loud.

"Two anglers were attacked by wild swans while they were out fishing in a rowing boat on Barton Broad... One man is seriously ill in hospital with injuries to his face and a broken arm... the other has a broken collar bone. Oh dear, perhaps we shouldn't let the two boys out on their own again."

That did it. No more rowing out to the reeds and trusting in the good intentions of a bunch of imperious, long-necked, chisel-beaked muggers. A few days later, I was given a Hitchcock-like confirmation that here was a bird with attitude. Something akin to the tooth and claw side of nature and capable of pecking your eyes out, or breaking your body with a mighty blow from its great wings – if it liked the look of the iced-bun you had in your mouth.

We had moored the yacht and taken the picnic hamper and chairs to a pebbly stretch of shoreline, which edged one of the smaller Broads – I think it was Salhouse. Ashley and I went running ahead to claim the last patch of ground on the hundred yards stretch of beach with an unfolding of our deckchairs, when a flotilla of white feathers sailed in for a plunderous attack on the feast of food laid out on the shore. There must have been more than twenty birds. They made straight for the most sumptuous looking of the half dozen banquets, scattering the holidaymakers with their hissing and flapping as they went for the sandwiches and cakes.

Not content with devouring everything other than the duck pate sandwiches, which had an unsavoury, fowl taste about them, they took possession of one picnic area before turning their attention to the others. I watched, terrified, as family groups fled to the higher ground. For fifteen minutes I prayed that some kind of Jurassic Park warden patrol might appear to rescue things and let my stomach have its fill of the goodies which the women had shopped for and spent the whole morning preparing.

"We've waited long enough. Those birds are here for the day. Get the chairs and baskets, quickly and let's get back to the boat. We'll have to have our picnic in safety."

Long after the salmon paste and Spam sandwiches were gobbled down my throat, the jelly and tinned peaches with lashings of evaporated milk on them were but a mouth-watering memory, the swans were still out there. Dozens of people were keeping their distance, forced to be onlookers while the feathered felons feasted on. A few brave souls attempted the occasional sortie to grab plates, cups, and ransacked baskets. Two swans fought for possession of a ladies' straw hat. The stylish wide-brimmed purchase, which only minutes earlier had topped the broad, summer smile of an elderly vicar's wife from Norfolk, was now fit only to frame the debauched face of Robert Newton in the role of a gin-sodden, God-forsaken beachcomber.

The rest of the holiday was an idyll of sailing along placid canals, under blue skies. That is until the ex-navigator, Stan Thomas, was given the chance to steer the yacht. It was late one morning on the last full day of our cruising. Everyone was resting down below and Uncle Stan – now promoted to Captain Horatio Hornblower in his own head – was alone on deck at the tiller.

"Hey you... Just watch where you are steering that bloody thing. You blasted idiot! You're coming straight for our nets. Ohhh... you bloody..."

My concentration on the game of draughts with Ashley, down in the cabin, was broken by the spate of Norfolk swearing coming from the riverbank above. We rushed to one of the small cabin windows and looked up just as the side of our yacht hit the bank of the canal. The boat shook from prow to stern. The swearing was now symphonic, as other voices joined in.

"You bloody lunatic. Look what you've just done! This is... was... an angling competition. We've been here since six-thirty this morning you bloody, brainless bugger, you... See what you've bloody well gone and done! You've smashed into our catches you clueless, bloody..." I had never heard so many splendidly intoned bloodies being strung together in my life. Uncle Stan could not abide swearing. Swear words and, worse still, blasphemy seemed to pierce his sensitive nature like the arrows St Sebastian had sticking out of him, when he was made a dartboard for the Emperor Diocletian's Imperial Guard. Uncle Stan said nothing, bearing the flow of foul language like a penance for his bad steering.

"Squashed to a bloody pulp... Squashed to a... a... useless, bloody pulp!" Uncle Stan stood silent and impassive as he received a broadside of profanities from the riverbank.

"You may be a little 'un, but you're the biggest fool I've ever seen in my life!"

That was it. The angler had used the one "F word", above all others, which found the Achilles' heel of my dignified uncle. For the first time during a one-way traffic of verbal abuse, I heard him speak.

"Did I hear you call me fool? Do you know what a fool is?"

"Yes, too bloody right I do... You are!"

Now, I know what you will be thinking. What any normal person would think... What's all the fuss about? Foolishness is, after all, part of the human condition. As Elvis put it "Now and then there's a fool such as I." To my ten-year-old way of thinking, Laurel and Hardy were a pair of fools. The Three Stooges went one idiot better. I loved such fools, and recognised one as soon as Bob Hope put on his pappy's six-guns and pretend to be a gunslinger in *Son of Paleface.*

Uncle Stan had a sense of humour all right, but I knew that he had a problem with this particular word, having been severely admonished for imitating the suave Grytpype-Thynne saying "You silly twisted fool, Neddy," in a bit of vocal nonsense following *The Goon Show* on the radio.

"Fool"... The word devastated him like a judgement from God. It was Christ's voice from the Sermon on the Mount. "Whoever calls his brother a fool shall be in danger of hellfire." Clearly all the condemnation of Jesus for the biggest bunch of lying hypocrites in his day – the Scribes and Pharisees – was being applied to him. Uncle Stan snapped. His father's demon, the old pub brawler Bogie Thomas, had been resurrected without a drop of liquor having passed my teetotal uncle's clenched teeth.

"Well, if it's a fight you want."

"Who?"

"You."

"Who, me?"

"Yes, you!"

"When?"

"Right Now!"

The man on the bank doing most of the swearing had noticed the growing gap of water between the side of the boat and dry land.

"Right now? How?"

"I'll show you how. If it makes you lot feel any better I'll fight the lot of you… one by one!"

Thank God, Albert had rushed up from below. He did the wise thing and used all his strength to push the boat away from the riverbank with an oar. Amidst all the shouting and bawling, the threat and counter-threat, a few mighty heaves got the yacht drifting back into mid-stream and the current began to save us from a good hiding. The last sight which the ranting, fist-shaking anglers had of Uncle Stan was the pint-sized Scouser still mouthing the word "fool" to himself as he shadow-boxed a bunch of imaginary fishermen on the rear deck of our yacht. He was keeping himself in trim for fear the current changed its mind and brought him back to be gutted and then kippered by the raving mad anglers of the Norfolk Broads.

CHAPTER 24

ARTFUL ARTHUR

The 1930s was not the best time for any working-class couple to get married. Mum and Dad lived happily on their own for a few years, before hard times drove them to move in with Pop and Nan Thomas at Fern Grove, off Lodge Lane. Uncle Stan had won a scholarship to the prestigious Liverpool Collegiate. He was still at school and beginning to think that family poverty was likely to deny him a place at university. There was no work for the two older men in the house, whose greatest shared pride was in going to Goodison Park, to watch Stan Thomas dribble rings around opponents for Liverpool City schoolboys. By the mid-1930s, my mother's excitement with her late marriage and the thought of having a family had given way to resignation and sadness. The deaths of her baby girls, in 1934 and 1936, left my mother bereft and empty of any sexual appetite. Mum had kept a secret from her husband, only revealed on her death certificate in 1951. The twenty-four-year-old Arthur Williams believed he was marrying a woman in her late twenties when, in fact, my mum was thirty-one. Now approaching forty, Nellie Thomas might have guessed her chances of having children were fading as fast as the desire to satisfy her younger husband's rough-and-ready idea of sex whenever he wanted it.

"Is Arthur off again? And where to... need I ask? Damn the man! He's only been home on leave for a few hours." Mum, possibly nursing me on her knee, responded to Pop's anger.

"The bombing is bound to start again soon and that bike's not safe on the streets in the daytime, let alone at night."

"If a forty-eight-hour pass can't keep Arthur at home, or in the air raid shelter for that matter, what hope is there for Nell and the baby?"

Once my dad was out of the door, Pop had found his voice. Everyone knew where Arthur was off to. However, it was the middle of the 1941 Liverpool Blitz and his wife was glad to have him home for a few hours at any price, so nothing was said to his face.

Arthur Williams was mustard-keen to get peddling away on the old Raleigh bike kept outside in the back yard. He had a five-mile cycle ride ahead of him before he could fall into the arms of Hilda, behind the locked doors of her prefab, in the mists of Childwall Valley. It was a bollock-breaking, Tour de France uphill-stage ride back, when his shagged-out countenance would have been noted by everyone other than me. I was knocked unconscious with half a tin of Cow and Gate baby milk down my throat. Snugly tucked-up in a large drawer, raised off the dry earth floor of the Anderson shelter in the back garden I was, at that moment in my life, beyond caring where the man may have been.

My father first set eyes on Hilda in the late 1930s, when he began working as a conductor on the Ribble buses. Whatever the dyed redhead clippie had to offer, he clearly could not get enough of it! With the war over, Hilda was still living in her prefab in Gateacre and now ready to divorce her first husband. My father began extending his occasional visits into overnight stays and long weekend sessions, suitably squeezed into his double-shift work on the buses. He did not want the unexpurgated truth of his adultery to be uncovered, because he did not want a divorce to end all his sabbaticals at Borrowdale Road and severely restrict his access to me. He enjoyed my mum's company and the attention she gave him, but his lust was still for Hilda.

The interludes spent by my dad at No.52 were marked by restrictions on what he saw as my holiday-camp regime with the Thomases.

"Who was that you were playing with up Garmoyle Road last night? I saw you. It was one of the Whittles. I don't want you playing with the like of him."

"How many bags of sweets are you going to let him eat, Nell? All that rubbish will rot his teeth... if the liquorice strips and pipes don't rot his bottom first."

"The *Dandy, Beano, Rainbow, Radio Fun, Knockout...* Dear me, he only needs a few tins of Condor and a couple of packets of Pop's Woodbines and he could start up a newspaper shop in that front room."

My dad was the only person in the house who cared to monitor the time I came in from the street at night and how many times I went to the pictures in a week. He would not allow table tennis on the front room dining table; neither did he approve of me rearranging the chairs and sofa to sail a pirate ship, with Ashley, in an ocean of living room cleared of all furniture. At the dinner table, he left strict orders not to allow me to load any more roast potatoes on to my Sunday dinner plate until I had finished the three or four already there!

"Nellie!... Nellie!... Bring me a towel quickly. I've sliced the top off my big toe. I'm bleeding to death!" My dad was home again, for a few weeks' pretence at being a family man and providing me with a bit of drama. Arthur Williams could be described as having most of the attributes of the all-round, modern, husband. He was a hard-working, reliable and very honest employee. He was also very practical; a top-class meat and pastry cook, he could iron, repair his own shoes and mend his own clothes. I once sat and watched him remove the red piping from the outside legs of his bus driver's trousers and then immaculately hand-stitch them back together to give himself a new pair of navy worsted, Sunday best. Such innovation was praiseworthy, but a lack of concentration when practising chiropody in the bedroom with a Gillette razor-blade had my mum ringing for an ambulance to take her husband to Sefton General.

Apart from one long spell of a couple of months after he was first demobbed, my dad never seemed to stay longer than a couple of weeks at No.52. No siren call, but a hurriedly written sealed letter, furtively shoved through the front door late at night, would summon him back to Hilda's flat in Garmoyle Road and he was gone. Suddenly martial law was lifted and it was open house, once more, as the Jolly Roger was re-hoisted in the living room! With the constant coming and going of Arthur Williams, I not only saw some dramatic changes in my own lifestyle, but also recognised the truth about the man's dubiety and inconsistency towards my mum. His unfaithfulness denied him the open affection my demonstrative nature was inclined to dish out. Although I loved him and secretly admired him for being a cool and modern sort of man, I was never comfortable with him, because of my deep suspicion about his motives. His nomadic habit of wandering between my mother's bed and that of another woman made him a forbidding, as well as an untrustworthy sort of guy.

"Something is coming." A fearful dread would enter my dreaming in the early hours, and I would be summoned from a warm bed to the cold air of the upstairs landing. The recurring nightmare was classic M R James. In the persistently repeated scenario, an unmistakable terror had been summoned from the darkness of my mother's bedroom. "Why can't my legs move? I'm not going to make it to the top of the stairs!" My legs were always stuck in a slow motion glue of my worst fears and escape was impossible. "Whoever or whatever's coming from the half-open bedroom door, it means me no good. Oh!... It's behind me now... getting closer with every step. Got to make it to the top of the stairs... got to jump... Ahhhhhhhhhh!" Thank God, I always woke up, as I was about to throw myself down the full flight of stairs into the hall below.

Several attempts at reconciliation between my parents had been wrecked by my dad's dishonesty and his reckless behaviour with Hilda. By 1948, my mum's reluctance to believe the worst of her husband had been worn down by a cousin's eyewitness reporting of Arthur's overnight stays at the prefab down in Childwall Valley. Broken by disappointment and disillusion, she was persuaded to divorce my father. The legal proceedings foundered on a lack of juicy, photographic evidence, even though a private detective was hired to try to do a *News of the World* job on the two of them. "This spying on me is out of order, Nellie," I heard my angry father telling Nan. He, no doubt, made sure that the evidence of harassment from the wife's family became part of his legal defence. Of course, my sensitive lugs had picked out threatening phrases like, "Legal custody of the child." No bloody wonder I had a permanently itchy arse.

With the failure of my mother's divorce proceedings, Arthur's mood towards the Thomases hardened. He decided to play an even bolder, nastier game to get nearer to me, whilst at the same time sticking like a greedy bear to the honey pot of Hilda's charms. Out of the blue she rented a flat just around the corner from our house in Borrowdale Road. The idea of being taken a mere stones throw to live with the horrible Hilda sent my sphincter into orbit.

"How are you coping, Nell? You look tired and worn out. I don't know how you can live with it." It was one of the many feet-numbing, street-corner conversations I became privy to whenever I was taken shopping with Mum. I would stand waiting for the topic of my father and Hilda to change to the price of a cauliflower, or the shortage of bacon, before I could begin to think of getting home. The woman we had just met had gone all Coronation Street camp. Nodding her head and directing her eyes down in my direction, she half-mouthed her not-so-secret words of sympathy. "I've seen them, as brazen as you like, out together in the park and on Smithdown Road. What a hard neck Arthur's got.... And as for her..." The voice went into a whisper, but I heard every word. I had become so skilled in the art of lip-reading that I asked for a ventriloquist's doll for Christmas.

My biggest worry in being taken out for the day with my dad was not knowing whether I was going to be delivered into the presence of Hilda. "And where did your dad take you today? Oh, the Kardomah café in Church Street. Very posh!... And did he meet anyone there? Did he meet a lady?... The one who sits in the kiosk at the Mayfair and gives him all the free tickets, so that he can take you to the cinema as often as he does." Even if Hilda had been meeting my dad, I could never have brought myself to tell Mum and become an accomplice to his cruelty. My poor mother, however, could not help herself. "You know who I mean, don't you? I wanted to let her know that I was clearly on her side by saying something mingy, but splendidly satisfying like... "Do you mean the one who looks like Bette Davis when she was Queen Elizabeth with Errol Flynn at the Grand... only this woman had a Technicolor face!" I was too young to get into horror films, but thinking of the whitewashed mask of Bette Davis, and then Hilda's vivid, high gloss finish, was as close as you would want to get to a scary movie while you were still in short trousers!

"Hello, Nell... Well here he is... His Majesty returned safe and sound." No sooner had my dad and I stepped off the tram from our trip to the pictures in town, we bumped into my mother doing some late shopping on Smithdown Road.

Mum was flustered all right. Taken completely by surprise, she did most of the talking. It was a rare moment, indelibly etched into my psyche, as my parents found themselves speaking to each other in public for the first time in many weeks. My mother's face displayed surprise and pleasure in her good fortune. It was lit up and made youthful by a look of extraordinary excitement in her eyes. "What have you be been laughing at today... Cartoons? Laurel and Hardy?... I hope it's not The Three Stooges. After he's been to see those silly dopes he and Ashley are ready to bang one another on the head and pull each other's ears and noses off... I'm only joking. He loves going to the pictures with you Arthur. I hope he's been good?"

Mum cleverly tried to snare my father with family matters he would not want to duck out of. "With Stanley's birthday coming up, will you be coming round to make the trifle, and blancmanges, like last year?" Arthur seemed as pleased with the invitation as he appeared to be enjoying the company of a woman whom he no longer wished to live with. They talked for a good half-hour; long enough to make me hungry for my tea, except that for once I did not mind about filling my stomach. This was the type of nourishment I had been seeking for ages.

"How are you feeling after your operation, Arthur?"

"I'm much better now, thanks Nell. The rupture had got so bad I couldn't drive. I had to take too many days off work. I still feel it when I've been in the cab for a few hours... How is Stan getting on at Oxford? I saw his cartoon in the *Echo* last week as a star of the Tranmere Rovers team."

"He's doing really well and loving all the sport, of course. He's hoping to get a second Blue for cricket this summer... Are you still doing those exams to be an inspector, Arthur?"

"I've passed the exams, but your face has to fit at Garston to get an inspector's job. Checking people's tickets requires a certain class of person." Mum smiled as Arthur added... "We'll wait and see."

Having exhausted the few things about my dad's private life she was at liberty to talk about, Mum took the conversation into the safer waters of what was on at the cinema and what she had been listening to on the radio. Hearing them laughing together at the "Oooh!... Well... Oh no Missus", and "Not on your Nellie" nonsense of new funny man, Frankie Howerd, on last Sunday's *Variety Bandbox*, made me wonder what all the business of separation was really about.

Suddenly, it was all over and so were my hopes that they still loved one another enough to try, yet again, to make things work. My dad said a polite goodbye and was gone. As Mum and I walked home up our street, artful Arthur was quickening his pace to Hilda's flat, only a gossip's whisper away. He would, of course, tell her nothing of our meeting. Why should he give Hilda the bullets to fire at him? It was enough that every time he returned from seeing me, she would be cool with him; make him pay for the time he had spent with those he had, once, cared for more than her. Painfully, she would re-test his devotion until she could be sure that all his attention was firmly fixed back where it should be; his mind decontaminated from any disturbing thoughts of his family around the corner.

What was going on in my poor mother's head? After the shock of seeing her husband appear out of the blue, like that and behaving like a young schoolgirl, she was going home to ponder on the slimness of her chances of ever getting him back. By the time we reached our front door, Arthur would have arrived back at Hilda's flat. Soon he would have his slippers on and be warming his hands in front of Hilda's posh new electric fire. He would have to settle for a less-than-comfortable evening with the woman he had left his wife and family for. There had to be some penalty for spending his time elsewhere.

For all the many commendable aspects of his personality, Arthur Williams had a major character defect. Having been born one of nature's deceivers, he now turned his art upon me. It was to be some twenty-five years before I could nail the lie he had forced me to live with concerning the cause of my mother's death. It was our first outing together following her funeral in the spring of 1951. We were sitting on the top deck of the No.60 bus taking us to Aigburth Vale and the Mayfair Cinema. "I want to tell you something, son. I've been out to see the doctors at Clatterbridge Hospital. I saw the lady doctor who treated your mum and she told me in no way could stress have caused the brain tumour which killed Nell." I had to quickly check my mental file of precocious facts for nine-year-olds to have at their fingertips. "Brain tumour? What's that?" My Vista Vision view of the mansion houses in Ullet Road clouded over with the thought of having something nasty inside my head. "It's something you're born with, son... It's a lump which grows inside your brain and it gets bigger as you get older, until one day it kills you." Had my father sussed out I was budding neurotic, or did he simply want to make sure that I became one?

A family of grisly thoughts, uncaged by my father's dark explanation of Mum's death, were now free to prowl around my subconscious, growling out loud insinuations about inherited illness every time I had a severe headache. My dad continued, "Your mum could do nothing about it and neither could the doctors, or anyone else. I couldn't, that's for sure... The Thomases are very wrong to try and blame me for your mother's death." Having exonerated himself from playing the lead in the drama of deceit during my mother's long illness, Dad switched the conversation to the film we were about to see. It was Burt Lancaster and Nick Cravat in *The Flame and the Arrow*. "Tonight you're going to see enough swashbuckling and acrobatic stunts for you and Ashley to have the furniture in No.52 turned upside down for a fortnight." He thought to himself, "Thank God I'm away from all that!"

CHAPTER 25

THE DEATH OF MY MOTHER

It was a bright, cheerful morning in April 1951. I was a happy nine-year-old playing a game of tick with the other kids in the street, when I saw them coming. What it was about the determined, plodding progress of the two uniformed men which disturbed me so much I could not at first glance tell. Onwards they came, walking in a heavy, ominous, military step up the pavement of the even-numbered houses of Borrowdale Road. A chill, so unnatural for such a mild and optimistic spring day, swept through my body; a sudden fear settled on me and I stopped running. Someone had flicked the switch on all the fun in life and I was swamped by a dark foreboding about the unspeakable news which the two policemen dared bring into the happiness of my home.

With a frightening inevitability the men in black turned up the front doorstep of No.52. There and then I knew the grim nature of the message they had reluctantly been despatched to deliver. "My mum... She's dead." I blurted the words out to Beth as I struggled to continue our game against the sequence of alarming thoughts, now flooding my brain. The unconcern of the other children rapt in their guileless play merely increased my sense of treachery and personal danger. All the harmless street fun, with life going on as if nothing had happened, did not fool me for one second. I had been given an icy forewarning that the unadulterated happiness of my childhood was over.

Unable to contain the growing sense of panic, I ran through the open front door of my house to find out the reason for such a grim-faced visitation. The policemen had been as brief about their solemn business as concern to avoid a complaint of callous insensitivity would allow. Indeed, they were ready to leave when I rushed into the hall, adding a child's look of fear and confusion to the alarm and distress already on the faces of my bedrock grandparents.

Nan was a phenomenon: an irresistible force of nature. She was the home's tireless skivvy: the one who ensured continuity and stability in the clockwork, day-to-day functioning of family life. She was also my indulgent second mum, under whose skirt I would seek to hide when in big trouble. There I could be certain of an unequivocal advocacy, no matter what charge the world had falsely levelled against my precious name. My stoic, indestructible Nan was standing at the foot of the stairs: a figure of utter despair. She was an immensely strong little woman, but her body had buckled under the shock of terrible news and a weight of tears. Equally disturbing was the sight of my grandfather trying to console his wife by taking her into his arms, for I had never, once, seen him offer his all-too-willing slave even the smallest token of affection.

My father never returned after the divorce proceedings of 1949. With Uncle Stan also out of the house, hard at work in his classroom at the Bluecoat Grammar School across Wavertree Playground, my grandparents had to take the brunt of the devastating news alone. Seeing me rooted to the spot with a stark look of fear in my face, they tried to shake themselves free of their initial stupor; for my sake they contrived a most implausible cover-up for news they found too unspeakable to tell me.

Oh, how I wished that my uncle had been present in that moment of crisis. His will and compassion would have committed the Thomases to the soul-freeing task of telling me the truth. In Dad's self-exile, Stan Thomas had become the guardian and mentor to his sister's child. He was not there, however, to deliver me from Nan's monumental error of judgement. By the time he arrived home, Arthur Williams had been contacted at the bus depot in Garston and my fate was sealed by Uncle Stan finding it totally unjustifiable to transgress upon a father's bounden duty to tell his son such terrible news. In her desire to protect me and stall for time, Nan concocted a lie so unconvincing that far from keeping my happy world intact, she ensured it would implode into a void of confusion and insecurity. I knew that all the camouflage was nothing less than a horrible lie, but was clueless about how to battle for the truth which would be so difficult to bear. "Your mum won't be coming home from the hospital next week. She won't be coming back for a long, long time."

Whenever I require a reference to prevarication or understatement, I need only think of this desperate and foolish attempt to strip death of his workaday clothes and dress the unworthy spectre up in some very inappropriate Sunday best. Nan, aided and abetted by Pop, had signed up everyone to a conspiracy, which forever changed my view of life and death. In their desire to protect me from unbearable hurt they tried to set my compass away from the tempest about to engulf us all. Instead, they steered me into waters as becalmed as they were bewitched by doubt and anxiety. Week after week, I waited for any sign of a breeze of truth to let me move my life forward.

Uncle Stan regarded the family as God's vehicle for man's spiritual transport through this earthly life. He was God's steward and guardian over us all. My father was seen by an undevout Pop Thomas – a man not normally predisposed to humbug – as a transgressor against all of the Ten Commandments with something to say about the sexual appetite. Stan found a genuine liking for his worldly, easy-going brother-in-law dangerously compromised by his own Christian beliefs. This was the late 1940s and not the post-Christian society of today. For good or ill, post-war society's willingness to conform to strict standards of moral and social behaviour had not yet been tested by the contraceptive pill and the late twentieth-century communications revolution. In 1946, most people still believed God to be in His Heaven. After all, had they not recently relied on Him to deliver them from the evil of Hitler? Most people went to Church with a vestige of religious conviction and my uncle did not stand alone in believing adultery to be a cardinal sin. His views were merely a refined, educated and articulate expression of what the vast majority of decent people would have thought about the way Arthur Williams had treated his loving wife.

Stan's Bible scholarship would have made him familiar with 1 Samuel Ch 2:

> *If one man sin against another, the judge shall judge him;*
>
> *but if a man sin against the Lord, who shall entreat for him?*

Evidently, my dad had placed himself beyond all human help. His pre-war affair with Hilda had continued after 1945 and was to last long past Mum's death. As a child playing in the street, I was aware that Arthur Williams's love life had become a juicy item of neighbourhood gossip and a public affront to my family's sense of common decency. Uncle Stan's championing of his sister's case throughout the long and unsuccessful divorce proceedings of 1947 and 1948 took up much of his precious study time. In the weeks before his Finals at Oxford he continually had to return home and be engaged in distracting, upsetting written and telephone correspondence on behalf of his sister. Being robbed of the First expected by his tutors should have made him angry and bitter towards my father. Stan, however, was never tempted to see his errant brother-in-law as some kind of devil. The two men in my life got on well together and I never heard my uncle express anything but sorrow for the mess Arthur had created for himself, as well as Mum and the rest of the family.

Following the late-morning visit from the two policemen, there was little desire to eat any tea or supper. For a kid whose eyes were always bigger than his belly this sent out clear distress signals. "How ill does Mum have to be for it to affect everyone so much and make them all lose their appetites?" I was put to bed earlier than usual with the rare dispensation that I could read my comics for an extra hour or so. I thought it to be yet more evidence of very odd, disquieting behaviour. I tried to escape into an Edgar Rice Burrows science fiction jungle, where an abandoned boy had not only survived losing his parents, but worked himself up from that low point to become King of the Apes. Dad arrived and I waited for the post-mortem to get going behind the closed door of the back living room. Hearing him defending himself, in the mock courtroom downstairs, I got out of bed and took up a listening-post at the top of the staircase, so that the angry voices inside a fiery kitchen furnace of condemnation could be carried more clearly to my Bugs Bunny ears.

The interrogation was quickly turning into a witch-hunt and Pop sounded as if he were relishing the role of a Cromwellian Grand Inquisitor! I had the vision of a scrap developing between a hard-punching middle-weight, forced to take on the seventy-year-old, ex-fly-weight champion of a chain of public houses in the Lodge Lane district of pre-First World War Liverpool 8, who had been pulled out of a long retirement to defend the family honour. A narrow slick of pale light was trying to squeeze itself under the living room door into the friendlier-looking darkness of the hall. As the bright slither struggled to free itself from the mounting gloom and tension in the small back room, it began to flicker to the movement of a pair of unlikely combatants. My anxiety was fused with an excitement strong enough to overcome the fear of being caught eaves-dropping; slowly and carefully, I edged my way down a few steps of the stair to claim a better seat, nearer the ringside.

It gave me a hollowed-out feeling to hear my father, a sworn despiser of cellulose cissies and lily-livered leading men crying bitter tears of remorse, as he surrendered under Pop's brutal impeachment. No one could contain my grandfather. Sober, he was a quiet and reasoning man, but now he was off his leash. Intoxicated with a rage that only ten pints of Bass used to give him, he let loose in a rare burst of anger punctuated with an unfamiliar profanity. "You and that bloody woman you chose to live with against the laws of God (Pop could always give God a mention when He was considered to be an ally) and common decency. Both of you killed her... You damn well know you did, don't you? Have you any idea of what you two scheming devils have done to my girl and this family? All the crocodile tears you choose to weep now, Arthur, can't begin to cancel out the years of your conniving... the distress and heartbreak you inflicted upon a girl who worshipped the ground you walked on. You made her feel worthless and although the divorce fell through, we are all witnesses to your shocking behaviour... I would have stopped your malarkey years ago, but Nell wouldn't let me. She was against the divorce and the hiring of that private detective because she wanted you back so much... I pushed for it, because you and that evil bitch are little more than a pair of scheming devils. Both of you played on her feelings so much you made her illness all the worse to bear."

There was a short pause in my granddad's long and loquacious bombardment of blame, before he resumed with another personal, revealing onslaught, "I told you your brains were in your dick. You and your shameless, senseless behaviour, Arthur, more than anyone or anything contributed to Nell's brain haemorrhage this morning and that woman you live with is as guilty as you are!" He could have gone on for an hour I'm sure but mercifully, the sweet voice of Uncle Stan intervened. "Arthur has had enough, Pop. That's it... that's enough. No more, Dad. He's taken all he can... That's it!... It's finished with."

It was a month of *Beanos and Dandys* falling through the letterbox before my father got around to telling me that Mum was dead. I had accepted that he was the one ordained to give me the terrible news, which was ancient history to my friends in the neighbourhood. The longer he put off his onerous duty, the more difficult his task became and the more I dreaded the evil day. It was like being in the dentist's chair, desperate for an end to all the misery and pain, yet not properly anaesthetised; sitting, traumatised by the fear that you were not numbed enough to cope with what was to come. Finally, four weeks after the funeral, Arthur was given an ultimatum by Uncle Stan to come round and speak to me. He arrived at teatime, when we were all seated at the table, to make a very poor stab at doing his duty in the presence of those he had so deeply wronged. My father pulled an extra chair up to the table and the room went as quiet as the grave. "I've got very sad news to tell you Stanley. Your mum will never be coming home from hospital. Your mother is dead, son... We are all very sad about it. You've still got your Nan and the rest of us to look after you." He was desperate to end his statement without any horrendous slip of the tongue. Thank God he didn't add... "So cheer up mate, and eat up all your tea!"

He mumbled something about having to go to work, said he would call to take me to the pictures in the next couple of days, and then he was gone. His departure left Pop with a look of incredulity on his face, which no words could express. It was also noticeable to a traumatised little boy that his father did not appear to feel grief like the rest of us. Arthur Williams had no notion of either a heaven or a hell and did not care to express a belief about where my mother had gone. It was left to my uncle's much firmer grip on theology, once my dad had departed, to make some sense of the wickedness of it all.

The mauling which my father received at No.52 made sure that he had no desire to confront the Thomases again, until forced to at the funeral. Never a man to let any emotion show, he had broken down under Pop's verbal assault and needed time to piece the bits of his shattered pride back into something resembling the Arthur Williams he could live with. He certainly had forgotten about his little boy, left in limbo. As much as the adults tried to keep the funeral preparations secret with their behind-closed-doors conversations, they were well monitored by a flapping-eared child who was beginning to feel that he was no longer at the heart of the family's concern. However, I was far too scared to start asking questions of people I trusted with my very life and soul. "Whatever is going on is being done for my good. It must be. If it isn't, then I'm having a terrible cruelty inflicted upon me... a quality of unkindness that only the dreaded Hilda might dole out to me, if she got the chance. But not from those who loved me... Surely?"

My dad, no doubt, had his reasons for leaving me so hopelessly cast adrift. He was also a victim of this family tragedy. For too long he had felt neglected and marginalised by his wife's adherence to her own parents. Many years later Nan's sister, Peg, thought it time to come out in support of Arthur Williams, who her large family all liked. "Your dad wanted nothing more than to live with Nell away from interference... I don't want to sound disloyal to your Nan, but she was very skilful at manipulating things to keep Stan and her daughter very close. Your mum and dad did have a nice house of their own for a few years in 1933-4 but there were no jobs and they moved in with Pop and your Nan."

"So did lack of money force them all to live together in Fern Grove?" I asked.

"Well, times were hard for us all... but the truth is that young Nellie couldn't keep away from her mother."

"Your brother, Bert, told me that Dad met Hilda when he finally got a decent job on the Ribble buses in 1938."

"I'm not trying to condone your dad's behaviour, Stan, but some might say that he was driven into the arms of another woman. Not many son-in-laws could have put up with the closeness of the Thomases, as lovely as they all were. My girls thought the world of Arthur and they believed he was driven away from his wife. He was a proud, confident man and he could not cope with playing second-fiddle to Nell's deep affection and... well, let's say it... her unhealthy relationship with her own mother. They were like sisters and most men would have felt as if they weren't needed."

Arthur could take no more battering of his self-esteem and went looking for attention, laced with some racy sex, from the big-busted clippie, Hilda. Mum's shocking death had both surprised and overwhelmed him. He thought his game of trying to get the best of both worlds would go on until my childhood was over, at least. Now, Arthur's confidence had deserted him and he was as lost as he had ever been in his life. We had a telephone. Even if he didn't care to put his face around the door ever again he could have phoned; arranged to see me and told me the truth about my mother. For all of my father's undoubted physical courage, he did not have the stomach for this task. He could not cope with a family situation fashioned out of his insatiable desire to have his cake and eat it.

As the hushed-up arrangements for the funeral went ahead I overheard a conversation between Pop and Uncle Stan, which had drifted in my direction, like the smell of Bisto. "Albert's mother is going to take Stanley away for the day next Wednesday. I do not like this at all, Dad, but the whole family will be there and the situation with Arthur is so fraught with tension... You know that he still hasn't told the boy, don't you?"

So Mrs Lilley, a close family friend whose familiarity allowed me to call her Auntie, took me off on a seaside outing to Southport. The fact that there was no Ashley to accompany me along the endless miles of sands was rather strange. We were inseparable and performed as a double act at all the Lilley family's Boxing Day parties. Did Ashley know something he shouldn't? Had he been placed under house arrest for the day? Except for having been mesmerised by the Jewish funeral of Mr Cohen, I was totally ignorant of such things and how they were organised. In spite of some disturbing thoughts, however, I repeated the belief that I knew how much my family loved me, and accepted the gift of a day out without particularly looking forward to it. It was only as the weeks passed without any conclusion to all the secret preparations that what had happened, finally, sank in... I had been given a holiday on the day of my mother's funeral!

It still numbs my senses to think that, while I was steering dodgems and firing air-gun pellets at moving tin targets, buying candyfloss and asking for another ride on the ghost train, my mum was being buried at Smithdown Road cemetery. The street watched the cortege leave from No.52. My friends saw it, and then ran home to get answers to questions I was unable to ask. All the family were present. Nan's brother Bert and her sister, Peg, with their large, respective families were there. Pop's two sisters, together with their married daughters and children, were present. They were joined at the graveside by close family friends to witness my mother's body being laid to rest. There was, however, no precious son and only child to see her lowered into the earth, so that he might remember the occasion like no other and truly accept that she was no more. Perhaps, then he could begin to shape an idea of his life without her.

"Ashes to ashes... Dust to dust... In the sure and perfect hope of resurrection to eternal life" I was denied the cathartic words of Christian burial, which for a little boy made aware of the importance of the soul through his uncle's teaching, would have helped him draw a clear line in the sands of grief and despair. The child may then have had a better chance of walking away from the graveside with a hope and belief in new beginnings.

In that Festival of Britain year of 1951, family and friends watched as I went from a happy, well-adjusted nine-year-old to an anxious, fearful, eleven-year-old boy, subject to severe mood swings, who displayed a selfish, spoil-sport mentality when things were not going his way. The backlash from Mum's death hit me very hard. My work at school fell to pieces under the emotional confusion. Disoriented and disheartened, I travelled quickly from a top seat at the front of the class to somewhere nearer the back. In desperation I resorted to cheating from classmates a lot dimmer than myself, in order to get through the day without ridicule or a punishment. Dovedale's commitment to sport helped me. Outwith the school's regime of discipline, my turmoil erupted in comical acts of petulance, when something loomed up to defeat my purpose. Nowhere was this Junior Jekyll and Hyde personality more likely to manifest itself than on the Old Farm Field at Sefton Park.

"Out... LBW!" The umpire's raised finger signalled its terminal message that my turn with the bat was over before it had ever begun. Unimpressed, I remained at the wicket, with my feet glued to the crease. It was the third time I had been either bowled or caught out in the first over I had faced and the patience of the other young boys gathered around me was wearing thin. Stubbornly, I ignored my uncle pointing skywards, suggesting referral to a higher judgement should I refuse to move immediately from the wicket. "Did you hear me, Stanley? Out, again, for the third time this over. Clean bowled this time, I'm afraid!" I still would not move. Uncle Stan was forced to apply some sardonic spin to his meticulous umpiring "Wonderful stuff Stanley. The first ball of Tony's over removed your off stump... the second brought a lovely catch at slip from Brian... the third and last delivery has just torn your stumps clean out the ground and the bails have vanished completely." For judicial support Uncle Stan turned to the other boys, whose faces could not conceal their enjoyment over the deep pit of humiliation I had thrown myself into. "He was nearly out that time, wasn't he... Eh, lads?"

As laughable as my pals found it, for me it was a moment of abject failure. "Sod this for a bit of fun. Fuck the lot of you!" Off I went at a canter with Uncle Stan's bat and as many wickets as I could carry. "That'll show you well-adjusted bastards not to bowl me out first fucking ball, when all this fucking stuff belongs to Uncle Stan and in a perverse sort of way, that means me too!" On and on I galloped homewards along Greenbank Drive, leaving John Arlott to inform BBC Radio listeners to the Second Test at The Old Farm Field. "The covers have just come on as a heavy outburst of little Stanley has halted play for the day!"

It was the same story when it came to our games of football. The loud groans from my team-mates were matched by the jeers and laughter of the opposition as, put clean through on goal, I failed to score. Without the customary hat trick to offer for keeping the one-and-only leather case ball, I cultivated the habit of snatching it up, tucking it under my arm and then running, Forest Gump-style, all the way home. The Barclay brothers began taking an extra ball along... just in case!

How my childhood friendships survived such nonsense I do not know, but prevail against all the odds they did and the next day's knock on my front door would be celebrated with wide grins all round. It may have been a mitigating fact that, in my uncle's absence from home, I was the sole custodian of all the sporting paraphernalia stored upstairs in the great sportsman's bedroom. My friends were so unusually kind and tolerant it made me wonder how much they recognised the loneliness I now felt in the years following Mum's death.

The last time I saw my mum, she was standing waving goodbye to me from the small, open window of one of the barrack-like wards of Clatterbridge Hospital, in the Wirral. Clatterbridge was a leading cancer treatment centre, but this was the era of primitive X-rays and limited radiotherapy. It was a lifetime away from twenty-first century medical technology with the all-seeing MRI scanner, which might have saved her life today. The strict nursing rules of those days would not allow young children into the wards. On this poignant Sunday visiting hour I was left outside to peep in through the open window and occasionally attempt to share in the cheery conversation around my mother's bedside.

Everyone was in high spirits. "Your mum has been given very good news, Stanley. She's going to be allowed home in a few days." Rejuvenated by rest and heartened by a hopeful prognosis, she had made everyone so happy with her optimism. Two days later, she was dead from a massive cerebral haemorrhage. Specialists from the Dark Ages of neurology could not see what their intellect had told them to look for. "Ta-ta, love... I'll be home soon." I still carry a mental picture of my mother hopefully waving out to me from the open window on that last day of sweet farewell. Her relaxed and smiling face became a tragic keepsake. Effortless to open and forever close to my heart, it is a constant reminder of the anxious, unambiguous love and fierce protection she gave to the only one of her three babies to have survived beyond the first weeks of birth.

The poet William Cowper described grief as a medicine. I have yet to collect my prescription, which is now well and truly past its expiry date. Had I been brought up amongst the close fishing communities of my adopted North East of Scotland, a lack of years would not have denied me the sight of my mother's body, unmasked to the cold reality of what death is all about. I would have been allowed time alone with the person who, until a few wretched hours ago, had given me a young lifetime of love and care. I needed that time, so that I might strip myself of any false strength and say my own positive farewell. I was never given time to let my sorrow flow.

To this day, I have never been able to grieve for my mother. There were no child's tears as I lay awake at night asking for it all to be some bad dream. Neither was I capable of John Lennon's anger and rage against God for His lack of love, when his own mother was so tragically taken from him. On a dark day, when I was too young to question the why of things, my loving mum was simply sidelined from the mainstream of my life. Nevertheless, she has remained smiling out from that hospital window, optimistic and believing in only the best for me. It is a picture that sums up my longing for what might have been.

My mother's death affected me so deeply that for much of my young life an enormous black hole opened up, disabling me from reacting calmly and rationally in times of uncertainty and stress. At the heart of every attack on my intelligence and strength of mind, there would be a visitation from the small boy inside me. "Why were you denied the truth when it mattered most to you?" Loving, overprotective grandparents, even the wise and priestly morality of Uncle Stan, could not prevent the surrender to my father's lack of control. Denied the right to see my mother's coffin lowered into the earth, I became very confused and frightened about illness, death and even life itself.

I was one child who should have looked death squarely in the face. I needed to see it stripped of all its mystery and fearful allure; uncovered in its plain simplicity as the one, certain truth of our human existence. My mother's death never properly registered within my soul. To me, she simply vanished, mysteriously and forever on that time-stopping day in the frailest of spring sunshine.

CHAPTER 26

ARTFUL ARTHUR STRIKES AGAIN

My father died in 1977. By then Uncle Stan had moved from Liverpool to become Head of Maths at a school near his new home in Taunton. In 1983 I took my wife and children down to Somerset for a holiday and our two families were picnicking in glorious sunshine on one of the lawns at Granleigh Manor Estate, where Penelope Keith made the BBC series, *To the Manor Born*. I had, at last, grown old and bold enough to ask difficult questions of the man whose moral authority over the family I still found inhibiting, especially when I attempted to talk about the past. My uncle refused to condemn people for human weakness, which was a matter for God alone. He could not, however, fail to correct a falsehood.

"Did you say that your mother died from a brain tumour? Where on earth did you get that from, Stan? Nell died from an aneurism… You say your father told you that?" My uncle stared at the grass and shook his head. "What a man! He has some nerve to deny that the worry and heartache he and Hilda put your mother through did not have a serious impact on her illness. I spoke to the same doctors as Arthur and they agreed that years of emotional stress would have increased the likelihood of a brain haemorrhage. There's no doubt in my mind that the two of them deciding to live on our doorstep had a serious effect on her health. It seems inevitable, to me, that the stress of it all shortened your mother's life."

"What a bugger!" I thought to myself. "The devious sod had altered his wife's cause of death to neutralise the effect of a decade of deceit and humiliation on the pattern, if not the prognosis, of her long illness"… It set me thinking about the times I used to come in from the street to find Mum, with her head down on the kitchen table, trying to ease the pressure and pain. She could have done without all the years of her husband's deceit and the arrogant disrespect which robbed her of precious dignity. Without my father's adultery on her own doorstep and the sight of Hilda and him, arm in arm, confidently strolling about the neighbourhood streets and shops she would, perhaps, not have needed the prescribed breaks in the fresh air of a Wirral sanatorium to rid her mind of the daily humiliation. In spite of everything, I have many good memories of my father, but his track record made him a difficult man to show real affection to. I loved the best of him, but hated the worst.

CHAPTER 27

DAD CONDUCTS THE TRAFFIC

The day in question belonged to my father and to a film, which compelled the imagination to keep the projector running with its black and white warning for mankind. It was not long after Mum's death in March 1951 and Dad had been paying greater attention to what I was doing and taking me out more often. One Saturday morning he had picked me up from No.52 and we had gone into town for our regular treat at the Tatler Cartoon Cinema. He also had some off-duty business to attend to, connected with his new job as a toll collector at the Mersey Tunnel, next to the yawning mouth which sucked anything with an engine and wheels under the murky waters of the river. That is how we came to be threading a pathway through the lanes of stationary traffic at the top end of Dale Street, where a bottleneck of hooting cars and lorries had turned this busy city circus into a scene from *The Day The Earth Stood Still*.

I was still reeling from the impact of the first science-fiction film I had managed to see after successfully sneaking my pair of short trousers past the Imperial uniform of the doorman at the Gaumont Allerton. It was a movie many years ahead of its time. Memorably gripping and thought-provoking, it starred Michael Rennie as an alien visitor from another solar system in our galaxy, who had been sent to warn earth's leaders about the contamination of outer space by the testing of H-bombs in the atmosphere. Like one of my more formidable teachers, taking out the cane and swishing it about a bit to make the class sit up to the consequences of any more bad behaviour, Rennie stopped the earth spinning and all our clocks working, as everything stood still for one hour of our earth time. Here at the top of Dale Street, I was back in the film. As far as I could see, both in front and behind me, all the traffic had come to a halt; so had the pavements of people, who seemed mesmerised by this Rubik's Cube of a jam. All I needed was Rennie's giant robot, Gart, to appear and sort out the mess. However, we didn't need him at all, because my dad was about to take the situation by the scruff of the neck!

Arthur Williams was a man who could not stand around in a crisis. He could not contain himself if he believed others were not doing enough to sort things out as quickly as possible. It, therefore, took him only a few seconds to imagine the banner headline, 'Traffic Chaos Blocks City Centre' already inking itself onto the front page of the *Liverpool Echo*. He planted me onto the pavement with a firm, reassuring grip on my shoulders. "You stay here a minute, son. Don't you move now! This situation is dangerous... There's not a bloody policeman in sight." Without the aid of a telephone box for the split-second change of clothing, he was off into the tangle of traffic, a vexed vigilante for the public good. Assuming an authority and precision of arm movements, which put my scout master's expertise with semaphore to shame, he took charge of the traffic chaos in the midst of a jungle of failed communications.

I stood amazed; a man, with no declared musical talent, was transformed into a Sir John Barbirolli of traffic control! Immediately, the clarion horns in the brassed off section of vexed vehicles ceased their tuning-up and settled down to compose themselves under his baton. With drivers now sensing the slightest hope of a welcome first movement, all attention focused on my father's hands, as he began to encourage a rhythm and flow out of the tangled knot of cars and buses. He must have stood directing operations for some ten to fifteen minutes, before the message got through to the nearest police station that coppers' jobs were becoming two-a-penny and a couple of officers were despatched to take control of the situation. My dad was applauded back onto the pavement and rather than take a few curtain calls, we marched off to Brown's café in Whitechapel, where I devoured a bowl of my favourite oxtail soup and a plate of steak and kidney pudding, before topping things off with apple pie and custard.

The most commendable thing about my father's unusual self-confidence in such situations was that it sprang from dire necessity. Normally, he sat a few seats back from the main action, preferring to let others make all the running. He had no desire to influence, let alone control, those who wanted to rush in, take all the flack and make most of the mistakes. "Never say that you are the fastest gun in the West, son," he told me. "There's no reason, however, why you can't admit to being the second fastest. That's pretty fast, after all. Fast enough to make you feel good and have others respect you... Best of all, it makes sure that no one will come looking for you, to knock you off your perch. Those wanting satisfaction will be out searching for the guy in black, who looks like Jack Palance and claims to be No.1!"

My father's big contribution to my protected upbringing, within a family overawed by the idealism and the brainpower of Uncle Stan, was his willingness to give me the type of down-to-earth, common sense and practical advice I would surely need to assimilate, if I wanted to survive the real world beyond childhood!

CHAPTER 28

GUY FAWKES NIGHT 1951: MY FATHER TURNS UP AS GANDALF

It was now well past six o'clock and we were all in a heightened state of readiness for the bonfire to be lit. I had rushed home from school and gobbled down an early tea, in case I missed out on any of the preliminary fun and excitement. By now, however, my patience had developed a fuse short enough to pre-ignite the wigwam of lumber placed against the rear wall of our house, halfway down the cobbled back lane. A couple of dozen children and parents, along with a few subversive teenagers, had collected in the narrow jigger which separated the back yards of the terraced houses in neighbouring Borrowdale and Lidderdale Roads. It was November 1951 and I had just turned ten. This was the first time that Ashley and I had been allowed out on November the Fifth, without an adult to watch over us. It was going to be a bonfire night I would never forget.

There were not many years of unauthorised street bonfires left for the two of us to get excited about. The biggest and best of Liverpool's hundreds of celebrations that evening were about to explode into life on the hundreds of bombed building sites which still littered the city's housing districts. By far the most spectacular event for miles around was taking place on the derelict, six-acre patch of enclosed ground at the corner of Smithdown Road and Greenbank Road. This bonfire was so big that the older, tougher gangs of boys from the houses above and behind the shops on Smithdown Road had taken all the weeks of September and October to collect for the biggest open-air blaze you could wish to see. It was, by far, the most exciting and dangerous place to be on a night of magical entertainment for both children and the many adults, who still seemed to be celebrating the end of the war. Certainly, there would be an army of small boys not seeking their parents' permission to head to Greenbank once their own, small, street affair had lost its sparkle.

Earlier in the evening, an attempt by Langdale Road boys to light a large fire in the middle of the street next to ours had been thwarted by the killjoy pressure-hoses of the local fire brigade. The relaxed City Council attitude to the hundreds of victory beacons, lit throughout every neighbourhood during the celebrations of 1945 and 1946, was now being replaced by a more sober desire to curb public excess on Guy Fawkes Night. The *Echo* was busy reporting how more and more teenage gangs were trying their best to recreate the street dangers of the Liverpool Blitz.

Although ours was a very modest bonfire, it, nevertheless, commanded our allegiance and devotion. All the boys in our tiny kingdom of four streets had built it; we had looked upon our finished handiwork, and pronounced it pleasing in our eyes. The caravan of fruit boxes, old clothes, broken furniture and miscellaneous household throwaways, which we had been transporting for weeks, was now stacked as high as possible against the brickwork of the back garden wall. Suddenly, without any fanfare, the fire was lit by one of the older group of boys who had claimed an unwritten authority over the celebrations. A blazing paraffin rag was poked into the nest of petrol-soaked tinder, which I could see peeping out from under a wicker of pirated junk. One final rag was tossed onto the top of the fire, successfully torching the trouser legs of the guy, who looked remarkably like Adolf Hitler. Five years had passed since he had bitten the Berlin bunker bullet, and we still wanted to burn the bugger… over and over again!

Wh… oosh! Within minutes we had a blaze to cheer about, as the young lieutenants of this pagan caper perched themselves on top of garden walls, edging themselves ever closer to the rising smoke and flames. None of the adults present seemed to want to challenge their daredevil supervision of all the fun. Only the random lobbing of a Jumping Jack, down into the frivolous screeching of a group of girls, threatened to spoil an evening where adults surrendered much of their authority to the young.

As the older boys fuelled the fire with an endless supply of lumber from back yard storage depots, small groups of people began to take it in turns to set off carefully selected items from their prized boxes of fireworks. I had my own humble, five shillings box of Paines at the ready. The modest purchase from Bassnetts had me worried because of the serious competition promised by Ashley, whose Aunt Mary had lavishly provided him with a crisp ten shilling note to send up in smoke. This was a big night for small boys to invest all their pocket money, as well as their pride, in. For the past three weeks, I had been regularly taking down my small treasury of explosives and dazzlers from the cupboard shelf in the kitchen. I would spend several happy hours carefully arranging them on the table in front of me, as if each firework were a miniature soldier standing ready to face the rigor of a parade ground inspection from his commanding officer.

Holding back on the moment to light my first firework stretched out the time to enjoy the bonfire in the full flush of its youth and energy. It was yet another conscious effort on my part to extend the trifling pleasures of life against a newly fashioned awareness, since my mother's death, of how short the span of an existence might be. On a clear, but cold night, it was good to look at the growing strength of the fire and feel the roasting heat melting away the early winter chill on my cheeks. From my side of the blaze I stood staring through the light of the consuming flames, marvelling at the shimmering distortions to the faces of my friends and neighbours. With what seemed incredible daring, boys began to step forward; like bold Shadrach Meshach and Abednego, before the fiery furnace of King Nebuchadnezzar, they stooped to light the blue touch paper with its first glowing sign of life. Suddenly, through the mist of gunpowder and bonfire smoke I got a glimpse of my dad, who had arrived from the bottom end of the lane. He was armed to the teeth with four or five very large, white, paper bags containing a Woolwich Arsenal of the most jumbo-sized fireworks.

Arthur Williams was a class act. He could not help give the Thomases a lesson in how to put on a good show. Watching him make the humble sandwich was a revelation in food preparation. In a late 1940's home, where a small amount of money had to go a long way, he created stratum monsters I did not know whether to eat or excavate! His love of glamorous food was inspired by the American culture he, alone in our family, seemed prepared to embrace. What a contrast with my Nan's need to give a similar proportion of meat the Kali worshipper's death of a thousand cuts, before spreading the economic portions across a loaf of thinly buttered bread, for distribution amongst the seated, expectant Five Thousand! The price I paid for having Arthur Williams prepare my tea was that he never made you more than one sandwich. Each was so monumentally delicious you desperately wanted another, but I never dared ask the family's answer to Gordon Ramsay for seconds.

When my father was at home to do the catering for my birthday parties, Ashley would talk about the food for days afterwards. Besides his delicious sandwiches, there were desserts to win prizes. He produced sweet tasting custard, so creamy and smooth that it mocked the rival claims made for a pint of Guinness, pulled in a Dublin bar; trifles with the succulence of tongue tingling raspberries, in their rich juice, dampening several layers of light textured sponge; pink and white blancmanges, made with a tin of Carnation evaporated milk, rather than the souring contents of an unrefrigerated bottle from Hanson's dairy. All were presented to us, as if we were taking high tea at the Adelphi, in its heyday, when it was one of England's great five-star hotels.

He was a five-star dad in lots of ways, but not where it mattered most; in the way he treated my dear mum, who loved him so much. I knew that Dad had come to the bonfire from Hilda's upstairs flat, around the corner in Garmoyle Road. Only minutes earlier he would have kissed the slightly twisted Bette Davis mouth, seeking some sign of approval in the cold, mascara-laden eyes that it was alright to give me a couple of hours of his attention.

So here he was, my fugitive father, with his large bags containing as conspicuous a collection of the biggest individual fireworks he could carry. He laid his remarkable tribute carefully down on the step of a back doorway, upwind of any of the fire's devilry. In hindsight, it was a careless act, to create such a small explosives depot, so perilously close to the haphazard behaviour of so many ill-disciplined sparks. Here was an incident just waiting to happen. I can imagine *The Fast Show's* Ron Manager, standing on the touchline, making notes for his after-the-match comments on a catastrophe in the making. "Well, you know... Small boys... dancing about a fire... pockets full of matches and bangers... mind's ablaze with mischief... not a policeman, or a referee in sight... father taken his eye off the ball, so to speak..."

There was an overwhelming, spontaneous combustion. It was a display of pyrotechnics bettered only by a Chinese rocket factory going up into the starry heavens from a densely packed suburb in Canton. The first big bang, from a firework the size of a tin of Heinz beans, blew a new back entrance for next-door's cat to saunter through at three in the morning. One by one, my father's carrier bags succumbed to the heat. Those people with the worst memories of the Blitz ran for their lives up the lane, as one side of the bonfire became a self-detonating ammunition dump of noise and flashing light. Roman Candles discharged their fireballs of red, green and yellow, like crazed traffic lights, sending a confusion of signals in all directions. Three or four huge rockets, each with a fuselage capable of carrying a monkey into space, launched themselves at the brickwork and ricocheted off the walls in a dangerous game of bagatelle. A dozen replicas of Mount Vesuvius, with as many cascading Fountains of Golden Rain, lit up the cobbled floor of the lane, turning it into a mosaic of grey, pink and amber fragments.

I had retreated from a Promenader's front row bombardment, to a position some way up a back lane now reverberating to cannon fire and eruptions of light. All that was missing to embellish the sound and fury of the occasion was a suitable piece of loud, classical music from our flamboyant neighbour Gerald Dunn. Eccentric, poncey Gerald should have been at home to draw back the curtains and throw open the windows of his downstairs living room. He could then have mounted the small wooden podium, which he had permanently placed facing his gramophone, and raised his baton to wildly conduct music suitable for the occasion. The short, boisterous allegro from Handel's *Music for the Royal Fireworks* would have done just nicely. Even the great Gandalf would have taken his tall pointed hat off to that!

My dad may not have been acquainted with Gandalf, but at this moment a Balrog was stamping around inside his head. He was beside himself with disappointment, having seen his plan to impress and please me suffer such a cruel sabotage. However, he need not have worried about the impact he had made on the proceedings. By accident, if not by design, he had ensured that, more than fifty years later, I can see still him standing amidst the mayhem of multiple explosions and illuminations. "Great show Dad. You can bring back Hitler, tomorrow, if the war was as entertaining as this!" More poignantly, when it was all over I was left with the bitter-sweet memory of the absentee father, who tried too hard, often in the most unnecessary ways, to let me know that he really loved and cared for me.

CHAPTER 29

DOVEDALE: THE VINTAGE YEARS, TAKEN WITH A DASH OF LENNON

In 1949 Dovedale Road School's catchment area included the respectable streets of terraced houses on the Wavertree side of Smithdown Road, together with the middle-class avenues and lanes of Mossley Hill. Fifty years earlier, this slice of Liverpool 15 and 18 would have been regarded as a residential suburb. By 1945, however, a creeping urban decay had ruined the look of the once-grand nineteenth-century homes of the merchant-bankers on Upper Parliament Street and was snaking its ugly way down Smithdown Road to infest the beautiful Victorian mansions on Ullet Road. Even though my childhood witnessed the decline of Liverpool 15, I grew up believing that being bombed out of Toxteth into a superior, council-commandeered property next to Sefton Park was an act of God which moved my family to a paradise on earth.

Such was the reputation of Dovedale for getting its pupils through the dreaded Eleven Plus that some of its three-to-four-hundred pupils, including John Lennon and Ivan Vaughan, came to school from the posh suburbs of Menlove Avenue and Woolton. Most of us, however, lived within a mile of the school and preferred to walk there and back, twice a day, if we wanted to avoid school dinners.

In the late 1940s, after five years of wartime restriction, it was an uplifting feature of the lives of people who lived off Smithdown Road to begin their morning with the chatter and laughter of hundreds of post-war baby boomers, as they filtered along the streets towards Penny Lane. We were headed for a day of rigour in the classroom with widely varying levels of enthusiasm, but with minds well rested on eight-to-ten hours of sound sleep, in bedrooms free from the intrusion of television and its insomniac, night-shift partner, the computer.

"Hey... youse guys... Does anyone want a slug of liquor before school?" We were being addressed in an absurd, speak-easy American accent by the simpleton who liked to join us on our morning route to school. He would appear from one of the side streets off Garmoyle Road to make an early start to a busy day of living in a world of his own. "Wait a minute... See what I've got. Dis'll whet your whistle for all dat readin', writin' and 'rithmetic you're gonna do today, pal." During my first year at Dovedale this redundant clown would trot alongside us, until we were forced to stop and give him his morning fix of foolery. "Look... I'll open the biggest bottle of lemonade you've ever seen." Time after time, the man would go through the routine of placing a finger in his mouth and making the loud popping noise of a stubborn cork being prised from the tight neck of a champagne bottle. "There's enough lemonade in my gob for a birthday party... listen."

The imaginary bottle was lifted up to a full moon of a face, disturbingly reminiscent of Charles Laughton. With a squint of what might have been his one good eye, the loony steadily poured an endless number of pints of invisible lemonade down his open throat. "Glug... glug... glug..." It was a good enough sound effect to have wooed the BBC's Radio Drama Department into employing him for the background to romantic scenes along riverbanks or during fraught, kitchen-sink moments when the taps flowed as strongly as the language.

I have the standout memory of taking a few rather eccentric, sauntering journeys to school on crisp, frosty mornings after bonfire night. Every post-Guy Fawkes, the pavements and gutters were littered with the empty, cardboard cylinders of spent rockets, squibs, whiz-bangs and discharged Roman candles. To the concerned onlooker, Ashley and I could have been mistaken for a couple of apprentice "nico-pickers", collecting tab-ends off the street when, in fact, we were merely behaving like connoisseurs of good wine, bending to select our trophies from the now deserted battlefield and give each one a long, unhealthy sniff.

"Ah, yes, Ashley old boy... the distinct, pungent bouquet of soot and fired gunpowder. There's nothing like the lasting finish in one of these extinct cones of a cascading Vesuvius to give you that early morning spark."

"Quite so, Stanley old bean... you can keep your Medoc clarets and Chateau Lafite Rothschild. There is not one of these provocative little nose-ticklers... from a Brock's firework box, I would wager... which does not have the vintage stamp of Houses of Parliament cellars, November 5th 1605 about it."

In September 1949, I entered my first year at Dovedale Road Primary School displaying the extrovert family genes which had not been suppressed by generations of Welsh Calvinism, followed by a brief spell of Victorian propriety, before the early twentieth-century fall into decades of unemployment, poverty and squalor. For a small boy with an urge to perform within the comfort of his own home, I did not like it one bit when put in front of a public audience. At school I quickly developed an innate distrust of teachers who, possessing no more than religious fervour or, worse still, a Training College Certificate, thought they had a licence to turn a Shakespeare production into a chimp's tea party.

"I want you to play Joseph in the school nativity play, Stanley... Oh now, don't look so glum about it. I've noticed great dramatic potential in your activity at break time. The little cardboard wings, so inventively tucked into the sides of your shoes... Jack Flash of *The Dandy*, isn't it? A pity you didn't quite get the take-off you'd hoped for from that high wall, yesterday. Did Miss Hayes bathe the knee for you?... Yes, I have great hopes for you as Joseph. You will not let me down now, will you?" I could hardly refuse. Such guile played upon the sense of duty I was already fashioning out of obedience to my uncle's high values. Joseph was no starring role, but all the Hollywood greats had to start somewhere. It also flattered an inner belief that I was taking my first steps to becoming the swashbuckling successor to Douglas Fairbanks Jnr. What I should have said was "No thank you Miss. My level-headed father says all film and stage actors are nancy-boys or arse-bandits." Having watched Michael Wilding in *Maytime in Mayfair* at the Grand, and then seen a big photo in the foyer of the Royal Court of someone called John Gielgud togged-out as Hamlet. I was inclined to agree with him. The added fear that God might punish me for turning down a part in the play "what He wrote" forced my hand. Reluctantly, I agreed to be Joseph in the Dovedale First Year Christmas production of *No Room at the Inn*.

"Good evening to you, innkeeper... Have you a room for us in your inn? My wife, Mary, is great with child and must lie down." The stiff, Victorian language did nothing to disguise a dirty secret as old as mankind and was an enormous embarrassment for me to utter. Being forced to say such a line might give people the wrong idea about the baggage of carnal knowledge I was lugging with me into the small town of Bethlehem. I wanted to turn and tell everyone I was still getting the *Teddy Tail Annual* for Christmas! Apart from a few pupils such as the worldly John Lennon, who clearly knew too much for his own good, most of us found the topic of sex and pregnancy as mystifying as working out who was who in the Holy Trinity.

Almost as bad as playing a forty-year-old man, who had put a thirteen-year-old girl in the family way, I was being forced to dress up in one of my Nan's sheets with a chequered tea-towel slapped on my head. Once the clip of a Ben Turpin moustache had been firmly shoved up my nostrils, the grandfather of Osama bin Laden was ready to make a respectable woman of the Virgin Mary! When I paraded in front of the family, only the thought of humiliating me into running away from home and joining Menachem Begin's terrorists to blow up the King David Hotel in Jerusalem, enabled them to stifle their laughter!

"Here, Joseph. Have one of these iron-hard, crusty cobs for your supper. We've a good dentist in Bethlehem who does a nice crown for a couple of shekels"... Not quite the line delivered, but a likely explanation for the chip I had just taken out of a precious new tooth. My mistake was to persist, rather like the ravenous *Inspector Frost*, in shoving a door-step butty between the bristles of the lavvy brush perched above my top lip.

Chomp... chew... gulp... chew... "Yes indeed, the roads to Bethlehem are a bloody nightmare at this time of year." I was fairly getting into the swing of Judean small talk, when the moustache, together with its torturous metal clip, was dragged from my nose into the swirling mix of bread and saliva inside my mouth. For a few seconds I thought that I was going to be the first member of the Holy Family to choke to death on Christmas Day! I saved myself by spitting the lot out in the direction of the audience. As one startled lady in the front row slowly removed her specs and began to clean them with a small handkerchief, she silently praised God for her short-sightedness and the newly-created NIIS!

Following that scene-stealing performance, six months later I was given one of the school's two-tone soccer jerseys and a Robin Hood-style hat with a long feather in it. My teacher must have thought she was a dab hand at theatrical costume "Oh... yes... yes, Quite the part. However, the Pied Piper was nothing without his magic flute, was he?" Play the flute... I couldn't even get a note out of the free-gift penny whistle, delivered with the *Beano* one Friday! Worse was to come when I was handed a do-it-yourself kit for a pair of medieval tights. To a seven-year-old who had seen so many screen versions of *Men of Sherwood* that he could spot laddered tights from the back row of the cinema, nothing could have been less authentic than the pair of thick, old lady's stockings which were handed to me by my teacher.

"Take them home, Stanley, and get your mum to dye the stockings separately. One of them must be crimson and the other old gold... the same colours as the football shirt."

"But there's no top to the stockings Miss... There's nothing in the middle!"

"Oh dear... And there was I thinking that you had bags of imagination. When the stockings have been dyed, tell your mother to stitch them to a pair of your underpants... once they have been washed, mind!"

There were no further instructions and even less consideration given as to how foolish I looked when stood in front of the long, wardrobe mirror in my Nan's bedroom. What an unsettling sight! The heavy woollen leggings were sagging down like pantaloons, forcing the fly of my underpants to open and shut with every movement I made. If it were true that the Pied Piper was a paedophile, then I was typecast for the part.

"I can't play the recorder, Miss. I can only make squeaky noises and they come in fits and starts... That's what my granddad told me to tell you." I gave the teacher a short demonstration of my uselessness, hoping that some school virtuoso, destined for the wind section of the Liverpool Philharmonic Orchestra, would immediately replace me.

I had taken the recorder home to try to make some sense of it and could hear the conversation of my mum, Nan, Pop and Uncle Stan being interrupted by bouts of aborted laughter. My granddad was scathing of the lack of common sense in, so-called, educated people. "Why can't the teachers get someone who can actually play the damn thing to stand behind the curtains at the back of the stage, while little Stanley pretends he's playing the clarinet in Geraldo's orchestra?" Nan then made a comment you would only expect from the mother of a violin prodigy when, at his christening, the vicar asked the baby to play one of his early Caprices. "It's not fair on the boy... It takes years of practice to play a musical instrument properly."

Pop reserved most of his sympathy for the general public. "I think we should spare a thought for the audience. It's not fair on those who have paid sixpence for a ticket and then been forced to look up into those underpants! The flies keep opening and shutting like the flaps of a tent in a force-ten gale."

Never again did I venture into acting at Dovedale. Nevertheless, I still liked to watch others and can remember going to the 1952 school production of *Treasure Island*. As the hall lights dimmed and the rustling of programmes subsided, the curtains drew back on Act 1 "At the Admiral Benbow Inn" introducing us to an energetic performance from an eleven-year-old John Lennon, who knew how to show off all right. He was Squire Trelawney and full of himself, strutting about the stage in a Dick Turpin hat, whilst brandishing a flintlock pistol. Lennon had big problems in his young life. He was no less disturbed by his own sense of social displacement than I was deeply traumatised by my mother's death. However, he seemed able to attack his fears and anxieties head on, whereas, I let them overwhelm me. His bravado as Squire Trelawney was no piece of acting. He was merely being himself.

In my time at Dovedale, the likes of John Lennon, George Harrison, Jimmy Tarbuck and Peter Sissons would march with their classmates, two abreast, all the way through Wavertree playground, for a swimming lesson at the Picton Road Baths. Even those of us less adapted to the life of a water-baby than Lennon appreciated an hour's release from a morning of forced labour in the classroom, a fact which seemed to quicken the pace, the nearer our noses got to Picton's warm, chlorinated water. When he cast his staff upon the waters of the Red Sea, Moses must have got the same feeling of self-importance as we did seeing the busy stream of traffic part, to allow us safe passage across Smithdown Road. Lorries, coal carts, trams and buses full of passengers were forced to stop and contemplate the endless procession of young swimmers. Each Dovedale boy carried a towel and woollen trunks, either neatly fashioned into a jam-roll and secured firmly under the armpit, or suspended over a shoulder by those who preferred to trust in the tightly-drawn noose of an elasticated, snake-buckle belt.

"Right, boys... Line up at the deep end, would you!" Mr Bolt had turned up to act as the official judge in our final attempt to gain the beginner's breaststroke certificate before we left Dovedale in the summer. "When I blow the whistle I want those of you taking the certificate test to line up at the edge of the pool... The rest of you go and sit down and watch." John Lennon had been so bloody pleased with himself at gaining this, his first ever award that he kept the elaborate art nouveau certificate in preference to his Sixties MBE which was returned to Buckingham Palace in protest at the Vietnam War. I also kept mine as a reminder of the day I thought I was about to escape the dreaded Eleven Plus by going down to Davy Jones's locker at the bottom of the Picton swimming pool.

Fred Bolt never actually taught me, thank God. He frightened me enough, though, as he passed by in the corridor, or when he made his determined way across the playground. Peter Sissons' brother called him a sadist and his domineering manner certainly did not endear him to pupils. Fred must only have been in his early thirties, but he looked older than my father, who was now considered too decrepit to fight the Russians, should the Berlin Crisis cause a Third World War. Combining a reputation for prison-camp brutality in his liberal use of the cane with the notorious, hybrid fascist features of bald head and black toothbrush moustache, he declared to the whole world his self-appointed role as school disciplinarian. It was only the fear of what this man might do if he decided that I was a coward which forced me to the edge of the pool. For months I had kidded myself that managing a breadth with one foot on the floor at the shallow end was adequate training for any attempt to swim the whole length of the Picton baths.

"You lad... Why are you standing there, shivering? Get into the water... Go on. Get going, or the others will be finished before you have even started."

"I can't swim, Sir."

"You can't swim! For the love of..." He struggled to keep God out of playing any part in my salvation. "Dive in, boy, or do I have to come and push you into the water."

I did not dare explain that my class teacher had been kind enough, over the last two months of swimming lessons, to leave me to my own devices once in the water at Picton Road.

"Oh mighty Johnny Weissmuller, 1928 Olympic freestyle swimming champion and Lord of the MGM and RKO jungles, save me!" Uttering this silent prayer I jumped in.

When I came to the surface, I was as surprised as a torpedoed sailor to still be alive. Choking and spluttering on great gobfulls of chlorinated water, I began thrashing out in the hope that a pair of useless, trailing legs would follow flailing arms without detaching like a couple of coal wagons saying ta-ta to a runaway steam-engine. Panting and spitting from drowning lungs, I began to inch down the pool until my nimble toes met the sloping floor and edged me, exhausted, into the shallows. Fred Bolt, distracted by the plight of half a dozen other terrified boys, all battling the waves in a desperate, last-gasp effort to finish, missed me travelling the last couple of yards on foot!

Fred Bolt appeared to have a dispensation to bully, in spite of the fact that bullying was seen as a high crime by Dovedale's florid faced, chain-smoking headmaster, Stanley Evans. This man's remarkable antidote for one venomous outbreak of school bullying was to set up a boxing ring in the middle of the playground, complete with ropes, corner-posts and wooden stools. Teachers acting as referee and cornermen completed the atmosphere of a pre-war, open-air championship fight. It was all very well stage-managed for the assembled pupils to witness natural justice being dished out to one of the schoolyard monsters.

Strict enforcement of Marquis of Queensbury rules meant that any lapse into ungentlemanly conduct by one of the playground trolls was impossible. The smaller, slimmer of the two boys had been granted a level playing-field, which allowed us to rejoice in the memorable comeuppance of a school lout. Without his normal reliance on eye-gouging, groin-kicking and biting off pieces of ear-lobe, the tormentor of innocents was a spent force by the end of the second round. Blow by accurate blow he was steadily, cerebrally picked off and punched into an impressive points defeat by the newly crowned Paperweight Champion of Penny Lane!

John Lennon was a bully. I doubt very much if he was ever caught red-handed, for he practised his art in the covert manner of a CIA operative. Any dirty work was done by others, gathered under the banner of his charisma to add a little physical coercion to Lennon's preferred style of verbal intimidation and cunning. It was little boy-stuck-up-against-wall stuff, where the victim would be forced to hand over his dinner ticket. That is, if the smell from the kitchens that day signalled chips were on the menu.

The replica Colt 45, which I had foolishly taken to school to show off to my classmates, was a choice item for any boy to own, with its impressive weight, gleaming barrel and buffalo-horn handle. The gun was a precious gift from my

Aunt Mina of Pittsburg, USA. It was part of a huge parcel, containing a cowboy suit, D.C. comics, Western novels and a month's ration of candy bars, sent to lift my spirits following the death of my mother, in that bleakest of springs, 1951.

Off I galloped around the playground at break time to the William Tell Overture playing in my head:

> *De de dum, de de dum*
>
> *De de dum... dum... dum...*
>
> *A fiery horse with the speed of light,*
>
> *Two pounds of potatoes*
>
> *And a small brown loaf*
>
> *It's the Lone Ranger.*

The gun's powerful hammer detonated a magazine of megaton caps as I chased an invisible war party of Sioux across the schoolyard. A lingering whisper of gunpowder smoke passed under the nostrils of the watchful Lennon. My demonstration of gunslinging was far too flamboyant an act of proud possession to go unpunished by the Jack Palance of this frontier town. A couple of his hired hands rode out to cut me off at Bollocky Bill pass. After a good kick in the balls I was unable to sit tall in the saddle for the rest of the week!

Following the death of my mother and despite being the centre of attention in a loving family, I entered a world of fear and anxiety. While John Lennon's reflex action to hurt and loneliness was to attack the feelings of others, I imploded and let the world upset me. Only my humour and tenacity saved me from losing all sense of belief in myself. Thank God for Johnny Weissmuller, Hopalong Cassidy, Captain Marvel, Superman, – Oh yes, and the Paperweight Champion of Penny Lane – I never, ever, lost faith in them.

CHAPTER 30

LORD SNOOTY'S ELEVEN V THE BASH STREET GANG

Dovedale Road County Primary School was not some kind of prep school for the up-market, suburban middle class. Most of the 400 pupils at the all-boys' school came from respectable working-class homes, at a time when family income did well to stretch beyond providing the essentials of food, clothing, and paying the rent. I, therefore, raised a smile at someone exalting John Lennon for being an eight-year-old rebel, who cast his obligatory school uniform to the dogs!

The truth is that, beyond the enthusiasm of the first-year intake, most of Dovedale's pupils did not wear any kind of regimented school dress. The only identifying form of school uniform I was anxious to be seen in was my A-team soccer strip. I was so bewitched by the high-buttoned, canary-yellow soccer jersey, with its badge depicting a white dove, that I could not bring myself to hand it in after the last game in the Championship-winning spring of 1953. Instead, it was smuggled on board the *Scottish Express* at Lime Street station, all the way to a Highland holiday in Ullapool, on the West Coast of Scotland.

Primary school football was a deadly serious matter on soccer-mad Merseyside, both for the pupils and their wide-eyed, impassioned teachers, who ran the many rival teams as if they were managing Everton or Liverpool. With so many boys to choose from, trials for the senior team were always over-subscribed and lasted many weeks into the new autumn term of our final year. Mr Bell, who was responsible for the A-team in the glory season of 1953 when Dovedale reigned supreme in South Liverpool, came into the classroom with a piece of paper as significant as the one Neville Chamberlain clutched in his hand when he arrived back from Munich.

"The final trial for the First Eleven will take place at Penny Lane next Saturday morning at 10 o'clock. I have managed to whittle down all the boys who have taken part in the series of games into two teams. The names of those playing will be pinned to the main notice board at playtime."

"Probables" versus "Possibles". Such an artful use of our native language kept us keyed up and completely in the dark about our progress and ultimate destiny. Were we future Wally Fieldings, destined for the Everton forward-line, or sad Accrington Stanley rejects, earmarked for an uncelebrated lifetime of hard work?

Football at Dovedale was the compelling activity of most pupils. There were a few, like John Lennon, who found the prospect of chasing a ball the length and breadth of a playing field somewhat disenchanting. However, for the vast majority of my post-war generation, including Jimmy Tarbuck, George Harrison and Ivan Vaughan, soccer was an even bigger part of our lives than it is for boys today. This was due, in part, to the everlasting popularity of the "Beautiful Game", but mostly because it faced no competition from the multiplicity of leisure pursuits open to the modern child. It did not register with us that we were being initiated into the greatest team game in the world at a time when the likes of Hungary's Puskas, Czibor and Hidegkuti were about to appear at Wembley and rip the hearts out of the three proud lions, on England's whiter-than-white shirts.

I would sit and listen as Uncle Stan and Pop got engrossed in disturbing kitchen conversations about the gravity of the foreign threat to our national game:

"Is England not the best football team in the world any more?" I asked. Pop looked across at Uncle Stan and winked. "It's a very serious situation, Stanley, when teams composed of temperamental Italians, untutored Uruguayans and backward Brazilians are challenging England's divine right to lord it over the soccer playing nations of the earth."

I knew where Brazilians came from. I said to myself, "Brazil? How, in the name of Tommy Lawton, did they manage to play football deep in the Amazon jungle?" The moment I bent down to lace up my new Co-op, Desperate Dan-endorsed, brontosaurus-hide football boots at the Grove Mount changing rooms, I could begin to share my granddad's worst fears. How were we, England's 1966 seedling hopes, meant to match the ball-playing skills of atheist Communists and gutless, emotionally unstable Latins, with such Cro-Magnon contraptions strapped to our feet? The steel-toed, high-ankle, stiff-as-fuck, clod-hoppers with studs like wine corks which we climbed into had not yet benefited from Stone Age man's ingenuity to work new wonders with the flexibility of leather. The hideous contraptions defied any pair of twinkling feet to cast their magic over a sodden, suet-pudding of a leather ball, loaded with lumpy laces to brand your forehead for a season, if you did not connect with it properly!

On Saturday mornings I walked the half-mile journey from my house to the hallowed, manicured pitches at Grove Mount in Penny Lane, where all Dovedale's home matches were played. The prehistoric, leather boots strung around my neck would have received their weekly scrupulous inspection from my granddad.

"There are a couple of studs which are a danger to both your own balance and another boy's kneecaps."

The offending studs with their bare nails would be yanked out and replaced with new ones on his cobbler's last. The boots would then be given a fresh coat of Dubbin, to make them a few pounds heavier, and even more suited to the British game played on mud-holes much loved by hippos, where mere humans needed legs of oak to be successful footballers.

When it was an away fixture, I would pick a window seat on a tramcar, or on one of the new diesel buses, and let it deliver me to a ninety-minute bruising on a grassless, stony desert such as Princes Park, or one of the winter quagmires down at Otterspool. I needed the half-hour seat with all the enforced stops to prepare myself, mentally, for these campaigns on foreign fields. I would stare, unfocused, through windows misted up by the coughs and barked conversations of Saturday morning shoppers. There were certain fixtures where you would have personal battles to fight, trying to match the crunching tackles of Toxteth hard cases, who sensed a soft underbelly in your preference for a more thoughtful and elegant style of play. Here, lying in wait, were your never-to-be-discovered Tommy Smiths and Norman Hunters; unrestrained native breeds that ran about their familiar concrete surfaces on empty stomachs. We were the Christian sacrifice in an arena where wild boys bit at your legs with the ravenous appetites of hungry young lions; headless and heartless, they careered about in their reckless pursuit of shins and ankles, rarely expressing any artistic desire, when finding the ball at their feet.

Uncle Stan knew that by providing me with the kit to play for Dovedale helped build up my frail self-confidence following the death of my mum. It also encouraged the Thomas sporting tradition to be handed down from one generation to the next.

"You should have an interest in all sport, Stanley, and a passion for at least one. It is when you are young that you lay down the foundations of a physical fitness, which will benefit you in later life. Also, being fit is a necessary complement to any intellectual qualities you might hope to possess." I thought of Roger Bannister, the Olympic athlete, who was studying at Oxford to become a doctor... He was about to become the first man to run a mile in under four minutes. This feat ensured that he remained one of my sporting heroes for the rest of my life.

At the end of the 1953 spring term, Uncle Stan was pleased to see me swap my school soccer and baseball strips for the blissful sound of leather on willow. My Pop, great footballer though he had once been, was fair-minded enough to impress upon me cricket's claim to sovereignty over all other team games. "Well now, Stanley... Football or cricket? You ask me which game is the better. Umm?... Let me see, now. That's not quite the same thing as asking me which one I like best and was best at. There's only one honest answer, my lad... Cricket is the superior game. Would you like to know why?" Pop, a dead-ringer for the late Pope, John Paul, was now well into a mood for a bit of his own pontificating, so I nodded and sat back, waiting for his erudition:

"When you play football you are constantly supported on the pitch by the effort and skill of ten other players all working in a common purpose to defeat your opponents. In cricket, however, you are at the crease alone. There is a real battle of wits going on out there, at the wicket, make no mistake. You will find yourself subjected to a physical and psychological intimidation which will test both your concentration and your courage."

"Do you mean demon-fast bowlers?" I asked.

"It's more complicated than that. You will have to face up to the equally withering alternatives of dangerously fast, body-line bowling or, deadly and deceiving spin. You may survive the first couple of deliveries and fool yourself into thinking you have concocted a cunning plan to prolong your stay at the crease."

Pop's enthusiasm for the game had carried him off into a test-match scenario. "You manage to sneak a single and get away from the relentless accuracy of one express delivery after another. The bad news is that, at the other end of the wicket, there waits another bowler with a slower, altogether craftier style, ready and able to undermine any unwarranted surge in your confidence!"

I interrupted his masterly soliloquy. "Uncle Stan told us that there's a lot of strategy in cricket. What did he mean?"

"Well... to add to your state of siege, the captain of the opposing side will most likely be a master of strategy, meaning he can out-think you with a multiplicity of tactics and settings. For a start, he will have surrounded your wicket with an inner-circle of vultures, called slip-fielders, all perched and ready to feed off any scraps you may care to edge in their direction. Worse still, these sharp-eyed scavengers are supported by an outer ring of equally alert catchers and fielders, who can uproot your stumps with a throw of sixty yards or more."

Before I could take a few seconds to imagine Superman scoring 1,000 runs a minute against this Lex Luthor of the leather-seamed piece of Kryptonite, Pop had launched himself into a final few deliveries on the virtues of the game where all the gentlemen were players, but not all the players were gentlemen.

"Good Lord, even the weather can be called in to defeat you. Just when you might think you are beginning to get on top of a sticky situation and, perhaps, win the game... down comes the rain and both teams are forced to accept a draw."

Pop paused, making sure that he had submitted all his evidence. "I, therefore, rest my case, young man. Cricket is by far the more cerebral game and a much greater challenge to an intelligent sportsman than is football, wonderful game though it is."

So, there I had it! Pop's sermon from the Mount of Marylebone. "Blessed are those who play cricket, for theirs is the Kingdom of Hutton, Compton, and Trevor Bailey." I was, henceforth, obliged to give this game, which sounded as if it had been invented by a Russian Grand Chess Master, my utmost concentration. Apart from the Sabbath, for most days of the week in midsummer, we were content to pace out new and untried wickets for ourselves on the grassy, uneven pitches on the Old Farm Field at Sefton Park; batting and fielding until a tired sun signalled bad light, and tilted his amber glow beneath the avenue of sycamore trees on Aigburth Drive.

There were a few occasions in the summer season when playing cricket for the school gave me the heebie-jeebies. Taking part in such matches convinced me that here was a sporting challenge more worthy of decorated war heroes; a game for crazy people, born blind to any mortal danger; boys who could look fear in the face without blinking! I had a real problem in making it to the 80 bus-stop, at the bottom of Ullet Road, when I knew that it was going to deliver me into the hands of the barbarians of Toxteth.

On one such a Saturday morning, in May 1953, I turned up at the gates of Princes Park; attired for some heavenly choir in my Nan's Rinsoed white shirt and flannels. There I met up with the rest of the Dovedale team, who were already gathering before the knockout cup-tie against the Bash Street Kids of Liverpool 8. To the boys from Toxteth's Granby Street School, who had been arriving in dribs and drabs, like a long-lost clan of ragamuffins, it must have looked as if Lord Snooty had abandoned his, unwise *Beano* habit of consorting with the lower classes, and turned up with a load of his toffee-nosed cousins from Eton.

The world is prescribed by your neighbourhood when you are young. Short journeys assume the scale of epic adventures. London was at least a thousand miles from Liverpool. Africa, where you hoped Johnny Weissmuller lived with Jane and Boy, was a moon-flight away in your imagination! There must only have been a couple of miles between Penny Lane and the wildlands beyond Princes Park. However, in terms of social outlook I had crossed mountains and valleys, forged rivers, and trekked plains, to get from my respectable, lower middle-class suburb to the uncharted inner-city jungle, where the more primitive tribes lived. I had transferred from the leafy parkland neighbourhoods of

Calderstones and Sefton, to the bombed dereliction of Toxteth, where "posh" little schoolboys might still be cooked in a cannibal pot!

Dovedale Road Primary School drew, mainly, on a healthy mix of working-class and lower middle-class families, where a man was still the family breadwinner. Denied the education, which their offspring were about to receive as a non-negotiable right, our parents possessed the under-utilised intellect and cultural awareness to provide homes which offered children a lot more than mere material possessions. Some were skilled tradesmen, with the clever hands to match their natural intelligence. Others were recruits to the newly nationalised industries of gas, electricity and rail. Many were council employees, at long last blessed with steady jobs in a land aspiring to provide full employment: keeping the streets, back lanes and parks clean; the trams and buses running on time; the thousands of newly designated council houses spick and span.

The Dovedale school catchment was certainly respectable, but the inclusion of some of the wealthier, middle class, semi-detached houses along Allerton Road and Menlove Avenue hardly allowed it to function as a school of privilege for the seriously rich. The truly affluent lived a little further out, at Woolton. Here, John Lennon was brought up in his Aunt Mimi's modest semi, where he rubbed shoulders with Liverpool's social elite of bankers, lawyers and businessmen. It was the reputation of Dovedale which insisted to Mimi that she should interview head teacher, Stanley Evans, over his school's suitability to begin the education of her surrogate son.

Both headmaster and school passed her rigorous inspection and young Lennon was despatched each day, to Dovedale, but most of us lived in the streets off Penny Lane and Smithdown Road. We were all privileged to go to Dovedale, that's for sure. In terms of supplying a never-ending stream of scholarship boys to the city's finest grammar schools and also in its superb record of sporting achievement, it was one of Liverpool's great primary schools.

That salient fact had nothing to do with so few of us coming from homes with professional parents. The footballing Barclay brothers had a dad who worked in a bank, a fact which explained the Hornby train set, fleet of Dinky model cars and a battalion of painted toy soldiers which, on rare occasions, I was allowed to play with. John P's father was employed in the local gas works near Penny Lane. Ashley's dad was a cinema manager: a very respectable job in those pre-television days, when Hollywood was king. That is, until a sudden brain haemorrhage left Ashley's mum alone, to bring up her two youngest children without a pension. Any home comforts Ashley enjoyed came from the time he preferred to spend with his, unmarried, Aunt Mary, who was a nurse.

I suppose I have the *Führer* to thank, for transporting me from a cramped terraced house off Lodge Lane, to the splendid comforts of No.52 Borrowdale Road. Many years later, whenever I was asked by my pupils to say a few kind words about Herr Hitler, in addition to making condescending references to the autobahns, full employment, and a natty set of black uniforms with high-heel boots for bent arse-lickers, I would also refer to his generous gift of the marvellous, four bedroom, double bay-windowed house, near the entrance to Sefton Park!

Most of the houses in my street were privately owned and the residents were a lot better off than the new tenants in No.52, a house recently commandeered from its private landlord by the wartime city council. There was a synagogue at the bottom of Borrowdale Road, at the entrance to Sefton Park, and many of our neighbours were Jewish shopkeepers. Men like Simone Cohen's father had turned the two-mile stretch of Smithdown Road into a thriving area of commerce as well as a daily source of entertainment for bored housewives who loved to nose and gossip.

A decade or two earlier, our family's poverty would have placed us near the bottom of the social heap. Uncle Stan had given us a restored family pedigree, based on his Oxford education, wartime heroics, sporting achievements, and his status as a teacher at the local Bluecoat Grammar School for boys. To the people of Borrowdale Road it was a pedigree which no amount of money could buy. He had what can only be described as "The Morse Effect" on the susceptibility of our more middle-class neighbours to a touch of culture and a top class education.

I knew that the Thomases did not slot easily into the social pecking order of the street. Stan Thomas was a social asset, of course, but there was clearly a lack of family prosperity at No.52. Indeed, I reckoned that we were at the top of the street league table when it came to possessing worn carpets, curtains with moth holes in them, plus an antique iron fireplace, in the kitchen, alive with cockroaches and armchairs that your whole body disappeared into when you attempted to sit down. When invited to one of the many children's parties, which were a familiar feature of our street life immediately after the war, I noticed the quality of the carpets and thick fireside rugs you rolled about on; the comfy-cushioned moquette furniture you sat on, and the posh polished sideboards laden with fine clocks, ornaments and delicate-looking crockery.

My father had no time for the office workers or so-called businessmen, who lived in Borrowdale Road. As they passed by in the street, in their dark worsted suits, they all seemed to have been fashioned from the same tailor's template. To complete the identikit image of the "city gent", each wore a trilby and carried a small leather attaché case.

"See those cases, son. Very impressive, aren't they? Until you look inside them... You would think they were all carrying secret papers of strategic importance to the nation, but they're empty of any serious intent to do a real day's work."

"What's in them then?" I asked, like the perfect stooge to a droll comic.

"Nothing more than a few rounds of thinly-sliced, tomato sandwiches... Not even a piece of cheese, from his tight-fisted wife, I'll bet."

Back in 1945, we may have just won the war, but we were a nation still divided by class, having failed to see off the scourge of nineteenth-century poverty, with all its dire social consequences. Lord Snooty in my *Beano* was a cunning piece of social engineering proclaiming that, in struggling post-war Britain, we were all in it together, just like when we were fighting Hitler. It did not fool me for one minute. All my pals knew a toff of an Eton schoolboy when we saw one. If Lord Snooty thought that he could make friends with the Bash Street Kids from Liverpool 8 then he had another think coming...especially when it came to playing a game of cricket!

"What are the teachers thinking about?" I asked myself. "We're not here to get our heads kicked in... so who wants us to dress us up like a Junior MCC touring team? Right now I wish we could swap these laundered, Lord Snooty whites for their Dennis the Menace outfits."

It was a bright May morning in 1953. Dovedale cricket team was about to get an introduction into class warfare when we turned up at the Princes Park gates for a game against the boys from Granby Street School. These scallys took one look at us, rigged out in our pristine whites, and saw a bunch of upper-crust tossers. I wished that I could have been grown up enough to explain my own circumstances and the anger I shared about the class-ridden society we lived in. No close examination of my respectable, Sefton Park neighbourhood credentials, however, would let these Toxteth lads accept me as being working class. One look at the turnout of the Dovedale team would be enough. To them I would forever be little Lord Snooty. Nothing said in mitigation by my one-time dockers' clerk, beer-swilling granddad and a Nan who, for a few shillings a week was still prepared to get on her knees and scrub out shops on Smithdown Road, could alter that. No matter how much I wanted the Granby Street Eleven to be merciful, I sensed that they were up for giving us all a good bashing!

For a start, these boys came from homes without a "bathroom", as I was privileged to call it. They were lucky if they could get the timely use of an outside toilet, shared by every cold arse in the street. Some had given up on any pretence at normal behaviour, but many tried hard to live law-abiding, family lives in

213

houses lacking the basic amenities promised to their grandfathers, back in 1918. The few, relative comforts we enjoyed would be exaggerated into the possession of noticeable wealth by the boys from Liverpool 8, who measured us against the injustice of their own deprivation. This game of cricket was an unnatural meeting across an intolerable social divide, which made us all too readily identifiable as the enemy who had to be thrashed, at all costs!

Dovedale boys certainly would not be envied by their Granby Street counterparts for the dubious luxury of being ordered by parents to take a warm, soapy bath. We would be sneered at for possessing a poorly furnished but distinctively bourgeois front room; one which had lace curtains on the bottom half of the windows and second-hand, well-worn squares of carpet, attempting to grace a surround of stained floor boards. In my home there was also the defining presence of a telephone and a piano, which only my mum could get a recognisable tune out of. Copies of the *Manchester Guardian* and the *Listener* were placed neatly next to the radio on a small fireside table. That last bastion of Liberal editorial statement, the *News Chronicle*, most likely folded open at the crossword page, could be picked up from one of the big armchairs in the back living room. Unfathomable to me, their obscure and serious presence betrayed the education and culture of the men in the household.

I was still too young to be properly clued-up about the lack of moral responsibility, on the part of all governments before 1945, for the poor quality of life these resilient, brave boys from Liverpool 8 were forced to endure. There would be no enlightening annual holiday to North Wales for them, where they could run along the grassy battlements of Caernarfon Castle. More in tune with their low expectations of a paradise away from home would be a day out to Sefton Park. Gangs of lads thought it a worthwhile holiday treat to bike all the way from Scotty Road with a bag of jam butties and couple of empty screw top bottles. At one of Sefton's many fountains, they would pause from their fun and drop packets of sherbet into bottles of the pure Welsh water to celebrate a rare day out with slugs of imitation lemonade.

The fierce-looking lads from beyond Princes Park were denied books and the experience of music; access to libraries and museums; occasional trips to the theatre – all of which were my family's natural instinct to bestow upon me. They wouldn't have thanked me, I know, for arriving like a reformed Uncle Scrooge at their front door that Christmas Eve with gift wrapped copies of *Treasure Island, Kidnapped*, and *The Coral Island* to hand out. They would have stoned me down the street, because society had failed to give them the education and home environments where they would not feel intimidated by learning. These boys from the inner city had been fed from birth on the Big Lie that their intelligence would always remain a prisoner to the undeniable, unalterable fact of their social condition. Thank God for the Labour Government of Clement Atlee. At long last, here were politicians, with the power over people's lives, who seemed to have a plan to effect change. My generation gained all the benefits from the Welfare State, but for those so far down the social ladder, the task of climbing up a few rungs was still an Everest. I'll guarantee that many of the grandchildren of these Toxteth lads are still struggling. I was a very lucky boy!

When it came to being turned out to make a favourable impression on people, these boys had their own interpretation of being dressed to kill! Back in the safety of Penny Lane, we could refer to them as "scruffs", although to say so to their faces, in the open daylight at Princes Park, would not be a good idea! I don't suppose a single one of the Granby Street tearaways had ever been spruced up in his life. Even if the money had been on the table, not one of those boys would ever have succumbed to being taken by two women to get togged out at the local branch of the Co-op, near Penny Lane, or on an even more expensive visit to T J Hughes in London Road.

The Granby Street team were uniformly dressed in crew-neck woollen jumpers, with no shirt or vest underneath. These garments had been given so many hot-latherings with carbolic soap that they had taken on the harsh, beaten-look of medieval chain mail. The warrior image was enhanced by all the boys having adopted the tribal signature of a basin haircut. This, no doubt, predisposed them to the view that only the nancified sons of effeminate poofters would come out of Bioletti's barber's shop in Penny Lane with the sissy-boy Walter hairstyles we were sporting. What was worse for our image, as unyielding opponents, in this Princes Park clash of civilisations, was that our mothers could be relied on to turn us out in freshly-laundered shirts and grey flannel trousers, pressed with a crease sharp enough to point your body in the direction your legs were telling you to go. Every morning, clean socks would be laid out by the side of my bed, having been darned into respectable usefulness immediately a hole appeared in either heel or toe.

Nan had an obsession with cleanliness and it was her desire for me to always be the beneficiary of sparkling-white underwear. Her fanaticism was born, partly, out of countless years of back-breaking toil as a washerwoman to other people's dirty clothes. Greater still, however, was the fear that, having been knocked down by a No.46 bus, I might cause a shocked ambulance man to make an injudicious public remark, about the size of the skid-marks on my underpants! I took all of this being looked after like a little gentleman for granted. Here, on the threshold of an epic contest, however, a sudden awareness of the care and attention which had been lavished on me in my pampered home life made me self-conscious, not to say a little embarrassed.

These Toxteth toughs were a stern, cultural challenge to my world of good manners and courteous behaviour. Was the fact they were so disrespectful, coarse and aggressive a matter of nature or nurture? The possibility of it being both was the thing that scared me most! The air began to ring with a barrage of the thickest Scouse accents, the like of which Harry Enfield would, one day, get a lorra, lorra laughs out of parodying. Our limited vocabulary of a few choice swear words was being enriched with every new utterance across the no-man's land of pavement separating the two teams.

The stand-off was broken by a Granby Street boy taking a few bold steps to get within spitting distance, before succinctly and profanely proclaiming, "Yer' a bunch of swanky twats, but can any of youse lot cope with ar' kid 'ere?" The team's gifted spokesman then pointed to a giant of a lad who was a few years short of joining the SAS. "He fuckin' well bowls at ninety fuckin' miles an hour, down dat strip of cement over der." The lad grinned as he pointed to a couple of acres of barren ground across the park, which was about to take the place of the pampered, test match wicket of Grove Mount, Penny Lane.

We had played these boys in a soccer cup-tie only a few months earlier, winning the game decisively, by two or three goals. How could I forget a victory, secured against a background of incessant, obscene chanting? A rent-a-crowd of hundreds of pupils, aided by dozens of dangerous-looking, highly inarticulate, older brothers, several fathers, and even a few fearsome-looking mothers, had been imported to augment an appallingly crude cantata of intimidation:

> *Hughsie passed the ball to Mowie,*
>
> *Mowie scored the goal*
>
> *And sent the poor goalie*
>
> *Spinning on his*
>
> *Holy, holy, holy,*
>
> *Three monkeys up a stick,*
>
> *One had his finger*
>
> *Where he should have had his…*

It was a song-cycle to make the suicidal Schumann glad he would never see his forty-sixth birthday! Our teacher, Mr Bell, gamely running one of the touchlines, was seen to shudder at the end of each raucous stanza:

Dick fell out of the window

Eating a bag of scollops,

He landed on the drain pipe

And paralysed his…

Cynically commissioned to harness the literary talents of the most ribald of the playground poets, its diabolical purpose was to inflict moral distress on the sensibilities of properly brought up young gentlemen. The endless chanting went on and on, for weeks afterwards, in a continuous loop within my head. In fact, it's still playing…

Bollocky Bill went up the hill

To have a game of cricket,

The ball went up his trouser leg

And hit his middle

Wickety Wong the Chinaman…

Dovedale's Championship-winning team of 1952-53 was unbeatable with the big leather ball placed at the flying feet of our electric-paced wingers, Brian Barclay, and the aptly-named Ernie Smallman who, when he could not flit past defenders, ran between their legs. Playing football, however, was not the same as having an explosive device hurled towards you at sixty miles an hour, by some eleven-year-old wannabe Freddie Truman!

I was in the team on the strength of my bowling and fielding, not to mention the permanence of the crease in my trousers! My early desire to be the next Dennis Compton had dissipated, one Saturday evening, at the sight of Uncle Stan returning home with another battered nose. It was broken, yet again, and plugged, in horror comic fashion, with two bloody wads of cotton wool. Stan Thomas was so fearless that, in the cause of opening the batting for Birkenhead Park, he was prepared to end up with a sporting-memory-of-a-hooter, which gave the family licence to start calling him Mr Punch! With Uncle Stan's expert coaching, however, I developed a precocious style of leg-break, allied to an even more unfathomable googly, which got me into the Dovedale team as a novelty act, as well as providing a rest for the two fast bowlers.

Toxteth had suffered badly from bombing and the featureless expanse of park in front of me displayed all the barren, uncultivated, appearance of a moonscape. I could hear my uncle's voice lamenting over yet another no man's land of a wicket, where batsmen could be decapitated as quickly and efficiently as French aristocrats during the Terror. I began to dwell on the mental image of Uncle Stan's battered, Saturday evening face and asked myself, "Do such things as broken noses run in families?"

To crank up my nerves a few more notches, the set mouths and dead-eyed expressions of the Granby Street boys suggested hearts and minds as stony as their wicket. The preparation these lads had been given would be negligible, compared to the hours of expert coaching we received at Penny Lane. However, a harsher home environment and far more brutal street life than ours had bestowed upon these Bash Street kids the look of the cut-throat mob arranged behind Mel Gibson, when he charged the English off the screen in his version of the Battle of Stirling!

Dovedale lost the toss and we were forced to bat. Our two openers strode out to dig a trench against the likely bombardment, as the rest of us arranged ourselves in sacrificial order, on one of the few remaining clumps of grass scattered about the bare public park. The first ball could have been developed in a Barns Wallis laboratory. It seemed to bounce an impossible number of times, before shooting up from a stony outcrop to hit Johnny Stephen, full in the chest, like a piece of exploding shrapnel! Johnny's lengthy spell of prostrate moaning, followed by several minutes of seriously administered massage, produced an unconvincing recovery. The very next delivery tore out his stumps. My stomach turned over and I knew, then, what Pop meant when he had talked about "cowardice in the face of the enemy."

The bowler causing all the consternation was supposed to be eleven years old, like the rest of us. The boy with the Wayne Rooney face was not a day under fourteen and I wanted to know why our teacher, Mr Holmes, had not demanded to see his birth certificate or, better still, smell his breath for the four or five pints of Worthington he had downed for his breakfast. I watched, open-mouthed. "Ooooh... This guy's running fast enough to take-off like Squadron Leader Neville Duke, in his jet plane... I hope he forgets to let go of the bloody ball and flies off to break the sound barrier over the Pier Head!" I was now getting quite agitated, as the fast fall of our wickets tolled my imminent call to the crease. "Oh, Jimmy... Jimmy and your magic patch... Now's the time to whisk me away from here. One ricochet from a boulder or stone embedded in that pitch and this Granby Street troll will disconnect every bone in my body!"

Given his venerable age, he could well have had the time to develop a political agenda. Perhaps, he belonged to a family of dockers: militant trade unionists, who had brainwashed him into carrying a fiery message to the fanciful, pseudo-middle classes of the Poshlands beyond Allerton. He launched each new delivery with a total ignorance of the rules of cricket. It was bowling so lacking in style and technique that, had he been playing for a public school, he would have been flogged, bare-arsed, in front of a roasting fire overlooked by the portrait of an approving W G Grace!

Alert to my impending doom, I was now sitting bolt upright, like a prairie dog sniffing the air for any sign of a crafty coyote. By the time I was strapping a set of pads to reluctant, uncooperative, legs, I had made up my mind to desert the crease before I landed up in Sefton General Hospital. "I'm a bowler, anyway, and the last man in. What shame is there, with the score at 23 for 9 wickets, in running away, Jerry Lewis-style, at the first sight of a ball which would give me a nose like Jimmy Durante?"

"No ball!" shouted the Dovedale umpire. The wild first delivery merely gave the Granby Street assassin an extra shot at doing me some harm. His second ball was a horrible full-toss. I jumped clear of its path, well to leg side. Mercifully, it took the whole wicket clean out of the ground and I became anaesthetised by the sudden vision of my ritual, Saturday lunch of a tin of Heinz sausages and beans with mashed potatoes. I was certainly in a happier state now, striding manfully back to join my defeated team-mates before throwing off all sense of shame along with my Blanco-whitened pads. I was mentally racing ahead to the bus and home; the dumping of my worthless whites; a quick change of heavily-stained underpants and then...

Hi-Ho, Silver

Here comes de Lone Ranger

It's off to the children's matinee, at the Grand on Smithdown Road!

I cannot help but think that the wrong social class was given the rulebook, along with all the paraphernalia of the game of cricket. What might England's future have been, had these young tearaways from Toxteth – and you might like to add the other inner-city neighbourhoods of Manchester, Leeds and Birmingham – been able to embrace this essentially (Yorkshire miners apart) middle-class pastime of rural England.

The idyllic, village green scenario also points to the Achilles heel of our national summer pastime. For all the emotional eloquence of the Oxbridge radio commentators who, throughout my childhood, waxed lyrical to get the game included in the morning prayers of every school in the land, cricket required the possession of acres of green parkland and a regimental store of equipment. You needed gigantic bags, packed with loads of pads, gloves, varnished stumps, seamed-leather balls and a couple of expensive willow bats. If you could manage to own all of that, you still would not be one of the boys without a club blazer, cap, flannels, boots and a V-necked cable-knit sweater so that Hardy Amis could dash off a few pencil sketches of you, standing with your back to the tea room, on the pavilion steps.

Such compulsory accessories put cricket well beyond the social circles these Toxteth lads operated in. On top of that, a player needed the time and money for a few rounds of Scotch in the clubhouse, after net practice, and a wallet full of notes for the post-match "No... No... Surely, it's my round, again, Sandy" socialising on a Saturday night. Could an inner-city version of the game for the likes of the no-nonsense, demolition men from Liverpool 8 have transformed the cerebral, languid, often dreamy quality of our great summer passion, with an injection of back-street cunning and fearless aggression?

Of course, it is possible that the game of W G Grace, Bradman and Botham might possess a few too many hours of mind-boggling inactivity, to have charmed these hyperactive street-wise lads away from evenings and weekends of gang activity, with the added thrill of petty crime. It's a nice thought, however, that any present-day gibes echoing throughout the Punjab, or Aussie sneers from the uptown bars of Melbourne and Sydney could have been silenced, forever, by recruiting a National Dirty Dozen from the council estates of Toxteth, Moss Side and Brixton, to shake up the stoic, but dreary soul of English cricket!

CHAPTER 31

HOW TO FAIL THE ELEVEN PLUS WITH STYLE

The dreaded Eleven Plus was the most terrifying watershed in our young lives; overcoming it was the passport to an academic education and a set of qualifications which would open the door to success in life. John Lennon succinctly put the merciless instrument of State selection into its true context when he once told foreign journalists, "There's an exam in England they hang over your head from age five, called the Eleven Plus. If you don't pass the Eleven Plus, you're finished for life."

There is still, within my soul, a remnant of the chill I felt that fateful morning of the Eleven Plus. My exiled father insisted on calling at No.52, dressed for driving his tram later in the day, to accompany me on that stressful, foreboding, bone-shaking journey into the city.

"Is he ready for the big day? Has he had a good breakfast?" Well, no. I wasn't bloody ready. Far from it... and most of my breakfast had been thrown-up in the sink.

"Have you got your pencils with you... and a rubber?" I nodded bravely, unwillingly bearing the weight of the family's hopes on my little shoulders. It was a year since my mother's death and I was still hopelessly traumatised by my loss and the events surrounding her funeral.

"OK, then... Let's get it over with. It'll be a piece of cake to a lad like you."

There was nothing I loved better than a nice, big slice of my Nan's home-made sponge cake. This was no piece of cake and even if it had been, I would have choked on the first mouthful! It seemed an interminably long and uncomfortable ride into town, memorably unrelieved by my father's sincere but often awkward, ill-chosen words of reassurance, and his unwelcome intrusion into my private agony.

He was probably as glad as I was to see his duty done and have me safely delivered to the portals of the Liverpool Institute, then the city's most prestigious grammar school. He hurriedly wished me good luck and was gone, leaving me to congregate with hundreds of other lonely, deserted, children whose parents had, likewise, made a quick get-away from the stressful scene with all its vain expectations and portentous consequences for the future prospects of their offspring. Thus, we were made to stand for fifteen minutes, too worried even to give each other a few whispered words of support. It was certainly a long enough wait to increase the sense of panic and raise the level of fear now welling up in hundreds of fast-beating little hearts.

Suddenly, three daunting figures appeared against the backcloth of the sombre, smoke-blackened, sandstone of the school building. They were formidable, scholarly-looking men, whose sinister, archaic dress of black gowns and mortarboards I could readily associate with cold and strict places of learning. Such were the disquieting, class-conscious places, epitomised in the film *Tom Brown's Schooldays*, which I had been taken to see, more than once, at the Grand. I loved such memorable entertainment, partly because I could thank God all our lamp-lit way home that I was not some prisoner of an alien class system. Best of all, I did not belong to parents who punished their children by sending them away to boarding school. I could, daily, enjoy the warmth of my mother's voice and the sweet comfort of my Nan's many indulgences, including her celebrated cooking.

The three austere, scholastic, gentlemen, suddenly barked their abrupt and co-ordinated commands. We were all herded along light-starved corridors into an impressive, oval assembly hall, turned cattle-mart for the day, and very reminiscent of a Hollywood style Roman amphitheatre. Such places I knew to be arenas of trial, torture, and agonising death. Here, we were given blunt instructions and new marching orders that despatched us, in strict military fashion, to one of the many designated classrooms, which were to serve as our prisons for the rest of the day. Securely placed under the strict surveillance of a gaze so intense and wicked it rightly belonged up in Sauron's Tower, we began the task of completing an elaborate set of exam papers, deemed appropriate as the true test of our intelligence in number, language and spatial relationship.

When Uncle Stan generously loaned me his Fleet Air Arm navigator's watch, I am sure that he meant it as an act of kindness to help me manage an anticipated struggle against the enemy of time in my battle with a battery of unfathomable questions. It was the watch that had repeatedly taken off from the bleak, deserted deck of an aircraft carrier and into the grim skies above a perilous Atlantic. The prayer constantly on the lips of the young navigator, seated in the cramped cockpit of his frail Swordfish, was, like mine, dedicated to survival and a safe return to the flight deck of his makeshift home on a wild ocean. The nautical face of this precious war memento now stared up at my stupefaction and lack of stiff upper lip. Sincerely donated to be both a practical and moral support in my hour of need, it merely translated into the constant reminder of Uncle Stan's unseen presence as the family's yardstick of intellectual achievement and supreme courage, against which I was about to be measured and found wanting. Suddenly, I lost all control of who and where I was. My engines had stalled and I was losing height fast. I, too, was all at sea; a little navigator lost and going down into a deep ocean of fear and panic. My traumatised brain beat in metronomic rhythm to the big wall clock, as its hastening fingers spelled imminent disaster.

Dovedale was, in the late 1940s and early 1950s, one of Liverpool's most successful feeder primaries for the city's finest grammar schools. In my A1 year, while only a minority of Liverpool's children managed to negotiate this Rubicon to success and prosperity in life, all the pupils in Mr Bell's top class passed the Eleven Plus, together with most of the boys in A2. My family were, therefore, devastated not only by my failure to get into the best grammar school, but by the incomprehensible fuck-up I had managed, in spite of being second in the top class of forty-five pupils. Uncle Stan, dumbfounded and upset for me, was able to use his influence as a teacher to have the feebleness of my performance verified. Only his relentless advocacy on my behalf, together with the submission of my school record by Dovedale, gained me a "recall" interview and a place at Toxteth Tech. Although they put a brave face on it for my sake, this outcome was well below my family's hopes of me attending the Liverpool Institute to sit alongside the crème de la crème.

Some of us are genetically better programmed to cope with emotional stress and have been provided with the brain impulses more predisposed towards survival. Anxiety and depression have long been features of my family's psychological profile. Undoubtedly, I was another victim and still am. As unremarkable a scholar as the records show John Lennon to have been at Dovedale, he passed the Eleven Plus with relative ease. Unlike me, John's attitude to the exam was driven by the same aggressive reaction he always made to any threat to his own status and self-belief. "That was the only exam I ever passed because I was so terrified," he later confessed. I used to wish that more people, including myself, were able to turn fear against itself like that. We would all achieve a lot more personally in life, no doubt. The problem with such mental hardness is that success, most probably, would be at the expense of others. That was always an inner fear, and having been brought-up "to do unto others as you would have them do unto you", I could not live with the moral consequences.

The "recall" was the one supposedly sympathetic element of the Eleven Plus. It was a safety net, set up for borderline cases whose school record justified their getting a second chance to convince a panel of three, sceptical grammar school headmasters about their true intellectual worth. My abysmally poor marks did not justify my getting any such dispensation. Nevertheless, Uncle Stan's connections inside the City Education Department set me up for a second bite of the apple and, yet again, I was about to bite off more than I could emotionally chew. My family, naturally, saw this interview as the God-sent opportunity to send my neurotic temperament to the seaside for the day, and this time to do myself justice.

Uncle Stan's plans for me to stun the interviewing panel with a precocious knowledge of the stars and planets was totally undermined by the first question I was asked. It had managed to squeeze itself out from between the nicotine-stained teeth of the smallest and oldest of a triumvirate of venerable scholars, whose briar pipe, comfortably positioned in front of him was about to be flourished in a bout of surreal questioning. The three men were seated, together, like Appeal Court Judges, behind a large oak desk in the headmaster's study at Quarry Bank Grammar School, where I had been summoned to attend for vetting on a fine morning in the late spring of 1953.

The nasty old sod had, I presumed, studied my medical file as well as my record of work. On reading, "Stanley has a tendency to panic and is subject to fits of anxiety, no doubt inherited from a long line of neurotics," he had decided not to engage me in some introductory, friendly, conversation about who I was and what my future intentions may be. Rather, he wished to inflict upon me a piece of mental arithmetic so bizarre and obscure, that it did not register with me as a question at all. "Now Stanley," the one with the nasty mouth and pipe to fit it began his cryptic question "I want you to suppose that I have a large cricket bag"... Well, that was just the inappropriate use of metaphor I did not need. My anxiety and over-active imagination swiftly combined to distance me from any possibility that I was merely being handed a theatrically dressed-up test of arithmetic. Unfortunately, what had spontaneously illuminated my brain was the image of Uncle Stan's cricket bag. There it was, sitting on the dark varnished floorboards of his bedroom at No.52 Borrowdale Road, begging Ashley and me to haul it downstairs to the group of eager, waiting pals, who would then compete for the honour of ceremoniously carrying it down to the Old Farm Field in Sefton Park which beckoned to us daily from the foot of the street.

Uncle Stan would often be at the head of our procession to the park. Looking like a benevolent Pied Piper, he would lead three streets of children carrying bats and wickets to an afternoon where they would be lost in the enjoyment of England's favourite summer sport. His troop of eager young cricketers would soon be split up into well-balanced sides to pit the ferocious Aussie pace of Ray Lindwall and the subtle antipodean leg-spin of Ritchie Benaud against the stone-wall defence of Trevor Bailey and cavalier batting of Brylcreem's pin-up boy, Dennis Compton. My uncle's great cavern of a bag was stocked up with all the essential cricketing paraphernalia. Two expensive bats, a set of wickets with bails, two sets of pads, two pairs of batting gloves and the standard requirement of a batsman's box – a strangely erotic item to us pre-pubescent boys – were all mine to indulge my friends whenever we wanted.

You will, by now, appreciate how far my mind had strayed from the real purpose of my conversation with the three, determined-looking, black-gowned gentlemen, whose sole remit was to ascertain my competence in handling a perverse, clever-dick question of mental arithmetic. I could only stare blankly back at my inquisitors, my mind transported elsewhere to a perfectly level, nurtured wicket of well-manicured grass. I was already "padded-up" and heedless of the health and safety precautions of your modern-day batsman with their "sissy-boy" titanium headgear, I took guard... "Middle and off please. OK... I'm ready as I ever will be to face up to one of Brian Barclay's sixty-mile-an-hour in-swingers or, even worse, one of Uncle Stan's cunningly flighted googlies."

I was momentarily brought out of my trance by the grim tones of the Witch Finder General. "Now then Stanley..." The voice of my inquisitor was clearly becoming less friendly and more judgemental in style. "Inside this cricket bag I have a set of pads, two sets of wickets, four leather balls, and...oh yes... two sets of bails." I was now back in the comfort of my stupor. "Did he say two sets of balls...or bails? If he said bails does that mean four of them...or six? Bugger! This is an even bigger cricket bag than Uncle Stan's. Surely that's not possible?" My head was reeling with the thought of what the gang could do with a bag that size. We could organise a cricket festival for the whole neighbourhood.

My torturer was still not finished. Indeed, like some Jesuit Brian Statham, he had simply been pacing out a long run-up for a very fast delivery. "Well Stanley...Let us conjecture that I will take out of the bag one set of wickets, two bails and three balls. What would I be left with in the bag, do you think?" Well I was bloody-well stumped if I knew, and I didn't think Mr Pestilence or his horse knew, either. What was it again...three bails and two balls? No, hang on...two bails and...Oh bugger! I'm a bloody goner, that's for sure.

I jumped out of the way to leg side, leaving my wicket unprotected and soon to be uprooted. The likes of radio commentators John Arlott or Brian Johnston might have been comfortable with all this use of metaphor, but could they do the bloody sums? I think not!

I sensed a look of alarm beginning to register on the faces of all three headmasters who, with every passing minute, were becoming more determined to keep me out of their respective schools. They held a brief confab to concur that I was not on the correct wavelength to receive a top-flight education. I had, perhaps, been listening to programmes like *The Goon Show*, or, *Take It From Here*, rather than be tuned into my maths homework. They decided that any further conversation about numbers might get me recommended for special schooling, and turned desperately to the matter of my hobbies, which they assumed were a simple enough topic for me to handle in my native tongue. This gave me some chance to redeem myself, by appearing to have the vestiges of some intelligence, and so I took them on a short trip round the known universe. Sadly, my uninterrupted discourse on Red Giants, sunspots, Saturn's rings, comets and the like did not do enough to wipe out the memory of my disastrous first innings. Although I escaped Rose Lane Secondary Modern, my inability to suss out the con trick of a devious set of clever buggers let me down. Yet again, I had failed to get into any of the grammar schools represented by the sickliest-looking three of the Four Horsemen of the Apocalypse.

Chance as well as nerves played an appallingly significant part in these momentous proceedings. Whereas my first question had completely unnerved me with its oblique references to the uncertain knowledge they were seeking, another Dovedale classmate, well below me in academic ranking, was immediately asked about his hobbies. In answering "Nature, Sir", he was given four trees to identify in the large garden outside the study window. On promptly sighting oak, ash, elm, birch, then adding sycamore, Douglas fir, two squirrels, and a magpie for good measure, he was immediately signed up on a £40,000 a week contract with one of the city's most prestigious grammar schools, the Liverpool Collegiate.

Beth's reaction to the Eleven Plus provided me with the only uplifting footnote to this dreadful episode in my life. Not only did it enlighten me about the obscure, proverbial reasoning which seemed to select heavenly bliss as the most congenial of partners for worldly ignorance, but it also gave me a defining memory of Beth's uplifting, optimistic, personality. I had returned home from the disaster of the exam a defeated and miserable fellow, most anxious that a disbelieving Uncle Stan and family understood the truth about my abject failure; that it lay in the personally ruinous impact of my mother's death.

Who, then, did we both meet for the first time out of our house, the day after the Eleven Plus exam, but irrepressible Beth. I winced when I saw her running up the street towards us. "Bugger! She'll tell him it was easy, I'll bet!"... Too late. He'd already stopped her. "Hello Beth dear... and how are you feeling today? Did you get on all right yesterday?" She hardly gave the question a second thought as she skipped on by with her shopping errand. "Oh, that? It was really, really easy. I think I've done really well." Of course, she failed like the great majority of those who sat. But to fail with such style and so little sense of guilt and shame! She had so much sunshine in her that it banished my cares and, in the months of recuperation which followed, it flooded our play together with my prayer that things could only get better.

CHAPTER 32

NO STANDING UPSTAIRS

I jumped on board the No.86 bus with Pier Head flagged up on its front destination window. It was one of the new diesel double-deckers, which were about to close the final chapter on the city's century-old love affair with a tramcar ride into town. The new, go-where-you-please, innovation in passenger transport would forever alter the overhead view from Liverpool's busy streets. Mine was the last generation of Scouser children to look up, in wonder, at the patterns drawn across their confined glimpse of sky by the endless miles of looping electric cable.

It was Coronation year 1953. I was now into my final year at Dovedale and regularly had to make my own way to school football matches all over South Liverpool, so no one objected to me going into town on my own.

The top deck of the tram gave me a bone-shaking, but safe and scenic ride into the main city shopping centre of Church Street, from where I could make straight for the *Tatler* cartoon cinema, or stay on to Dale Street and nip down to the Wizard's Den in Moorfields. When Ashley was with me we might choose to spend an afternoon plying the lifts and escalators between the exotically furnished floors of Lewis's department store, where we could pass an hour gazing at the many items of home comforts which we would never dream of possessing.

My dad was one of a group of tram drivers selected to take the city's first fleet of green buses on to the streets of Liverpool. However, while being trained to steer trackless wheels in the right direction he did time as a humble ticket puncher. I had, by chance, got onto my dad's bus. I caught a glimpse of him bringing order to the common steerage downstairs, as I made for the steel staircase and wound my way up to the non-smoking, top deck. Having been brought up with a passive preference for my father's Craven A and Pop's Wild Woodbines, I was not trying to escape upstairs into a nicotine trip to town. I was simply making a beeline for what I considered to be a first class window on the world below. Having chosen a time well clear of the rush hour to travel, I hoped to have first choice of the vacant seats overlooking the cavalcade of human activity on the pavements below.

I pulled up at the top of the stairwell. "Bugger!" I was forbidden to swear, but using such a wonderfully expressive word sounded a hell of a lot better than the, "Drat" and "Doggone" Desperate Dan came out with in the *Dandy*. The only available seat was next to the aisle at the rear of the bus. I was as desperate as Dan to get to the Wizard's Den, and buy myself a pack of magic cards, which were the current craze at school. There was no way I had the patience to wait the extra few minutes for another bus to come along. Reluctantly, I sat down to make the best of the half-hour journey to Church Street by trying to guess how young or old, attractive or ugly, happy or miserable-looking, each of the passengers in front of me might be, judging by the back of their heads. At the next stop, along Smithdown Road, a middle-aged woman was forced upstairs by the crush on the platform and to her dismay, found all the seats occupied. However, she must have rated her chances with the small boy in the seat next to the stair, who looked as uncomfortable as he was undecided about how to react to a lady's predicament. My problem was the notice, visible to all passengers, which clearly stated, "No Standing Upstairs." There was not even the soft soap of a "please" or "thank you"; just a stern public order, to be obeyed without dissent. I decided to sit tight.

The woman had one of those stuck-up faces, which suggested an indecently swift ascent up the social ladder had quickly taught her how to behave badly to people whom she deemed to be a rung or two below. It could only be worse for those whose feet were firmly planted on the ground. She was someone who staked her newfound status on a working-class deference, which she prayed had survived the unity and egalitarianism of wartime struggle. Such a woman would expect the surrender of my seat to be as certain a gesture of good manners as the doffing of my cap, and the opening of a door for anyone in a skirt.

Standing one step down from the top of the stairs, but still high and mighty enough to command attention, Mrs Hoity-Toity leaned over the rail and gave my short trousers a look that was clearly trying to prise my arse from the comfort of the brown leather seat. I knew nothing about middle-age decay in females, with its accompaniment of swollen ankles, varicose veins; even less concerning the torment of hot flushes and the dread of a prolapse. However, Pop and Uncle Stan had instructed me plenty about being the courteous little Sir Walter Raleigh to all women, whether the claim to be a lady was genuine, or not.

As a ten-year-old in 1951, I was not aware of my right to the seat, under the Liverpool City Council Transport Order of "No Standing" on the top deck. It was printed in bold, black letters and stuck in a prominent place at the front of the bus. For the first time in my young life I took the notice to define the legality of my position. "I might only be ten, but God gave out Ten Commandments, and that looks mighty like one of them to me!" There was much confusion in my head, for under the burden of a rigorous home training in good manners I had resigned myself to giving up the seat. Indeed, my legs were bent and my bottom already a good couple of inches off the leather, when I heard the conductor's voice from the top of the stairs. "Don't move an inch, son. You just sit yourself down. That's your seat and you stay on it!"

I had not seen my dad in weeks. Suddenly, like Sabu's genie he was at hand, bringing with him a hint of a future full of civil liberties. "There's no standing allowed upstairs, madam. You will have to come down. Hopefully, you will get a seat downstairs at the next stop." The woman clearly thought her possession of a few middle-class comforts such as a mortgage, a Morris Minor and the latest in walnut radiograms, gave her the edge over a council employee who had to subject himself, every week, to a knock on his front door from the rent man.

"The little boy has kindly given me his seat. Can't you accept that, conductor?" It was the way she half-closed her eyes when she uttered the word "conductor" that rang the wrong bell with Arthur Williams. "Yes lady" – he had dropped the pretence of calling such a person madam – "I am, indeed, only the conductor but, like you, I have to conform to the City Council Regulations above your head. No one is allowed to stand upstairs!" Hyacinth Bucket turned a wounded profile to try and catch the sympathy of the passengers behind her, but they had accepted my father's blank expression as one of firm resolution. "Oh, you silly man! This is all so unnecessary, especially as the little boy, there, wants to give me his seat... Don't you dear?" She turned the spongy features of an over-powdered face towards me and managed a horribly forced, pleading smile; like a thin smearing of jam trying to squeeze out through two heavy layers of cake. I could visualise this women getting home to write a strongly worded letter to Alderman Braddock, demanding my father be sacked, or at least demoted to cleaning out the lavatories at the Garston Bus Depot, unless she got her own way about me knowing who my betters were.

My dad made sure he had the final word. "If you don't come down at once I'm going to ask my driver to stop the bus so, that I can ring Penny Lane for an Inspector.".... "An Inspector?" I thought to myself. "Does this mean the police are going to arrest her for wanting my seat?" I was highly embarrassed by all the fuss, which my simple desire for a tip-top view of the world had caused. High-hatted Hyacinth was now in retreat, to wait for a seat downstairs, amongst the loud conversation and winter coughing of the riff-raff. The thought of an Inspector calling was too serious a threat to the lofty self-esteem she had begun the day with, as she received her husband's daily homage of tea and toast in bed.

The half-hour journey ahead was, suddenly, made more bearable by the person sitting next to me getting off at the top of Smithdown Road. I took my chance and slid quickly across to the window. I cleared the condensation with the palm of my hand and rested my head against the glass, so that I could gaze down at the perplexing, over-regulated world of adults. It would be many years before I could get into an X-film, drink a pint of frothy beer, or put my mark on a ballot paper. However, I had just been granted a delicious freedom from one of the decaying conventions of the class system.

From now on I would use discretion, whenever I had to think about surrendering my seat to anyone on a bus, or tram. It goes without saying that I would still give up my seat to the elderly, the infirm, or to those in a real predicament, and of course, any pretty girl would, soon, get me standing. Never again, however, would I get up for those who had no more right than myself, but made the assumption that every seat had their imperious name on it.

CHAPTER 33

HEAVEN IN THE SCOTTISH HIGHLANDS

On several occasions when we were holidaying as a family in North Wales in the late 1940s, Uncle Stan would leave us at the end of the first week. He was off somewhere mysterious and I would miss him. He conjured magic out of the most dismal days of perpetual rain at places with the most unpronounceable names, like Pwllheli; the two of us stripping down to our swimming trunks and running around the holiday camp three years before Gene Kelly was to turn such pranks into an art form. When he departed, all the fun of playing cricket, football and crazy golf went with him. On his return home, it was clear from his frame of mind and the stories he brought back that he had been somewhere wild and wonderful. In the spring of 1952, a year after my mother's death, Uncle Stan took me with him on the five hundred mile journey, by train and bus, from Liverpool 15 to the beautiful wilderness of the North West Highlands of Scotland.

I was ten and knew of no schoolboy who did not confess to an interest in trains, whether it was a buffish obsession with model railways, an anorak's addiction to the rigours of train-spotting, or simply having to make do with jigsaws and books full of pictures, annotated with encyclopaedic information. It was my good fortune to have a childhood which embraced the last decades of the golden age of the steam locomotive.

The children in our neighbourhood streets would continually break from their play to wave at the ordinary, journeymen engines pulling their coal trucks and freight wagons along the railway line at the top of Borrowdale Road. There was even greater excitement at the screeching whistle which heralded the approach of an express, hauling its passengers to and from Scotland and Southern England. I longed to get a fleeting glimpse of one of the galactico steam locomotives, such as the *Flying Scotsman*, the *Princess Elizabeth* or the *King George VI*, all resplendently lacquered in their glorious regional company colours. Unfortunately, so many of these regal steam engines moved in different circles to me, stoking up the mania of young boys who stood alongside the railway lines of the Eastern, Great Western and Southern Railways.

In late autumn, early darkness turned the cavalcade of brightly lit carriages into a moving picture show; strange faces at the windows peering out, wrongly believing that no one cared to question who they were and why they might be travelling such long distances, so late at night.

Never in a month of Mallard-spotting Sundays did I perceive of anything as inspiring as a rolling convoy of carriages, stuffed full of mail and wide-eyed sorters, all caged together on the long night-shift to Scotland. As I dreamt on, past midnight and into the unearthly hours of morning, strong-limbed postal workers stood and grappled within a speeding, swaying workplace to decipher and then pigeonhole thousands of letters and parcels; rectifying misspelled names and addresses so that they might reach their true destinations without mishap. They were the covert, front-line troops of the GPO's delivery system, locked in a battle to punctually deliver the mail onto thousands of front-door mats beyond the far and mysterious border of Scotland.

My imagination was allowed to dwell on the secret, travelling company of midnight mailmen, all working on the nation's behalf, when I saw the hypnotic and beautiful film, *Night Mail*, which had come on at the Grand Cinema as filler, before one of the big pictures:

This is the Night Mail crossing the border,

Bringing the cheque and the postal order,

Letters for the rich, letters for the poor,

The shop at the corner and the girl next door.

The rhythmic poetry and the music of the GPO-sponsored film belonged to W H Auden and Benjamin Britten, respectively, but the star was the magnificent, steam express, tearing north from London to Edinburgh. No wonder I was in such awe of the great steam trains. They were heroic creations, bravely battling through the night and the weather; steeling themselves to the task of negotiating hills and vales, winter blizzards and snow blocked tracks as they rushed by in all their rhythm and drama, while I slept soundly in my cosy bed.

Such was the romantic background to my excitement when I learned that I was about to take a long journey by overnight sleeper from Lime Street Station to Inverness, the capital of the Scottish Highlands. I had never slept in a bunk bed before, let alone one confined to the compartment of a train. I lay for hours in the top bunk above Uncle Stan, staring out at the surreal night images, flashing past the carriage window and tunnelling on, through my brain, like a film on fast reel; sounds and visions from a dark, unending mural of towns, villages and spookily lit ghost stations, empty and dead to the world. My mind was fired up like the fireman's coke oven with the wonderful delirium of it all. As I lay on the hard, thin mattress I could feel my body moving to the chugging strain of the great steam engine in front. It was impossible to trust my mind to sleep with the scary rattle of the coaches constantly reminding me that I was being dragged, at breakneck speed and without any respect for my safety, along a perilously narrow tightrope of steel. Slowly, the hypnotic rhythm of the carriage wheels began to work like a tranquilliser on the senses; ears shut down to the eerie whistle blows; eyelids closed on the white clouds of smoke trailing past my window like creepy will-o'-the-wisps, feeling against the glass for a way in. Against all the odds, I succumbed to a deep sleep, which blanked out the unending blur of passing fields, hedgerows and slumbering farms of the disappearing English landscape.

I awoke in the Highlands of Scotland to the activity of my uncle preparing himself for the final leg of our journey, as the train slowed down in its approach to Inverness in time for an early breakfast in the station cafeteria. Still bleary-eyed, but with my stomach well prepared for the long day of travel ahead, we transferred on to a single-decker bus for my own Magical Mystery Tour through misty glens and past mighty, rugged peaks to arrive in a mesmerised state at the Presbyterian Manse in the west coast fishing port of Ullapool.

I was getting my much-prized holiday courtesy of Uncle Stan's wartime friendship with a young naval padre, the Rev. Alick Macaulay and his wife May. What a glorious awakening to the unappreciated, natural world beyond the narrow confines of Liverpool's grey streets and grimy buildings. There was a king-sized generation of kids growing up amongst the drab, uninspiring ruins of 1940s Merseyside who would have given their eye-teeth to go on such a mind-stretching adventure and share in such a life-changing experience.

Within forty-eight hours of leaving Borrowdale Road, I was in a rowing boat being taken to the far shore of Loch Broom. Other days would find me sitting down to exchange family stories, rich in pleasure and laughter, as we picnicked overlooking the beautiful Summer Isles, or rested on foothills of moss and heather, next to the towering, serrated majesty of Stac Polly. Encouraged by my Spartan uncle and when the heat of the noonday summer sun suggested a more eccentric, mad-dog style of behaviour, we stripped down to our swimming trunks and sat up to our waists in the testicle-numbing waters of a fast-flowing mountain stream. I sensed adventure at every turn of the pathway as we walked for miles through damp, scented pine forest and tramped across fragrant, blooming heather. I stood transfixed on high moorland, tracing the soaring flight of a golden eagle as she monitored our intrusion into her domain.

Not until our appetites for spectacular views and jaw-dropping vistas had been fully satiated would we return home, ravenous for food taken locally from land and sea to the Manse kitchen. Eggs brought straight to the breakfast table from the hen house. Potatoes lifted from the good soil of the Manse glebe to be boiled in their jackets and then gobbled down, with large knobs of butter, alongside freshly cut slices of cured ham. On my favourite food days it would be a chicken or maybe a rabbit, killed only a few hours earlier, to provide us with a wonderful roast or stew.

More to my uncle's taste, as a worthy accompaniment to the earthy freshness of his tatties, were a couple of soused herring, plucked from the salt-water barrel in the back-yard. On one memorable occasion, Uncle Stan was left in charge of four hungry children, while Alick and May were away in Dingwall. He demonstrated his numskull city ignorance of Highland life by serving up the Silver Darlings uncooked, straight out of the tub! The incident made him the butt of ribbing for years and did little for his claim to be only one great-grandmother removed from true, Gordon clanship. However, it said much about the self-discipline and Christian obedience of the three Manse children that they managed to cope with the painful sight of their guests eating succulent pieces of ham, whilst they suffered their raw, scaly meal in monastic silence. There are those in the fishing communities of my adopted North East of Scotland who would say that such a glorious fish as the herring can be eaten and enjoyed in any way it cares to present itself!

The Manse was a stronghold of virtuous Calvinism, but also a place of family love and much laughter with the Minister always ready to tease his Liverpudlian friend's naivety about Highland life. "Well, now Tommy (This was the name Alick had bestowed on my uncle down in Portsmouth, during the War), here's the fellow who's been making all the noise and bothering us these last few days." Alick rose from his knees at the fireplace in his daughter's bedroom. His face and navy pullover were covered in soot, as only seconds earlier his head had been stuck up the chimney! In his powerful hands he clutched a deranged seagull, which must have fallen down the stack when shot by the minister defending his chicken coup from aerial attack. Over a period of days the bird had become frenzied with fear and crazed with hunger.

The grin on Alick's face widened into a wicked intent as he seized upon my uncle's discomfort at the wild bird being deliberately held so close to his face. As tough and brave as Uncle Stan was, he did not like the glint of madness in the scurry's eyes. "Dear me, Alick… That large snapping beak could take an eye out in a second." The high-spirited Reverend, however, was set on having some fun at his friend's expense. "Here you are then, Tommy. Would you like to say hello to this angry wee fellow, then?" Alick thrust the bird at Uncle Stan's crop of wavy black hair and chased his pal in and out of the bedrooms and then down the stairs into every room in the Manse "Alick! Alick!… That bird is dangerous…

That's enough! It's gouging pieces out of my neck and ears. I'm being eaten alive! Call the blessed thing off... Alick... Please!"

It was one of the few times in my life that I had seen my dignified uncle have his own feathers ruffled. He was clearly upset with the bites at his neck and at having his new Moss Bros jumper pulled to ribbons. "Tommy, man... It's just a scavenger, after one of my chickens. Well, he won't get any more, and that's for sure!" Alick had finished with his fun and went outside to wring the wretched bird's neck. He came back still grinning from ear to ear at the state a mollycoddled Sassenach had got himself into over the attentiveness of a squawking gull.

To make quite certain we each appreciated how pampered our lives were down south in Liverpool, Alick put us to work on the glebe. This son of a Hebridean farmer loved to see the sweat pouring off two unemployable, city wasters forced to face up to the pain of cultivating the land. "You English boys don't know what it is to have to do a hard day's work. If you had been brought up with me, Tommy boy, you would have been sweating from sunrise to sunset." Pretending to be at one with the few acres of land attached to the Manse was exhilarating fun, but to live such a life for hundreds of years of unremitting peasant labour was another matter entirely. Alick wanted us to take back to Liverpool a glimpse of where he had come from; that devotion to being the parish minister did not deny this man of the cloth his roots amongst the unsentimental, toiling crofters of North Uist.

I certainly got a different perspective on life, standing mesmerised on the hillside at the back of the Manse, watching rabbits being shot by a man of God, of all people. I learned the hard way about recoil, as my first attempt to fire a gun threw me backwards into the long prickly grass. I watched disquieted but spellbound at the actions of knife and wrist, as Alick opened up the stomach of a dead rabbit on the kitchen table. The clean, swift butchery revealed five foetuses of an unborn litter, resting inside the body of the once fast-running, pregnant female. The pathetic, lifeless things were laid out before my squeamish eyes only long enough for the family sheepdog, Lark, to sniff them out. Raising herself up on stretched hind legs and with a few licks of her selfish tongue she quickly gobbled down the tiny morsels in a couple of tasty, "Thank you very much," mouthfuls.

My holidays in Ullapool taught me how trivial material things are; how little we really need to live a contended life, provided we have our health and are surrounded by good people. I was made aware of the healing power in the beauty of the unspoiled, natural environment. I had been transported to a world which was a cure for the curse of urbanisation; uncontaminated by pollution and overpopulation; unaffected by twentieth century materialism and the madness of an emerging consumer society.

The Manse stood on a hillside overlooking Loch Broom. You simply slipped out of the back garden and then climbed a few hundred feet to stand on top of creation, looking down on some of the finest scenery in the world. One lovely spring morning in 1952, I was sat on that hilltop, staring at the distant mountain peaks and listening to the conversation between my uncle and a young missionary who happened to be in Ullapool during our stay. The missionary was about to go to Africa and while much of their talk was steeped in theology, it was also about the down-to-earth struggle for human dignity and social justice in the slums of Glasgow, Liverpool and London.

As I sat listening and looking out over the beauty of Loch Broom, there was a defining moment of my stay in Ullapool. All those hours of Sunday school scholarship suddenly presented me with the Biblical account of the transfiguration of Jesus. I thought of Peter, overwhelmed by the spiritual experience on the mountain top, blurting out "How good it is that we are here!" Such a spontaneous outburst summed up my moment of special awareness, in a place where I was never far away from God. OK, some of it was to do with the emotional turmoil I was fleeing from back home. Here, in Ullapool, I had the wonderful Manse children to play with and help me forget the recent trauma of my mother's death. I was in love with the life of a Manse family and the daily routine of goodness; grace before meals, prayers before sleep and church twice on a Sunday. It was all part of the ritual of a rich, profoundly Christian experience and I could have stayed there forever. I had felt an awakening in my soul to the presence of God all about me; in people, places and things. In Ullapool I realised that it was my dear uncle who had nurtured the love of God within me, which I now recognised as an undeniable part of my being.

Given such a role model to look up to and love as dearly as any father, how could I not try to live up to his over-optimistic expectations, not just for me but for everyone? How could I not try to excel in sport and in my school work when, quite often, my heart was not interested in hours of study? The downside of having such a seemingly faultless person to look up to was that, whenever I failed to measure up to my own meagre expectations, I often experienced an exaggerated sense of failure.

It was only later in my life, following the deaths of my father in 1977 and then my uncle in the early 1980s that I began to realise what I had signed up to, all those years ago in childhood. I had surrendered much of myself in trying to fashion a life on the blueprint of my uncle. It was lamentably late in life that I began to shake myself free of the conflict of love and loyalty between him and my father, which had plagued me throughout my youth and childhood. Slowly, I began to assert self-control over my personality and behaviour. I remained complex, full of eccentricity and contradictions, but I had, at last, begun to throw off pretending to be someone's son and become my own person.

I was so much happier and healthier for realising that much of my young life had been a pointless struggle trying to imitate virtues which were not my own. In attempting to clothe myself in my uncle's goodness I did, however, acquire a sense of what it means to strive to be a good person. Uncle Stan's compassion for others was based on his belief in a God who has made us so interestingly, yet perplexingly, different. Our individuality must, therefore, be precious. It was only when I finally freed myself from the burden of imitation that I began to relax in the knowledge that my worth was in being myself.

CHAPTER 34

THE SPECTRE OF LOCH BROOM: UNCLE STAN
SEES A GHOST

All children like to be frightened by the idea of a world of monsters, witches, goblins and ghosts. By the time I came to spend my last childhood holiday in Ullapool, in the summer of 1953, my primary school fascination with such things was being beefed up with a secret devouring of the graphically illustrated *Tales From The Crypt* horror comic. I also had Uncle Stan's approved reading of the more perceptive, but no less terrifying, R L Stevenson, the Brothers Grimm, as well as the seasonal visit from Dickens's Christmas spirits.

However, all this was pure fiction... wasn't it? There was a small part of me which hoped that these outlandish tales of the macabre were a little more than that; a condensation, perhaps, of pure ectoplasm oozing from the pens of those gifted to lift the veil on the possibility of a world of the supernatural. I was a sucker for stories to test my famed credulity, as well as stir the imagination, at a time when emotional intensity was beginning its steady rise to the teenage boil. I had been brought up to believe in a life after death, blessed by the eternal presence of Jesus, which was a totally different proposition to an unseen world of disembodied spirits, most of whom seemed hell-bent on tormenting the living into an early grave. Imagine my astonishment, therefore, whilst on holiday up in Ullapool to hear Uncle Stan, of all people, claim that he had seen a ghost.

It was well after 10pm in the Old Kirk Manse. I was comfortably propped up in bed, racing through the pages of yet another Angus McVicar novel under the magical glow from a lamp attached to the headboard, when I heard a commotion in the hall downstairs. Uncle Stan and his fiancée, Margaret, had arrived back from their late-evening walk.

The Rev. Macaulay's resonant, North Uist dialect travelled up the stairs to interrupt my reading. "Hello, both of you. Have you enjoyed your walk? Would you like a cup of cocoa before we all...?" Margaret could not be contained. "Oh, Alick. It's more than cocoa we need. If this wasn't a teetotal manse, I'd ask you to get out a bottle of whisky. We've just seen a ghost. Both of us... really Alick... We've seen a ghost!"

I was out of my bed like a shot, to listen in at the top of the stairs. "What's all this nonsense now, Tommy...? Ghosts indeed... Come through to the kitchen both of you." Alick glanced up to the landing. "There are too many pricked-up ears around for my liking." He pointed to my less-than-ghostly form, crouching at the top of the stairs. His wife, May, had now joined him in the hall and the four adults went through into the kitchen, closing the door on the spellbinding conversation, which I was not allowed to hear first hand.

Word quickly spread amongst the four children that "Tommy has seen a ghost!" Our pestering produced heavily censored pieces of information, thought to be the most suitably circumspect explanation for all the fuss of the night before. I can remember going back to Liverpool and telling Ashley that Uncle Stan and Margaret had seen a ghost, but feeling cheated that l could not terrify my pal with enough creepy details. It was years later, when I was at university, that I heard, in full, the true story of the Ullapool ghost. Whilst on a weekend visit to my uncle's home in Mossley Hill we ended up, one evening, talking about past family holidays. I returned to the mystery of Ullapool and took the chance to ask him what had caused such a stir that night, ten years ago.

Uncle Stan and Margaret had only just got engaged when they took me with them up to Ullapool. Unlike my previous holidays with Uncle Stan, when I had him all to myself, this time I had been marginalised by the presence of his bride-to-be. It proved to be no real problem. The great joy of my holidays in Ullapool was the time I spent with the three Macaulay children Margaret, Roderick and Donald.

The bond of Christian friendship and understanding between my uncle and the Macaulays was as genuine as it was obvious. It was a mutual admiration society based on the deepest affection and trust. Alick's respect for Stan's intellect and sense of moral purpose was as absolute as my uncle's admiration for the indomitable faith and mental courage of his friend, the Church of Scotland parish minister. Talk of ghosts, however, produced the expected reaction from a man who felt the need to temper such dialogue with some Presbyterian common sense.

"Oh come on now Tommy. There's no such thing as ghosts. You, of all people, should know that." Uncle Stan, however, had been obliged by the fresh turn of events to alter his philosophy on the matter.

Having left the house well after nine o'clock for a romantic stroll before bed, my uncle and Margaret walked for about a mile along the main Dingwall road out of Ullapool, before turning back when they saw darkness begin to settle on the still waters of Loch Broom. The couple rounded the final curve of the road on the outskirts of the village, and came in sight of the Old Kirk Manse on its hillside stretch of glebe, sloping down to the road. Beyond, lay the shingle beach of Loch Broom.

Arm in arm they were remarking to each other how peaceful the small fishing port looked, set against the tranquil water of the Loch. The moon was almost full and the beach lit by moonlight. My uncle's attention was unexpectedly taken by a lone figure, walking up the slope of pebbles away from the water's edge. Wearily, it trudged up the shingle and as it did so, he noticed that it had a towel over its head. To my Spartan uncle, a midnight dip in a freezing Highland loch was not an improbable act of foolhardy eccentricity to be ridiculed by the likes of you and me. Alick had, on many occasions, chuckled to himself from the comfort of his deck-chair or ground blanket, as Uncle Stan attempted to freeze my bollocks off with unnecessary ventures into Arctic sea water or the refrigerated currents of wild, mountain streams.

Suddenly, it struck him. It was no bather. Not some he-man, like himself, coming ashore with all the senses frozen. As he related the moment of terror his words chilled me to the marrow. "It was an old woman… and not a towel, but a shroud draped about her head and shoulders. The hairs on the back of my neck stood on end. I stopped dead in my tracks and turned to Margaret, who had jolted to a halt, and was staring ahead. She, too, had seen it. Together we exclaimed, 'I've seen a ghost!'"

Margaret clung to her fiancé's arm. They stood, rooted to the spot, as the apparition continued its slow walk up the beach, with the moonlight seeming to shine through it. When the figure came to a small escarpment, where the beach rose to meet the road, it disappeared from sight. The couple waited for whatever it was to reappear and cross the road, but it had gone. They climbed down onto the beach and found a water overflow tunnel running out from under the road. The figure would have had to crawl into it to vanish so completely. Unless, that is… it was not human and had simply passed through, like a spectre dismisses the solid wall of a house.

Uncle Stan and Margaret climbed back up from the beach. Facing them at the far end of the tunnel, and on the opposite side of the road, was an old cemetery with its stone wall and raised burial ground illuminated in the moonlight. That was the moment when they both knew for certain that the thing walking back from the water was going to its resting place in the old graveyard.

It had taken more than an hour of serious discussion, with the kitchen clock ticking on to midnight, before Alick was forced to take his guests seriously. The Reverend's study of theology and scripture left little room for a world of spirits and ghosts. However, he came from a Western Isles crofting culture, centuries old. There were many odd tales that had been carried down through the generations; unexplained, unnatural occurrences in the lives of a people where second sight went hand in hand with man's intimate relationship to the land and sea; when the proximity of death produced a belief in the sixth sense. As much as the rational scholar in him said poppycock to such things, Alick could not go in for a final, lofty dismissal of what we, loosely, call the supernatural.

Stan and Margaret made it their business to ask local people about the figure on the beach. The woman had been seen by others, coming up from the waters' edge and trailing back to a grave in the ancient cemetery.

When my uncle had finished telling me his story, I asked, "What do you think it was that the two of you saw that night?"

"I do not challenge St Paul's view of a hidden, spiritual universe. Like Paul, I am personally convinced about principalities and powers beyond this physical existence. However, I have never believed in ghosts until I saw that sad, old woman."

"Sad... Why do you say that?"

"There was something tragic about the figure. It looked worn down by sorrow. There was a local story about a fishing boat being lost out on the waters of the loch... and a grieving woman paying homage to a dead husband."

As I lay in my bed that night, I could not rid my mind of the spectre of Loch Broom. Who knows what kind of energy is produced when the heart is so badly broken and a passion for a lost loved one is matched by an intensity of grief. Perhaps, distress and melancholy had struck at this woman's wretched soul with such force and pain that it left behind an earthly remnant to continue her mournful pattern of obsessive ritual.

CHAPTER 35

JOINING THE SCOTTISH SCOUTS

It must have been the autumn of 1953. My uncle was in a whirl about his wife-to-be, Margaret Heath, who pained his heart by living in Stoke. Much of his spare time was now spent writing long romantic letters and masterminding weekends together when they could plan a Liverpool wedding for the following summer. When my uncle left No.52 Borrowdale in August 1954, he took with him all the restraining influences on my teenage behaviour.

Even though September 26th would merely signal my twelfth birthday and the world was not quite ready for *Shake Rattle and Roll,* I was, nevertheless, desperate to escape from the house after tea rather than knuckle down to the regime of daily homework from Toxteth Tech. The evenings were getting too short for a meaningful game of football. Every Monday night I could go down to the newly created St Columba's Youth Club and there was always the choice of the Plaza, Abbey or Grand Cinemas at the weekend, but I wanted yet another excuse for avoiding too much study.

"I'm going to join the scouts... the Scottish Scouts." If Pop thought I sounded grand it was because the idea was the most preposterous I could come up with to a son of John Thomas, a migrant Welsh quarry worker turned master builder who had moved to Liverpool from North Wales in the 1860s. My grandfather married Nellie Mansell Dawkin, a Scouser in all aspects save having been born within the sound of Bow Bells and, therefore, as cockney as any Cheapside sparrow. His daughter then married Arthur Williams, whose own grandparents came from Llandudno in North Wales. Unless there was a McWilliams or a MacThomas hiding out somewhere in the household, I had no more claim to be Scottish than the Liver bird could pretend to be an ostrich. As Pop so eloquently put it, "We can all claim descent from Adam, Stanley, but that does not give us the right to walk about without any clothes on!"

I had made the lofty announcement to my grandfather while we sat together, after tea, in the back living room. Pop was highly amused and continued to tease me. "Your sudden interest in the scouts Stanley... I suppose it has nothing to do with the fact that Ashley joined such an outlandish organisation only a few weeks ago, and has been seen wearing a kilt and playing the bagpipes ever since?" My granddad had, of course, hit the nail on the head. The thought – worse still the sight – of my best pal in church on a Sunday, dressed ready to march out at the head of a Scottish Highland Regiment and raise the siege of Lucknow, was too much for me to contemplate. I had to be rigged out like that, pacing alongside him at least one day during the week and all day on a Sunday!

"Anyway," Pop explained "You are not Scottish enough my little Wacker. Your Nan's mum's mum… Got that?… Your great-great grandmother… was born in Inverness, but that's not enough to let you put up the goalposts for Scotland, never mind playing for them at centre-forward!" I was downhearted about my prospects for days, but Ashley was pal enough to take me along to see the leader of the exotically labelled Twelfth, Liverpool Wavertree Scottish Scouts, at their local headquarters in Greenbank Lane, next to Sefton Park. Captain Legge was no longer in a fit physical or mental condition to be in charge of anything, especially a group of pubescent boys in kilts, with nothing underneath to save their balls from being fondled apart from a flimsy, tartan jock-strap. He had enlisted as a young soldier in the Boer War and looked completely knackered from having fought two wars in a young lifetime. Now over seventy, arthritis had reduced him to walking with the aid of a Harry Lauder stick – all knots and gnarls with a big knob at the top! The scoutmaster's features were as gaunt and deadly serious as those of Peter Cushing, bending over a coffin in the crypt of Castle Dracula. He was in full regalia when he interviewed me. Indeed, I never once saw the man out of his scout uniform, a fact which should have disturbed me as much as it did Uncle Stan.

"And where did you say your grand… great-grand… Oh dear, still not quite there… great-great-grandmother was born… Inverness? A White, you say and a member of the Gordon Clan. How fortunate, that we wear the Gordon tartan?" He paused and looked at me hard across the table of the scout hut. "Ah well, it's all a bit shrouded in the mists of time… Your ancestry, is it not? No matter. I shall have to check with the regulations, but I think it might be stretching things a bit… having to go back five generations to find some true Scottish blood." When I told my family the sorry news that my credentials were not good enough, Pop put his jibes about my mongrel past to one side and took my rejection as a personal slap in the face. I heard him tell Uncle Stan that Hitler had gone back five generations in order to prove someone Jewish enough to kill them! "If the likes of that Anglophile fop David Niven can get away with playing Bonnie Prince Charlie then why shouldn't you wear the kilt?" He winked down at me. "We'll see young Stanley… We'll see."

If there ever was a book of regulations, then it had been torn up years ago. Old Legge was going to let me in, all right. Membership of his troop had been declining for years and he had become too decrepit to do anything about it, apart from forgetting about such things as rules and regulations.

A few days later, Mr Legge appeared at the front door of No.52. He was invited in for a lengthy discussion with Uncle Stan in his front room study. I could hear my uncle asking awkward questions about the quality of the troop's leaders and their qualifications for supervision of the boys; the facilities for instruction, camping and the like. The scoutmaster was more than pleased to get out of the house without having to declare his sexual preference. My request to join had been dallied with, but thanks to my uncle's assertiveness, I was in! I had succeeded in joining the Scottish Scouts but only, it seemed, for the Tartan Special Effect! Mr Legge's meeting with Stan Thomas had more than made up for my lack of the Scots granny Ashley had been so unfairly blessed with.

As a life-enhancing experience, scouting turned out to be a personal disaster. I returned to Civvy Street within six months wondering why so many millions world-wide considered their participation to be such a boon and blessing. In spite of the novel uniform, the church parades and the beneficial training boasted to my uncle, I cannot remember being given one test for a scout's badge. I never saw a single reward for all that eclectic endeavour of fire-lighting and flag-struggling semaphore; burning sausages in a frying pan to a state of desecration and then tying unfathomable knots in old pieces of rope with hands still greasy from camp-fire cooking; applying tourniquets, splints and bandages to the feigned injuries of unhappy volunteers… Not one friggin' badge! What did the beret, khaki shirt, kilt and sporran mean, without an armful of badges to say you had been there, done that!

The two defining occasions of my short career as a jaundiced, failed scout were both related to the perils of camping. The first camp I attended was a weekend practice at the scout field in Greenbank Lane, where the Twelfth Liverpool Scottish had an old hut, hidden away in a secluded field. It was my first experience of roughing it; living in a tent and cooking for yourself; making sure that you had a wash and a shit every day without your mum having to tell you where your face and arse were. Catering for the ablutions and bowel movements of a couple of dozen tearaways, prematurely sectioned from the supervision of their mothers, was a major problem of public health.

The fact that Uncle Stan's splendidly Jewish nose had been broken more than once by various cricket balls did not prevent it sniffing out something frail and untrustworthy in the old scoutmaster's command over his young troops. His hooter followed its hunch and made a surprise visit to our campsite on the Saturday afternoon. I was far from happy at having to give up my weekend of morning football followed by the children's matinee at the Grand Cinema. It seemed to be a poor exchange for learning how to put up a bivouac, make a campfire like Stone Age man and, worst of all, build an emergency latrine – a luxury the inventor of the fire-stick clearly felt he could well do without.

There was certainly a whiff of something ripe in the air at the camp site. "What are those boys supposed to be doing in that patch of long grass next to the hut? There's a terrible stink all over this field, Stanley... What on earth are those lads in kilts digging about in? You can hear the spades squelching." The three boys had been told to dig a cesspit for the waste from the latrines. Without any careful directions, they had chosen to dig up an area of the field which had been used to bury shit ever since Baden Powell sat down on a field latrine at Mafeking to write the first Chapters of *Scouting for Boys*. It was a quagmire of sewage Shrek would not choose to throw little Lord Farquhar into. Suddenly, the boys surrendered to the odorous nature of their task and began sucking one leg after the other on to dry land. "Oh, no... no! This is not the place for you to be tonight, Stanley. Come on... get your stuff. You're going home."

Shortly after we got back to No.52, Mr Legge arrived at the front doorstep. He spent a good half-hour, perched on the end of his stick with no apparent concern at having left his scouts by themselves in the dangerous ecosystem down at Greenbank Lane. I was not allowed to go back that weekend and succumb to the toxic mix of Captain Legge's campfire Irish stew flavoured by the aroma of bog shit, with the promised afters of Billy Evan's sulphur fart pills, primed to go off in the tents late that night!

The fart pills were Billy's party trick. He had bought them from the *Wizard's Den* and began to take them as a nightcap at a previous weekend scout camp. For the good of mankind, his failure to read the prescription instructions carefully enough had been reported back to Uncle Stan.

"Now Billy, I've called you in to ask about the scout camp out at Childwall a few weeks ago. Ashley and Stanley have told me that there were lots of nasty smells in the tent at night... and the same thing happened at Greenbank. I believe it was so bad they had to keep putting their heads outside in the middle of the night for fresh air... Is that correct Billy?" The lad was astounded by the blunt openness of the questioning on such an unheard-of topic of conversation. Farting in public had not been turned into the art form it is today. It was deemed such an uncivilised offence and so lacking in social decorum that it was an act to be perpetrated in total secrecy. This ruled out every room in No.52, especially the echo chamber of the upstairs bathroom! I could only imagine that every time Pop and my uncle needed to fart they would discreetly remove themselves from the house and jump on a bus or tram to the outskirts of the city. Only when they had found a dense enough forest, or some high and windy hill, could they feel free to let rip and contaminate the atmosphere with no feelings of moral responsibility.

"What are you up to, Billy, with those pills? I know you like to take them with you to scout camps." Billy gave me a sideways glance which suggested that such betrayal deserved a good beating when he got us both outside. Farting in a tent was his private business and nothing to do with me, or my uncle, who continued with his interrogation. "Look, Billy… these are the sulphur tablets I took from Ashley and Stanley." The offending pills were held out across the big desk for the three of us to examine. "These two silly blighters got them from you and I was quite nauseated by the consequences I can tell you. I think you enjoy taking them to scout camps to make a few… well more than a few… ghastly smells, don't you?" Billy's head dropped. "Yes, Mr Thomas, but I didn't know how many farts there were in one pill and at the Childwall camp I swallowed lots of pills."

Seated behind his big desk, Uncle Stan did his best to stifle a smile with the same degree of discomfort as he managed to hold in his own farts. He then put on his most judicious expression. "Breaking wind in company…" Billy looked across at me for a translation. "… especially within the confined walls of a small tent is not a pleasant experience to inflict upon others. I'm sure you realise that, don't you?" For a moment I thought we were going to get a breakdown of the earth's atmosphere during the Jurassic period of the great, methane-blowing dinosaurs, followed by a dire warning about the dangers of striking matches within the close confines of a scout tent. However, the matter was quickly closed as Billy went for the safe option of a contrite apology and departed to forever remember a man small in stature, but big in grasping the nettle of farting as an issue of our time. Billy chose to leave the scout troop a few weeks later. No doubt he wanted to fart as often and as freely as he felt like, without the fear of a Crown prosecution. A few years later, when Tex Ritter and Gogi Grant both had versions of *The Wayward Wind* in the Top Ten, I could not help but think of Billy every time the record was played.

I was surprised to be allowed to go camping with the Twelfth Wavertree Scottish in Wales during the summer of 1952. The fact that Ashley was being allowed to go helped sway things, but his presence was to prove no guarantee of my welfare or happiness as we set up camp; putting up the tents and digging yet another latrine; eating more burnt sausages and hard boiled beans around a camp fire; washing socks which had only been on my feet for a day and seemed fit to remain on my feet for the rest of the week. It all made me want to go home.

Things got worse on the second day, when I was stripped to my underpants and then staked out on the grass, to have my body anointed with a two-pound jar of strawberry jam! The whole pot was emptied and smeared over me for dozens of Welsh wasps to come and sample. As I lay there, baking and fuming in the noonday sun, I could see the masochistic old sod, Captain Legge, walking around in the background, hands behind his back, glancing and smirking at my discomfort. He seemed to be luxuriating in the primitive culture of initiation and chose to ignore the type of things a young Joe Stalin might have liked to inflict on his little friends... "You're unable to organise a bloody bun fight, but willing to let me get stung to death in some foreign Welsh field." When, later that evening, the insurrection took place, old Legge had lost my vote. I was with Fletcher Christian on this one.

The latrine was a three-walled canvass cubicle, giving very little privacy to hover a desperate arse over a three-foot deep hole, dug out of the grass field. A group of traitorous boys had skilfully sabotaged the bushwhacker's trestle-and-bar lavatory seat. The primitive support for any sudden lowering of a hefty pair of bare buttocks was nothing more than a set of twigs held in place with a couple of feeble knots no granny would own up to. When Captain Legge paid his last visit to the toilet before retiring to his tent for the night, sabotage sucked him down into the slimy bottle-neck.

The old scoutmaster shouted until he was hoarse, but "Lights Out" had been called and for all I knew, such signals of distress might simply have been a test of my discipline to obey camp rules. More boys left their tents to join up with the rebels, who marched around the latrine chanting "Our scout master needs a rope around his neck and we'll all give a jolly good tug." After a disturbing silence, which lasted all of fifteen minutes, those behind the plot relented and pulled him out of the cesspit? I watched through the flap of my tent as he struggled up to the top of the field, where he cleaned himself up at a water tap on the wall of a farm building.

Early next morning several hasty phone calls were made, and that evening, adult reinforcements arrived to re-establish control. I suppose it said something about a nation which had just seen off Hitler that instead of being put in front of a firing squad, we were merely confined to camp for a few days. Although I had not taken any part in the mutiny, I had seen enough anarchy to feel personally threatened. I fell back on the image of Uncle Stan as a fly on the wall of the latrine and then buzzing over to give me full permission to leg it back home.

"Sir... Mr Legge... Sir! Williams is running away. He's packed up his kit and he's run off up the field to catch a bus to Birkenhead!" Ashley said that I had almost made it to the big bar gate at the top of the field when I was tackled from behind by one of Mr Legge's Doberman deputies and brought back to the camp, where I was forced to endure another five days of torture.

Once I got home I never went back to the Greenbank scout hut. My uniform was neatly folded and delivered to Mr Legge by Ashley. Predictably, a few evenings later, the thrawn old Scotsman arrived at our front door in an effort to persuade me to return. I was watching from the front room window and noted that, although the Captain was not invited in, he had come prepared for a long siege, making a great display of tucking the knob of his walking stick firmly into the pleats protecting the puny cheeks of his bony backside. His shaky old legs were thankful for any support, as he rambled on and on.

"What a determined old bugger!" My dad had called in at No.52 to take me to the Tatler and he joined me at the window where I was squinting out at Uncle Stan manfully trying to wind up my affairs with the Twelfth Liverpool Scottish. "If that man Legge suffers from piles, son, they'll be well and truly cured by now. He's been sitting on that stick for nearly half an hour and the knob... plus about two yards of pleated kilt... have disappeared up his arse!"

That was the end of my venture into scouting. It was most unfortunate that my fascination with all things Scottish, from Rob Roy, William Wallace, the Loch Ness Monster and the real *Flying Scotsman*, Billy Liddell, had turned me into such a sucker for wanting to wear the kilt!

CHAPTER 36

BETH: THE PRETTY NURSE OF PENNY LANE

I was many years and hundreds of miles away from my childhood days spent in Penny Lane. I had, in fact, returned with a group of young teachers to one of the "St Brendan's" bed-sits we so happily occupied in the swinging Elgin of 1967. Some three years earlier, I had managed to escape from the catarrh and incessant wisecracking of Liverpool's friendly streets, possessing little more than my professional qualifications and the strong desire to teach in Scotland. My dubious calling card was a hand-stitched, navy serge Beatle-suit, complete with black, winkle-picker shoes. A conspicuously new and raw recruit to the staff at Elgin Academy, I was given asylum within the school's fraternal social life as a pitiful scouse refugee from the Mersey mania now sweeping the nation.

Our fine fettle that Saturday night was the product of a memorable ceilidh, up at Grantown-on-Spey in the heart of distillery country. The unkind licensing laws of the early Sixties had forced us to leave the intoxicating atmosphere of wild music and drink far too early. As choice consolation, however, we had departed with the warmth and flavour of a selection of the exalted local malts to sustain us on the short journey home.

"The night is young and the moon is yellow... Before I sing the whole of Stagger Lee, what we need right now is a few more drinks and some music." In an effort to kick-start the party spirit someone switched on the transistor radio to a moment of sorcery from the Beatles. It was their latest single, *Penny Lane*, with its catchy piano, baroque-like trumpets and the vivid picture-book message it delivered about my childhood in Liverpool:

Behind the shelter in the middle of the roundabout

The pretty nurse is selling poppies from a tray

And though she feels as if she's in a play

She is anyway

The magical Lennon contribution to what is, essentially, a McCartney composition hit me like a piece of Scripture revelation. The spellbinding, evocative words were not a product of John's psychedelic exploration with LSD, nor were they the piece of impulsive fantasy-scribble Paul, perhaps, imagined them to be. They belonged, instead, to an indelible memory from our shared teenage years back in Penny Lane.

Observant and like-minded about the precious permanence of a special moment in time, we had simultaneously recorded it on that "inward eye" to store away as riches. Now, all these years later Lennon's creative genius had found the perfect context to restore and fashion our yesterday into an enchanted, mislaid, musical post-card of a place and person I instantaneously recognised. "It's Beth!" I shouted out, startling the warming conversation of my bemused friends. "The pretty nurse... the poppies in a tray... the whole bloody thing! I was there. He's singing about Beth!"

Beth and I were pushed around the shops on Smithdown Road by our respective doting mothers. Being unexpected, late babies and only-children, we seemed to create in both women a common purpose for our protection and sound development which placed us continually together as suitable playmates. We were but a twosome in the swarm of toddlers who began to infest the Liverpool streets in 1945, as the proud justification of our parent's unfounded optimism and careless passion in those dark days of wartime leave in the Blitz.

The streets off Smithdown Road were still occupied by redundant brick air-raid shelters that served us well as dark and secret bolt-holes for our earliest games of hide-and-seek. Bombed building sites scarred the neighbourhood like the defacing aftermath of some virulent pox. Strictly forbidden to us they were, nevertheless, compelling places full of awesome and exotic devastation. None was more alluring as a doorstep adventure playground than the great area of destruction at the corner of Greenbank Road. We were drawn to the apocalyptic landscape of the razed ten-acre site, accepting the desolation as a preposterous gift from Goering's defeated Luftwaffe. It offered endless possibilities for our unbridled imaginations to mock a future where children's lives would be diminished by the greedy possession of expensive and superfluous toys.

"Dinner time!... Come and get it!" Beth was shouting the boys in from her commanding position on the hill next to our tin hut. She had drafted Ashley and me, together with a few other boys, to help in the building of a technically sophisticated covered den from the Legoland of bricks, pieces of wood and corrugated iron which lay strewn over the ground. We played our war games on a Mons-like landscape of trenches and scrubby hillocks, while Beth made better use of her time in setting up a primitive, but recognisable, imitation of vital home-comforts. As we wearied of endless strategy, and our tireless energy suddenly seemed battle-spent, she would time to perfection the welcome break for dinner.

250

"Come in for your dinner! I'm not calling you again. You can take it or leave it, but I've never heard of soldiers fighting on an empty stomach." The one who got to our den first would put his hands up to his mouth and make the bugle call of "Come to the come to the cook-house door boys... Come to the cook-house door!"

No little Mrs Beaton could have created better make-believe menus out of stones and gravel. No expletively gross Gordon Ramsay could conjure up better, locally scavenged gourmet dishes of dandelions and rye grasses, aesthetically embellished with the luxury of a dock leaf or two. All were arranged in best haute cuisine style on the improvised remnants of Welsh slate. I would have been sorely tested to imagine the wonderful mime as my Nan's best Sunday cooking, but instinctively knew when not to offend a female who had just struggled for hours in the kitchen on my behalf!

Beth was an all-action tomboy and more than a match for other seven-to-eleven-year-olds in our endless enjoyment of the great running and catching games like "Re-Allio." After picking well-matched teams and sanctifying the "den" at the top of Borrowdale Road with a ritualistic chant, a frenzy of runners would operate through the labyrinth of linking jiggers, streets and gardens, all inextricably leading to Sefton Park with its magical, leafy, camouflage of the Fairy Glen. Our mothers did not need to constantly seek us out with the present-day anxiety of parents for the whereabouts and safety of their children. The only people we were wise to stay clear of were the watchful guardians of civic pride such as park keepers and helmeted, patrolling policemen who seemed to be on every corner. A whole summer evening would pass by before the leading chasers brought in the last solitary captive, taken wandering and perplexed on the outer edges of our known tribal world at the Big Lake in Aigburth Vale.

It was a salient fact of our intoxicating and inclusive childhood that boys and girls played so much together. It was Beth who educated me into the mystery and complexities of females: sensibilities; and what made them go off in such an untimely and unexplained huff, that they simply refused to play with you for days on end; interests, and what made them read the sissy *School Friend* comic rather than the prescribed *Wizard* or *Eagle*.

"Do you want to be one of the Silent Three?"

"I thought only one of the three wise monkeys couldn't speak?... No, thanks!"

"They are three girls, silly. They're on the front page of *School Friend*."

"No thanks, again... That's a girl's comic. I don't read sissy stuff."

"Boys can read these stories too, you know. The Silent Three are girl detectives at a private boarding school. They hold secret meetings and dress up in gowns with hoods to do detective work. They even solve murders! You can be the only boy member."

"Give me a loan of the comic, then... but it's not something I'd want to tell Ashley about."

"Well don't... Oh, if you do decide to join there is an initiation ceremony where Margaret and I tie you to a chair and then kiss you six times each." At ten I knew I liked girls very much. Margaret Jones was that one year older and developing fast. I signed on the dotted line.

I was surprised by the enjoyment I got out of a girl's comic. *Belle of the Ballet* was a bit too much for even the likes of Billy Elliot, but it was a revelation to realise that girls also had passions and interests similar to us boys. Most young boys were hopelessly ignorant about sex. Thank God we had Beth to give us the most fulsome explanation of what men and women did to one another when they stripped off naked and jumped into bed together. The image of the pretty nurse brings wonderful, humorous memories of the innocence of inquisitive children's games like "doctors and nurses", played in an age where children were uncorrupted by the modern over-exposure to adult behaviour. Within the licence to practise and consulting room respectability of my mum's front room, Ashley and I would, with feigned indifference, submit to the routine of an inoffensive medical examination by Beth, who would have expertly assumed the manner of a benevolent school nurse. "You can leave your underpants on young man. We've no time for that sort of thing in my hospital. Now open your mouth and say... Ahh!." We did so because of the scope it then gave us to conduct a reciprocal, but much more thorough scrutiny of the mysteries of the female body! "This is a much more serious case than we first thought... Don't you agree, Doctor Ashley? I think that we will have to pull these knickers down and take a really good look at the problem."

As far as I was concerned, "carnal knowledge" could have been to do with how to repair the rides at the fairground. Ashley had a sister, but with me it was all to do with curiosity about gender. What's more we were safe and protected by rules and moral frontiers which we were not inclined to violate. It was all as innocent as the street games we played. The girls were the star performers, endlessly and effortlessly skipping whenever they decided to vary from their addictions to hopscotch, statues and the erotic athleticism of handstands against the wall. I especially loved to watch them when they chose to skip into the big rope to an accompaniment of street songs and rhythmic chanting. I would marvel at the stinging cord of woven hemp being spun ever faster; the whirling of dextrous hands dictating the pace and pattern of their dancing feet.

Yellow matter custard

Green slop pie

All mixed together

With a dead dog's eye

Spread it on a butty

Nice and thick

And swill it all down

With a cup of cold sick

The young John Lennon would never have heard such a vulgar proletarian chant out in the sedate avenues surrounding his posh Aunt Mimi's house in Woolton, where the refined fresh air was stifled by a pall of quiet respectability. His productive intelligence would have first noticed it in the playground of Dovedale Infant School and logged it for future re-fashioning. Later, as the Beatle scribbled in a venomous rage at his own social displacement, he let the yellow matter custard drip, steadily, from the dead dog's eye in a simple, startling, re-mix of childhood imagery.

Penny Lane was not only the street along which so many of us five-to-eleven-year-old boys trekked to and from our school at Dovedale Road. It was also the name locally bestowed on the circular market area of shops with its attendant tram and bus terminal. A daily trip on one of the city's depleting fleet of antiquated, but sacred tramcars would bring the young John Lennon and my pal Ivan Vaughan into Penny Lane, from their neighbouring homes in Woolton. On fine summer days they would ride to school seated on top of an open top-decker, as it sped along the grass-carpeted, hedge-lined track which ran down the middle of Menlove Avenue and Allerton Road. From such a lofty vantage point they could let their young imaginations escape from dark thoughts of the classroom and plot their daily mischief with the tired metal of the old bone-shaker rattling its loud camouflage for their dangerous talk and conspiracy.

They would pass the entrance to beautiful Calderstones Park on Menlove Avenue, where a few years later a fourteen-year-old Lennon, very much the young Ted now, would throw his flick knife deep into the grass between my open legs. This was John's bullying, cynical style of asserting his intrusion into my company with Beth. He had served notice that it was time for me to depart. "No one gave you permission to sit there talking to Beth until we got here... Now fuck off before I get annoyed with your presence."

Once past the sentinel fire station set back a mere stone's throw away along Allerton Road, and having negotiated the heavy, ring-road traffic on Queens Drive, Penny Lane would suddenly be upon them with its Woolworth's, Bioletti's barber shop, corner TSB bank, and the imposing St Barnabus Church. Penny Lane was a beating heart at the centre of our neighbourhood life. As such it was a rendezvous for most young teenagers like Lennon, Pete, Beth and me, who found in its bustle and diversity an irresistible, magical charm and attraction.

"I need a haircut. I'm off to Bioletti's... I'll be back for dinner time."

Bioletti was Master Barber to a young Paul McCartney and by special appointment to Reggie Bevins, Harold McMillan's Post-Master General whose ministerial worthiness, when he appeared for his monthly grooming, allowed him to be deferentially ushered to a raised seat of ceremonial importance, sanctified within a privately curtained cubicle at the front of the shop.

"I'll need a shilling for the hairdressers, Nan."

"A shilling!" The Sayer's iced bun, with its wad of butter in the middle of it, failed to reach my granddad's welcoming mouth. "Where are you going to... the salon of Madame de Pompadour? It's only sixpence for schoolboys down the street at Philips."

"I'm not going near him again. He took the electric clippers down the back of my collar last time I went there and nearly sliced off the mole on the back of my neck. I've been going to Bioletti's in Penny Lane for more than a year now... There's a young Greek hairdresser... He's called a stylist and everybody wants him, because he can give you the best Tony Curtis in Liverpool."

"Twelve months of National Service and a regulation short back and sides would cure him... and Tony Curtis... of all his fancy for style." Pop was still shaking his head. "Oh dear, oh dear... a stylist... is that what you call him? I have a fairly good idea what I would call him if I got a good look at him."

I did not stay to find out what camp creation my grandfather had conjured up to offend his Edwardian image of what every true barber should look like. I was off to Bioletti's, the Mecca of style for hundreds of local teenagers in the districts of Liverpool 15 and 18.

So that is how I came to be in Penny Lane on that bright, late-October morning in 1954. Beth was there too. I could see her standing against a backdrop of the terminal tram and bus shelter, her appearance turning the normally Technicolor world of the shopping parade into an irrelevant monochrome. She was dramatically attired in her cadet nurse's uniform to sell her blood-red poppies for the Annual Earl Haig Poppy Day Appeal. They were in a tray, suspended from her neck, in the style of one of the siren ice-cream girls who, in the strange twilight of interval at the nearby Plaza Cinema, would entice the audience from their seats in a ritual of death by chocolate.

I have such a clear memory of being similarly lured across the busy street to find out what she was up to with her little piece of theatre. I remember John Lennon and his gang joining us, possibly from a successful bit of shoplifting in Woolworths across the road. Beth was thirteen, like me, but her hormones had raced ahead of mine encouraged by her own precocious sexuality. She was now a part of John's teenage social scene through her romance with Pete Shotton, John's best friend, whom she later married. Beth was, therefore, the tenuous link between my pubescent boy's life of sport, the cinema and American comics and the far less naïve, sometimes dangerously adult preoccupations of the aspiring Teds who had just joined us in the shelter in the middle of the Penny Lane roundabout.

"What are you up to, little Florrie Nightie-gale?"

"I'm collecting for Armistice Day. For all the... "

"You mean for all the dear, dead soldiers, so that they can rest in pieces."

"Don't be cruel John. My father fought in the Great War."

"No war is great... but gizza poppy anyway."

Some of us coughed up a few pennies and we took a little flag from the tray.

"When you go to the Cadet Nurses what do you all do? Do you get to help in hospitals? See operations... see dead bodies, like?"

"Only if there's an 'r' in the month... but we get trained to cope with bad accidents by being made to stare into a big bucket of blood every week." The joking and laughter carried on for a few more minutes then Beth told everyone that she had to get on with her important task. There was something about the whole experience which drilled itself firmly into my memory for the rest of my life.

As John's *Pretty Nurse of Penny Lane* Beth Davidson, for that was her childhood name, offers a bright and blithe cameo to set against the bleak despondency of Paul's *Eleanor Rigby*. These knowing and prescient lyrics conjure Beth's delightful play-acting into proper place within the greater cosmic drama of the Beatles:

255

And though she feels as if she's in a play,

She is anyway

Growing up with Beth in our infant years meant continually dressing up and putting on small concerts for our loving, sympathetic and accommodating families. Beth and Margaret Jones were the stars of plays and concerts at St Columba's Welsh Presbyterian Church at the bottom of Lidderdale Road. There was also the Grand Cinema on Smithdown Road where, before a Saturday afternoon children's matinee, the owner Max Heilbron would often organise a talent-show to encourage kids to try out their music hall repertoire.

I was sitting with Ashley and Beth in the den we had made for ourselves inside the wall of a garage at the top of Borrowdale Road, when another member of our gang, Anita Scott, ran out from her house opposite to make an announcement which would shape our play for the next twelve months.

"Guess what? My dad says he's going to build me a theatre in the back yard of our house. It's going to have a stage and curtains… and footlights!"

"Is it going to have a roof over it?" I said, in my desire to create the smoky darkness of the back stalls at the Grand.

"Why are boys so silly? No, stupid… It's going to be an open-air theatre like the ones in Calderstones Park and Sefton Park."

I wasn't too sure about all this amateur dramatics in a backyard. I had instant recall of my ambivalent reaction to the post-war children's concerts at the open-air theatre near the big café in Sefton Park. Here the grandfathers of Bungle, Zippy, George and Geoffrey gave me advance notice of the fathomless depths to which adult behaviour will sink when driven by a set of faulty genes and emboldened by hundreds of excitable children, all starved of entertainment by five years of being cooped up in an air-raid shelter.

"You're not going to dress me up like a pumpkin on legs and get me to sing 'I'm a little teapot, short and stout'…"

"No we won't do silly, baby things. We'll put on proper plays and concerts… and make people pay to come in."

"Margaret's got a John Bull printing set. We can get tickets printed and charge everyone a penny."

There was great excitement about the unexpected and most unlikely project. To my amazement, however, the whippet-like Ken Scott used the garage at the side of his kitchen in his backyard as the carcass for a marvellous raised stage, and furnished it with a back-cloth, lighting and curtains, which I noted, were far better than any of those on the windows in my own home. Beth, Margaret and Anita wrote and produced little plays and concerts, for which the rest of us had to audition. If you did not have a part to play then you paid a penny entrance fee and took your place in one of the three rows of old wooden seats in the yard.

In the summer of 1982, after many years away, I made a nostalgic return visit to Liverpool. Tommy Hill's small repair shop was still there at the top railway end of the jigger and open for the backbreaking business of resurrecting clapped-out bangers. From force of old habit, I climbed the familiar, greasy, staircase to revisit the loft above the car pit where, some thirty years earlier, Beth and I sat in the dim, inspiring light with other members of our gang. We would share jokes and tell stories enveloped in an intoxicating atmosphere of petrol fumes and engine oil. At weekends, financed by our meagre pocket money, the cocktail of garage smells would be enriched with the pungent aroma of chips soaked in vinegar, accompanied by communal swigs from a big bottle of Dandelion and Burdock, as it passed quickly between lips eager for its unique pre-Coke bouquet.

It was here, in our favourite hideaway, that Tommy told me the terrible news.

"Beth is dead, Stan... Oh yes, she separated from Pete and came back home to Lidderdale in 1977 or 78, I think."

"What happened. Was she ill when she came home?"

"She seemed fine. She went out and enjoyed herself. You know what a happy social person she was, but then she got cancer and died. She was only thirty-five. It's a terrible, terrible thing... So sad."

Neither of us spoke for a minute. Several days of my family holiday were lost as I tried to shake off the impact of the tragic and shocking news. I felt such a deep and personal loss even though we had not seen each other since the Christmas of 1964. By then The Beatles had arrived and it all began to happen for "The Fab Four" just as Beth had predicted.

Of all life's stages, childhood surely should be blessed with its cherished, golden moments to be treasure stored. Now a lifetime away from my seedling roots, in my mind's eye, I still love to visit that special October day when Beth had her image trapped within the lens of Lennon's creative imagination. She was the focus for our attention, drama and fun. Above all, she was the sweet childhood friend who helped unlock that small doorway to self-belief.

So, Beth, pretty nurse selling your poppies from a tray, you can no longer be my personal and private knowledge, my slumbering secret. You have been awakened and revealed to belong to the present, as an elixir and incandescent spirit. Most important to me, you are the constant reminder of our unique and privileged childhood, and of that lost age of freedom, safety and day-long happiness, spent under those blue suburban skies back in Penny Lane.

CHAPTER 37

TEEN REBELLION AT ST COLUMBA'S

As we grew up through Sunday school, Bible Class and Christian Endeavour our church responded to the surge of hormones in the early 1950s by creating a youth club to keep us out of trouble for one night of the week at least. The couple of hours of table tennis, darts and billiards mixed with crisps, lemonade and a little religious chat was tame stuff, I suppose. It's easy to forget that we were the first generations of teenagers let out of the home to mix socially and it was all a bit new and innovative at the time. Always there was an accompaniment to our activities in the Country voice of Slim Whitman drifting into every corner of the hall from a scratched 78, turning slowly on an old, wind-up gramophone.

Attending St Columba's Youth Club on a Monday evening at 7.00pm presented me with a serious clash of interests, because it coincided with my favourite radio programme *Journey into Space*. This was the first science fiction radio serial and it had come on the air in September 1953, just a few days before my twelfth birthday. The eerie music and the echoing voice of the narrator David Jacobs made it compulsive listening. I would wait until the latest episode of "Operation Luna" was finished before heading down Lidderdale Road to meet up with Ashley, Beth, Margaret Jones and the rest of the neighbourhood's twelve-to-sixteen-year-olds.

This all came to a sudden, unhappy end in November 1954 when John Lennon and Pete Shotton inspired Beth to orchestrate a mass walkout. One Sunday, Pete Shotton spied Beth coming out of church and took a real fancy to her. That was the start of their teenage romance and explains how John and Pete, along with the rest of their gang, began to come down from Penny Lane and drift into the Monday night sessions of the club. They appeared on the scene for only a month or two and when they came into the church they did not stay long before going on to either Capaldis café, or the chip shop opposite the Brook House pub, but what a devastating short-term impact they made on my fledgling teenage social life.

On the evening of teen rebellion, Ashley and I were in the main hall and had taken no part in the discussion group activity in one of the small rooms, where the youth club leaders were determined to engage this bunch of intruders with some sort of gospel message. John would be keen as mustard to stir things up and I can guess how the conversation might have gone.

"And just what do you believe?" Such a provocative question from the tiny, but determined, Mr Lowe would have been John's cue for a ding-dong verbal contest.

"I believe for every drop of rain that falls someone gets wet."

Totally ignorant of the Frankie Laine hit which had dominated the new Top Twenty for the past six months Mr Lowe, the club leader, would have vainly tried to press on with his outreach.

"Do you believe in God, John?"

"God?... You mean the old man in the sky with the white beard and sunglasses? He's either dead or he's taking a very long kip in heaven."

"He's certainly not dead... neither is He asleep in heaven. Do you think there is a heaven, John?"

"I imagine there is no heaven, it's easy if you try. Hey! What a great line for a song. Just a sec. while I scribble it down..."

It all probably started with some clever, cheeky banter and then, as the frustration of the adults took its toll on their patience, degenerated to the point where words like, "Fuck off, you silly old sod" were used and more obscenities were bandied about by the boys. They were asked to leave. Beth was outraged for her boyfriend Pete and came into the hall like a good shop steward to rally support for a walk out.

We were not yet affected by the Rock'n'Roll youth-quake, and James Dean's rebellious screen performances. This was the year of Brando's film *The Wild One,* but many of us were too young to take real notice of what a bunch of American hoodlums could do to a small town. I still can't figure out the herd mentality which persuaded forty of us to down darts and dominoes, and walk out of St Columba's, never to return. In one ten minute fit of teen tantrums, the church lost all its youth. John, Pete, Beth and Margaret Jones had taken much bigger and bolder steps towards growing up than I, and the world of the liberated teenager had opened its doors to them. I remained in a limbo of wandering the streets, going to the cinema, visiting the same few loyal school friends until, in my fifth year at Toxteth Tech, John P and I both landed very lucky with wonderful girlfriends and their company kept us organised and happy for a few years.

CHAPTER 38

ON HEARING ROCK'N'ROLL FOR THE FIRST TIME

It happened in October 1955. In those days my hair grew like a lawn which had just been given the Evergreen Complete three-in-one treatment and I was returning home from my regular Saturday morning visit to Bioletti's barbershop in Penny Lane. My fourteenth birthday had just given me the licence to walk at least half an inch taller. I was also feeling good about the haircut Andre had given me. There was plenty of opportunity to admire the young Greek hairdresser's interpretation of a Tony Curtis from the countless sideways glances I had been giving myself in an endless line of shop windows along Smithdown Road. Having served out a year's probation, I now regarded myself as a fully-fledged member of the Teenager Club and was happy to be wearing a new pair of narrow, Terylene long trousers. Mine was not the home in which to break the mould of the fashion-unconscious and attempt to wear jeans. Even my more modern father detested denim. "Your real Teddy Boys won't wear denim, son... They may be nasty bastards, but they know how to dress." To my dad, denim was the identifiable garb of the American hobo and older, lawless teenagers desperate to imitate the style of American juvenile delinquents.

Anyway, I was pleased as fuck with my grey nine-inch bottom trousers with the razor-edge crease. They were a huge improvement on my first pair of flannel long trousers; hideously thick, woollen affairs, which made you feel like you were trapped inside two pieces of rolled-up carpet. I had a hunch that wearing such things may well have lost Harold's Saxons the Battle of Hastings.

The haircut had been a triumph for Bioletti's young Mr Teasy-Weasy. I might not have looked so cool, however, had I been unsuccessful in the Saturday morning lottery to get Andre. Mr Bioletti was a good barber, but every teenager wanted his young Greek stylist. You sat in line and took your chance. "And who is next?" All the young heads would turn with the timing of synchronised swimmers in an Olympic final, as a long line of worried faces indicated that Andre was still busy. "Come on, now lads... who needs a haircut?" No one dared offend Mr Bioletti with a personal refusal, for fear he would pass you on to his 80-year-old father. Now here was a barber to frighten any fourteen-year-old; someone who combined the mad urges of Edward Scissorhands with the body vibrations of Shakin' Stevens. Blood was often offered up to Kali, goddess of a thousand cuts; necks were nicked and ears pierced by the dancing blades, which seemed to have a life of their own in the old man's unsteady fingers.

As I made my way down Smithdown Road with yet another surreptitious glance sideways at my classic coiffure, I was singing something from the Top Twenty to keep myself amused... "Oh such a night. It really was such a night." Yeah... it could easily have been Johnnie Ray's No.1 smash hit of 1954 that I was trying to imitate. Johnnie Ray was someone distinctly different: a very interesting and salacious fellow. He was one of the few pre-rock ballad singers a teenager might be prepared to listen to: a sort of balladeer John the Baptist preparing us for the seX-Factor in Rock'n'Roll. My grandfather hated him. Every time "cry-baby Johnnie" came on the radio he would react. "Switch the thing off... Switch it off. I can't stand that blubbering! The man wears a hearing aid for heaven's sake... That should tell you something." Perhaps Uncle Stan had tuned in to the ambiguity of the man's camp style and personality, because he did not care for him either. Only my progressive father had a decent word to say about good-old Johnnie Ray. "He's a great performer, son. I've seen him at the Empire and he was electric!... Unlike the dead piece of driftwood, known as Perry Como!" Decades before the safety and comfort of the panty-liner, Johnnie Ray was the first of the crooners to get so emotional during his stage act that all the women (together with the many closet gays in the audience), would have wet knickers to match their tear-stained faces.

On the other hand, I might have been singing something sloppy like *The Black Hills of Dakota*. I loved Doris Day and went to see Calamity Jane three times. She must have been thirty, but looked as determined to re-direct your hands away from her breasts and stocking tops as any of the well-brought-up young ladies in our neighbourhood. Of my teenage friends, only Gill Baldwin had a portable Dansette record-player. Gill's parents, however, were older and posed as somewhat refined people, so you had to put up with Harry Secombe or a guy called David Hughes singing light classics, if you wanted to sit in her front parlour and watch a pair of ripe, heaving bosoms rising and falling to the system's amazing technology, as the stacked 45s decided to play themselves.

My music, therefore, came from the movies or from radio. In those days radio meant the BBC Light Programme. The other two BBC stations, the Home Service and the Third Programme were for middle-class farts and eggheads, respectively. The Third Programme was the highbrow wavelength with such an uninteresting location on the dial that I never once tried to get in touch with Beethoven until long after Chuck Berry had forced him to roll over. By then, in the late Sixties, his sonatas and symphonies were being played on the renamed Radio Three!

Teenagers were compelled by a lack of choice to listen to popular music dominated by white American ballad singers like Johnnie Ray, Frankie Laine Guy Mitchell, Perry Como, and Eddie Fisher. British artists such as David Whitfield, Dickie Valentine and Jimmy Young were all doing their best to break up an American monopoly of the early pop charts, but it was not sexy to sing with an English accent. Thank God we produced Lonnie Donegan, The Beatles, The Stones and Punk to create a role-reversal which stuffed Yankee heads with the desire to mimic the accents and sounds of "Cool Britannia!"

Radio Luxembourg began the first Top Twenty in 1949, when I was a few years too young to be truly in the groove. By the early 1950s I was attempting a rearguard action to listen to pop music at home by joining Pete Murray's regular, late Sunday night audience of millions, on those occasions when the adults at No.52 did me a favour by retiring early to bed. However, the Luxembourg chart was still based on the sale of sheet music and did not represent what was happening in the teenage world of the hit-single:

Sun- tanned, wind-blown,

Honeymooners at last alone.

It used to piss me off having to listen, week after week, to Bing Crosby and Grace Kelly riding high at No.2 in the Luxembourg Top Twenty with *True Love* from the film *High Society*. I knew that it was the likes of Haley, Presley and Frankie Lymon and The Teenagers who were topping the real teenage charts, based on record sales as printed in the *New Musical Express*. There are echoes of this dual charting today, where downloading off the Internet produced a revised twenty-first century index of popular taste which, finally, killed-off *Top of the Pops*.

Even worse for my generation of teenagers was the fact that all popular music played on the radio had to be sanctified under the strict moral code, laid down by Lord Reith back in the 1930s. It was, no doubt, a relief to the BBC that manic Little Richard's *Tutti Frutti* – a wild, but heavily sanitised version of his much more risqué stage routine – was a B-side number, which was never played on steam radio.

Answer me, Lord above,

Just what sin have I been guilty of?

Frankie Laine's first studio version of the November 1953 smash hit had to be toned down for release to a far less contentious broken-hearted plea of *Answer me, Oh my love*. As late as 1959, Elvis was in trouble with his studio rendition of *One Night Of Sin*, which was amended before release to *One Night With You*. I'm sure the parents and leaders of church youth clubs hoped that such a desirable change in the lyrics would make their young people think more in terms of a quick grope on the back row of a cinema, rather than a juicy, all-night session between the bed sheets.

Not all pre-Rock'n'Roll music was worthless. Frankie Laine's voice was powerfully operatic and had a vibrant sex-appeal. Mario Lanza put sex into classical music and nearly blew the Abbey Cinema's sound system apart when it showed *The Great Caruso* to packed houses in 1952. In 1953 I went to see Martin and Lewis in *The Caddy* and could not stop singing the Dean Martin hit *That's Amore* for weeks afterwards. There were plenty of good tunes to sing, but at an age when someone had just put some lead in my pencil, I was impatiently waiting for the guy who put the "ram" in the "ram-a-dam-a-ding-dong" to turn up and turn me on!

So there, written on the back of a fag packet was the context of my interest in popular music that late autumn of 1955, as I found myself swanning down Smithdown Road towards a life-defining moment when *Rock Around The Clock* came blasting out from a radiogram inside the door of a G-Plan furniture shop. It stopped me dead in my tracks; for a few minutes my teenage world stood still. Out of the blue, like St Paul on his road to Damascus, I experienced an eclipsing mono-moment of teen awareness. There was no blinding light and I had no horse to fall off, but I was electrified and given a complete re-wiring with the one, two, three o'clock Rock'n'Roll of Bill Haley and his Comets.

I was riveted to the pavement by a sound, which instantaneously confronted the predictable, obedient, pattern of my life and made me question a lot of the ideas I had about who I was and what my place in society might be. It certainly would make me challenge those who thought they knew and understood me better than I did myself. Only my Presbyterian upbringing prevented me from raising my arms towards heaven and proclaiming, "Hallelujah… I have seen the fucking light!"… before tumbling backwards the rest of my delirious way home!

Rock'n'Roll created a new life for us teenagers. At last we had something relevant to talk about at school and to listen to in those coffee bars which had made the wise investment in a juke box. A school pal invited me to his youth club in Anfield, which was a couple of bus journeys away from my home. It was well worth the journey because I learned to jive, an experience I described to my uncle as "Flying without an aeroplane!" For me, dancing was the other great, liberating thing about Rock'n'Roll. Fast, furious, and encouraging syncopated communication with your partner, it encapsulated the music-driven freedom of being a teenager in the 1950s. It made use of the wide open spaces of the Locarno-style ballrooms which our parents had packed onto before the war.

When the Sixties explosion of Beat moved millions into the smaller clubs and cellars inspired by the music of The Beatles, dancing became a restrictive occupation. It translated through the predictable gyrations of Twist and Shake to the pile-driving Pogo of the Punks, who clearly wanted to express themselves, but no longer had the bloody room to do it. Perhaps the lack of ballroom freedom of expression explained their need for the striking hairdos! My generation got everything; the NHS, free education – with free school milk thrown in, huge university grants and the unrestricted space on ballroom floors to dance the night away in the decade of the jive.

Such was my sheltered existence with BBC radio and my uncle's classical taste in music that, struck down on that pavement in Smithdown Road, I did not know what the Bill Haley sound was or where it had come from. The single *Rock Around the Clock* had, in fact, been kicking around the charts for nearly a year, but was now about to explode into our lives as it established itself at No.1 in the charts. I had not seen the film *The Blackboard Jungle*, which was shown only in the big, well-policed cinemas on Merseyside. The newspapers were full of the associated Teddy Boy violence, but not everyone was lit up by the sound and appearance of Bill Haley. John Lennon, for one, was not over-fussed by the former yodelling Country and Western singer who had been aptly described as looking like a pie salesman. The film with Haley's backing track was, however, a sensation. It had released something socially energising and transforming into the lives of the nation's youth.

As the soundtrack to *The Blackboard Jungle* story of American juvenile delinquency spilled out from cinema screens onto the streets of Britain, youth was challenged to react to music in a way it had never done before. Bill Haley was nowhere near being the best exponent of the new music. He was merely a catalyst; the best was yet to come with Presley, Chuck Berry, Little Richard, Jerry Lee Lewis and Buddy Holly.

Now since my baby left me

I've found a new place to dwell.

Down at the end of lonely street

At Heartbreak Hotel…

I heard Elvis coming out of the living room radio for the first time in the late spring of 1956. As his voice moved from tenor down to a shuddering baritone and the plaintiff lyrics echoed through the empty downstairs rooms of No.52 Borrowdale, I felt the hairs on the back of my neck rise up. "Fucking H…aley! Who in this new universe of music is that?" I was compelled to turn up the volume and risk giving a heart-attack to my terminally ill Pop, slowly dying in his prison of a bedroom, upstairs. Perhaps it should have been *Hound Dog*. Forget euthanasia… What a way to go!

It was the sublime Presley of the Sun Label and the early RCA years who stirred the likes of John Lennon. "When I heard it *(Heartbreak Hotel)* for the first time on Radio Luxembourg it was the end for me… Once I had it and got into it, that was life there was no other thing." Presley affected us all because he was a cosmic symbol of sex as well as music; his appeal cut across culture and gender. Several months later, via the cinema newsreels, I got my first censored view of an Elvis stage performance. I thank you, Bill Haley, for your pavement revelation, and rejoice that you were no pie-in-the-sky man, but a wake-up voice in the wilderness of Fifties popular music, preparing the way for the King and the Golden Age of Rock'n'Roll.

Dale Street in November 1950. This was taken only weeks after the occasion when my dad left me on the pavement to step out into the middle of the road and sort out a colossal traffic jam, which stretched back one way down Dale Street and the other beyond the Mersey Tunnel entrance.

My local cinema, the Grand, on Smithdown Road near Penny Lane. I must have spent a few thousand hours of my childhood amongst the smoke and nicotine world inhabited by the gods and goddesses of the silver screen. It is now a petrol station.

Captain Hook's ship *The Jolly Roger* anchored next to Peter Pan's statue in Sefton Park in the late 1940s. Within a few years it had been sunk by pirate attacks from gnawing rats and vandals.

The Pivvy, as I remember it in its late 1940s decline - a seedy, run-down remnant from the glory days of the old Victorian music hall. By the time I was at secondary school, with its decadence relieved only by a more wholesome Christmas pantomime, the Pivvy had degenerated into a venue for dirty old men, not to mention an eye-boggling peepshow for randy young teenagers.

A delightful photo of the Penny Lane roundabout in all its middle-class pomp and splendour, soon after it was built in 1927.

Winter wonderland in Sefton Park. Not the great freeze of 1947/48, but a 1967 reminder of the magical effect of ice and snow.

Approaching Penny Lane from Allerton in the early 1950s. I can imagine John Lennon's small gang of would-be Teds dodging around the open counters at Woolworths - just out of sight in the right foreground - before coming across to talk to Beth, who was standing with me dressed in her cadet nurse's uniform to sell Remembrance Day poppies from a tray hanging from her neck.

I will always remember coming back on a ferry across the River Mersey, late one spring evening in 1957, from a skiffle contest in Birkenhead. It was getting dark, but the bright face of the Liver Building's clock reassured me that we would make the last bus home from the Pier Head.

St David's Welsh Presbyterian Church in Princes Road, Toxteth. Also called the "Toxteth Cathedral", it was designed by George and William Audsley and built in1865-68 by my great grandfather, John Thomas, as were many of the houses in the adjacent streets of the so-called "Welsh District," which lay between Princes Road and Park Road. The congregation left after the First World War and it now lies in a ruinous state waiting for the spirit of 2008 to restore it to its former glory.

The splendid interior of St David's Church. An imposing, beautifully designed place of worship, with a set of organ pipes capable of turning The Phantom of the Opera into an Archdeacon.

The wondrous Palm House near the Fairy Glen in Sefton Park, as I remember it in 1950. The glass had been restored following blackout restrictions during the last war, when the many panes were covered with a non-reflective paint to prevent it being a target for the German bombers. One of the nine bronze and marble statues of famous explorers and naturalists, which stand on guard around the building - that of Andre Le Notre, designer of the gardens at Versailles for Louis VIV - seems to stare out at me, possibly looking for the little boy I used to be.

The bandstand near the Big Lake in Sefton Park. In the summer months, after the Sunday evening church service, Beth and I would be taken to play on the grassy slope next to the trees, whilst our mothers enjoyed a chat in the gentle warmth of the dipping sun.

A typical late 1940s Saturday afternoon's entertainment at Sefton Park Cricket Club's splendid ground. Note the many bicycles lying on the grass. The same mode of transport was used by ice cream vendors who used to peddle their refrigerated drums of the life-supporting stuff down from the cafe's on Smithdown Road.

St Columba's Welsh Presbyterian Church on Smithdown Road, Liverpool 15. This was a centre of community activity for the rows of streets adjacent to the Ullet Road entrance to Sefton Park. Only its tower now remains as part of a sheltered housing scheme.

This is a poster celebrating the 1934 opening of The Tatler News Theatre in Church Street, as the first provincial cinema of its kind in Britain.

This photo of Wavertree Playground, taken in 1970, looks from the swings at the Wavertree Road entrance across to the Royal School for the Blind and the Blue Coat Grammar School, where my Uncle Stan taught in the late 1940s. The locals preferred to call it the Mystery because the name of the nineteenth century benefactor, who gave the park to the people, was unknown. What the 80-acre gift of land did insist upon, however, was that the park should not be a Victorian promenading place but somewhere to play sport, which in my day meant dozens of soccer pitches, as well as a home for the tents and arenas of the annual Liverpool Show.

The Cameo cinema in Webster Road, which lies across from the Toxteth Park cemetery on Smithdown Road. The photograph was taken in 1960, when this dark little flee pit was closed down. It will be forever remembered as the scene of the murder of the cinema manager and his assistant in March 1949. George Kelly was later executed for a crime he may well not have committed. The Big Lake in Sefton Park was drained to find Kelly's gun and 65,000 local people were questioned by the police, including my mum and Nan.

The open-air theatre at Calderstones Park 1958. There are deckchairs at the front for those who merely want to fall asleep in the sun. At the back young mothers with their prams enjoy an afternoon chat, whilst keeping an eye on their children who are supposed to be watching a magician perform on the stage.

The smaller Greenbank Park, next door to Sefton Park, was another oasis of lake and greenery on my doorstep. Looking at the man in the boat reminds me of the time I fell in when my dad was rowing me up and down the lake. He was clearly mad at having to walk home with his little son dripping a trail of water all the way back to No.52 Borrowdale Road.

Dad and I would get off the No.86 bus at Church Street and make straight for the Tatler News Theatre for a programme of six or seven cartoons, a Pathe Newsreel and then a Laurel and Hardy or Three Stooges "short".

CHAPTER 39

THE FAIRGROUND IN SEFTON PARK

Whenever I hear Paul Anka's *Diana* or the Everly Brothers singing *Bye Bye Love*, it immediately conjures up the Sefton Park fairground of the 1950s. The new transatlantic sounds of The Platters, Conway Twitty, Marvin Rainwater, Connie Francis and a host of others seemed to offer a perfect complement to the noisy teenage world of the dodgems and roller coaster. It was stellar nursery stuff in a universe of teen nostalgia; a place and a time synonymous with Rock'n'Roll; of being forever sixteen and on the look-out for girls.

At thirteen, if I wanted to listen to pop music, I was forced to choose between the miserable menu of fuddy-duddy records played over the BBC radio, or the sanitised selections at our church youth club. The Sefton fair offered me a summer of non-stop Rock'n'Roll, played for free. The fairground gigolos who operated the main rides were also the first DJs of an open-air clubland, where an irresistible blend of Wurlitzer, soft drinks and candy floss was set against the background noise of spinning waltzers. Like the prairie wagon-train pioneers, we felt safe and comfortable within an encampment of caravans, encircling a horseshoe of brightly lit arcades and crowded stalls.

There was nothing quite like being on a waltzer when *Great Balls of Fire!* was blasted out in an endless sequence of 45s. Played, continuously, from summer teatime until well after dusk, the heady mix of carousel and constant hum from huge electric generators travelled easily on the still air of summer twilight. Haunting melodies drifted across the expanse of the great park to accompany us home through the streets of Liverpool 15. From my bedroom window, in the distance like a turned-down radio, I could still hear the melodious, lovesick voice of Buddy Holly:

> *The stars appear and the shadows are a-fallin'*
>
> *You can hear my heart a-callin'...*

On such late, lush evenings for fast-beating teen hearts, there would be a few young romances brokered or broken at the Sefton fair. Teenagers went to the fair for the heady cocktail of Rock'n'Roll, shaken and stirred with an intoxicating fairground buzz; served in the hope that you would meet up with someone you fancied. All the girls over fourteen I knew were much too decent for anything more than a bit of fun. They might let you inside their bra, if they were in the right mood, but that's about as far as a proper upbringing would allow their hormones to take them. For the braver-hearted, concealment in the long grass under one of the large trailers provided the opportunity for "going all the way", as the too-good-to-be-true Pat Boone used to sanctimoniously refer to the shameful sin of shagging. That is, if you knew who to be with, and had the guts to ask for a packet of Durex at your local barber's shop... "And is there anything else you would like, Sir? I've tidied up the Duck's Arse at the back and blown away the bum fluff on your face. Would Sir be requiring anything extra for the weekend?" Some bloody chance, when a long line of your dad's and granddad's pals were waiting to see if you had both the inclination and the guts! The background noise of the fair was excellent camouflage for sex in the long grass behind the caravans, or at the back of the stalls. More than a few teenagers lost their virginity at the Sefton Park fair, including Ringo Starr... "It was very weird: two girls and a friend of mine on the grass at the back of the fairground, and there was all the fairground music and Frankie Laine and millions of people around and *Ghost Riders in the Sky*!" Ringo had the advantage of coming from the Dingle where, at thirteen, boys didn't need the incentive of a bar mitzvah to start behaving like their dads and order contraceptives along with the trimming of their fledgling sideburns.

Even at the prodigiously cocky age of fourteen, most boys knew that they were far more likely to knock down a row of coconuts than make some girl think of sweet surrender in the grass. My nibble at more adult entertainment came from popping into one of the many sideshows, which added a bizarre element to the magical setting of the summer fair. In the immediate post-war years, there was a lingering public taste for a last vestige of the travelling Victorian freak show. By the time I was in my middle teens, these menageries of monstrosity were gone. I would have to wait some fifty years for twenty-first century geneticists to fascinate and scare me quite so much! Mind you, there is always Gerry Springer and Jeremy Kyle to remind me that the public's fascination with the fairground freak show is not completely dead.

"Who do you know with a beard, Stanley?"

"Father Christmas and the old sailor, who came to see Nan... the man with the peg leg."

"Uncle Billy, your Nan's cousin, you mean... OK... but have you ever seen a lady with a beard?"

This conversation was taking place fifty years before I could refer Pop to a couple of very odd ladies from the *Little Britain* sketches...Today I might have replied "Not since Aunty Jean came to see us," but I simply said, "No."

"Well then, step inside the tent over there with me and I'll show you one."

It was 1948, and I was only a few summer weeks away from my seventh birthday, when my grandfather decided to introduce me to a very fat, bearded lady. She was sat in a tent like a waxwork, unperturbed by the continual procession of people who stopped to stare at her untrimmed Van Dyke. A few years later I was back, unchaperoned, in another darkened tent and listening to the grunts and whoops of a "Wild Man of Borneo". The dim lighting, no doubt, helped prevent someone recognizing their unemployed, next-door neighbour, rattling and banging away on the bars of his cage. The Ape Man of Allerton was probably only as wild as a crate of Guinness allowed him to be. He certainly needed some bottle to transform himself into a small, first cousin of King Kong. Without a skinful, one look in the caravan mirror would have been enough for him to call in a shooting party from the rifle range, next door!

There were other tents with more ethically challenging exhibits: gruesome items, most likely stolen from the pathology lab of a university hospital. Creepy, foetal evidence, including the disquieting sight of Siamese Twins, locked in a death embrace inside a jar of preserving fluid. Where the two-headed calf came from I don't know. In my Pop's way of thinking, two heads were always better than one, but the fact that the identical pair of chewing faces looked at me and then mooed, fairly put me off the cream-crusted, half-bottle of school milk, which Lidderdale Road Infants served up at break-time every day.

The banner across the entrance to one tent was an overpowering invitation to meet the gender-bending Victor Victoria. "Roll up, roll up, ladies and gentlemen... including you two wide-eyed seekers of knowledge and truth down at the front there." The owner of the sideshow had taken note of our arrival on the fringe of a small crowd, who were enjoying his free, warm-up patter. The man was standing on a platform alongside the entrance to the tent and seeing a few small fish to fry he directed his gaze and words at me, and my pal, Ashley. "If you're old enough to be curious, then you're old enough to see things for yourself, that's my way of looking at it! As for the rest of you... No one is ever too old to learn something new." With no policemen about, the huckster was only too willing to take our pennies and not unduly concern himself over the moral welfare of a couple of ten-year-olds in short trousers.

"I invite you to see for yourselves this unfortunate... " He hesitated, winked, and then added "or, for those of us who may be that way inclined, lucky accident of nature." A panoramic grin was followed by another knowing wink towards the young men in the crowd. "Victor Victoria. That is what the young…" he paused again, as if hoping a medical dictionary would, magically, fall open alongside him at a suitably exotic entry "…person you are about to see, likes to be called. You are not going to be tricked with mirrors, or deceived by doubles. What you are about to get, is both Adam and Eve. Two, for the price of one! Where on madcap Merseyside can you get an offer like that?"

Without the bat of a shyster's eye-lid, we were admitted to the tent. When the curtains of the small stage were drawn back I could only marvel at the tall, androgynous apparition who proceeded to slip out of a long, Chinese robe and then stand with one side facing the audience. OK, I may have been an exploitable ten-year-old, but most of us in our last year at Dovedale had a good idea about what they wanted Betty Grable to look like in the nude. I was fairly confident that the shapely leg, rounded hip and alabaster arm on view belonged to a woman. Helping me scale a mountain of disbelief was the sight of one amply filled brassiere. He, she or whatever, lifted the robe back on to a slender shoulder and then turned to give the crowd a butcher's at what was on offer on the other side of this "buy one, get one free" package. Unhelpfully, an empty bra-cup hung down in front of a flat chest, which had the look of a busted sofa, hurriedly tidied up for the visitors. My mind boggled at what a drum-rolled, full-frontal would expose me to! The thought of facing up to some fiendish, laboratory blunder of a human being, straight out of a *Weird Tales* comic, was a lot scarier than seeing the Siamese Twins and another two-headed calf again!

We got little more than a flash of Victor Victoria's strange asymmetry. It was enough, however, for one wide-eyed wisecracker to shout out, "Where's your cock, mate? I'll bet it's either a peanut inside those little pink pants of yours, or else you've got a huge one and it's tucked away, like a Cumberland sausage, between the cheeks of your arse!" Under Uncle Stan's moral tutelage, both Ashley and I had been protected from any language below the level of Shakespeare, Milton and the Authorised King James Version of the Bible! We were grateful, nevertheless, for the reassurance given by the comically crude, but pinpoint observation. The joker in the pack clearly knew an out-of-work poofter when he saw one!

There could be no ambiguity about the sex of the pretty young woman, seemingly lying asleep in a glass coffin, pretending to be Snow White. I was now at the pubescent stage of getting an erection every time I sat down on the throbbing seat of a double-decker bus into town. I was with a gang of young boys who spent most of their dreamtime fondling Ava Gardner's tits, so they were easily persuaded to part with the sixpence entrance fee for a gander at the not so white-as-snow, fairy-tale icon of purity. In the centre of the empty tent, on a large table, lay an attractive young woman. She had been placed under a huge glass lid, like a delicious slice of confectionery in a baker's window. Someone, who appreciated how suffocatingly hot it can get lying there motionless, in a transparent tomb, had persuaded Snow White to behave more like the wicked Queen and take all her clothes off!

Wartime rationing must still have applied to dwarfs, as Snow White had to make do with two, tiny attendants, each dressed in Santa's Little Helper outfits. "I don't like the look of either of them. They give me the creeps," I whispered to Ashley. Once, when I was still young enough to be allowed to sleep with my mother, I fell out of the sheets to find myself staring into the face of an unfriendly-looking little Rumplestiltskin, dancing his midnight socks off in the doorway of the bedroom. After such an unforgettable performance, malevolent dwarfs were a regular feature of some of my worst nightmares.

Neither of the two fairground midgets could be called Happy, that's for sure. Each stared gloomily from opposite corners of the small tent, possibly cursing the lack of inches to give them a better look at the nubile fantasy, stretched out in front of them. "Where were the other five dwarfs?" I whispered. "Away playing in Scotland's forward-line at Hampden Park," was Tony Brooker's sharp reply! Snow White was naked, except for a tiny G-string, but sixpence was a stiff price for staring at the mantelpiece when what we wanted was a warming look, if not a poke, at the fire. Predictably, we were all gathered at the foot of the coffin, like six lechers at the wake of a stripper. "Can you see what I see?" The excitement and promise in Tony's voice directed all eyes south to fix, in goggle-eyed wonder, on the crop of dark pubic hair spilling out of the flimsy cloth triangle covering the girl's crotch.

My mind had wandered a long way from Snow White's face, but I looked up sensing that the girl in the deep coma was now wide awake and taking a keen interest in the proceedings. Suppressing a strong desire to laugh the lid off her coffin, she was craning her neck to enjoy the seamless expressions of fanny-fixation on the drooling faces of her young admirers. I was in the middle of the group and had a line of vision any gynaecologist would die for. However, the flimsy triangle of modesty covering the great mystery of her sex made all the difference to me benefiting from my first erotic experience. Instead of getting the growth-stunting fright of my life, I was able to enjoy many months of pleasure in thinking long, and often hard, about what lay waiting for me to explore, deep down in that forest of fuzz, one day when I was more up to it!

There was nothing sexy about the fairground boxing booths of the late 1940s. Coming from a respectable, working-class home with its high moral tone, so clearly defined by the Christian principles of my uncle, I was expected to give all low forms of entertainment a wide birth. The fairground boxing booth, with its sawdust-ring atmosphere of blood, sweat and bad language, was a million miles away from church Christian Endeavour meetings which, together with lots of sport, were Uncle Stan's preferred type of social activity for me. I can't remember when boxing disappeared from the carnival life of the fairground. However, licences for what was little more than a regulated street fight, were still being granted in the early 1950s, when I stood at the front of a large crowd, hoping to see some local tough-guy volunteer to dim the lights of the fairground champion.

I was never a scrapper, unless cornered and fighting for my life, or when someone wanted to take the sandwich away from my gaping mouth at school break-time. Uncle Stan's abhorrence of violence was acquired through too many bad childhood memories of his own father, the drunken brawler, Teddy Thomas, arriving back home from the pub to abuse wife and family. My adulterous father was neither a boozer, nor a wife beater. He was however a very physical man. He loved boxing and would let me stay up to listen to a Freddie Mills or Bruce Woodcock fight on the radio. Perhaps it was my dad's strong defence of the "Noble Art," as he called it, which encouraged me to see something weirdly respectable in a contest where two men, protected only by padded gloves and operating within strict rules of behaviour towards an opponent, then tried to punch one another's heads off! My dad got very articulate and technical about it all. "That's what the wireless can't show you, Stanley, the footwork and the defensive techniques to draw your opponent in… the feinting and jabbing with a left, and then plonking a lovely right-cross on the chin of an utterly bewildered adversary."

Pop added to my curiosity about the fairground's interpretation of Marquis of Queensbury rules, by having a spat with the owner of one of these boxing booths. He had taken me to the Sefton Park fair for the first time in the summer of 1947, and had just won me a goldfish in a glass bowl on the hoopla stall. We were preparing to walk back home when some unfinished business with another of Aneurin Bevan's newly designated State pensioners put paid to the afternoon lull in fairground activity. Sporting a natty bowler, the man was taking some air, whilst finishing off a lunchtime cigar outside the entrance to his boxing booth. Clearly, the pair had not quite satisfied themselves over some matter from their younger days of alehouse skirmishing. What followed was a parody on one of Robb Wilton's music hall monologues:

"I hope that you are not coming in here, later, Teddy Thomas.

And who might you be talking to, Billy Hughes?

You know who.

Who?

You!

Who, me?

Yes you.

What's it to you?

What's it to me? You'll soon find what it is to me.

Would you like me to try, Billy?

You're more than welcome to try, Teddy... If you'll let the boy hold your coat and look after your new pension book as well as that goldfish.

Don't you worry yourself about the goldfish... You'll have a fluke's gob on you when I get over to you!"

My grandfather had his jacket off in a flash, so, as a precaution, I placed my goldfish down behind it, on the grass. Pop's detachable collar was whipped from its neck studs and the waistcoat followed, as the right sleeve of his striped shirt was rolled up for action. My head was whirling with the excitement of being able to report back to Ashley that I had seen a re-run of the Victor McLaglen, Cary Grant, punch-up in *Gunga Din*; the two elderly veterans of the trenches having attracted a small crowd of people, no doubt believing that they were in for a free preview of the evening's entertainment.

The whole thing fizzled out when a fairground woman intervened. "Come on now the two of you. Give it a rest Billy. He's going to have a heart attack and you look as if you're about to have a stroke. I don't know which looks the hotter, Billy, your face, or the cigar! Here stick it back in your mouth and come inside for a cup of tea." The woman handed the boxing man the butt end of his unfinished smoke and lead him away. We continued on our way home, where I felt it my bounden duty to report back to my Nan with an amazing tale. I don't think she found my story at all improbable. Her reaction was to go on about the dark world of drink and brawling for so long, it made me determined to investigate the art of fisticuffs for myself. All the enthusiasm shown by my sixty-six-year-old granddad for a bare-knuckle scrap suggested I would have to disregard Uncle Stan's abhorrence of any type of street violence and take a peep at what went on behind the heavily curtained entrance of the fairground boxing tent.

"Do we have someone in the crowd willing to throw his hat into the ring for a crack at the fairground champion? Is there a sporting gent amongst you... any fit young man ready to go the distance with Barry Kinsella, here? Only twelve months ago he was the North West Area Middleweight Champion, but injury has forced him out of the professional ring, just when he was shaping up for a crack at the British title... Nevertheless, he is still fit and keen to take on anyone who feels capable enough to stay the distance of three, two-minute rounds with him. At five foot eight and just under twelve stone, he's not a bit worried about how big and strong some of you lads think you are... Isn't that right, Barry lad?" The promoter turned to get a nod of grim assurance from the chisel-featured veteran of more ring brawls than I'd had hot dinners! "You only need survive for three rounds and a five-pound purse is yours. Knock Barry out and a ten-pound prize is yours!"

Ashley and I were hoping to see an imitation, no matter how poor, of Errol Flynn's antics in *The Fighting O'Sullivans*. We were not going to be let down. "Yes, you sir... I do believe we have someone making his way towards the front right now." Whoever was coming forward fairly caused a stir of conversation in the crowd and gave the green light to transport dozens of paying customers into the tent. We were admitted, half-price, to claim a ringside view of proceedings without any thought as to whether the police, our parents or the Superintendent of St Columba's Christian Endeavour would approve.

The challenge had been taken up, not by any of the young men in the crowd, but by one of Smithdown Road's legendary characters. I never knew his name, only that he was a permanent fixture near the Lodge Lane junction of traffic lights at the top of Smithdown Road, where he scraped a living whistling for taxis and selling the *Liverpool Echo* in hail, rain and snow. He was a lively old bugger, I'll give him that! All the years of dodging trams, buses and cars as he peddled his evening papers enabled him to spring into the ring without a thought for the wooden steps, which helped set the canvass ring some three feet above the grass and sawdust floor of the tent. He almost fell out of his worn, gabardine mackintosh as he stripped down to a pair of tissue-thin trousers and a vest, which hung on his skeletal frame like an item of wet washing on my Nan's clothesline. "Ex-e-Echo! Ex-e-Echo!" or "Pink Finaal!... Get yer Pink Finaal!" was the distinctive, throaty cry which helped him sell hundreds of post-match football editions to over-the-moon or under-a-cloud supporters making for the buses, trams and the pubs on a Saturday evening.

"Now ladies... I do believe I can see three or four of you in the crowd and most welcome you are too... and gentlemen. Please give your generous applause to the plucky challenger here. Not quite in the first flush of youth, I'll grant you... But, if you can come home from Flanders with your body in one piece and your head on the right way around, then you're either lucky as hell, or very fast on your feet! By his appearance I would say that his luck has long run out, so let's hope he's not called the Randy Turpin of Tunnel Road for nothing!... I jest, ladies and gentlemen... I'm sure our challenger, here, is up to the task and will give our champion a severe test of nerve, over the next few minutes in the ring." This mickey-taking raised a few laughs around the ringside as the promoter continued his merciless ribbing of the no-hoper, who couldn't punch a hole in a wet *Echo*. The fairground boxer was a fit, strong-looking man in his early thirties, whereas Smithdown Road's King of the Down-and-Outs was sixty, if he was a day, and weighed in at less than seven and a half stone, dripping wet with Wavertree rain.

"I notice that our brave challenger, here, is wearing his famous Russian boots." I looked away from the loose-tongued showman, basking in the success of his ballyhoo and across to the challenger's corner, where I could see what was left of his shoes. The toecaps were peeled back from their paper-thin soles, like two tins of beans curled open and ready to go into a pot. "They're called Russian boots because they've been especially designed for the weather in Liverpool... They let the rain rush in and then rush out again!" The joke caused another wave of laughter to ripple around the tent and our Belsen-like hero did a little Chaplinesque dance to show off how well-ventilated his feet were. Suddenly, I felt uneasy. The audience had become too cynical for my ten-year-old taste buds and seemed to have switched on a raw appetite for blood and guts. I was worried that all the fun I was hoping to get out of this David-versus-Goliath contest was about to turn into a bad accident waiting to happen.

If anyone in the crowd was hoping that the fairground champion might show a little charity towards someone old enough to be his father, their wishes were quickly dashed. The bell sounded for round one and punches rained in on the pathetic challenger. He took a bigger battering than an order for twenty haddock suppers in a packed fish and chip shop. Jab after jab, interrupted with crosses and hooks were delivered from all angles. Each blow was flavoured with loud snorts and sniffs from the seasoned ex-professional, making him sound more like a champing racehorse than a champion boxer. The old paper-man's nose had begun to bleed and one of his eyes had closed up. Would he go down? Not on his luckless life he wouldn't. Years of standing in the pouring rain and biting wind at the exposed corner of Lodge Lane had fashioned him into an extremely hard nut to crack. With his dirty vest building up vivid patterns of splattered blood, he began to look like the victim of a return of the Nazi air raids to Liverpool 8. However, he stuck it out until the end. The final bell had him hanging on to his public executioner like a legless, out-of-his-mind boozer; drained of all but one, last, monosyllabic grunt to be carried home to bed.

A great bout of cheering erupted to make those outside the tent wonder what drama they had been missing. On a system of points, the knackered old challenger had been demolished, but the contest rules demanded only survival, and so he was a winner! The crowd continued to cheer for several minutes, as showers of silver coins came splashing into the ring from all directions. I could now rejoice in a sad victory and watch the dogged old bugger set about trying to pick up every single coin; first filling the pockets of his raincoat, before making profitable use of his leaky old shoes.

As if selling a few newspapers, in all weathers and probably feeling crap for most of the time, was not a hard enough way to make a living. More than likely, he had forced himself into this bone-crunching sideline to secure some drinking money for the next few weeks. In the 1980s, Mrs Thatcher and Norman Tebbit would have held him up to the nation's three million unemployed as a shining example of innovative capitalism!

I still like to watch professional boxing on television and have seen some amazing contests over the years: Ali v Foreman, Ali v Frazier and Thomas "Hitman" Hearns v Sugar Ray Leonard; the marvellous Marvin Hagler and the courageous, battling Barry McGuigan. Nothing, however, could match up to what I witnessed in the 1952 fairground triumph of a needs-must victim of an unfair world. For once in his life, the pissed-upon old news vendor had been flogging his evening *Echos* on the sunny side of the street.

CHAPTER 40

THE KOP AND BILLY LIDDELL

I started going to Anfield in the relegation season of 1953-54. When you fall in love with someone the timing of the madness takes no heed of health wealth and circumstance. So also with a football team; its success, the quality of its players and the lack of civilised toilet facilities in the stadium are as unimportant as being a Michael Jackson fan and having to listen, hour after hour, to his Mickey Mouse voice as well as coping with the latest knob transplant into the middle of his face. To the faithful and the obsessed, such challenges matter not a fart! The governing law of footie-fixation dictates that the scale of a supporter's affection and loyalty is inversely proportional to the status and fortunes of his team. The worse the predicament of his club, the greater is the test of true loyalty and devotion.

My Pop had hoped to make me an Evertonian, like himself, by taking me to the more impressive Goodison Park with its substantial, mock-Tudor stands and a uniformed commissioner standing guard in the marbled, main entrance to the club. I enjoyed the times I went with him, but found the experience a little too neutral. The Everton crowd was always vocal and humorous, but seemed to be too serious-minded for my liking; too studied and conversational about the game, for my more emotional and perturbable nature. Not for nothing was Goodison Park knows as "The home of soccer science". It is a significant and betraying fact about the psyche of the Merseyside soccer fan that so many of the great home-grown, stand-up comics, Arthur Askey, Ted Ray, Ken Dodd and Jimmy Tarbuck, have all been Liverpool supporters. Unfortunately, for the rest of the country, Scousers believe that God created each and every one of them to be all-round entertainers. Being a Liverpool FC supporter, however, does seem to require a special talent!

I was switched on to the passion and comedy of tribal football one Saturday in October 1953. I was twelve and had recently attended a Christian Endeavour meeting at St Columba's, where the guest speaker was the Liverpool team captain and Scottish international winger, Billy Liddell. There I was, staring up from my second-row seat, at the most prized face in my cigarette card collection of famous footballers. Pop would often pick up my treasured set of soccer stars and find the excuse to wax lyrical about the likes of Wilf Mannion, Hughie Gallagher and Raich Carter. He always gave the picture of flaxen-headed Billy Steel a long. hard look, as if he begrudgingly recognised someone who was an even better inside forward than himself. There were some great Scottish footballers in my collection, but the favourite was Billy Liddell.

Here he was, in the flesh, addressing a group of no more than thirty youngsters in the small Bible-study room of our church. I could not take my eyes off him. He had a hair-style any 1930s film star would have died for, with a centre-parting as straight and well-greased as the signal points at Edge Hill railway junction. All of my childhood heroes seemed to seek me out rather than me pick them... And quite right too! Why should any self-respecting demi-god stand in an endless Pantheon line-up, simply to risk not getting into a snotty-nosed schoolboy's All-Time Greatest Football Eleven? In a team of mediocrities, such as Liverpool boasted in the mid-1950s, Billy Liddell found it an easy job to be idolised. Like Dixie Dean, a decade earlier across Stanley Park, he would have been an exceptional footballer in any age; a world-class player, in spite of having to, week after week, sustain a struggling collection of uninspiring journeymen.

We listened in awe to the man whose exploits had persuaded the media to rename Liverpool FC "Liddellpool". It was an epitaph which well-suited Liverpool's slide to becoming one of soccer's run-of-the-mill sides. Now wearing the No.9 shirt, Liddell was worth more in goals and points to his team than the rest of the players put together. He spoke modestly, in a calm, matter-of-fact manner about football and his faith in Jesus Christ. The story goes that the church at the top of Oakfield Road, opposite the Kop entrance, put up a big evangelical poster asking the question, "What would you do if Christ came again?" One irreverent wit had added the cogent advice "Move Liddell back to the left wing and play Jesus at centre-forward!"... After the Christian Endeavour meeting, Ashley and I decided that it was Anfield for us on Saturday, at the next home game!

A few days later we took a tram to the top of Smithdown Road. Here, for the first time in our lives we crossed the border from our own neighbourhood in an endless line of covered wagons the city council insisted on calling buses. After a lot of whistle blowing and directing of traffic at the Lodge Lane junction lights, we were off on our pioneering journey to a land which promised the pilgrim faithful a better life in the lush pasturelands of First Division football. Along with a tribe of converts as fanatical and vocal as John Smith and his Mormon Tabernacle Choir we were travelling to a spiritual home where false hope and misplaced optimism sprang eternal out of the well-manicured blades of Anfield's prairie grasses.

We claimed two seats on the top deck of a bus, which was already filling up with the very characters comedians like Ted Ray and Ken Dodd owed their living to. "Where are youse lot standing today? I'm giving the Kop a rest... Yer can't get to the toilets... After the last game I went home, again, with my trousers bleedin' well soaked though from those rolled up Echos being used by the dirty sods standing next to me. Maureen thinks I'm starting to piss myself... so I told her... Yeah, I must be getting inconti...inconsti..." There was a burst of laughter. "Tell her you were pissed-off with the 4-2 defeat by a useless bunch like Lincoln City, more like!"

Another supporter began to poke fun at his two mates in the seat in front of him. Tweedledum and Tweedledee looked like the pairs mutton pie-eating champions of Wavertree. They sat with wide grins of satisfaction, their cupped hands supporting two enormous beer bellies straining at the imposition of XXL vests, half a century before being morbidly obese made such T-shirts a regular off the peg purchase for football supporters... "If you stand between these two fat-arsed getts, no one will be able to piss on you for a radius of ten feet." This golden shaft of Wacker wit produced more laughter, and gave two little boys permission to enjoy the rude but very funny conversation of men so refreshingly different to Uncle Stan. "Thank God he isn't on this bus," I thought to myself... "He would have rung for an emergency stop at the first whiff of any 'lavatory humour' and that would have been the end of it." We would be travelling back home on one of the town service buses, returning respectable women from Saturday morning shopping in the city centre.

With excellent timing the last burst of laughter had signalled our arrival at the Oakfield Road bus stop some two hundred yards from the ground. At this customary point of disembarkation, we were decanted onto the pavement to be swept along by a tide of supporters all making for the looming edifice of the Anfield Kop.

We became more excited with every accelerated step, as we tried to keep up with the one-way flow of human traffic along Oakfield Road. People were coming together from all directions as tributary side-streets delivered more and more jostling, eager punters into a rush for the entrances to the ground at Walton Breck Road. I had the vision of not making it; crushed and trampled to death by the enormous herd of camels, which were about to be threaded through the eye of a turnstile needle. However, mounted policemen on horses as big as Agincourt chargers herded us into regimented queues; pressing us like cattle into the narrow turnstile gates and onto the more open foothills of the Spion Kop.

We seemed to be climbing the endless stone steps of a giant pyramid; pulled ever upwards by the noise bellowing from beneath the looming corrugated-iron roof of the Kop. Finally, like Sir Edmund Hillary and Sherpa Tensing on Coronation morning, we stood at the summit to take our first panoramic view of the Anfield pitch. Having got there a good forty minutes before kick-off, we were able to watch the ground slowly fill up in a patchwork of red and white. It was like watching a newly sown lawn, recorded by slow-action camera, thickening and spreading by the second in front of our eyes. To our left was the great expanse of the giant terracing, which would soon hold more than 20,000 swaying, singing, chanting souls. I had staked my claim to my own tiny plot of standing room, high up on the Kemlyn Road side of the Kop. I sensed I would soon become one with this gathering army of supporters, whose expectations for the next ninety minutes were as unzipped as my own. The marvellous thing was that I did not need to introduce myself. The host of voices in the huge chancel of the stadium had been expecting me for some time and knew just who I was. I had, finally, made it, to take my rightful place as the latest, junior member of the Kop Choir!

The genial soccer-mad Scousers, whose unrestricted conversation I so much looked forward to on alternate Saturdays, throughout the winter months of the mid-1950s, were taking part in a dying expression of working-class culture. These football followers were part of a nation still relaxing from the stress and hardship of six years of war. The national game seemed to symbolise, not simply a return to normal social behaviour, but also the triumph of freedom over tyranny. For the last half a century this jewel of a game had become the sublime metaphor for what the nation could achieve through an application of self-discipline, skill, energy and team-work. Football was also the State's favoured alternative to alcohol as a weekend safety-valve for controlling the frustration and suppressed anger of millions of working men who woke up each morning to a depressing lack of personal fulfilment.

It was an unacknowledged fact of life that the coalfields, steelworks and shipyards which had fathered and resourced the game in the industrial heartlands of the North of England and Central Scotland were finished by the time I stood on the terracing at Anfield. The feast of football served up to Scousers in the 1960s and '70s was an invitation sent out by Balthazar. The moving finger had already scrawled its apocryphal message auguring the extinction of Britain's old working class, as millions of jobs were lost in a revolution of new technology and cyber communication. The consumer and leisure revolution was about to change the habits of the nation at weekends, and sociologists predicted the death of soccer as the supreme, elevating, working-class experience.

I'll bet those sociable soccer men, who kept me feeling so comfortable and well-brought-up every other Saturday in the 1950s, could never have conceived that the day was fast approaching when middle-class values, and the issue of crowd safety would force the replacement of the swaying, singing terraces of the Kop with plastic seats to help people behave with a little more decorum.

I had no fear of standing with such men. I had come to the conclusion that I would be a lot safer surrounded by this bunch of friendly, protective if somewhat compulsive grown-ups, than in the caged area known as the boys' pen, squeezed high up in the corner of the ground, at the side of the mountainous Kop. Did the abbreviation stand for "penitentiary", I wondered? It looked, to me, like the Ape House at Chester Zoo. Should any young boy want to stand, surrounded by a bunch of twelve-to-fourteen-year-old silly buggers, with a few genuine, hard-case hooligans thrown in for good measure, then I took my hat off to him. I decided to take my chances in the ocean of heaving bodies, where momentum could carry a hefty man up and down a dozen or so of the terraced steps when Liverpool attacked the Kop goal. Corner kicks created a Tsunami of movement as the crowd pushed down and then surged back up the terraces, enjoying the fear and exhilaration of surfers trapped in the embrace of an arcing, suffocating swell.

There were reassuring moments of spectacular drama when the vast crowd performed a Snowdonia mountain-rescue operation to pass the prostrate body of a collapsed spectator down from the dizzy heights of the top terraces to the waiting St John Ambulance men on the touchline. I often thought of faking illness, underneath the high canopy, just to get a downhill toboggan ride over a forest of helping hands.

The only other serious threat to life and limb came from giant wooden rattles, which were brought onto the terraces for special occasions like derby games and FA cup-ties. During a replayed cup-tie against Manchester City in 1956, I was eternally grateful to be small enough to duck one such swirling piece of mediaeval thuggery, as the man next to me took it full in the face. Needless to say, he was no longer interested in the game! Had Bonnie Prince Charlie employed a few thousand extra Inverness Caley Thistle supporters with such lethal weaponry at Culloden in 1746, we may well have been spared the next 150 years of Hanoverian rule and families in England, today, might be sitting down to haggis suppers every Saturday, served at elegant Jacobean dining tables!

It was Pop who educated me into how the Kop had been named after the Relief of Ladysmith, a famous battle in the Boer War, when a hill was defended to the death by 300 British soldiers. The original Kop terracing of 1906 had been rebuilt in 1928 as the largest cantilever single-span structure in English football. Some 425 feet wide, by 131 feet deep and nearly 100 feet high, it had seen occasions when 28,000 (nearly half the ground's capacity) had packed behind one goal-mouth. The Kop dwarfed the other terracing and stands at Anfield. Its high cathedral vault acted like giant lungs to gather in the bellowing noise of the crowd before forcing the sound up into the corrugated iron roof. Here the thunderous roar was amplified and transformed into a mighty wind driving the Liverpool team forward as they attacked the Anfield Road goal. Billy Liddell told us that the Kop was reckoned to be worth a goal start to the team. At corner kicks there were thousands who claimed to have helped suck the ball into the opponents net!

I didn't go to Anfield for the football alone. In those depressing, mid-Fifties seasons of always finishing short of the points needed for promotion that would be expecting too much! Like tens of thousand of others with older, more sophisticated tastes in entertainment than myself, I was attracted to the spectacular open-air theatre, where a Shakespearean crowd played its part; often putting on a much better show than the boys down there on the pitch! I went to Anfield for the music hall atmosphere and to experience the most inventive, spontaneous vocal support of any ground in England.

There was a man who got out of the crowd to entertain the Kop with a performance fit for Danny Kaye in *The Court Jester*. He began his routine outside the eighteen-yard box by dribbling and mis-kicking an invisible ball, before tripping and awarding himself the deliciously executed mime of a penalty-kick, which sent him sprawling in the February mud of the goal mouth. He headed umpteen invisible corners into the top of the net to tremendous roars of encouragement from spectators who were pleased to think they possessed all the pieces of the jigsaw and not just the bit with a part of Dopey's face on it! Week after week, he turned up to do his party piece, winding up his act by kicking a shoe over the bar and into the Kop. On my way home, I often used to think of him. Where did he live? Was he as much appreciated by the wife and family who had to put up with his behaviour the other six days of the week? Or, was the fortnightly five minutes of crowd pleasing, self-deprecating comedy the only thing that kept him going in a sad, lonely existence. Whether he was simpleton, or an eccentric Professor of Theoretical Physics, it did not matter a proton. Once a fortnight, if only for a brief few minutes of fantasy football, his star shone as brightly as any of the great players who had ever worn the red shirt of Liverpool. He made us all laugh and united the spirit of the crowd with a set-piece of clowning so predicable, yet amazingly fresh, each time he played the fool in front of us.

The Anfield crowd was always sporting, especially to opposition goalkeepers, who enjoyed a rousing reception when they came to throw their caps down into the back of the Kop goal. They were also very sympathetic to the wholehearted players. In those lean years of Division Two, many were second-rate like the winger Fred Morris, who cost the club the princely sum of £7,500 from Mansfield Town, in 1958. The Kop knew a comedian when they saw one and were ready to applaud the fruitless endeavour as Fred charged, mindlessly, down the right-wing in more than forty First Team appearances that season. Unable to change speed or direction, never mind stop to cross the ball, he would often be forced to throw himself, headlong, over the touchline wall into the crowd. At the end of one singularly unproductive, mad dash down the wing, a deathly hush fell over the crowd as Fred went arse-over-tip into the Kop. A lone voice seized its chance to peal out the blunt appraisal of the winger's performance. "Fred... You're playing with your dick out!"

Although the tradition of Roman Catholic support belonged to Everton, the city's Irish heritage of singing in pubs and as an accompaniment to children's street skipping games was taken onto the Kop where it was developed into an art form. There was both a mystery and mystical quality about the Kop's singing and chanting. In the Sixties the BBC's *Panorama* team came searching for the phantom who conducted the Kop Choir to a standard rarely achieved by the Liverpool Philharmonic Chorus. Like the Loch Ness monster, the legend of an invisible maestro grew to become a focus of serious academic research into the paranormal. The choral outbursts were so well-orchestrated and so perfectly timed that they produced moments of concert hall brilliance:

> *Dyson pinched the ciggies*
>
> *Dyson pinched the ciggies*
>
> *Ee Aye Adio,*
>
> *Dyson pinched the ciggies*

The Kop had unplugged itself as quickly as it had switched itself on. Terry Dyson, the Spurs inside-forward had, indeed, been a naughty boy when he was caught smuggling fags through customs on his team's return from a European game. The Kop had not failed to pick up on the piece of tabloid gossip. They were in top form that Saturday, in April 1963, and their response to the Tottenham pre-match kick-around was a warm-up of their own original and instinctive vocal humour.

Jimmy Greaves was highly amused by the Kop's genius for improvisation and signalled his approval to the terraces before helping Spurs go 2-0 up. This was the new Liverpool of Bill Shankly, however, and Ian St John put on a magnificent display of centre-forward skills to transform the score line into a 4-2 lead for the Reds. Suddenly, the Kop responded to the raised baton of their invisible Von Karajan and were off again, this time to the tune of Old Macdonald's Farm:

Old Bill Shankly had a farm,

Ee Aye, Ee Aye, O

And on that farm he had St John,

Ee Aye, Ee Aye, O

With a flick, flick here,

And a flick, flick there,

Here a flick, there a flick,

Everywhere a flick, flick...

Ten more verses followed, as every Liverpool player was given a personal tribute. A fifth Liverpool goal went in! Next, the Kop plucked a children's nursery rhyme out of the ether:

London Bridge is falling down,

Poor old Tottenham!

Not even enough lines and rhyme for a stanza, but pure magic! The creative genius of the Kop to think on its feet had, yet again, been given a uniquely humorous collective voice, anticipating future concerts of vocal brilliance to be ushered in by Beatlemania, and the singing, Swinging Sixties. Exiled in Scotland, I missed out on all the euphoric excitement of the Shankly revolution and the great nights of early European success at Anfield. However, as a Koppite in the 1950s I had my own glorious moments, too, and none better than the home game against Notts County, in November 1957.

On paper it looked a very ordinary fixture, against a team sliding fast into relegation and soccer oblivion. However, it was a very special day, both for me and my hero, the ageing legend, Billy Liddell. Known as the *Flying Scotsman*, Liddell had made his name and taken his rightful place amongst the truly great players of British soccer as a fast, powerful, marauding left-winger, able to cut inside a defence and unleash a cannonball shot. As Bob Paisley, a man of few words, so succinctly put it. "If Billy couldn't get round a defender then he'd go through him!" Now, for the only time in his one-club career, he had been dropped from the First Team. The sports editor of the *Liverpool Echo* had his phone buzzing and his mail-bag bursting with letters expressing outrage and doubts about the sanity of manager, Phil Taylor. On hearing that the pressure of public opinion had restored Liddell to his rightful place in the forward line, I was determined to be among the 52,000 fans, who turned up praying to see him triumph.

That day, I was with friends who had forced me to desert my normal Kop vantage point for the smaller, Anfield Road goalmouth terracing. I don't know what had prompted me to do such a thing, but providence was about to bless my change of habit. You could feel the expectancy of the crowd whenever Liddell received the ball out wide on the left-wing. A fanatic standing in front of me had clearly defied the doctor's advice not to leave his hospital bed. Half of the man's body was encased in plaster with the rest in bandages. He could not stand without the aid of crutches. The thought did cross my mind that if Billy Liddell scored, we might have an emergency – even a death – on our hands. His only hope lay in containing himself like an Egyptian mummy watching Tutankhamen Town playing Rameses Rovers in the Pharaoh's Cup.

The game was goalless and then, suddenly, Billy Liddell was given the ball just over the half-way line. Running at the County defence, from some thirty yards out he unleashed a powerful ground shot which the keeper let through his hands and into the net right in front of me. The crowd went into an ecstasy such as Moses must have experienced when he came back down from the mists of Sinai to tell the children of Israel that he had just got the Ten Commandments from God for nothing! The mummy's crutches were launched into the air; receiving instant healing he shouted out an Eleventh Commandment, "Thou shalt not take the shirt of Billy Liddell and give it to a tosser!"

Never again would I experience such an outpouring of joy and emotion from a football crowd towards a player respected and adored above all others. Billy Liddell scored another two goals that day, and tens of thousands of euphoric, vindicated supporters made their happy way home thinking "Stick that up your arse, Phil Taylor." Taylor would be remembered not only as the last mediocre manager before the arrival of the Messiah, Bill Shankly, but a man stupid enough to drop a thirty-five-year-old centre-forward, who was not only one of the all-time greats of British soccer, but had another twenty goals in him that season!

CHAPTER 41

WALKING TO SCHOOL WITH ADAM FAITH

Every morning classmates Griff, Charlie and Brad would call at No.25 Gainsborough Road to collect John P for their communal walk to school. Outside the invigorating season of spring and the warmth of summer's most honeyed days, I preferred to take the bus. Rain and wind easily put me off an 8.00am, two mile walk to the toil of the classroom, whereas, the vagaries of the Merseyside climate never seemed to bother my four, foul weather friends. I liked to pick my times for joining them; the pleasant, crisp mornings in the dying days of winter; dew fresh, bud bursting spring mornings, with the gardens of the big houses full of birdsong; the rolled up shirt-sleeves, coat-over-the-shoulder mornings of late May and June, when I could feel nature's promise in the early heat and sunshine, which came dancing through the broken canopy in Ullet Road's long avenue of trees. These were the good-to-be-alive days, when I felt up to meeting all the challenges ahead; days of youthful optimism, which ran like a rich vein of silver through the conversation, as we journeyed forth to our studies at Toxteth Tech, in the Dingle.

All the way along our well-trodden route, from the first crossing of Smithdown Road, up Arundel Avenue and then into Ullet Road, the five of us would shoot the early morning breeze. Skirting Princes Park, we took a short cut to the school gates down Sandringham Drive or, occasionally, went for the longer stroll down Linnet Lane so that John and Brad might pay homage as they past the home of the brash, flash jazzman, George Melly. We talked about anything deemed worthy, or unworthy, of our teenage minds. With no television to harass our wits and senses, we relied mainly on the radio, the *Daily Mirror*, and the good old *Liverpool Echo* to give us the basics, so that we could begin to form opinions on some of the major issues of the day. I, alone, came from a home where *The Manchester Guardian*, *The Observer*, and *The Listener* could be found lying around to invite my cautious attention.

"They've had race riots down in London... in Notting Hill. My granddad thinks we're only a few years away from the same trouble up here."

We were now sixth formers about to leave school a decade before Enoch Powell had his vision of a re-routed, swollen River Tiber lapping Birmingham's pavements with the blood of ethnic conflict. We could never imagine, as we walked to multiracial Toxteth, that parts of Liverpool 8 would go up in flames less than twenty years later!

"Do you fancy going to see Brigitte Bardot on Friday night, at the Forum in town… *Et Dieu Créa La Famme.*" Griff was in a show-off mood, having just read *La Guerre de Trente Ans* in the original French.

"Et Dieu… what?"

"And God Created Woman Well, that's what it's called in America. The British censors think God had nothing to do with it and have called it *And Woman was Created.*"

"It'll be in sub-titles, though won't it?"

"The dialogue may be, but her tits won't. Who's keen to go?"

We were blessed to be teenagers in the era of Bardot. Her next film had a title we could not pronounce, but we got the message about what she might be up to from big posters, in plain English, announcing *The Night Heaven Fell* – a suitably decorous reference to someone bringing the ceiling down during a violent orgasm. Many years later, I discovered that every time one of us swore blind to getting a clear glimpse of French fanny, the very non-public Brigitte was also insisting on remaining non-pubic by wearing a body stocking. Thousands of uncontrollable erections didn't deserve to be short-changed like that!

Brigitte Bardot was the cinema's main assault on our raised hormone levels, but we were often calm and rational enough to discuss the world's biggest events as they impacted on our lives. The range of topics was as varied as it was historically significant. From America there was the attack on human rights at Little Rock, along with the equally savage mugging of popular music by Presley, Jerry Lee Lewis and the outrageously magnificent Little Richard. It was important to know if there was a link between U2s and UFOs and which we should fear the most. Religion and faith were under attack from the new secular society but, suddenly, there was a loveable, redeemable papacy under Pope John XXIII to confuse the jaundiced opinions of my atheist pals about the existence of God and the relevance of the Church. There was always jazz. I was the Rock'n'Roll outsider but, nevertheless, I was curious to know how Brad, Charlie and John were finding room in their Trad jazz cellar minds for the likes of Miles Davis as well as Dixieland.

By the late 1950s, only John P had a television set in the home. With ITV in its infancy and considered by many to be merely a transitory experiment, the first TV commercials were a novelty. One of the most memorable depicted a lone, Harry Lime-type character, whose craving for a particular brand of cigarette was screened so often it must have taken a good few chain-smoking years off the actor's life. With raincoat collar pulled up against the night and any annoying gusts of wind, he paused to light a fag under a street lamp. His casual resignation about having been stood up by blonde, leggy Olga, the East German agent who was his whistle blower in more ways than he cared to admit, was meant to re-assure the less-than-choosy smoker, "You're never alone with a Strand."

Television may have been latest thing in home entertainment, but the primitive technology of the 1950s was a drawback to it ever claiming the social control which it exercises today. I can remember John's father proudly installing his 12 inch, rented, Pye table model for the Nottingham Forest v Leicester Cup Final of 1959. Our viewing pleasure was severely blighted by the limited number of fixed cameras. These were incapable of giving the TV audience any better a view than Cecil B De Mille's mountain top shot of insect-like armies doing battle down in the valley below.

"Edie... Edie... Where-the-hell are you? The bloody electricity has run out. The television is off! For God's sake... quickly woman! Get a shilling or the game is ruined." The only goal of the game was scored just as the money in the meter box ran out. All of John's dad's cursing and his wife's Olympic sprint down the hall, clutching a shiny refill, was in vain.

Going to the pictures was still our best, non-sporting form of entertainment. Besides being a main source of conversation, it was the place where you took your girlfriend for a good grope around her bra and a twisted neck from snogging in the dark. Unbelievable as the passage of time and changing tastes might make it seem, there were marvellous moments, in packed cinemas, when side-sore audiences acclaimed Jerry Lewis to be the funniest man in the world. In a decade of Hollywood innovation, which gave us a couple of flash-in-the-pan years of 3-D, and then a production line of wide-screen blockbusters in Cinemascope, with the choice of Technicolor, or new Eastman colour, we had great films to talk about.

Westerns still packed people in, and there was the gunfight to end all gunfights: Kirk Douglas and Burt Lancaster, with the sun at high noon, orchestrating two sets of flashing, tombstone teeth to first dazzle and then blow away the Dalton Gang, at the OK Coral. All 6'5" of Christopher Lee made his first major screen appearance as the Prince of Darkness. John Wayne had, alarmingly, thrown away his Stetson and pulled on a mangy racoonskin hat to save his fledgling nation from an army of swarming, swarthy Mexicans at the Alamo. We shared with our History teacher, the 5'6" Mr Dottie, his secret, boyish fascination for muscleman Steve Reeves, who was flexing his pecs at the Forum in Lime Street, as *Hercules Unchained*.

There was much more serious conversation after seeing *Room at the Top* and *Saturday Night and Sunday Morning*, which after a decade of glorious Technicolor revived a taste for the more socially realistic black and white films. They also directed us back to the novels of John Braine and Alan Sillito, where we could search for bits of ourselves in the new northern, working-class heroes like Joe Lampton and Arthur Seaton.

The 1950s bestowed on youth a dynamic, cultural importance which gave us unaccustomed influence as consumers and commentators on the society we were about to help shape. However, by accident, or design, we were anaesthetised against any Angry Young Men criticism of the State and what its real intentions towards us might be. The 1944 Butler Education Act and Labour's Welfare State made us heirs to opportunity for personal wealth and happiness undreamt of by our parents, and postponed judgement on whether we could obtain salvation by virtue of a middle-class lifestyle. We could no longer see ourselves as prisoners to a centuries old class system.

Approaching middle age in the Thatcher eighties, many of us woke up to the emptiness of the, so-called, affluent middle-class society, which not only widened the gap between North and South, rich and poor, but claimed pride and virtue in the accumulation of wealth. Poverty was something about which all of us should have retained a powerful moral conscience, because that is what we rubbed shoulders with when we were young.

All the angst of being seventeen and having to study hard was there, of course. We were, however, the first generation of children from working-class homes who had been given a passport to some degree of self-fulfilment and success in life. We were a blessed generation, liberated from many of the old parental controls and restrictions; rescued from dismally predictable futures of toil in dark, depressing places of sweated labour. All that and a bottle of Hanson's dairy milk delivered to your desk at school each day – what more could a Bevin boy want! Proudly and happily we walked to school, the elite new beneficiaries of peace and social enlightenment; sensing that we were a special breed and talking freely of many things "of shoes – and ships – and sealing wax – of cabbages – and kings."

"Hey... Who's this guy George Adamski? Is he some sort of a nut?"

"D'you mean the American who's written the book *Flying Saucers Have Landed?*"

"Yea, he's a Polish immigrant... He claims to have seen space ships and spoken to aliens out in the Mojave Desert in California. He drew a map of our solar system in the sand for one of them. He then pointed to the third planet,

Earth, and placed a finger on his own chest. The alien pointed to the second planet, Venus."

"What did he look like?... Not the Emperor Ming, I hope!"

"Adamski said that the aliens were tall, human-like, with long blond hair and tanned skin."

"It's no bloody wonder they looked like that... They've spent all their friggin' lives roasting next to the sun and taking baths in sulphuric acid."

"Sulphuric acid?"

"Sulphuric, hydrochloric, nitric... It's the morning routine if you live on Venus, pal."

"Adamski's been overdosin' on Dan Dare in the *Eagle*. That alien is a dead-ringer for a Theron."

"What's a fuckin' Theron?"

"They're the good guys from the northern hemisphere of Venus"

"So, we're OK then are we? These guys'll save us from the Russians, eh?"

The pictures and stories in the *Eagle* were so impressive that rumours spread about the chief artist, Frank Hampton, having been inspired by a Close Encounter of the Third Kind. Did the urbane pipe-smoking Hampton know much more than he was letting on? Had he, like George Adamski, been on speaking terms with seemingly benevolent, extra-terrestrials?

Following the publication Adamski's best seller, a flood of UFO literature and movies from the United States gave us the excuse for continued debate about life out there, beyond the stars. *The Thing* – an unsubtle, but clever film title suggesting endless sequels like *The Thing with no Face... The Face with no Thing... The Thing with a Face on its Thing... The Thing with a Thing on its Face* – provided us with our earliest attempts to test the X certificate rating on these black and white masterpieces of comic, Dr Who-style, sci-fi.

Behind all the culture-led hysteria about little green men from outer space, there was a far more rational, earthly explanation of our fixation with the threat of alien invasion. Superpower confrontation had created a propaganda industry to combat the post-war Soviet threat. In the witch hunt for "Reds under the Beds", Cold War architect, John Foster Dulles (a man with the uncompassionate and deadly look of Pope Pius XII) and rabid, Republican Senator Joe McCarthy, wanted us crawling on our knees, examining every filled-to-the-brim chamber pot. The Americans had seriously overestimated the capability of the Soviets to produce their own weapons of mass destruction. To keep us on our capitalist toes, they had us scouring the heavens for the first signs of bug-eyed communists from the Red planet, commanded by the heirs of Emperor Stalin. The creators of the *Eagle* may well have been trying to tell us that not being alone in the universe was far from being the biggest worry for earthlings, on both sides of the Iron Curtain.

Politics was a taboo subject on the school curriculum, for fear it stirred up ideas of class warfare in the new egalitarian Britain of State-sponsored education. However, that fact did not prevent the H-Bomb from severely limiting our chances of having any future. There was a David Low cartoon at the time, which borrowed heavily from Dalí and depicted a towering, cross-like mushroom cloud, casting its giant death-dealing shadow over a doomed planet. When you are seventeen and think that you have a divine right to live into ripe old age, then something likely to reduce your life span by a biblical three score years and ten is bound to grab your attention.

We talked about Hitler and the Nazis a lot; Auschwitz, Dachau and Buchenwald had seen to that. I think it was Brad who introduced us to Lord Russell of Liverpool's best-seller of the mid-1950s, *The Scourge of the Swastika*. As Deputy Judge Advocate General, British Army of the Rhine, this brilliant barrister was responsible for all the war crime trials in the British zone of Germany from 1946-1950. Once the war had been won, he set about presenting to the civilised world, an intellectual and moral condemnation of the Nazis so overwhelming because its message was through the personal and intimate power of the written word.

There was a hatred of the Nazis in post-war Liverpool, which meant that most of my generation of Scouser teenagers, perpetuated a suspicion of all things German. As late after the war as 1957, I can remember going to Anfield to watch an England v West Germany Under-23 International. Liverpool's current left-winger, Alan A'Court, had been selected to sweeten the support of the Kop, which proceeded to give the Germans a good introductory five minutes of a 28,000 arms raised, fingers under the nose, Nuremberg style, Zeig Heil salute, before serenading them with another five minutes of "We won the war. We won the war... E-aye-adio... We won the war."

Going to cinema so often in the late 1940s and early '50s I did not need Technicolor to know that the ice-cold eyes of German actor Anton Diffring, strutting about the prisoner of war camp in his SS or Commandant uniform was telling me to beware our new European partners. In the early 1950s there seemed to be either a war or prisoner-of-war film on every week at the Grand. *The Way To The Stars, In Which We Serve, We Dive At Dawn, The Cruel Sea, The Cockleshell Heroes, The Wooden Horse, Albert RN, Stalag 17, The Colditz Story.*

It was like having a continual boy's serial, to remind us of the heroism and sacrifices made in the name of freedom.

Spike Milligan, who could never forgive Hitler for depriving him of five years of writing *Goon Show* scripts for BBC radio, gave us many of our laughs on the way to school. There was hardly a boy at Toxteth Tech who, at the drop of a hat, could not produce a repertoire of *Goon Show* characters. Major Bloodnok, Henry Crun, Minnie Bannister, Eccles and Bluebottle, were all impersonations that spontaneously leaped out of pupils' mouths in the classrooms of the most tormented of our teachers.

Once, during registration at Toxteth's second year annex in Garston, an easily led, Mr Blobby of a boy called Jerry Anderson, was bullied into being the first and only pupil to put on the voice of Eccles and reply with a "Y... urrp", instead of a plain "Yes", when the class names were read out. It was enough for Mr Parker to stop the roll call and take Anderson out into the corridor for a good morning thrashing. As Peter Sellers, deploying his suave, George Sander's voice to give us Hercules Grytpype Thynne, would say to the toadying Count Jim "Thighs" Moriarty, "You gullible, twisted, little fool, you!"

Our teachers were rich pickings for our fast-developing appreciation of cynicism and satire. There were still a few amazing old wankers, grimly holding on to teaching posts before the Sixties clearout of dead-wood brought a new professionalism and fresh ideas into the classroom. Major 'Pongo' Phillips, Head of English, was an Oxford man. However, that was before the First World War had mummified his brains with the sands of the Nile, rendering him incapable of teaching us anything which might help us pass our O Level exam.

"You boy. Whad'ycall... Sit up and get on with reading the next paragraph out to the class."

"Who me, Sir?"

"No not you. Whad'yacallhisname... the boy sitting next to you. Yes you at the front. Whad'ycall... Come out here, boy. I'll show you not to provoke me."

Pongo was past the modern retirement age and both his mind and manner were still seated on a camel in the middle of the Egyptian desert. With this scourge of the Turks pretending to be Lawrence of Arabia, rather than helping us get to university, I learned nothing of English grammar. Mind you, I could reel off the thirty verses of *Gray's Elegy Written On A Country Churchyard*, including the Epitaph!

The Pongo experience left me with dozens of poems tucked away in my head, which I was able to call upon, later in my own teaching career, to frighten pupils into a better focus for work. If the level of classroom noise became an obstacle to concentration I could always come away with the first verse of Keats's *Ode to a Nightingale*. The sudden silence of woodland before dawn suggested that the class had drunk copiously from a bucket of the poet's home-made hemlock. "You may well shrink into your seats, you noisy little sods. There are seven more verses where that came from... Or, would you prefer a couple of minutes of *Kubla Khan*, by Samuel Taylor Coleridge?" Whereas I loved poetry and found it invigorating, it seems to have the effect of a general anaesthetic on today's pupils, subduing them far better than the prescribed Ritalin and guaranteed to send even the most hyper into deep and undisturbed sleep.

Thanks to our inspiring English teacher, Geoff Williams, who ran school Drama, we had plays to discuss and perform in. We all suspected that he was gay, but it was never an issue in his relationship with pupils. He was both good to and for us. We went with him to the theatre to see *The Crucible* and *The Glass Menagerie*. He took the school cast of *Hobson's Choice* and *Pygmalion* to the cinema to see how Charles Lawton and Leslie Howard set definitive standards of performance for us to aim at. Geoff's friendship allowed us a peep into the unexamined, private world of the schoolmaster. He gave me some much-needed self-confidence and allowed us all to sample his sophisticated and cultured tastes in music, art and literature. He was the one member of staff who wanted to recognise the fact that we were maturing young men.

Geoff's friendship left me the precious legacy of having read the plays of Arthur Miller, Tennessee Williams and Eugene O'Neill. They taught me that the language, intelligence and imagination of Shakespeare had successfully migrated across the Atlantic. At last, I was offered a more wholesome bite at American literature than the Action Comics I had devoured as a child. I could now let Uncle Stan know that they were not the standard by which he should judge all transatlantic contributions to the English language!

Outside the classroom, if it was not drama inspiring us then it was the DIY music of skiffle, which dominated our activity. That is, with the exception of Peter Griffiths – Griff – who clearly had more refined musical tastes, preferring finger-style, classical guitar to the three chord tunes of Lonnie Donegan. Although he showed a clear disdain for Rock'n'Roll, he had a startling look-alike problem, which turned our walks to and from school into a true test of his musical integrity. The lantern-jawed, straw-blond sixth former was a dead-ringer for the pop star, Adam Faith. I did not rate Faith's celebrity. He was no more than an office boy and failed skiffler, like me, who had got lucky. However, he had been sharp enough to seize on an opportunity to make a career for himself out of nothing. Apparently, he had been the leader of The Worried Men skiffle group, down in Soho. I could make a good guess as to what they were worried about. His weak, put-upon vocal chords vibrated uneasily to a background of pizzicato strings, making him sound like Patrick Moore playing the xylophone without the aid of his monocle. Griff's affect on teenage girls, however, was amazing and being in his company was like having a fan club by association.

First schoolgirl: "Look, here he comes. Hello Adam."

Second schoolgirl: "Say what you want and I'll give it you, darling."

Third schoolgirl: "Wish you wanted my love… baby."

The pretty faces were all pressed to the railings… cheeks flattened and lips pouting through so invitingly it was all I could do to hold myself back from having a sample. Against my better judgement, I began to look forward to the shrieks of delight from the girls of St Hilda's, in Arundel Avenue, as Griff passed by with the rest of us in tow, leaving their silly, fluttering hearts pinned to the iron bars.

Unusual for seventeen-year-olds, we talked little about soccer. To Griff, Charlie and Brad, football was an irrelevance. However, in John P I had someone as passionately enslaved to the misfortunes of Liverpool FC as myself. We had little hope of impressing our companions as we bravely bore the cross of following a mediocre Second Division team, who were second-best to Everton and going nowhere. From my viewpoint on the Kop, the Reds' First Team shirts looked as washed out as were the hopes of some 50,000 supporters for a Championship-winning team. On the other hand, Manchester United were establishing their status as the dream team of not just the nation, but the whole footballing world:

Manchester,

Manchester United

A bouncing bunch of Busby Babes,

They deserve to be knighted

So went the catchy, calypso-style song played, incessantly, over the radio to annoy the fans of every other football team in the land. Unmoved by the passion of the masses for football, my companions were, nevertheless, shaken to the core by news, shouted down from a passing lorry, as we walked to school down Ullet Road one crisp February morning in 1958.

"Hey, lads. Have you heard the news? The Manchester United team have been wiped out in a plane crash at Munich Airport."

The driver had slowed to a curb crawl to solicit our undivided attention. With the passenger window wound right down, and with one hand on the wheel, he stretched his body across his cab, like a Manx TT pillion-rider struggling to balance the recklessness of his companion when taking hairpin bends.

"Worst of all... Duncan Edwards is dead!"

The man was, literally, beside himself in his desperation to repeat the ice-cold message to a word-of-mouth world, which knew not the joys of texting. To me, it was as numbing a piece of news as the death of Buddy Holly, in the same unfriendly month, a year later. It trashed radio's, earlier, breakfast bulletins about Mao's Great Leap Forward, the launch of another Russian Sputnik, and the less likely report that a mouse of a fishing nation, Iceland, had roared at British trawlermen in the disputed cod filled waters of the cold North Atlantic.

There was no mercy in the fact that the man's chilling words had exaggerated the scale of the tragedy, which on that snowbound runway, all but destroyed the greatest football team in England. Eight of United's young first team – all boys not that much older than us – were among the twenty-three dead. The manager, Matt Busby, clung to life for days in intensive care. Miraculously, he pulled through to rebuild a team of new Immortals, including Law, Best and Charlton and fulfil his dream of lifting the European Cup. Only then could the leg-weary shades of Duncan Edwards, Tommy Taylor, David Pegg, and the other much lamented Babes, cease their haunting of the Old Trafford pitch in search of the glory which should also have been theirs.

These never-to-be-forgotten lads were about to become football's first pop superstars and challenge the likes of Cliff Richard, Tommy Steele, and Adam Faith for the attention of the media and the idolatry of millions of teenagers. The world-class wing-half, Duncan Edwards, had more talent in one toenail clipping, than all the twitching sets of tortured tonsils paraded on the new, ITV Rock'n'Roll extravaganza, *Oh Boy!* It was on Jack Good's Saturday evening, teen rage show that Adam Faith would have the bloody cheek to sing his first UK No.1 hit, *"What Do You Want If You Don't Want Money?"* Any Manchester United fan – indeed any true football supporter – knew the answer to that!

CHAPTER 42

MONSIEUR TERRIER AND THE DINGLE TEDS

It was sometime in the spring of 1954. I was still in my first year at Toxteth Tech, located like some Wild West cavalry fort on the untamed frontier of notorious Liverpool 8 and the equally lawless Dingle. It was mid-morning interval, and I had just sat down against the sandstone brick wall of the schoolyard when a gang of Teddy boys made their spectacular incursion from the Colebroke Road gate. The visitation was an unexpected and unsavoury interruption to my only moment of real pleasure in the school day. This came at break time, when my ravenous appetite could be appeased with the daily treat of wolfing down Nan's tidily prepared snack of cheese and marmite sandwiches.

The post-war urban phenomenon of the Teddy boy, and growing public concern over the rising levels of juvenile delinquency, were regular topics of family conversation in the cosy, but unadorned, back living room at No.52 Borrowdale Road. It was an enlightening, if sometimes puzzling, forum for a small boy to be privy to. Mum and Nan would occasionally chip in, but the conversation was dominated by the three most important men in my life. Uncle Stan would often bamboozle me with golden shafts of erudition way over my head. More to my comprehension was the plain speaking of my uneducated, (by my uncle's high standards) but intelligent, father who, trained in the duties of wartime RAF ground crew, was often forced to recall his brother-in-law's Fleet Air Arm language of the stratosphere back down to earth with some common sense and a more modern, secular view of society. All would defer, however, to the patriarchal presence of Pop Thomas, whose strongly entrenched Edwardian perspective on life was now struggling to cope with the speed of unwelcome and unsettling social change.

"Do you know what these blighters need?" My granddad was speaking from behind the screen of his newspaper. He was busy digesting the unpalatable contents of an article about teenage gang violence from last night's *Liverpool Echo*. His voice spilled over from the reporter's words of condemnation for modern youth, as he made utterance from the comfort of his dilapidated leather armchair, carefully placed within accurate spitting distance of the constantly banked-up, roasting fire. The red-hot coals were religiously tended by Pop with his trusty steel poker. This duty allowed him, when the more decorous members of the family were out of the room, a clearer, steadier aim, with which to propel the occasional, nasty mouthful of Woodbine-generated phlegm into the sizzling bull's-eye of the leaping flames.

There was no reply to his first salvo of morning conversation. "Well, I'll tell you, seeing that you're all so dull today." The wireless twittered away in the background, and then went silent, perhaps anticipating one of his edifying late additions to the next Home Service news bulletin. "These so-called Teds are an affront to the name Edwardian," Pop continued from behind the dugout of his newspaper. "They should all get called up for National Service. Two years in the trenches with me and Billy Windsor would have filled the holes in their heads with a few bullets." The reference to his old drinking pal Billy Windsor was to remind us about the qualities of a "real hard case", who won the VC in the First World War for single-handedly destroying a German machine-gun nest. My dad, of course, went out of his way to remind me that you were not, truly, a hero if you did not know what you were doing, and Billy was, by general consensus, a few pence short of being the full shilling. Pop raised his head above his precious paper, to see what type of fish his angling for some attention had landed him. It was a Saturday morning, however, and there was no one with him in the house, but me. I was busy reading my freshly delivered *Eagle*, but still managed to cock an ear to every word the venerated old man uttered.

So, when six of my granddad's favourite hooligans appeared in the Toxteth Tech schoolyard that morning, I already had a clear frame of reference and some very good reasons for being apprehensive. I took a hard swallow on my cheese sandwich and dismissed all anxious thoughts of Ollie Clarkson's Chemistry test, due after break and guaranteed to be unrelated to any of the work done in class. My mind and gaze were now firmly fixed upon these gladiators of the back streets, as their fearsome reputation cut an uncontested pathway through the mêlée of excited pupils, who had caught the whiff of bloodshed. The gang was making for the small outside toilet at the far end of the school yard, to deliver summary execution on one of the senior boys who had been foolish enough to violate the jungle law of the Dingle.

A tom-tom message had been relayed to the hidden prey who, precariously balanced on the edge of a cold lavvy seat, was sucking his last lungful of comfort from a cadged butt-end of deadly, contraband Woodbine. He would have less than one minute's grace to choose between scaling the rusty, fractured drainpipe, stretching uncertainly upwards to a frightening drop over the school wall, or setting his face into a mask of stoic serenity to accept a likely dismembering in front of a few hundred ghoulish onlookers.

Each member of the gang was a showpiece specimen of the pedigree breed, in striking draped jackets with matching velvet lapels and pocket flaps, set above the regulation six-inch drainpipes.

"What do they call those pencil-thin jodhpurs they wear....even though they've never been near a horse in their lives?"

"They're called drainpipes, Pop."

"Is that what they put on to climb up rain spouts and break into people's bedrooms at night?" Pop claimed the skin-tight trousers had to be peeled off blood-starved thighs by foolish doting mothers. I was struggling to raise a smile at his lampooning of such a fearsome bunch of hatchet men. It was hard to imagine any one of these thugs pliantly draping himself across some dimly lit stair banister, to be relieved of his stubborn trousers, while gentle moonlight from the landing window played softly on the odious features of his scrawny arse.

More intimidating than hearsay reputation and dressing up to kill was the weaponry carried by each warrior member of the gang. The one who passed nearest to me had a crowbar in his left hand, leaving the other free to push any offending obstacle aside. Another had a bicycle chain wrapped around his clenched fists with the ends left dangling to rattle a venomous warning of approach against any passing railing or lamppost. One pace ahead of the rest, the leader of the pack was trying to contain a very large and uncivilised Alsatian, which was taxing every muscle against the taut length of dockers' rope, lashing it to its owner's hand. The encumbrance, choking tight at the dog's neck, seemed to give the animal an added appetite for the tasty-looking flesh of one or two of the plumper, short-trousered boys. "Heel, you bastard... Heel!" There was clearly a struggle for supremacy going on between the dog and its heartless-looking master, with the aggressive beast giving as good as it got. The rear was brought up by the smallest member of the gang, a monkey-like proto-type of Gene Vincent, displaying an amazing set of sideburns, successfully cultivated down to his shoulders. In his wake, he trailed a long and heavy chain, which looked like it had been hacked from the abandoned anchor of some passing cargo ship down on the nearby Cast Iron Shore.

The unwelcome news of our uninvited and unwholesome guests had, by this time, broken the siesta of the dozen or so teachers who took their morning tea and cakes in the small staffroom overlooking the rear of the school. Drawing the short straw by dint of his role as Toxteth's own Judge Dredd and deliverer of school justice, Mr Blair, Head of Geography, was forced to put down his half-eaten Eccles cake and rise from the comfort of the one, commandeered, armchair. He made his usual bold appearance on the rear entrance steps and rushed down to yet another routine policing of irksome unruliness. He was about to confront

318

something a little more testing of his mettle than the occasional classroom naughtiness of biddable little boys.

He pulled up short of a suicide mission when he got his first glance at the unsinkable nature of his target. Blair was no fool. He was quick to assess how his bristling moustache adding macho seriousness to a steely countenance, together with all those countless, wasted years of whacking thousands of small, pliant bottoms, had totally failed to prepare him for such a nemesis. He could imagine only one outcome to the collision course which his reputation had set him on. There would be the inevitable assault on both his dignity and pride. Even more painful would be the severe and humiliating kicking-in, witnessed by hundreds of his future customers for school punishment who, never again, would be so easily subdued by the mythology of his strong-man image and the mighty swish of his cane.

The gang's leader let out a few feet of slack in the taut rope, allowing the Alsatian a restrained leap in Blair's direction. His response was disappointing. To my Pop's way of thinking it was the waffle of a skedaddler. "I've more sense than to lower my dignity and get tangled up with the likes of your kind." This was the reply we would have expected from the likes of sappy Mr Ousby, or the decrepit First World War blusterer, Major 'Pongo' Phillips, scourge of all infidels south of Gibraltar. We were at least expecting some low-budget movie thrills from the school's own Action Man, with his flailing right arm.

Surely, the tweed jacket would be removed and handed to a second. He would then take time to confound his opponents by carefully rolling up his shirtsleeves, before taking the upright stance of an Oxford man trained in the noble art of fisticuffs. It would not, of course, be some unrefined dogfight or street free-for-all, but an exhibition of sporting prowess, under the Marquis of Queensbury rules, and a lesson to all bounders and scallywags. I was desperately hoping for a re-run of my favourite movie, *Gunga Din*, and the bit where Cary Grant bobs around, desperate to hand out a bare-knuckles pasting to Victor McLaglen. I dropped my head, saddened by Mr Blair's abject surrender, and disappointed that yet another one of my authority figures had feet of clay.

One of Pop's favourite expressions was, "Cometh the hour, cometh the man." Suddenly, it meant so much more than the keenly anticipated remark, down at the Old Farm Field, in Sefton Park, when he would summon himself to take over the flagging state of the bowling, with Uncle Stan at one hundred and sixty five not out! The new French student teacher, Monsieur Terrier, appeared from nowhere to rescue my limp assessment of the manliness of the teaching profession. Until this defining moment of his brief stay at Toxteth, the young Frenchman had been universally declared a "Froggie puff". Pupils had strained to listen in to the whispered conversations of other teachers, as they made regular comments about the continental dandy, who was livening up the stuffy school corridors. Their relayed gossip had delivered us choice new words and phrases like "effeminate" and "effete". Most intriguing of all was, "He smells like a ponce's handkerchief", which sent us scurrying off for the nearest dictionary. To sexually curious twelve-year-old boys, such irresponsible talk suggested that Monsieur Terrier was already a few stages beyond a "mammy's boy" and well up the list of persons you had been warned by your Sunday school teacher to keep a very watchful eye on. Worst of all for me, bought up in a sporting household and well tuned to the exploits of Finney, Compton, Zatepek and Marciano, Monsieur Terrier had played netball for France! What more evidence did I need? The man was clearly only a sit-down pee away from being lifted for soliciting in one of Liverpool's infamous city lavatories.

Unable to construct any sort of meaningful sentence in their, newly crowned, Queen's English, the six hooligans from the Dingle would have made no sense of Monsieur Terrier reverting to his native tongue. "Come here you little pieces of shite," he commanded, giving them the added puzzlement of his Marseilles accent. My first year French was good enough to pick up "little pieces" and, of course, "merde" was one of the first rude words we had scurried away to discover in our new, French pocket dictionaries.

The Teds were still in cultural shock when the pretty-faced Frenchman sprang at the one with the heavy chain. One amazingly deft body-movement had the thug disarmed and pinned to the ground. The Alsatian reacted, snarling and snapping its pleasure that, at last, someone wanted to make a meal of things. Monsieur Terrier, however, was more than a match for the junkyard Rin Tin Tin. In the style of a Parc du Prince fullback, he leapt up from one vanquished opponent and booted the brute-of-a-dog under its chin and into touch. The animal whined, and then whimpered its notice to quit. It lay down, head between its outstretched paws, and stared straight ahead, as if its brain was getting an unrequested, action-replay of the whole sorry incident.

The school bell sounded the end of the contest, and I was back into an anti-climax of apprehension for the chemistry test in Ollie's smelly lab. The leader of the gang had collapsed in on himself, like some dying star, sucking the dog into a black hole of humiliating defeat. The proudly painted notice, "Love me love my dog", would have to be removed from the front door of his house, where the broken beast had, until now, lived a privileged canine life as one of the tribe. He and his much-chastened brute were led off with the other fallen Teds, back into the school building. They were now being surrounded by a phalanx of teachers who, suddenly, felt it safe enough to show their faces. The remnant of the gang was left to make an ignominious withdrawal from the schoolyard and await a speedy visit from the local police. There was no outbreak of spontaneous applause for the brave Monsieur Terrier. Perhaps, it was because we did not want Blair and any of the other latecomers to be the beneficiaries of such acclaim.

Monsieur Terrier, where are you now? I would dearly like to tell you how you still have a cult status inside my head. It turned out that you were fooling with us a little, *n'est ce pas*? You were, in fact, a Judo black belt were you not? That is not the point, however, is it? No, most important to me, was the lesson of life you taught me that day. Never again would I judge anyone on the hearsay of others. Never again would I underestimate someone, nor let superficial appearances prejudice a natural unfolding of the truth. Not even if the person was a gently spoken young French teacher, with film star good looks, who was inattentive enough to let mad Gordon Bain come out from his seat in class and stand behind him at his desk to sharpen a pencil. I will never forget Bain's raving, unfocused eyes, staring from behind M Terrier's head at the transfixed faces of his gob-smacked classmates. He seemed to take an eternity to put a needle-sharp point on a tiny pencil stub with a two foot machete! The deadly jungle knife had been endlessly removed from his trouser leg and then swished to and fro, lower and lower, nearer and nearer to the oblivious Frenchman's precious curls. Gordon Bain was soon to realise just how perilously close to death he had come that day!

CHAPTER 43

NOBBY TAKES A TUMBLE:

"Can you tallest boys move a few places along into the centre of the row please? That's lovely... Could you get that little fellow who's completely lost between the two Billy Bunters at the end of the fourth row to move down one step. OK, that's fine... There are a couple of boys down on the second row not wearing school blazers. Can someone move them to either end of the row... The big lad up there? Yes, you with the Everton scarf around your neck... Take it off and hand it to the teacher."

The man who turned up every year to take the Toxteth Tech school photograph was usually the star of a very unspectacular show. This Cecil Beaton of the City Education Department sported a pronounced limp which, along with a tripod and moving lens camera, he took into every school on his Merseyside itinerary. One leg was very much shorter than the other and had a boot on the end of it which could have been nicked from Boris Karloff, while he was having a monster nap between film takes. It was mesmerising to watch him go about his business of arranging pupils into the most presentable composition a monochrome mind could conjure up; his body rising and falling... up... down, up... down, with the hypnotic timing of a fun-fair merry-go-round. The colourful impediment added a little interest to the otherwise dull routine of four hundred boys remaining still as statues, while the limping camera man placed us in an order of height and smartness of appearance to reflect most credit on the public image of the school.

With the rest of my third year classmates, I filed into one of the middle rows of a hastily erected grandstand of platforms and benches. The older fifth and sixth year boys were positioned and ready for the off on the highest back rows of an impressive bank of terracing, which gave the narrow school yard the look of the final furlong at Aintree. I stood watching and waiting as the school's most presentable first year pupils took up their places behind the front seats reserved for the twenty or so teachers.

This was an opportunity for the teachers to parade in their full academic regalia. It was only on occasions like this, and at the splendiferous presentation of school prizes in the Liverpool Philharmonic Hall, that a discerning pupil, brought up by a Keeble College man, could pick out the Oxbridge graduates from the redbrick brigade. No such scrutiny could be made of the coloured, fur-trimmed academic hoods of the PE and Technical teachers, who were sorely disadvantaged in having to dress up in nothing more distinguishing than a training college blazer and tie. Such casualness betrayed a lack of scholarship in the days when Firsts were awarded only in leap years to a glittering few, and Lower Seconds were the common currency preserving the 2.1 status of most university lecturers. To have an Oxford or Cambridge Third in the staff room of one the great city grammar schools, such as the Liverpool Institute or the Collegiate, must have been a severe handicap to being treated like a fellow member of the human race.

"At last! Right everyone... I think we're ready to take your photograph now." The man with the limp took a minute to explain how the slowly travelling lens would pan across the faces of hundreds of boys, ordered to do nothing for the next few minutes other than contemplate its unblinking eye. "It's very important that you all remain quite still for the camera to sweep its way across the whole school. Oh, dear... Oh, dear me." Suddenly, the photographer remembered that someone very important was missing. "We can't begin without your headmaster, can we?"

Toxteth's assembled ranks relaxed into low conversation as we continued our restless wait for the commander-in-chief to make a grand entrance in front of his troops. Stanley Conway, or 'Nobby' to the pupils, got his name from a glistening baldhead, which added an aerodynamic look to his aquiline features. Apart from the ritual address at morning assembly, and his regular monitoring of the flow of bodies along the corridors at break times, he spent most of the school day in his small, wood-panelled study off the main staircase. Pint-sized and slightly built Nobby was always on the run, seeming to be in a constant struggle with an outsize flowing gown, which was forever slipping off his shoulders. He was a fair man in his dealings with the pupils and took a personal interest in the writing of their reports. A well-respected JP, he had an over-riding passion to see justice and fair play precede a good whacking.

"Stand up the boy in the front desk with his face covered in ink."

Nobby had been summoned down from his office to administer summary justice in the classroom of Mr Ward who, after a minute's absence, had returned to find a boy with his face splattered in ink. Such a gross and mystifying act of criminal behaviour quite clearly required the instincts and analytical flair of the nearest thing the school had to a legal brain, namely Stanley Conway JP. Nobby would certainly be unfamiliar with Tyrone Power slashing his signature over Basil Rathbone's face in *The Mark of Zoro*. However, the unmistakable sign of vengeance zigzagging from the boy's forehead down to his chin produced an echo from the silent cinema of his younger days, when Douglas Fairbanks Snr.

etched his version of the masked swordsman's calling card on every villain's front door in nineteenth century Spanish California. "Sit down boy. You look like Montezuma II, before he went out with his Aztec army to fight Cortés." Nobby drew the teacher to one side and whispered, "I have seen enough to suggest that well-merited revenge might be the motive here. Now, may I ask the perpetrator of this act to, please, stand up?"

When I rose from my seat, the Head of French clutched at his Fair Isle jumper in shock and disbelief. The man had taken me to be a first year of promise and a boy beyond reproach; the type of pupil who gave him a scrap of encouragement in his impossible task of getting Toxteth pupils to speak a foreign language with a little more flair than they applied to their own native tongue.

Nobby seemed to recognise me. "Is it Williams?... The boy to whom I handed over all those subject prizes at the Philharmonic Hall only a few weeks ago! There is a strange, somewhat perverse, aspect to this case, I fear, Mr Ward."

Displaying the circumspection of King Solomon, adjudicating the case of a eunuch accused of making the Queen of Sheba's handmaiden pregnant, Nobby opened my defence. "Why did you do this Williams? Were you in any way provoked?" This was my cue to wax lyrical on how my loose shoelace had been furtively removed under the anaesthetic of a tense preoccupation with an important test and then how, disbelievingly, I had watched it being stuffed into the inkwell on the desk. Finally, I painted the vivid picture of bottled-up frustration, and righteous indignation in wrenching the shoelace from its inky pot to produce a piece of spontaneous expressionism fit for exhibiting in the Walker Art Gallery.

Nobby stared hard at the decorated face of my victim. He put his hand up to his mouth, concealing his enjoyment of an image of the boy's gob-smacked amazement, which had just flashed across his mind. Showing only the faintest trace of a thin smile, he fingered his fine features as if he was about to take pleasure in his next utterance. "Do you disagree with anything Williams has said about this bizarre occurrence?" The word "bizarre" was deliberate and suitably beyond the stunted vocabulary of my Steble Street classmate.

"No Sir," he wisely replied.

"Does your answer signify compliance... or were you, indeed, the instigator in this matter of the ink?" These were the glorious days of teaching when you could baffle, even terrorise, pupils with big words. Two more beauties in the same breath finished off any desire my classmate may have had for a fair trial.

"Having listened to the most salient facts of this peculiar case I find Williams' action to be one meriting a great deal of understanding... This is, clearly, a case of poetic justice." With that pronouncement, he swept out of the classroom, his gown already making its own way back to his study.

Stanley Conway's years of sitting on the magistrates' bench had impressed upon him the need to teach his pupils to speak Queen's English, if only to enable a few of them to avoid a jail sentence once they left school. "I can no longer put up with listening to your pathetic attempts to sing the morning hymns. Your appalling pronunciation has dragged me from my office to prevent any further savaging of the school hymn-book." Mr Ward was the unfortunate teacher taking the morning assembly. He lowered his head, ashamed to have presided over such unchallenged disrespect for the language of the King James Version of the English Bible, which had just been read out to us by one of the senior prefects.

"Hand me a hymn-book, please, Mr Ward... Thank you... Now where's the first hymn I heard you desecrating... Ah, here we are." With the clear diction which had sentenced so many of his fellow citizens to a few months behind bars, he began to read the first morning hymn:

"For the beauty of the earth,

For the beauty of the skies,

For the love which from our birth

Over and around us lies."

"The word at the end of the first line, you uncivilised lot, is earth. Do you hear me? Earth... Earth... Not EERTH!"

I could see Geoff Williams, the English and Drama teacher, who was standing at the side of the hall, trying his best to control a fit of Welsh giggles.

"The same instruction applies to the second hymn, which you also brutalised a few minutes ago:

"Now Thank We All Our God,

With hearts and minds and voices."

God, in His wisdom, has chosen to bless even Liverpudlians with voices so they might be understood as well as heard by others. I concede that none of you can sing like Gigli, or speak like the Talking Clock. I am certain, however, that the Almighty will not thank you for the unholy, Dingle desecration of hymns which have Christianised countless millions of His peoples, from the icy shores of Hudson Bay, to the sun-kissed islands of the South Seas. Now let me find the most offensive of your mis-pronunciations... Yes here we are. Will you all look at the third and fourth lines of the first hymn:

> *"Who wondrous things hath done*
>
> *In whom His world rejoices."*

May I remind you that it is His world... Not the vulgar WEEERLD of your vernacular!"

The effort Nobby had put into the extended vowel sound almost forced his false teeth from a mouth which had the hinged look of Archie Andrews about it. Stanley Conway had started something he knew he might not be able to finish. Nevertheless, he pressed on in his finest diction.

"Now, repeat after me... World... World... Earth... Earth!"

His incantation sounded so purifying and good to his ears that he served it up again.

"World... World... Earth... Earth!"

Back came the eternal Scouse reply, with an extra helping from mouths gaping wide like the Queensway entrance to the Mersey Tunnel.

"Weerld!... Weerld!... Weerld!... Eeerth! Eeerth! Eeerth!"

Enough was enough. Stanley Conway's mortarboard was snatched from the lectern and placed firmly back on his head. He could see humiliation staring at him from four hundred faces, and handed the task of being Professor Henry Higgins back to Mr Ward. We had several extended assemblies over the next week, but it did not make one single boy more honey-mouthed in his morning praise of God. We were all hopeless, Cast Iron Shore cases. Fast-forward forty years and you had 400 applicants for a Harry Enfield "Three Wackers" sketch. Education may be able to take the boy out of Liverpool but it can never take Liverpool out of the boy!

I liked Nobby Conway. He was a decent, approachable man. Born in the last decade of the Victorian era and carrying many of the values of that age around with him under his flapping cloak, he made a good fist of trying to understand where this post-war generation of young people were coming from.

He was out of his seat like a greyhound from its trap when I took a header off the stage on the first night of the school production of Shaw's *Pygmalion*. At the end of that term he wrote in my school report: "As Henry Higgins, he surpassed himself on the stage." My father who thought he knew a thing or two about actors and their habits, read the comment and remarked: "Surpassed yourself... eh? You must have been travelling at some speed to do that. I presume that he is referring to your bout of Alec Guinness over-acting, when you tripped and flew off the stage, to great applause and much concern. The *South Liverpool*

Weekly News got it wrong when the reporter asked 'Is this the new Albert Finney?' He should have asked 'Is this the new Norman Wisdom?'"

The ordeal of waiting for Nobby Conway to turn up and get his picture taken with us was nearly over. "The headmaster is coming. I have just caught a glimpse of him on the steps of the school's rear entrance." With mortarboard at the jauntiest of angles and his black gown flapping like a bat's wings, he danced down the back steps with the light-footedness of Jimmy Cagney in *Yankee Doodle Dandy*. The sun was shining... his boys were waiting for him... he felt like getting his photo taken... the day was looking good! What both headmaster and pupils were not aware of was the death trap which awaited him at the bottom of the school steps. Earlier that morning, thirty sacks of best coking coal had been delivered down the coal hole and into the boiler room. By accident or design, the steel manhole cover had been left off.

Below the school yard, in the choking atmosphere of coal dust and furnace heat Crewe, the janitor, turned abruptly from his fierce shovelling to see a bleached, sepulchral leg sliding down the coal chute and into the cellar. A First World War infantryman's reflexes had not deserted him. Instinctively, he yelled "Bosch!" and took the polished edge of his shovel to it. Well, that's the story John P liked to tell in the pub, years later when we began re-creating the myths of schooldays.

It was a fact, however, that the whole school witnessed Stanley Conway's leg going down the open coal-hole. Everyone stood in freeze-frame, not knowing what to do next. The poor man rolled about in great agony, clutching his leg and trying to stifle the kind of sounds which normally emanated from behind the closed door of his study during the morning punishment session. Suddenly, Mr Ward remembered the job application he had in the post, and for the sake of a decent reference leaped up from a front seat to rescue his stricken boss. Picking Nobby up in his arms, he carried him back up the school steps, in the style of Bella Lugosi returning home with a tasty bit of supper.

The school photo of 1955 was finally taken. Several members of staff were missing, including Nobby Conway and a few other senior teachers who wanted to be around their stricken Caesar. The photograph was printed, but never given out for pupils to take home.

"I'm afraid you can't allow the pupils to take this photo home with them, Mr Conway." The school secretary had been chosen to be the bearer of bad news to her recovering boss.

"I'm not that indispensable, am I, Mrs Jenkins?"

"It's not your missing face that is causing concern, Mr Conway. It's the fact that one boy seems to be on the photo twice… at both ends of the back row."

As soon as the moving camera had captured his image at the beginning of its slow arcing progress across the hundreds of fixed expressions, one daring boy had dropped down to the ground behind the raised benches. Dashing along behind the backs of his schoolmates, he climbed back up into place at the other end of the row to squeeze his face into a second mug shot. Stanley Conway put on his glasses and bent over the photo which had been placed on his desk.

"Where is the boy Mrs Jenkins? At this end you say… and also over here, at the far end of the row. Do we have a transmogrification Mrs Jenkins?"

"Yes… Whatever you say, Mr Conway."

"Ah! Not quite, Mrs Jenkins. I'm looking at the lad on the far right. There is what appears to be a balloon-like face… but without any features!"

Not satisfied with his act of sabotage, the boy had blown a giant bubble of gum to create the camouflage of a Bertie Bassett-of-a-face, but devoid of Bertie's tasty, liquorice mouth, eyes and nose! He was quickly identified by the enormous Desperate Dan of a chin, which had refused to be eclipsed by a packet of Hollywood Stars bubble gum.

Over the past forty years I have stood in wearied silence for dozens of school photos. Always the big problem has been trying to raise a smile from people who have to return to a disrupted lesson with a class of unwilling pupils. In the Fifties no one would dare to – some would not care to – raise a titter if the headmaster came a cropper like that. Today, a similar misfortune would have the whole school whistling and cheering. There would be shouts of "What's he like, eh… Just what is he like?" The hi-tech majority would make sure they captured the moment on their mobile cameras for world-wide distribution on the web.

CHAPTER 44

THE PIVVY: A WORLD OF PEEPSHOW AND MOUNTAIN MUSIC

The Pavilion, or "Pivvy" as we affectionately called it, sat quietly back from the stir of narrow pavements and busy, small shops at the Tunnel Road end of Lodge Lane. To my post-war generation, growing up in the peace and freedom of the Smithdown Road-Sefton Park continuum of neighbourhoods, the Pivvy was a magical curiosity; a left-over from a fast-fading Edwardian world of old-fashioned values and tastes. Well-timed for my unchaste, teenage turn of mind, the Pivvy's programme of entertainment had sunk to the level of the peepshow world of dirty old men and their seedy pleasures.

"Let's try and get into the Pivvy sometime this week... The nudes are back!"

"A whole bunch of us will never get past the ticket office. We'll have to go on different nights and one at a time."

"Don't worry about that," said a streetwise scally from Park Road called Mowie. "You could get the whole school in at one go, if you wanted to... No one gives a toss." This inspired Moses Street turn of phrase produced a bout of raucous, dirty laughter. "There were boys a lot younger than us in the audience a couple of weeks ago!"

Now in my second year at Toxteth Tech – renamed Toxteth High School in the summer holidays – I was listening to the Monday morning break time conversation of a group of worldly-wise classmates who, in their dreams, had sailed round Cape Horn backwards, having first sampled the delights of all the brothels in French Indo-China on the way home to Liverpool 8. Mowie continued to entertain his salivating classmates with dripping descriptions of the selection of silent, motionless, nude women he had been privileged to ogle at on his last visit to the Pivvy. For me, a secret trip to the Pivvy carried the grave risk of giving Uncle Stan the fit of an Old Testament prophet. However, with every new and hornier reporting of such readily accessible sexual delights, it became an irresistible urge to sit comfortably within the protective darkness of the Pavilion's auditorium and cast my eager eyes on a bevy of women Danny Kaye would describe as being "as naked as the day that they were born."

"Have you seen what is on the bill again at the Pavilion? Just look at what is being served up for music hall entertainment." From his fireside chair in the back living room, Pop was about to tell us, whether we liked it or not. "According to the *Echo* blockhead reporter, here, the Pavilion's entertainment is defined as 'erotic and tasteful'." My grandfather lowered the newspaper onto his lap. We sat for a moment in silent anticipation until he pulled the switch on a very long stare into infinity and looked over his specs at my Nan. "Is this the society I was dragooned into defending in the mud of Belgium?" The curiosity of a twelve-year-old for matters that should not, yet, concern him had been aroused by Pop's use of the word "erotic".

I never thought of my Pop as being, in any way, religious. The Bible was not a book this extremely literate man would choose for his fireside reading. Neither did he pay any attention to his son, my uncle, leading the family in grace at mealtimes. Save for the odd family christening and a couple of weddings, I never saw him attend church. However, a quick gander at the Pivvy's programme for the coming week had him contriving the tortured expression of St Benedict catching a monastic brother secretly scoffing a pork pie behind the altar during Lent. From his lexicon mind he fished out another couple of fruity words to appeal to my awakening libido. "Erotic isn't a word this fool of a reporter understands. This type of entertainment is nothing but depravity and moral turpitude." I had once heard saintly Uncle Stan use the word depravity when, out of intellectual curiosity, he had picked up my dad's *News of the World* and subjected his pure heart to the hair-raising contents of its lurid reporting. The religious tone of our family life was set by Uncle Stan alone. The nearest my own father ever got to being in any way religious was to take me to see *The Robe* and then only because of his fascination with the new, wide-screen Cinemascope.

My father was drawn to the *News of the World's* front-page motto "All human life is here." What a Sunday morning pleasure ground of titillation it provided. Its succinct, understated catchphrase of journalistic intent also signalled why it was forbidden reading to me. I would, nevertheless, sneak behind the lines of my uncle's censorship into its world of murder, prostitution, blackmail and corruption; not to mention the preposterous threat posed to Hollywood leading ladies by Errol Flynn's "18 inches of dangling flesh". My ears fairly pricked up, therefore, when I heard the temptingly tasty word "depravity" being repeated by Pop.

"Moral turpitude" did not seem to have a filthy enough ring about it to excite me quite as much. It sounded more like something God used to clean his brushes, when he decorated the living room of one of His many mansions in heaven. Pop's advocacy of an elevated code of personal behaviour did not allow any peeping at bare nipples and hairy arses, but fell short of adding the guzzling of a barrel of draught Bass to his long list of taboos. He certainly sent out mixed signals. Had he not dressed his language in a cloak of Victorian respectability, but simply said that what was on at the Pivvy was a load of tits and bums, I would have risked an exorcism and booked my ticket for the next show.

Given the natural inclination of most fourteen-year-old boys to seek any excuse for a good wank I felt compelled, before the end of the school term, to have a nibble at this local feast for lecherous Liverpudlians. Much more satisfying than any fair-ground side-show, it involved the audience, in between a turgid flow of end-of-the-pier variety acts, being treated to a sequence of tableaux where naked women posed like Greek statues, frozen in body as well as time.

"Can you see anything? Can you see their fannies?... 'Cos if you can't it's not worth risking getting into trouble for."

"You can see their hairs. If you've got a pair of binoculars you could count every one!"

"Fuckin' great, eh... Better than my dad's *Health and Efficiency* where all the fannies are brushed out."

"But are you sure we can get in?"

"Us... get in? It's more bloody difficult to get into a Frankenstein film and it's fuckin' cheaper. Boris Karloff may scare the tits off some people, but he doesn't give you a hard-on for ninepence."

Within a few months I plucked up the nerve to go to the Pivvy behind the backs of the guardians of my soul at No.52. The bashful conscience I took with me into the theatre was quickly sucked to the edge of his perch on my shoulder, bug-eyes out on stalks, searching for the slightest movement of naked flesh in one of the tiring, statuesque females. As far as the law was concerned, if the lovely ladies did not flex a single muscle, it passed for Art. Any hint of movement, however, turned the whole thing into pornography and the local magistrates could rush in a posse of policemen and close the theatre. Boys took peashooters, whilst those with the guile and ingenuity of John Lennon smuggled in catapults to ensure a lively movement of torso, hopefully followed by a lingering look at a proud pair of chilled nipples, or a quick flash of forested crotch.

In a sad and odious parallel to our worshipful fascination with the female body, dotted all around us in the darkness of the afternoon matinee performance I was aware of a collection of solitary, rain-coated figures, slumped well down into their seats. These were the dirty old men of a mother's worst nightmare. Some were not so old you could gain comfort from their decrepitude. Indeed, they were all disturbing and scary enough to keep at a safe distance. We knew what they were up to, but couldn't speak about it until we were on a bus and well away from the place. I could not bring myself to look too closely at the respectable enough office types, sat with their flies undone, jerking-off into handkerchiefs under the cover of strategically placed trilby hats. Big John P once spotted a sad old sod using his bowler hat for cover. He must have been a member of the Orange Lodge; probably one of the local magistrates, with a whistle ready to blow if he didn't come before the ice creams!

At Christmas time, the real spirit of the theatre returned to the Pavilion, in the shape of a family pantomime. The biggest and newest stars of variety were always in residence at the Empire or Royal Court, in town. Nevertheless, the Pivvy was on our doorstep and some famous radio stars like Derek Roy and Issy Bonn, as well as great veterans of the music hall such as Robb Wilton, turned out to reprise their acts. Pop had been an unsuccessful song-writer for the old music hall. Indeed, in the late 1940s he was still receiving acceptable cheques from The Performing Rights Society. Out there, in some God-forsaken place, where the sun had not yet fully set on the British Empire, a tea-tanned remnant of some "It Ain't Half Hot Mum" jungle concert-party must have been desperate enough to be singing one of his comic songs. It was Pop, therefore, who made sure the family's cultural experience was annually enriched by a trip to the panto.

"We're not going to the pantomime this year, Stanley."

My face fell to my boots. I couldn't have felt more despondent had Adolf Hitler burst onto the wireless to say "Hello playmates! The reports of my death in a Berlin bunker were just a bad joke… I'm here to let you know that my lads are taking over Britain tomorrow and within a week you'll be reading Mein Kampf instead of the Beano." I looked forward to the family Christmas treat, ever since my first annual visit to the Royal Court two years earlier. Watching Albert Modley, Norman Evans, and the young Ken Dodd was a magical experience. I sat propped up in the gods, mesmerised by the toy theatre antics taking place on the diminished stage below.

"Don't look so glum, young fella. We're off to something special this year, instead. You know how much you like *Rocky Mountain Rhythm* on the radio. Well, this Christmas it will magically relocate itself from its log cabin home on the Light Programme to the equally unlikely setting of the Pavilion in Lodge Lane."

"Is Big Bill Campbell coming to the Pivvy?"

"Yes siree. You'll be able to see him in the flesh surrounded by all his Rocky Mountain friends. As Big Bill would say, 'It'll be mighty fine… mighty fine!'"

"Big Bill Campbell and his *Rocky Mountain Rhythm* was the talk of the school playground at Dovedale. OK, so these hillbillies weren't Hopalong

Cassidy but, together with *Riders of the Range*, they were the nearest thing you could get to having cowboys on steam radio. I am, therefore, as certain as I can be that Wild West fanatic John Lennon, with his passion for the sounds of the accordion and the harmonica, would have pestered his snobbish Aunt Mimi to let soft-hearted Uncle George take him the three mile tram journey on the 5w tram from Woolton to the Pivvy for the 1948 Christmas Show, even though she would regard it as an evening of vulgar, vaudeville entertainment.

Like me he would have spent the tram journey home contemplating the sight and sounds of the "Yodelling Buckaroo" and "Sergeant O'Doherty of the Mounties", who could summon up a chorus of Redcoats at the flick of a radio switch!

I can hear John's Uncle George asking, "And what did you like best of all?"

For me it was the little Western dramas in between the musical acts: the trick shooting and skills with the lasso, but not for John.

"I liked the man with his Old Squeeze Box best."

He would have been referring to accordionist Ronnie Brohen, who had the whole theatre audience clapping their hands and tapping their feet to the rhythm of home-made music.

The Pivvy's days as a music hall theatre may have been numbered, but throughout the Fifties it continued to remain a part of our neighbourhood culture. The nude shows were memorable, but so were the superior, late night jazz concerts with the Ken Colyer and Chris Barber bands. During his twelve-month sojourn at Liverpool Art School, Lennon couldn't resist taking some college pals back to the dying theatre. Here he introduced them to one of his favourite comedians, the great Robb Wilton, whose style of inventive, ridiculous verse was meat and drink to his own surreal sense of humour:

He said, "I'll punch your head!"

I said, "Whose?"

He said, "Yours."

I said, "Mine?"

He said, "Yes."

I said, "Oh!"

He said, "Want a fight?"

I said, "Who?"

He said, "You!"

I said, "Me?"

He said, "Yes."

I said, "No!"

Robb Wilton: Monologue extract

Robb Wilton and my Pop knew one another. Born in the same year, 1881, they grew up to be equally partial to a skinful of draught Bass in one of the local pubs in Lodge Lane. Pop's failure as a music hall songwriter must have left him a little envious of Wilton, who became a huge stage success in the 1930s and '40s. In his prime, Robb Wilton often came home to star at his local theatre, but he must have been in his late-seventies and living near the Pivvy in virtual retirement when John Lennon took in one last reminder of the wonderfully nonsensical Wilton monologues which influenced Lennon's own whimsical writing:

I call my budgie Jeffrey

My granddad's name's the same

I call him after granddad

Who had a feathered brain.

He flies about the room sometime

And sits upon my bed

And if he's really happy

He does it on my head.

John Lennon: extract from The Fat Budgie – "A Spaniard in the Works"

The main auditorium of the Pavilion Theatre was burned down during the Toxteth riots of 1981. Sadly for Liverpool's cultural heritage, this wonderful relic from the genuine old music hall is no more. What remains has been re-fashioned into a bingo hall. The only "Full House" now is the one marked down on the card of a screeching, bleached-blonde beautician, who is going to blow her £5,000 winnings on a ten-day, girlie holiday in Ibiza. Access to the Internet and the purchase of magazines so explicit they would put a lad from the 1950s off his dinner for a week, have robbed young teenagers of the joys of a stumbling, fumbling path to sexual knowledge. Whenever I take a long, reflective look at one of Renoir's deliciously mature and fleshy nudes I can, happily, think back to some of the ample females I had the privilege to gaze upon, in the magical days of the Pivvy's decline as a focus of local culture.

CHAPTER 45

SKIFFLING AT THE PIVVY WITH LENNON

The Pavilion Theatre closed down in the 1960s and today any visitor would fail to take a second glance at the tarted-up façade. However, its leftover remains from the heyday of the Victorian music hall have many stories, which the dumb, retentive stones would dearly love to tell. "Listen. Do you want to know a secret?" Words they would want to whisper in the ear of any wide-eyed Beatle fan passing by, on their Pilgrim's Progress through a Holy Land of Beatlemania. They groan and sigh for someone, simply, to put up the commemorative plaque saying, "John Lennon made his first stage appearance here in April 1957 with his group The Blackjacks – Stan Williams and The Satellites were there too!"

I went to answer the knock on the front door of No.52 Borrowdale Road. It was Brian Hollins who lived across the street at No.51.

"Did you see the advert in the *Echo* last night? There's goin' to be a big talent contest at the Pivvy next month."

"A talent contest?... Well I suppose I could climb into a pair of me Nan's black tights, stick a cushion up the back of me jumper and give 'em 'Now is the winter of our discontent'."

"Yeah and with that nose you wouldn't need a false one, like Olivier, to win. Seriously, they're allowin' skiffle groups to take part as well as singers and dancers. This is our chance... I think we should have a go."

It was the early spring of 1957 and the management of the Pivvy, struggling to maintain a vestige of dignity in what were the death-throes of the old music hall, but desperate to put a few bums on seats, had begun to live dangerously. Rather unwisely, in a city so littered with wonderfully absurd personalities, they were inviting all who believed they had talent to a Saturday-morning audition for a forthcoming Carroll Levis-style "Discovery Show". What an irresistible challenge to your typical Scouser, assured at the Temple of the Mersey Muse that an adenoidal, catarrh-ridden voice would hold audiences spellbound; maliciously misinformed that, underneath the plumber's overalls, there lurked a personality and a line of tatifilarious patter in the true Wacker tradition of Wilton, Askey, Ray and Dodd.

"I hear Edna's going to enter and sing Doris Day's *Ready Willin' and Able*... 'cos I have it on good authority that she's all three and she doesn't charge much either... Is that right Edna?" The other girls laugh and there are sly winks from the men at the table in the staff canteen.

"You hard-faced sod!... You should have a go yerself. With that Tab Hunter crew-cut you've been given by some mad, Apache barber you could sing *Young Love*". Dave's new all-American-boy haircut was as horrendous as his voice. Like Tab Hunter, who never had another chart success after his 1957 smash hit and went back to making B movies, Dave knew his limitations; a thousand other mad Scousers didn't.

Skiffle had been created for a bit of interval fun in the rather highbrow background of the jazz clubs. In 1956, Decca released a Chris Barber jazz novelty number, *Rock Island Line* with banjo player, Lonnie Donegan, as the lead vocalist. Throughout 1956, the BBC gave the record plenty of airtime and it was a smash hit, selling one million copies by the end of 1957. My pal Brian across the street bought Donegan's first 78 and so did John Lennon. This was a train we all wanted to ride!

Rock'n'Roll had arrived, Hurricane Rita-style, in 1955/56 with Bill Haley's *Rock Around The Clock* and Elvis's *Heartbreak Hotel*. However, the demi-gods of the new music and culture were way out of reach across the Atlantic. Filling the gap for a brief two or three years, while British rock music found its feet, came the phenomenon of Lonnie Donegan and skiffle. Thousands of us got the urge to make music, with most not having a clue about what to do! It was a whirlwind of DIY music, which caught teenage boys up into a fantasy world of pretending to be musicians. In its style, skiffle was ridiculously unpretentious music and open to a disarming ridicule. No one did it better than Peter Sellers:

"I'm here in the studio speaking to Mr Lennie Goonigan, the renowned King of Skiffle... Mr Goonigan, the words of your songs are derived from the Deep South. Have you ever been to the Deep South?"

"Yeah man... I've been all over the Deep South man. I've been to Brighton, Portsmouth, Truro, Penzance... I've done the lot man!"

"What are your songs about?"

"I sing songs of the people and the peasants, man."

"Um, Yes. Very appropriate for a man in a fifty guinea suit!"

"Puttin' on... puttin' on... puttin' on the style... and I don't like this style man. In fact, I'm going down to the tailors to get me a new style. One with a bit of velvet on the collar and a drape in the back, man. Ohh... Puttin' on... puttin' on... pt... puttin' on the style... Hum the chorus man."

"I don't hum."

"Don't you believe it, man, ha, ha, ha!"

My dad felt he need not worry too much about me being influenced by someone who could have the piss taken out of him like that!

As a soul-satisfier, skiffle was never in the same league as the music of Elvis Presley, Chuck Berry, Little Richard and Jerry Lee Lewis, even though they all shared the same roots in rhythm and blues. Neither was it ever likely to challenge Rock'n'Roll as the cherished symbol of the raw, sexual energy of liberated youth. However, Glasgow-born Donegan's nasal reworking of American folk songs had caught the imagination of teenagers and the approval of our parents who decided that, in comparison to the godless corruption and sexual euphemisms of Rock'n'Roll, the wonderfully inoffensive skiffle seemed a perfectly respectable thing for us to do! It is noteworthy that on that memorable day of June 7th 1957, at the St Peter's Church Fête, Woolton, both the local vicar and the ultra-respectable Aunt Mimi could beam their approval up at John when his Quarrymen took a giant step in the metamorphosis to becoming the Beatles.

So many groups were being formed in our neighbourhood alone that it was essential to be the first to go public with a name. We had no problem in being both quick off the mark and highly topical. "Bloody hell, Stan. What's that coming up the street? I mean up there in the sky." Brian almost added the obligatory "man"... "Look... Over Sefton Park and it's heading straight towards us!" Brian and I stood in the middle of Borrowdale Road and watched the first Russian Sputnik, travelling at what appeared to be the speed of a fast plane. It passed directly over our heads and continued northwards into the black, night sky beyond the flat expanse of Wavertree Playground at the top of the street. "Fucking amazing... It's the Russian Sputnik glowing red. They'll be ready to go to the moon way before the Americans." Brian was so impressed by the launch of the Soviet Sputnik 1 that he called our group "The Satellites".

Brian Hollins stood uncontested as our leader, being that vital year older at sixteen and appearing clever enough to assume an intellectual authority over us, as he was in his sixth year studying A level Maths and Physics. He was not clever enough for my Uncle Stan, however, who taught him Maths at Old Swan Tech and was constantly at pains to impress upon me that the O levels would soon be upon us. "You be careful, Stanley, about how much of your time you give to this skiffling lark. From what I see of Brian's work at school there's a serious lack of 'quantum' in the amount of Physics your pal is studying, when compared to the countless hours he devotes to skiffle." My uncle was right enough, of course. It was the hours of strumming and learning complicated chord changes which impressed John P and me. He was our greatest, indeed our only asset; someone able to replicate the finger-picking solos of Donegan's lead guitarist Denny Wright.

Meanwhile, on the Allerton Road side of Penny Lane, using his mum's house in order not to wear out Aunt Mimi's patience with the new, home-made music, John Lennon was organising a future career for himself by starting up his own skiffle group. At this time, the sixteen-year-old "pretend" Ted and would-be rebel could no more play the guitar than Donald Duck could speak the King's English. The great thing was who gave a fuck? Skiffle was a wonderful experience simply because it was handy and cheap. All you needed was a washboard, a tea chest with a broom handle and a £3.10 shillings guitar from a mail order advert in one of the daily newspapers. It was a simple way into music because a lot of the songs had just two chords; the maximum was three, a fact which freed skiffle from the snobbery about musical training.

Brian was in the Army Cadets and a chat with a local TA sergeant enabled him to magically appear with a bass drum from the nearby Wellington Road barracks. "Look what I've got. I got it for nothing because one of the skins has been damaged. If we can fix this I know where to get my hands on a snare drum, some cymbals and a foot pedal."

Enter Brian Bradshaw, school pal and eccentric boy genius. He was, by the length of every World War Two fighter and bomber plane stretched propeller-to-tail across all the landing fields of Europe, the greatest maker of model aeroplanes in the known universe. Brad had every British and German aircraft of the Second World War filling sideboards, bookcases and tables at 9 Talton Road. Some were gloriously suspended, as display masterpieces, decorating the ceiling of the model aeroplane shop on Lawrence Road.

"You'll never repair that, lads, but we can make a new skin, no bother. First of all though... seriously like... Don't you think you should paint it and get rid of the British Army union jack from the frame before we're all dragged into sectarian strife with left-footers, in Liverpool 8." I couldn't stand the thought of being taken for a member of the Orange Lodge, who still paraded with all the irreverent swagger they could muster and so I went straight down the road for a tin of white gloss.

"Has your Nan got a nice white cotton bed sheet in one of her chest of drawers upstairs... one that she wouldn't miss?" We did have some very thin sheets. I knew that. They went with the old, lumpy mattress and the washed-out, weightless eiderdown, which since childhood had invited Jack Frost to creep into my bed in the dark, early mornings of winter. We were certainly poor enough for her to miss a newly washed bed sheet all right, but no one was left at No.52 now to put the brakes on my impulsive behaviour. Anyway, needs must and Nan was a soft-hearted lump.

"Help me cut the sheet to size, Stan, and then we'll paint it with this stuff."

"What is it? It doesn't half stink."

"It's aeroplane dope. If you were in an enclosed space with a bucket of this stuff for long enough you could open a window and fly off to fuckin' well bomb Germany, by yourself."

"How is this goin' to make us a drum skin?"

"Well squire, once we've painted it and let it dry, we'll stretch it with weights… then we'll rub it down with sandpaper and start all over again. I reckon about half-a-dozen coats should do the trick."

All this was done with an unnatural patience borrowed from our perfectionist master craftsman of the balsa, tissue paper and glue. The process took us most of the week and I was high enough on solvent to be able to rattle-off a two-hour History essay in thirty minutes before Brad could pronounce both the tension and sound of the new skin up to scratch. When our leader, Brian, was happy with the progress we had made, he produced all the other items of a basic drum kit; only then did he tell me that I was to be the drummer! I was more than a little perturbed by the news, having just listened to a couple of jazz drumming records at Tony Brooker's house.

"Friggin' hell Brian. I need to be whisked away pronto to New York for a few months' training at the drum school Cozy Cole has just set up with Gene Krupa!"

"I'll teach you."

"You'll teach me? You?… You daft get."

"Yeah, me… Didn't I teach you to jive?"

"Yes you fuckin' well did! Like Frankenstein's monster at a Halloween Ball. I was the laughin' stock of that youth club in Anfield until a guy there showed me how to dance properly, you sod."

"You couldn't dance a bloody step of Rock'n'Roll until I showed you how. Look at you now, the best jiver in the street… Well, on your side of the street, anyway." He gave me a patronising nod of the head. "Don't you worry… They won't notice you once I give them my solo." I had two weeks to rid myself of the eccentric sense of rhythm which would have alerted any neurologist watching.

"I'll pop down to the Maypole on Smithdown Road. The manager is sure to have a few big tea chests lying in the store." John P had volunteered to play the tea chest and the sound he got from that big box and a taut piece of string was truly amazing. As rehearsals progressed, the home-made bass became a revelation under the deft plucking of big John. Once his evening ablutions were completed, he would join us for practice, a gleaming face laundered to match the pristine cleanliness of an immaculate white shirt, freshly ironed off the kitchen clothes-pulley by his long-suffering mum. The black hair would be plastered back 1920s jazz style, but he looked more like the Lime Street Odeon's film-poster of Christopher Lee's Dracula. John was still only fourteen but going on forty. Like all vampires, he still looks no older today!

John was a traditional jazz buff and he could see himself plonking away to Chris Barber, Monty Sunshine and co. on late-night radio. The bare-naked plywood of the band's most primitive-looking totem was a perfect symbol of the makeshift quality of the music. "We need to brighten this thing up with a good eye-catching design and let people know who we are... that this is not just some hillbilly band from the Ozarks." I wondered how wise it was to trumpet a name when we were so bloody clueless about what we were up to.

We lavished all four sides of our precious tea chest with several coats of expensive lacquer, providing a black diamond edging to a vivid yellow background. Finally, the name 'The Satellites' was emblazoned in bold, black enamel letters across the front. Great minds were obviously thinking alike, because Lennon and his pals Ernie Griffiths, Rod Davies and Pete Shotton were also in the throes of painting another tea chest to more than rival our own. As if to go one better than us, someone's father had cut out silver musical notes, together with a treble clef, and stuck them on hoping that, in a skiffle competition, a bunch of arty-farty judges might be more inclined to give them better marks for artistic impression. They had finally chosen a name with a suitable hint of coercion to lean heavily on the judges at the Pavilion audition. "The Blackjacks" had Lennon's hard-edged, intimidating ring of authority about it.

Desperate to create a studio effect for rehearsals, our Brian managed to connect the radio in his front room, where we practised, to the radio at No.52 across the street. I had completely forgotten about Pop's extension-speaker in the upstairs bedroom linking him to a daily supply of news from the wireless in the back living room, downstairs.

"Right then, lads," said Brian. "In E... Ok... One, two... " Ching, ch-ching, ch-ch-ch-ch-ch-ching-ching... ching, ch-ching, ch-ch-ch- ch- ch-ching-ching:

She came down from Birmingham

On a cold December day,

As she rode into the station

You could hear the people say,

That train from Indiana

She's long and she's tall,

She's a handsome combination

Called the Wabash Cannonball...

More Ching, ch-ching, ch-ch-ch-ch-ch- ching...

So it came to pass, one Saturday morning in the early summer of 1957 that a mighty rush of engine called *The Wabash Cannonball* arrived, unannounced, in the bedroom of a seventy-five-year-old terminally-ill man, whose taste in popular music had died with George Robey. He survived the experience, but within a month had taken *The Midnight Special* to that place with the only known cure for lung cancer.

The skiffle virus completely overwhelmed any preparation I was supposed to be doing for my mock GCEs. Uncle Stan's belief in education was as enduring as his faith in God, so I feared retribution from On High for any waywardness of purpose. To compound my feelings of guilt and foreboding about such a prodigal use of my spare time, there was the nagging doubt that we were not a credible item without a lead singer. There was no one amongst us with the assertiveness of a John Lennon, capable of belting out numbers such as *Don't You Rock Me Daddy-O*, or *Bring A Little Water Sylvie* to the accelerating, two-chord guitar rhythm of a freight train running out of control!

As an ex-golden-voiced choirboy, I could compete with the best of them. However, my refined tonsils were far too pretentiously preened by years of church singing. There was the added handicap of the hours I had spent imitating Gigli, whose glorious voice managed to escape, undiminished, from its HMV prison in the stack of Bakelite 78s on the old wind-up gramophone in my uncle's study.

Uncle Stan had a beautiful tenor voice and was always out performing in church oratorios and concerts across the city. Entertainingly, he sang whenever he took a bath and then our house took on the atmosphere of a concert hall, his lyric tones flowing down the stairs to drench my activity in a priceless contentment. He was at his glorious best when stripped to the waist for shaving. Lathered up like an out-of-season Santa and showing scant regard for the menace of the lethal, cut-throat razor in his alarmingly expressive right hand he gave this little shaver, gazing in at him from the upstairs landing, a fear of the barber that even the magical atmosphere of Bioletti's could never quite dispel. The bathroom window would be lifted up and neighbours given free tickets to Puccini, Verdi and always, as an encore, the Brylcreemed bonus of 'O Sole Mio.

My angelic treble had finally broken at fourteen. Along with the urge to shave off an insubstantial amount of bum fluff every day, I was now desperate to imitate my hero, Mario Lanza, and hit a top C from the other side of a Steinway piano which would blow the accompanist's toupee clean off! I did not, therefore, dare risk mockery from my pals with any strangulated attempt to reproduce the phoney Yankee Doodle of the one and only Lonnie Donegan.

Without a singer, what fat chance did we have of making it to the Pivvy audition in a few weeks' time? In our desperation to find a front man, John and I had become reckless enough to tout around at school. We got the response our foolishness deserved. Mel, a worst case scenario if ever there was one, introduced himself as the only applicant for the job.

"That's a great name you've got for yourself... Mel Donnegan. Is the name real, or are yer havin' us on?"

"There's a double 'n' in the surname," said Mel, who clearly wanted to succeed on his own merits.

I looked at John and shrugged my shoulders "So what... it sounds the bloody same doesn't it."

The skinny fifth year was an uncanny look-a-like for Sixties silly bugger, Freddie Garrity of "Freddie and the Dreamers". Mel had the same nonsensical expression, held in place by a pair of heavy-framed specs. He was clearly chuffed with his name, that's for sure. In that spring of 1957 it was the only thing he had going for him. His beaming face had the pleased look of someone with a couple of platinum discs tucked away under each armpit. "Oh, yer, it's real all right, 'cos it's in the family, like." This guy had handed us a couple of spades to dig a colossal hole for ourselves and we began shovelling like two frenzied, Tex Avery cartoons.

"I don't suppose with a name like that there's any chance you can sing skiffle, is there?" Mel didn't need a split second to clear his Edge Hill shunting-yard throat. There and then he was off into an utterly tuneless and lyrically wayward rendition of *Rock Island Line*.

My head sank deep into my shoulders and I glanced around praying that, away in the far corner of the yard, no one could hear what was going on. Mel was absolutely dire. His voice made Sid Vicious murdering *My Way* sound like Pavarotti singing *Nessun Dorma*. He had the looks to deny us the meanest scrap of female attention, but possessed the one redeeming asset of a hard neck with which to willingly stick his unruly head of black hair into a lion's mouth. "You're in, Mel. That's if Brian agrees. We'll ask him tonight!"

On the No.60 bus home from Aigburth Road that evening, I had second, third and fourth thoughts about Mel, whose face kept materialising in the intermittent darkness of the bus window as it moved in and out of the shadows down the length of tree-lined Park Road. "I know he doesn't look the part, but the great thing about skiffle is that it's not about sex appeal… is it John? Presley's face, a golden-toned delivery and swivel hips are not, in themselves, essential requirements for the job in hand… are they?" John's reply was direct and to the point. "It would help if he could bloody well sing, and he hasn't even got a guitar."

We said nothing to Brian that evening, but the next day we got hold of Mel again at school. "Er, Mel… Bad news, I'm afraid, mate. Brian says you can't be in the group if you haven't got a guitar… And you haven't got a guitar… So, sadly, that's that." We were ready to walk away, congratulating ourselves on a very near escape, but Mel did not give us the chance. "Is that important, like? Being able to play the guitar, I mean?" The guy had no self-awareness and even less shame. We could have tried giving him the X-Factor treatment with a mouthful of personal abuse, but it would only have been translated into the friendliest form of constructive criticism. In a last, despairing attempt to put him off, we began to invent the most impossible terms of employment that the two of us could think up.

"Well, if you can get a guitar by tomorrow's rehearsal, OK."

"Mind you, you'll have to learn to play it quicker than Johnnie B-Goode and within the next couple of days. Brian's shit-hot and he'll throw you out if you're no good."

"You'll need to get a copy of *The Lonnie Donegan Book of Skiffle Songs*, and learn them all by the weekend, OK?"

"That's if you can really be bothered taking a six-mile journey to and from your house to rehearsals… three nights a week, plus Saturdays?" Mel looked at me for a second opinion.

"Oh, yer, it's six miles all right and the last bus runs early in the week."

We had put together a vaudeville routine and almost finished with *Bring Me Sunshine*.

"So, if all that's all right with Brian then you're in, but it looks as though there seem to be so many problems …"

"A guitar? Get the Donegan song book? Learn all the words by Friday?" It sounded ominously like he was ticking off a shopping list. "No probs! In fact, I'll buy a guitar tomorrow… Look, I've got the readies." Mel pulled three crumpled pound notes out of his trouser back pocket. "This is just great, this… I'll send away for a guitar as soon as I get home. There's one advertised in the *Daily Sketch* for three quid. I've a cousin who'll give me a loan of his for a couple of days to practise on and I'll bring it to rehearsals. My dad says that skiffle is a load of old tosh, anyway. He says it's full of bloody, one-chord wonders an' I'll pick it up in a flash!" Whether we liked it or not, we now had our singer – the unbelievable Mel Donnegan. He was, truly, diabolical!

The next evening, he turned up at Brian's house with an ugly, tuneless guitar, and a few days before the "Pivvy" audition, he received delivery of an even more characterless mail-order model. If there was a manager of a Waterworth's green-grocer's shop, somewhere out there, who had gone into his back store, emptied out a few boxes of oranges, and then cobbled together an instrument to truly reflect the voice and personality of its owner then that's where Mel's order had gone to by mistake.

On the morning of the audition we unloaded our ship's luggage of guitars, amplifier, tea chest and drums off the No.86 bus at the top of Smithdown Road and joined the queue, backstage, at the Pivvy. Our name, "The Satellites", was added to the list of skiffle groups before we were told to take our place in a long line of singers, tap-dancers, jugglers, ventriloquists, magicians and the obligatory music-hall acrobat.

There were plenty of other skiffle groups present, but that did not worry me until I saw John Lennon standing with his nattily-attired Blackjacks at the other side of the stage.

"Oh, fuck! He's into skiffle too!"

"Who?"… Brian had only moved into the neighbourhood in the last couple of years and did not know who Lennon was.

"It's a guy called John Lennon with a group and they seem to have more idea about a stage image than we have."

We may have had an out-of-this-world name, but we were attired in a very down-to-earth, workaday assortment of checked shirts, jeans and trousers. I could see that John's lot were a couple of judging points up on us already in their black jeans with green stitching, white shirts, and obligatory baddie's boot lace ties. John looked more Rock'n'Roll than skiffle with his slicked-back, Ted hairstyle.

"We're relying on your guitar solo more than ever now, Brian, to make that lot forget the way we look."

"Who are you talking about?... The guy Lennon?"

I was referring to the three judges, hunched like spectres in the dimly lit auditorium, some five or six rows back from the stage.

We got our turn to impress the judges before John's Blackjacks. Given skiffle's limited repertoire, this was a good thing because a skiffle competition could produce half a dozen groups all singing from the same bloody hymn sheet! "OK, next," said a disembodied voice in the front stalls. "You are the... er... Satellites, yer? Come on then lads, show us what you can do." It took a few minutes to get organised on stage. Mel was agonising about whether his fingers could negotiate the only two chord changes he knew, and had been fucking up all week. John P, with his jazzman's cool was relaxed, fingers poised over the taut string of our standout tea chest.

Brian kept us all waiting by making deliberate adjustments to the controls on his amplifier and twiddling with the knobs on his Hofner. He wanted to make sure the three people that mattered knew that we were the group with the space-age technology to go with our name. Calmly, he stepped towards the front of the stage sporting a Canadian lumberjack shirt – the perfect colour to match his tousled mop of flame-red hair. The heavy-rimmed, Buddy Holly-type specs furthered the impression of a quiet, courteous manner and must have given the judges hope that they were going to get a break from the brain-numbing routine of *Freight Train* or *Bring a Little Water, Sylvie*, with something a little more interesting and eccentric; a snatch of music born out of the home-made fun and hearty laughter of the timberland log cabins above the snowline of Oregon.

"We're goin' to do *Maggie May*." This caused a lot of laughter from onlookers who could imagine a ship load of drunken, shag-happy sailors promising as much down at the Pier Head. Nothing more was said. Brian stepped back into the safe obscurity of our underwhelming stage presence and made one last nervous re-adjustment to his amplifier. "One, two..." The dreadful Mel was unleashed and steamed into the well-known Liverpool seafarers' song about Lime Street's most celebrated prostitute:

Oh Maggie, Maggie May

They have taken her away

And she'll never walk down Lime S...

Someone down in the bunker of the front stalls had heard more than enough to deny Brian his solo. "Thanks boys... I think we've got all we need." That was it. "Don't ring us, we'll ring you!" We quickly shifted our equipment off the stage to watch John Lennon and his Blackjacks, hoping that they would be as shit-awful as us. They were simply young guys we were growing up with. In the routine ordinariness of living a teenager's life, you can't possibly know when you might be in the company of undisclosed genius. What chance had a sixteen-year-old, future rock-god to convince me that he was, indeed, a cut above the rest of us? Give the lad a break. His first five-quid guitar had not yet arrived in the post!

The "Pivvy" audition had come a little too soon for John. A raw recruit to musicianship, he was still being weaned off his mother's four-string banjo and far from confident about playing the guitar. The great-man-to-be had, therefore, chosen to sing and play the bass, whilst sporting a natty pair of black, leather gloves. The Blackjacks' tea chest was a brilliant centrepiece, painted and decorated with a final, confident, flourish of silver musical notes; a suitable prop for main-man Lennon to claim attention.

John Lennon's flat cadence rolled across the footlights and into the semi-darkness of the theatre. "We're goin' to do Maggie May as well, like," he said, laconically raising an eyebrow to signal a certain carnal awareness. There was more laughter from the wings. "What a bloody goer. Nine shags in ten minutes... She won't be able to walk down Lime Street for a month!" John waited for the hilarity to die down, "One, two..."

Oh Maggie Maggie May

They have taken her away

And she'll never walk down Lime Street any more.

The Judge he guilty found her

For robbing a homeward...

Lennon had succeeded in escorting a staggering Maggie a few more doorways further down Lime Street than us. This was possibly a concession to the way, when announcing the number and refusing to wear his specs, he had given the judges the famous, unfocused, unyielding, hard-bitten stare.

In a delightful way, skiffle was a Trojan horse into the authority of parents and school over our lives. It so liberated and possessed me that I, willingly, signed up to an abandonment of school to go on a great musical adventure. As far as Brian, John P and I were concerned skiffle was nothing more than an escape from the tedium of working for O Levels, followed by two years of A-Level study for a place at university. For John Lennon, however, it signalled a serious divorce from formal education and the beginning of his pursuit of fame and fortune as a rock musician.

The great bonus of skiffle's wholesome social image allowed us the opportunity to play at church concerts and youth clubs, but the big event was a skiffle contest and there were more of them than there were choruses to Donegan songs. On one memorable occasion, the four of us trundled all our equipment, from Sefton Park's Ullet Road entrance to the Pier Head. From there we took a ferry across the Mersey, and then another bus to the Odeon in Birkenhead, which was one of the biggest cinemas on Merseyside. It was the venue for the local premier of Elvis Presley's first film, *Love Me Tender*, and the theatre was promoting the event with a Grand Skiffle Contest.

The adjudication took place both before and after the film. As we waited behind the black side-curtains to be brought back on stage for a reprise and the judges' final comments, I found myself staring up at Elvis in all his magnified glory, on the giant screen only a few feet away. It was nothing more than a two-dimensional, black and white flickering image of the real thing. Yet, such was the impact of motion pictures and Rock'n'Roll in my life that I found myself overpowered by the close-up of that unforgettable face, and the intimacy translated into an awesome wonder. I wanted to reach out and pass my hand through the gimmickry of the dancing projector light to touch the flat, lifeless surface of the silver screen and make sure that it was not Elvis, but me who was the real flesh and blood. "The fifth act you heard tonight was The Satellites and here they are again"... Brian said to our new singer, Ray Ennis, later of The Swinging Blue Jeans, "We're in a desperate situation Ray... Do something to make them take notice of us." Ray's sprint from the wings took him into the leap of Rudolf Nureyev looking for his best pair of tights. We all stumbled on stage behind him to take our encore. The backstage spell was broken. I was real all right, and was struggling to control an urgent bowel movement to prove it!

We did not win, of course, but who cared? On the slow, homeward journey back across the river I sat shivering in my cotton-print leopard-skin shirt, staring out through the passenger rails from one of the slatted, wooden seats which decorated the airish, open-top deck of the late ferry. I had my legs astride the bass drum to stop it rolling off into the murky-grey Mersey and beating its own watery retreat in the churning froth of the boat's diagonal path back to the Liverpool landing stage. Anxiously, I watched the illuminated clock face of the landmark Liver Buildings, silhouetted against the eerie, yellow haze of the city's night lighting. Slowly, its fingers began to win their struggle to let me make the last bus home from the Pier Head.

"Are you goin' to school tomorrow, John?"

"Oh yeah, sure... Doc Ashmore is setting up an experiment. We're preparing nitrogen dioxide from copper and concentrated nitric acid. If it doesn't stink the place out it may well blow us all up! He'll go bonkers if any of us aren't there."

"I've got a Maths homework to hand in to Barrington, but I can't do it now. I might not go in... We'll see." Of course, I did not go in.

"Hello lads. Well, it's been a glorious summer afternoon of... what's it called?... Yes, yes, skiffling, of course!" We had been asked to play at a Liberal Party garden fête, out in West Derby. "Well, thank you for coming today, boys. It's been a great success. All the stalls have done really well and you have played your part splendidly." We hadn't a clue who the guy was, but he had a posh voice and seemed more interested in the fact that we were young men than in our music. "If you're all free this evening we would like you to come back to a party that Julian... over there... is having for all those who helped organise the fête. Please come." We ended up in a big house, somewhere in West Allerton or Grassendale; a novelty item brought along to provide some fun for a bunch of bemused adults.

Many years later, I found out that we had been in the home of Julian Holt, a great-nephew of Alfred Holt, founder of the Blue Funnel shipping-line. He had invited us back to whet the appetites of a few of his gay friends. We were hired to sing a song of sixpence and then, who knows, present a dainty dish before a few old Liberal queens! Four fresh-faced, perspiring lads, naively belting out such dangerously appropriate songs as Leadbetter's *Diggin' My Potatoes* with its rich, horny, Donegan-enhanced lyrics:

I crept up to the window,

I thought I heard a moan

I heard somebody say, Ohh!

You're sucking my sweet bone!

The words to the Viper's version of Cumberland Gap kept me on my toes all night...

> *Lay down boys and take a little nap*
>
> *Only fifteen miles to the Cumberland Gap.*

However, the next morning we left unharmed and untouched, such were the dire social and criminal consequences, in those days, for letting your sexual preferences get the upper hand. Julian Holt gave us the ten quid for having our eyes opened to a few of the pleasures of adult behaviour.

My finest memory of the whole evening had nothing to do with skiffle, under-age drinking, and the ample pair of forty-something inch breasts which I was lucky enough to watch someone fondling. It may well have been the heat coming off the couple on the sofa in the living room, which sent me out into the back garden for some fresh air. It was a crystal clear, starry night, and as I looked up into the heavens I got the most spectacular view of the new comet, "Arend-Roland". It seemed to hang there among the stars; a high-flying, celestial kite set against the black void of space. Under the spell of some solar magician the fanned, white tail of dust and ice had been set in place to reflect the light of earth's sleeping sun. Soon it would rise to encourage a wide-eyed, teenage anticipation of another day, gloriously empty of the sobering responsibility that goes with the killing process of growing up.

CHAPTER 46

HELPING HILDA MOVE HOUSE

In the spring of 1957, my father decided that six years was more than enough respect for my mother's memory and married Hilda in a hush-hush Registry Office affair, attended only by Hilda's sister and her husband. The childhood dread of my father's mistress one day replacing my mum had, finally, come true. However, the woman who had haunted a little boy's worst nightmares now needed to be far more wary of someone who, at sixteen, was no longer frightened about what she might do to him.

Uncle Stan had married in the summer of 1954 and was now pre-occupied with a production-line of baby girls up in Mossley Hill. Pop was confined to one of the upstairs bedrooms, where he was slowly and painfully dying from lung cancer. It was in such opportune circumstances that Arthur Williams took it into his head to come back to No.52 Borrowdale Road. This time he came with Hilda, whom the law had fashioned into a real-life wicked stepmother for me.

"Whose idea was it, Nan, for them to sneak into No.52 and take such advantage of your soft-heartedness? What a hard neck!"

"I don't know why she could ever think of coming here, Stanley. I don't want Hilda in my home. It's a cruel thing to do to me, but your dad says that they have nowhere to go."

My father had a track record of utter selfishness in his dealings with my mum, but he did keep a genuine affection for his mother-in-law. Perhaps Arthur's scheming new wife had ground down his resistance to a proposition which ranked alongside the meanest thoughts Hilda had ever harboured towards the Thomases.

Late one Sunday evening, under cover of darkness, they moved in like squatters to occupy my mother's front room with all the speed and precision of a SWAT team. Having secured their downstairs living-quarters, they quietly annexed my mum's old bedroom, upstairs. In one of life's terrible ironies, Hilda found herself retiring to bed in the room next to her arch-enemy, Pop, who continued coughing up his lungs, unaware of the violation to both his home and his honour. Having the hard neck to enjoy a good night's sleep in the most fraught of situations was no problem for a woman able to claim such a cheap tenancy on the wreckage of a family's relationships. Only my dad and Hilda would have the barefaced cheek to ask for help from someone whose happiness they had both conspired against. Taken completely by surprise, my seventy-five-year-old grandmother was beyond any contest of wills. Shocked and intimidated by the fait accompli, she had surrendered to powerful invading forces and could only pray for a peaceful occupation.

"No, no, Stan. Don't do anything now. It's too late. All their belongings are here. With your Pop upstairs sick I don't want any more trouble. Arthur has promised me that this is just a temporary thing and they will be gone soon."

By the time Uncle Stan knew about the situation, Nan had been persuaded to give her trespassing ex-son-in-law a dispensation of six months in which to find a new address for himself and the second Mrs Williams. Uncle Stan, with a wife and two babies to look after, was relieved to surrender anger and outrage to his mother's yielding disposition.

Nan and I were, suddenly, confined to barracks in the back living room; my years of roaming freedom at No.52 were over. Nellie Thomas had to cope with Hilda taking over her kitchen. The woman who liked to cook up so much mischief for us all made it clear she wanted to stir her magic brews alone, on the new gas cooker. I had the appetite of a horse and my stomach could never forgive Hilda for the disruption to the pattern of our mealtimes. I retreated to my uncle's front room study to do my homework and play my small, bizarrely accommodating selection of Gigli and Lonnie Donegan 78s on the old gramophone. I was sustained in the belief that Hilda feared me as much as I hated her. Now in my fifth year at school, I was no longer the infant push-over.

Nellie Thomas did not know how to deal with people skilled in the art of deception and underhandedness. How my soft-hearted Nan, a person free of ill-will towards others, truly felt about her daughter's tormentor now seeking comfort in the family home, I could not begin to imagine. Nellie Edith had enough on her plate caring for a dying husband, as well as cooking and washing for a free-wheeling teenager, to want to stir up deeply buried feelings of hurt and animosity. To do so would only prevent Arthur Williams from taking an all-too-late responsibility for his son.

One evening, not long after the two intruders had settled in to No.52, there was an almighty flare-up. Nan and I were drawn to the door of the back living room by the sound of a struggle in the hall. With arms raised to protect his eyes, my dad had his hands full trying to contain a crazed attack from Hilda. "Will you take a grip on yourself… you stupid woman… or I'll not be responsible for my actions." Blood was running from his left eye, which had been punctured by a swipe with a sharp piece of cardboard. As he backed his way down the hall, he turned his head and managed a wink to let me know that, in spite of all the evidence to the contrary, he was in control of the situation. Suddenly, he stopped retreating and stood his ground. In front of his son, and a mother-in-law he had once had to defend from domestic violence, he could take no more. "I warned you. I'm not going to let you humiliate me in front of my son and Nellie… You mad, stupid bitch!" He hit Hilda once. It was a copy of the thirteenth-round punch with which Rocky Marciano salvaged his heavyweight title-fight with Jersey Joe Walcott, presenting boxing with one of the greatest ring photos of all time. One right cross, but what a beauty!

Hilda travelled the length of the hallway before slumping down against the closed door of the vestibule. I could hear Uncle Stan's Barbirolli recording of the Hallelujah Chorus bursting forth in my head. I hoped that my Presbyterian upbringing would stop me doing a sequence of Southern Baptist, Holy Roller tumbling, all the way down the hall. With arms raised to heaven, I would have somersaulted over Hilda's body and cartwheeled out into the street, shouting like the Negro slaves of old "Free at last! Free at last! Thank God Almighty… Free at last!"

For the rest of that week, my Nan did all her housework with an extraordinary surge of energy for her seventy-five years. She seemed to wring teardrops of water from bed sheets and towels, as if her powerful hands were, at long last, getting to grips with her daughter's tormentor.

I did not have a clue how to handle the situation. Forced into a corner, however, I became a dangerous and resourceful opponent as I tried to battle my way out. Hilda's paranoia had persuaded my father to put a padlock on the door of Mum's parlour. I knew that something had to be done to open up the prison she had created in my home. "Do not enter" and "Beware of the mad bitch" were notices I thought of pinning to the door. Rather than bring my father racing to his wife's defence, I resorted to more obscure, sleight-of-hand tactics, redolent of the sinister behaviour so favoured by Hilda in the past.

I waited until she was away for an afternoon visiting her sister in Woolton, before turning into Stan the removal man. It was a spur-of-the-moment idea to remove my mother's prized 12' x 12' square of good carpet from under Hilda's feet and replace it with the threadbare, collector's piece which lay in my Uncle's study. The idea of repossessing my mum's best carpet – the only quality item of furniture in the house – seemed a small, but suitable act of revenge against her smug occupation of No.52 Borrowdale.

I used Hilda's absence for the whole of the afternoon to painstakingly exchange the carpets, taking great care to replace every item of moved furniture back in its original position in my mother's room. In a flourish of domesticity I made good use of Nan's Ewbank carpet sweeper, dusting every surface to remove all signs of criminal activity, such as fingerprints and the misplacing of ornaments. Finally, I was satisfied. To me, the room looked exactly as it had done an hour earlier with the exception of Uncle Stan's shagged-out pretence at a carpet, which lay perfectly re-positioned on the floor. I stood in the doorway admiring my Pickford's technique. Brilliant! It could have been the handiwork of elves or pixies. I screwed the lock back on the door and having lit the blue touch-paper, I retreated to wait for the fireworks when Hilda returned.

Hilda arrived back from her sister's just before five o'clock. I was in Uncle Stan's study, across the hall, playing a Lonnie Donegan record:

> *Railroad Bill,*
>
> *Railroad Bill,*
>
> *He never worked*
>
> *And he never will,*
>
> *I'm goin' to ride*
>
> *Old Railroad Bill*

I heard the vestibule door opening and then a fiddling with keys, until Hilda found the one which would unlock her lair. She went inside and closed the door… So far, so good! There followed a long period of silence. I turned off the gramophone, wanting to tune into the mind of a woman suddenly mesmerised by an inexplicable alteration in her circumstances. Surely the earth must have shifted slightly on its axis while she had been on her bus ride to Woolton. Something was dreadfully wrong. It did not feel right under her feet. She looked down at the floor… "Oh, My God!"… The carpet! The only item of furniture in the room she desired and which toned in so well with her newly purchased Freeman, Hardy and Willis slippers, had undergone a wicked transformation. Uncle Stan's threadbare Persian purchase from a second-hand shop in Smithdown Road – a carpet so much better suited to his Christian rejection of affluence and the more scholarly surroundings of his study – had been transported to her fireside by some unwelcome piece of hocus-pocus.

"Is this an Act of God? Is it the price I have to pay for all the calculated harm I've inflicted upon them at No.52?" Hilda was far too insensitive to believe her presence in the house might turn the very stones against her. She stared down at the travesty of a floor covering and asked herself the question, "Apart from things which go bump in the night, who on earth could have done this mischief to me? Who could have executed such a discriminating swap? Oh, Oh. Stanley... Stanley!"

"Stanley! You're in... I know you are, because I heard your music playing." Hilda was shouting from behind the closed door across the hall, the pitch of her screeching having set the fingers on Uncle Stan's mantelpiece clock moving for the first time in many years. In a glory of anger and frustration she raised her voice one octave over the eight, "You are a very bad boy. You should be punished for this. Just wait until you father gets home from his work... He'll sort you out, my lad!"

My dad, however, knew how far he had pushed his luck in bringing Hilda to No.52 and had no desire to sort me out. A fair exchange of carpets was deemed to be no daylight robbery. With Mum's carpet back under my feet in my uncle's room, I was on more solid ground and inclined to think that Hilda could less easily settle into a life here with me and Nan. My dad told me, years later, that he had taken secret amusement at what I had done. Some three weeks after I had stolen our carpet back, she and my father left for a new furnished apartment in town and I had the satisfaction of knowing that my emboldened spirit and eccentric personality had forced her to call it quits. You would have bet heavily against their chances of being together for Christmas dinner. Unbelievably, some five years later they were tied into a tormented marriage, with my father still dancing to the tune of Hilda's spiteful belligerence.

CHAPTER 47

"HAPPY" – THE DESERT RAT

John P and I got great pleasure from observing our respective fathers. Both men were blessed with the dry, caustic sense of humour which is such a hit with teenagers. John's dad was so unintentionally comic that popping in to No.25 Gainsborough Road when he was around was a guarantee of some memorable repartee. Mrs P, a caring, attentive wife and mother, had learned the art of self-survival in her husband's world of indifference to the inconsequential matter of daily communication with his family. Taking the maxim, "If you can't beat them, then join them" to heart, she used Mr P's droll, unemotional response to life, and his cynical wit, as a weapon against him. The long-suffering Mrs P gave as good as she got by making the man whom she had knuckled down to live the rest of her life with the butt of her own humour. She shared this wily subterfuge with John and me by means of winks, nods and other under the counter gestures.

By the time John and I were in our teens, there appeared to be little in the way of reciprocated interest between man and wife, other than a polite, muted acknowledgement of the part each played in the roles of breadwinner and housekeeper to the family. If ever there had been a hint of love and affection in their marriage, it had vanished by the time the tall Irish guardsman returned home from his war with Hitler. He came back from Monty's North African campaign armed with military trophies, such as a German helmet, bayonet and trench rations, together with a new dislike for human beings. In a stark re-evaluation of his relationship with his fellow man, John's dad, like Rudyard Kipling's cat, now preferred to walk by himself, treating all people and places with the same detachment and disdain.

I did not have to live with Mr P, so hero worship came easily to a sixteen-year-old who could only marvel at the man's audacity and sarcasm. There was substantial working-class resentment behind the mask of wit he so freely used to protect his raw, innermost feelings. Gaunt and determined, Mr P walked every day to his job at the local gas works, looking like a Lowry pencil figure on the landscape of Liverpool 15. In step with millions of other fathers returning from the war to Civvy Street, he strode out to do work clearly unworthy of his high intelligence. Like so many working-class men of his generation, he showed the resilience of a Zola hero, enduring the grind of rising at 6am to clock on to a stupefying, daily routine of unfulfilment. He would then walk home along

Smithdown Road to his evening meal and a read of the *Echo* for an hour. Finally, he might revisit the pages of *Bleak House* before an early bed put him out of his misery for a few hours. With the exception of a short summer holiday, plus a day's respite at Christmas, the same process would be repeated, over again, week in, week out, forever and ever, with no Amen.

John's dad was not given to small talk. Conversing with others about local gossip, sport, the weather and last night's *Take It From Here* on the radio was for idle beer-swillers, or chattering women, gathered outside the doorways of the many shops on Smithdown Road. As with Jehovah, his thoughts were not our thoughts. No one could take a peep into the mind of Mr P. No one was allowed a glimpse at his troubles, least of all his deferring, dutiful wife, who with consummate grace had learned how to react to the slightest twitch in her husband's frame of mind.

Any minor adjustment in facial expression produced an immediate strategy from John's mum for coping with "the joyless old bugger", whose real name was Jack, but whom she wickedly referred as Happy. Predictable of habit he might well have been, but his indiscernible feelings gave her no warning of when to duck from the slings and arrows of his shifting moods. The kind and gentle-spirited Mrs P, therefore, thought it no skin off her back to act upon her husband's every whim and send him off to bed, as early in the evening as possible, so that she could have the kitchen to herself. Once in bed together, John assumed that Happy no longer gave his wife any physical attention, apart from pulling the bedclothes off her, as he turned in his sleep to deal with another division of Panzer tanks.

Mr P was a lover of newspapers and books, especially the works of Charles Dickens, on whom he was an authority. His head was full of the characters which inhabited the pages of *Great Expectations, Oliver Twist, The Pickwick Papers*, and the rest. Harold Wilson's age of "The White Heat of Technology" would soon be upon us, but our parents belonged more to the nineteenth century world of Dickens. They had not been gifted a Welfare State to liberate their intelligence, and allow them to break free from the old class system. While John's father was being payrolled by a Government that wanted his eldest son to stay on at school and, hopefully, take a degree, there was inside his head a university of language and ideas, which he would never utilise to better himself. He was forced to satisfy any secret, dream of a brighter personal tomorrow by inwardly rewarding himself with the mighty progress of his eldest son. For a whole pre-war generation, this sad fact, together with what he had seen men do to one another in war, probably explained why he talked so little. When he did decide to speak, however, he was often the most tersely funny man I have ever known. If he could make his point effectively, using as few sardonic words as possible, then he would.

357

"Charlie has got hold of an ex-army bivouac. He says it's waterproof, and big enough to hold six of us. He fancies us all going for a spot of camping in North Wales... What do you think?" John had been persuaded that Charlie's leaky old piece of tarpaulin, together with an oilskin groundsheet was enough to turn us into the Pioneer Corps, with a mission to trek across the Mersey into the hills of Clwyd. Eventually, the gang of us ended up on the rain-drenched slopes of Moel Famau, where the adventure turned into a monumental disaster! We were pissed on from the greatest height for the best part of a week. Our tent, foolishly pitched on ground sloping to a nearby stream, had us sleeping on water beds decades before affluence and a growing appetite for sexual indulgence refined the idea into a more reliable, sensuous toy. All we could do was idle away our time in the little village of Llanferres and steadily eat all the rations away. John, the biggest appetite amongst us by at least a couple of cooked breakfasts and three fish suppers, decided to throw his survival at the mercy seat of his father. On the third morning of the flood he rose early and went dripping down into the village to dash off an ET message home. It was unfortunate that he could only find a sunshine picture-postcard of the wettest hillside in Wales to communicate the seriousness of our predicament. Knowing his dad's fondness for succinct communication, he chose to write in the laconic style thought most likely to solicit a favourable reply. He felt pleased with the SOS, which read:

Dear Dad,

No mon. No fun.

Your son

He sent it first class post. Two days later, just as we had decided enough was enough and were about to pack up camp in pouring rain, a postcard arrived at the village shop. True to form, the unceremonious reply from Happy read:

Dear John,

Too bad. So sad.

Your dad

A few days later, after a wringing-wet bus and ferry journey home to Liverpool 15, we were back in the kitchen of No.25 Gainsborough Road where John got the chance to tackle his father over the lack of good humour in the sapping, stingy reply, delivered so speedily to that sodden hillside in North Wales. "Good God, John... Money isn't the answer to everything! Were there no hollow trees or small caves for you to shelter in? You ask for money... for food? I was a Desert Rat, John. You must remember that I had to travel the length of the

358

Sahara on one dry, salt biscuit and a tin flask containing a half pint of germ-ridden water, squeezed from the roots of a date palm, south of Tobruk."

One afternoon, John and I found ourselves locked out of his house. Undaunted, we went around into the back lane and negotiated the rear wall to find the kitchen window left invitingly open. We thought ourselves fortunate to find a wooden ladder, lying on the half-dozen sacks of the coalman's best nutty slack, thoughtlessly dumped under the window. The idea was for me to cat-burgle my way into the house. Presumably, I would scamper up the rigging in the style of Burt Lancaster as the Crimson Pirate. I would squeeze my body through the small opening at the top of the window and then tumble onto the floor to receive a perfect set of tens from the five invisible Olympic judges sitting in the far corner of the room.

"The ladder doesn't look too safe with its feet in that coal." I was not too happy with the awkward way John was manoeuvring it into position.

"Don't worry. I've got a good hold on the bloody... Whaaah!"

We hadn't allowed for John's size twelve feet and his fourteen-stone frame, making it impossible for him to replicate the acrobatic performance of Lancaster's diminutive, screen partner, Nick Cravat. In true Oliver Hardy fashion, John lost both his footing and a grip on the ladder, leaving it to crash through the upper pane of glass of the kitchen window. We stood for a few moments, admiring a piece of vandalism, straight out of a Dennis the Menace cartoon caper, before getting into the house and tidying up as best we could. After making our apologies to his mum, when she came in from the shops, we sat back to wait for Mr P's return from work.

John's father arrived home, on the dot, at 5.15pm. With the soulless expression of someone who had just seen his winning pools coupon blown up the blazing chimney by an unkind gust, he passed through the living room and into the small back kitchen, making no comment about the real and unexpected blast of cold air chiselling away at his balding head and Henry Fonda-like features. Not one hair of an eyebrow was raised in recognition of the disturbance to his world of fixture and habit. He washed his hands in the sink before coming through to his customary place of honour at the kitchen table, where he sat down, stiff-backed underneath the gaping hole in the window, to receive his customary five-star hotel service. As indisposed as he was to acknowledge the damage to council property, he was mustard-keen to note his wife entering bang on cue, and carrying the one sustaining, melting moment of his humdrum day. Sadly, he was unable to enjoy the aroma of freshly cooked liver wafting its way towards his nostrils. A refrigerated, late October gale from the Pier Head was howling around the rim of his plate and beginning to play havoc with the raw passages of his sinuses.

The meal was eaten in total silence as John's dad sat bottling up a vintage, seething anger over the deteriorating condition of his steaming plate of liver and onions. Even from my more sheltered seat at the far end of the room, I could see a skin, ominously forming on the once piping hot gravy so carefully poured to cover all of Mr P's potatoes; slowly the mash was acquiring a finish any French polisher would be proud of. John's dad ate every scrap of his dinner, spooning the last morsel of home-made apple pie down his throat in the rigid, upright posture of a man with a severe bowel disorder he would soon be forced to deal with. Mannered to the very end of his tether, he allowed himself to say, "Thank you Edie", as he handed back two plates, licked so clean they hardly seemed worth a soapy rinse. Stiffly, he rose from the Arctic micro-climate which had settled over his seat underneath the window. In total silence, he walked passed the three of us and closed the kitchen door firmly behind him.

We sat like church mice, waiting for the roof of the bell tower to fall in, as we listened to Happy's slow tread on the stairs. John's mum, smiling from ear to ear, stood with her arms folded in front of the fire, holding her breath, waiting for her husband to press the self-destruct button. Upstairs, Mr P was in meltdown; standing in his bedroom, taking in the cost of a new pane of glass and the ruination of the only fifteen minutes of pleasure in his immeasurably dull day. For me, it was like being in the *Tatler* cartoon cinema, watching Bugs Bunny light the blazing trail of gunpowder, which with a welcome predictability would send the deadly demolition snaking on its rollercoaster ride over a Rocky Mountain range of endless, snowy peaks. In the kitchen at No.25, suspended in a state of gleeful anticipation, we waited for Pistol Pete's log-cabin hideout upstairs to be blown to smithereens!

A chair was the first item of furniture to be thrown across the bedroom. During the next three or four minutes of unorchestrated destruction, John's dad hurled things around in the style of any early Who concert. Downstairs in the kitchen, Edie was still standing, arms folded, with the grin of a Cheshire cat waxing wider by the second, as more than a decade of pent-up reaction to the madness of Happy's war with Rommel finally erupted into a suitable self-expression. Suddenly, all went quiet on the African Front as this intelligent, unfulfilled man of inordinate self-control, attempted to purge the guilt for such self-revealing anger with forty winks of battlefield shut-eye.

CHAPTER 48

JAZZ AND NORTHERN COMFORT AT NO.25 GAINSBOROUGH ROAD

As we walked to school in those final years at Toxteth Tech, I had to put up with long, obscure conversations about jazz and be continually nonplussed by the sophisticated musical taste of my seventeen-year-old pals. In my rock'n'roll ignorance I was too dense to sense the significance of every new vibe John P was getting from Milt Jackson and the MJQ. Off the top of my head, I could not think of one good reason why the improvisations of Miles Davis should be considered so superior to those of Eddie Cochran. After all, Eddie had taught himself to play, in blues style, and passed on to the likes of Joe Brown and a young George Harrison his secret of the unwound third string, with which to "bend" a note. He even played and sang all the parts on *Summertime Blues*. C'mon everybody, give a rock'n'roller an even break!

Having been brought up by a deeply religious man and influenced by his love of classical music, it seemed a sacrilege to mess around with the likes of Bach. Was Brubeck not good enough to bloody well play the great Johann Sebastian properly, or was he just a pretentious git? In 1958, and up against the mighty master of Rock'n'Roll, the great Buddy Holly, whatever modern jazz claimed to be, it was not for me! Although, nowadays, I am a sucker for a bit of baroque, back then I much preferred the *Be-Bop-A-Lula* of the anarchic Gene Vincent and his Blue Caps to any jazzed-up baloney with Bartók.

As teenagers, music was the inspiration for so much of our happiness. Rock'n'Roll rescued us from the old-fashioned ideas of parents and gave teenagers a new cultural independence, based on our love of music. By late 1957, in a rush to embrace the new music, countless thousands of British youngsters were into home-made, hands-on skiffle, which allowed us the unselfconscious pretence of being musically gifted. This common misconception created mile upon mile of animated talk, on the way to school, about the Lonnie Donegan phenomenon, and Johnny Duncan's Blue Grass alternative to Lonnie's plundering of the American folk library. The others regarded my taste for Eddie Cochran, Little Richard and Jerry Lee Lewis as the clearest evidence of my being intellectually challenged. They were as condemningly wrong about my music as I was unjustly suspicious of theirs. However, their self-approving, zealous commitment to jazz lasted but a few years past university, whereas my faith in Rock'n'Roll will travel on with my immortal soul.

"What about the pics on Saturday night John?"

"Sorry... Brad's got tickets for a Mick Mulligan concert at the Pivvy on Sunday night."

The Pavilion Theatre was the venue for some great Sunday night traditional jazz concerts. Although only fourteen, John P's size meant he could gain easy admission to the stomping music of Ken Colyer and Chris Barber. Together with the enigmatic, curiously disconnected Brad, they attended Sabbath evening concerts at the Pivvy with the zeal of brainwashed Southern Baptists, on their way to kiss a few rattlesnakes in the name of the Lord. Here they found themselves in the like-minded company of the saved; ecstatic amidst a fellowship of brethren and ready to extol the extemporisation of these travelling preachers of the true gospel of old-time Dixieland. One such Elmer Gantry of the Trad Revivalists was Mick Mulligan, whose band offered the faithful a bonus in the slim, ragtime tonsils of a young and, in those days, far less flamboyant, George Melly.

After a Pivvy jazz concert, my pals would meet at John's house, to talk in tongues and listen to Blues and the chamber jazz of the MJQ. I made an effort to understand their music, my curiosity turning me into a name dropper, in the same league as Larry Adler, as I tuned in to rapt conversations concerning the virtuosity of Monty Sunshine's clarinet playing, the sweet notes of a Pat Halcox trumpet solo and the soft, expressive tones of Gerry Mulligan's baritone sax. I was a welcome guest to an exclusive club, who turned up not because I thought being a little pretentious was the cool thing to do, but for the home-from-home warmth and easy atmosphere of the small kitchen at No.25 Gainsborough Road. The peace of mind I got from just being there made me more than willing to disconnect myself from the more technical and abstract language of jazz talk. It moved me not one inch of a slide trombone that the names of Barber and Colyer were talked about less, as those of Charlie Parker, Gerry Mulligan, and the exotic sounding Thelonious Monk eased comfortably past them as preferred listening on the black, twelve-inch 78s. It was their scene, their music, and they feasted upon it well into the wee small hours of the morning. However, I was far from being left out. The magical accompaniment of static; the tick, tick, ticking of the steel needle, grooving steadily across the Shellac, mightily working against centrifugal force, as it inched its way, in ever decreasing circles, towards the familiar Prestige label; the mellowness of those after midnight sounds, crackling through the ether from the foreign radio stations over the wireless, were all meant for me.

Jazz at No.25, with its tireless, deep-into-the-night conversation, was a wonderfully contrived attempt to bring a sense of maturity and culture into our schoolboy lives. For a brief interlude, I enjoyed the amusing sight of John and Charlie smoking pipes as a prop to looking more erudite and sophisticated. Our appetites were fed beyond any hopeful expectation of a bite of supper. John's kind and long-suffering mum, would be forever pouring us big mugs of tea from a huge pot, which she placed at the edge of the fire to brew away next to the ever-present, overnight elixir of seeping senna pods. The miraculous, ever-present plate of pilchard butties began to take on a Galilean reputation, as half a dozen ravenous appetites threatened the tasty little fish with extinction.

These rich evenings held off the loneliness, which had entered my life and my dealings with other people in those years prior to university. They were not just about jazz. We talked about everything that mattered to seventeen-year-olds in those golden, watershed years of teenage liberation. When the conversation inevitably switched to jazz, my interest quietened. I kept my ears pinned, and against a background of ripening notes and voices, slipped away to a distant place. I moved my consciousness into neutral, happily fixing on the roasting heat of the banked-up grate of coals. Under the hypnotic spell of a fire, which refused to diminish, I let go of all unwanted, tangled thoughts, watching them drift and unravel before they vanished into the purifying flames. Here, in this small back room, so deficient in modern day comforts, but set aside from the complications of my life, I found a respite from emotional stress. My insecure, all-at-sea personality found its acre of barren ground. Despondent thoughts, created by the disintegration of my family and the emptiness of the once vibrant childhood home, which stood only a few streets away, could be put aside. I had a place of safety, blessed by the understanding of a true friend and the kindness of his tolerant, good-hearted mother.

CHAPTER 49

A VERY MERRY UNBIRTHDAY PRESENT

In my first year at university I made an effort to see more of my father. I wanted to know him better; try to decipher the enigma that was Arthur Williams. By 1960, he had married Hilda and the two of them were caretakers of a stylish set of flats, created out of one of the old mansion houses in Devonshire Road, near Princes Park. They enjoyed free rent of a comfortable ground-floor apartment in return for a small number of undemanding duties, such as keeping the hall stairways clean and checking for minor repairs. Although not a lover of housework, Hilda responded to the challenge of keeping wood and brass polished until the smell of lavender wax and Brasso rivalled that of the garden outside. Tending to the neat beds of flowers and regularly mowing a lawn, which looked as if it had been transplanted from one of the well-watered greens of Woolton Golf Course, should have been a doddle to my dad. He was, after all, a man who craved a little peace and fresh air, away from the noise and fumes of the Mersey Tunnel, where he sat for eight hours each day in a toll collector's booth. It should have been a little slice of paradise, but Hilda had decided to turn their life into a hell on earth.

I visited my dad on three or four occasions at the Devonshire Road flat, before I could take no more. The sinister, inhibiting presence of Hilda was too much for me. She had become the dark, unbalanced keeper of my father's soul. For his sake, I returned a few times after my first visit, but the sense that he was becoming a prisoner to his wife's cruel and vindictive behaviour frightened me off. Hilda rarely spoke during my visits. A benign disposition towards me could not, however, disguise the nature of the demonised vendetta she had begun to wage against the man who, for more than twenty years, had been both her passion and possession.

I quickly learned that Hilda no longer looked after my father. Being left to fend for himself inflicted minimal hardship on someone who could cook, sew, wash and iron without ever doubting his manliness. A far more discomforting fact was the arrangement of plastic covers over all the furniture, with the exception of one restful armchair, facing the TV. This was where the upright Hilda sat, her blank expression inspired by the sincerity tripping off the lips of quiz-inquisitor Michael Miles and phoney showman Hughie Green.

"There seems to be only one armchair in the room not covered up."

"Yes, son... That's where she has enthroned herself, eating chocolates and silently challenging me to dare sit anywhere in comfort." Right enough, newspaper pages had been spread out across the carpet and onto the surrounding linoleum, from where the paper chase continued into the kitchen. It was behaviour which might be excusable had she possessed a St Bernard with a dose of the skitters. Dad looked across the room. "The tabloid trail seems to be marking out a clear pathway for my contaminated feet to take." As Arthur Williams tried to navigate his way about the small apartment without, leaving a foot or fingerprint to say he existed, the poor bugger must have realised that he had jumped from the frying pan of an unsatisfactory family life, but one where he was idolised by my mum, into the bubbling cauldron of Hilda's devilry.

Hilda appeared to be sinking into the state of mental illness, which would have persuaded a less tolerant man to trigger a clinical referral. She was only one more caretaker's appointment away from escalating her madness into bold, savage attacks on my father with pointed combs and scissors; finally, there was an Anthony Perkins-style attack with a kitchen knife. For someone who could handle himself in a scuffle, Dad took some terrible knocks. The KGB kicks to his varicose veins were straight out of the Rosa Klebb School of Foul Play. I met him, more than once, in town, carrying the embarrassing evidence of dangerous looking, long-nailed assaults to his eyes and cheeks. I stopped going to see my dad at his home, as I could no longer cope with his acquiescence in such degrading punishment. I wondered if he took it all as some sort of penance for his sins against my mum.

To avoid the psychotic Hilda, I began to meet my dad in the city, usually for a lunchtime snack in St John's Gardens, next to his work at the Mersey Tunnel. I was never tempted to tell him about my problems. I knew what a mess his life was in, coping with the deranged Hilda. Sitting, together, in the sun – chatting about this, but never that – was a temporary escape from my prison of unproductive study in the Central Library, across the road. Most likely, I would have been counting down the minutes to any break from a mind-bogglingly boring reference on the periglacial research of some bearded anorak, whose findings no one gave a U-shaped toss about.

"I've got something special for you, son. I want you to have this for your twenty-first." The impulsive nature of his surprise cautioned me against telling my father the bad news that he was a year too early with such misplaced generosity. His memory had clearly stalled, back in December 1940, as he threw his RAF beret, greatcoat and trousers over the bedpost. A few moments of Christmas-leave passion with my mum had not only managed to move the earth for him, but had so displaced the dates in his calendar that only Salvador Dalí could tell him what time it was. I opened the lid of the black velvet box he had given me, and gazed at a splendid-looking, gold hand watch, attached to a chain. It was the kind of impressive timepiece Captain Mainwaring would pompously lift from his waistcoat pocket, to more effectively dress down young Private Pike on the matter of his lack of punctuality. Will Hay would, no doubt, have received the like, on his retirement from forty years as the village stationmaster.

I was seriously disinclined to give my pleased-as-punch father news which would quickly wipe the beaming smile off his face. However, the likely chance of getting the same present next year, after he had pondered the effect of German bombing on his memory, forced me into blunt honesty. "It's… very nice, Dad." Again, I clicked open the case of the watch and read the engraving on the inside. "To my dear son, Stanley, on his coming of age." The word "premature" was missing, making the inscription as inaccurate as, no doubt, were the small springs and cogwheels within the impressive casing. "Oh dear, I've got to tell you… I'm not twenty-one. I am only twenty next Tuesday!" All the pride and pleasure in his features drained away into the navy serge of his Mersey Tunnel uniform. "That's a bloody lie! It's not true! Don't tell me I can't remember the day when you were born… September 26th 1940!" This classic piece of, "Now, I'm your father and I know better than you because I made you," only stiffened my resolve to put the record straight.

After all, if I did not have the written proof of my own date of birth, safely locked away in a wooden box at home, then I was as stateless and hopeless as the East German refugees who, at this minute, were tunnelling their way to freedom, under Khrushchev's newly built Berlin Wall. "Dad, I was born in 1941, not 1940! I'm twenty next week… not twenty-one, as you so clearly want me to be." In the midst of all the noise of the Mersey Tunnel traffic, a silence fell, and tumbleweed drifted across the graveyard of our conversation.

My father took his Mad Hatter's unbirthday present back before any more words from me could heap further embarrassment upon him, and lest I became a little too attached to its glitter. "I'd better have it back, son. It's obviously not the right and proper time to give it to you." I never saw the elegant watch again! Artful Arthur probably took it straight back to Birkenhead market, where he was told that the sentimentally foolish whim for an engraving prevented him from recovering enough cash to decorate Hilda with a new hat and coat! I don't remember getting another twenty-first birthday present from my dad. A welcome fiver, perhaps, but no presentation package to cause him more humiliation, as he struggled to recall the exact timing of his wartime journeying between the beds of the two women in his life.

CHAPTER 50

THE GREATEST BEATLES PHOTO NEVER TAKEN

In the last few weeks of my second year at university, and suffering excruciating agony with toothache, I had taken the first crack-of-dawn bus into town from the newly built Lee Park estate on the outskirts of Liverpool. It was to this soulless puzzlement of new and partly built streets of council houses, with their muddy and uncultivated gardens, that my Nan and I had been shifted in the summer of 1960, when No.52 Borrowdale Road was handed back to its pre-war, private landlord. I had walked the floor all night, until I became demented enough to let some ill-practised undergraduate at the School of Dentistry try and yank out my rotten molar. As soon as dawn came up, I took the first bus out of the Lee Park terminus into town.

That is how I found myself, at six o'clock in the morning, sitting opposite the Fab Four in all their 1962 waxing glory. We were in a deserted Lime Street station cafeteria, long before the hour when even the most conscientious tea-lady would feel obliged to turn on her machines. There was no one else around, just me and them. No one spoke. Lennon stared across at me and I returned the compliment. For once, disengaged from any intimidation by the misery in my mouth, I was able to match his intensity of gaze. This was not the time to say the first "Hello" in years and chance getting my face bitten off by the uneven temperament of the main man, John.

It was the end of term in early June. Exams were over and if it hadn't been for the pain in my face I might have been tempted to say something, if for no other reason than getting an autograph for my girlfriend's young sister, who was already a fan. Anyway, they looked far from being sociable enough to bother anyone, and I was too blitzed by toothache to begin wondering why they were sat with me at such an unsocial hour of the day. Had they just returned from The Star Club in Hamburg? Were they waiting for an early London train to do the EMI audition for George Martin? If so, they had every reason to look apprehensive and withdrawn. They were tired and speechless, even with one another. The lacklustre collective personality of Merseyside's new super-band made their denim and leather look even more stunning, with George taking first prize in a magnificent brown, hide jacket. The whole bizarre incident left me with a burnished image of the classic Beatles' photo that was never taken.

The Beatles were obviously a cut above your average local Rock'n'Roll band. However, on Merseyside alone, there were so many others making similar claims for themselves, that I was reminded of the all too recent days when the lot of us were into skiffle, with so much enthusiasm and so little talent. Just how much better than the rest were John and the other three? Beth had encouraged me to go and see the Beatles at the Cavern, a place I was familiar with from the years of skiffle, when the group I was in got to play on the famous box of a stage. I still identified the Cavern with Fifties jazz and folk music and like John Lennon I could cope with neither, finding his remark, "Jazz is shit", to be supportive of my own less-complicated tastes in popular music. As a teenager, I had been surrounded by too many pseudo-intellectual pals, who seemed to think jazz was the only legal currency of musical tender.

Of course, I listened to music. I knew Elvis was back from the US army and that Dylan had arrived from another planet, but I was ignorant of what was happening right under my own nose. Perhaps I did not want success for someone as familiar as John Lennon.

I suspected those closest to John as a teenager were in awe of him. Beth often argued a good case for John citing his soft side, humour and – once you had penetrated the hard outer shell of self-protection – his acts of generosity and kindness. Both at Dovedale and as a teenager I had plenty of opportunities to reflect on his behaviour and I could not take to his aggressive, bullying personality and cynical put-downs. When the music started, therefore, I found myself prejudiced and had to be won over by the prolific brilliance of his partnership with McCartney. However, even in the breakthrough year of 1962 I remained unconvinced, judging him to be a prophet without honour in his own country.

How was I to know that he and the thoroughly decent-looking Paul McCartney were both musical geniuses? One immense talent in a band is enough, but two for the price of one? As Harry Hill would say "What's the chance of that happening... Eh?" In October 1962, just when I thought Kennedy and Khrushchev were going to vaporise me, EMI launched Paul's double-header, *Love Me Do/PS I Love You*. Sure enough, Beth had the last laugh on my scepticism and polite disinterest. She had proved herself to be as good as the oracle at Delphi with her prophecy of success for John and the Beatles.

CHAPTER 51

NEW YEAR 1965: AN OPPORTUNITY MISSED

In the autumn of 1964 I waved goodbye to my childhood roots as the Scottish Express pulled out of Lime Street Station taking me beyond the Grampian Highlands to a new life as a teacher at Elgin Academy. What appallingly bad timing! Here I was, a rock'n'roll Koppite, leaving the singing, soccer-mad city of my birth, just as Bill Shankly, Harry Catterick and the Mersey Sound were about to turn Liverpool into the soccer and music capital of swinging England.

On Christmas Eve it was not surprising, therefore, to be dashing back south to the seasonal comforts of my uncle's home in Mossley Hill, Liverpool 18. The next few festive days of overeating gave me the desire for a long walk. Hopefully, it would stop the 57 varieties of Aunt Margaret's stuffing from manufacturing enough gas to take Phineas Fogg and me "Around The World Twice In Eighty Farts". That is how I came to be in Smithdown Road, where I bumped into Beth, getting off a bus from town. The last time I had seen Beth was in the summer of 1963. She had just been to Paul McCartney's twenty-first and I picked up some lively snippets of information from the pop world she had entered since the success of *Love Me Do* in October 1962. Whenever we met, the recognition was always mutually joyous; instantly throwing a switch on the magic and happiness of our shared childhood in these friendly streets off Sefton Park. We exchanged seasonal greetings and enquired about our respective families.

"How's your mum?"

"How's your Nan and Uncle Stan? Married with three little girls and another on the way. Blimey. Still waters, eh."

"Yes, I love teaching and love it in Scotland. No, the kids can't understand a bloody word I'm saying. No I can't understand a word they're saying either. It probably explains why the Romans built Hadrian's Wall."

"What about John and the Beatles then, Stan? What have I been telling you for years now? You don't know what you are missing being away from this city at the moment... It's all happening!"

How could I argue with her? Gerry and the Pacemakers, Billy J Kramer and The Dakotas, The Swinging Blue Jeans — all seemed to have secured a permanent place in the singles charts. Even more impressive were The Beatles, who had claimed the Number One spot on no less than six occasions in the past sixteen months. Beth was exuberant at the worst of times and the rest of our conversation was about the startling success of John Lennon. "You know they're in a big Christmas Show down in London, don't you? Well... John is coming up to our house at New Year." She gave me a warm invitation, with a Cilla-like, "Now you will come, won't yer?"

Did I take up her offer? Of course I did. Wouldn't you? The chance to see Beth and her mum for a few hours was a good enough inducement. The bonus of being in the company of the great and the famous was, however, not so attractive. Could the leopard, Lennon, change his spots? I was a big boy now, but would John's cock-sure cleverness still unnerve me? It was worth the bloody risk, surely... and what a tale to take back north of the border to my pupils at Elgin Academy!

After finishing a couple of midnight cans of beer at John P's home, which was just a few streets away, I left for Beth's. As I made my way to Lidderdale Road, the echoes of a burst of New Year tooting from a couple of Mersey tugboats drifted over my head from the river at Otterspool. The chill air of new born January was resonant with expectancy and I was wider awake than I had been for days. Any doubts I may have entertained about the presence of royalty at Beth's were dispelled by the swanky, black limousine taking up most of the room outside her house, at the top end of Lidderdale Road. The front door of No.71 was slightly open and spilling out Gerry Marsden's *I Like It* on to the street. I hesitated, and then rang the bell.

"What a bloody din! No one will hear me above this." I rang again... and then a third time. I should have gone in. It was New Year after all: a time when access to a neighbour's home can be guaranteed. How much more so for a life-long friend, especially one who had enjoyed the run of this house as a child. From my Dovedale and teen years however, there was still a residual suspicion of Lennon. Foolishly, I let it overrule my desire to be in his company. Quick as a flash, I was in retreat down the street and off home to Mossley Hill. What a pathetic Hogmanay to report back to my friends in Scotland. Had I been up in Morayshire – the land of King malt whisky and the ceilidh – I would not have gone to bed for a week!

Two days later, just before my train back to Elgin and for the last time in my life, I met Beth again in Smithdown Road. "Hey, where were you the other night? You missed a wonderful time, Stan."

"Well I did come round. I rang a few times, but there was so much noise and after so many years did not like to come in."

"You came round and did not come in. You silly bugger! We must all have been in the back room. What a night you missed. John was in great form. He was hilarious."

"Yea... Well you know what it is about Lennon with me. Even when he was OK, I felt that he was holding fire... Waiting to have a go, like."

"He's not like that really. You should have come in and seen for yourself. He's very funny. Very witty, Stan. You would like him if you got to know him properly."

I then got a quick résumé of some of the stories John had brought back from the London party scene, where the Beatles had become the darlings of the rich and famous. His funny observations about Jewish control of the world of entertainment; the brag of a shag from the diva of British pop, Alma Cogan. "It was like having the Queen," he had quipped to roars of laughter. It all sounded like make-believe stuff, but these lads now belonged to high-octane world of showbiz. They may have been part of my growing up, but fame had transported them to another planet.

Beth had been wise to believe in John and the Beatles. They were, after all, no one-hit wonders. Indeed, Lennon and McCartney had proved themselves to be exceptional musical collaborators, who might even be touched by genius. All this current hysteria, though. Where was it taking them? Where would it all end? In April 1970 Paul declared, somewhat prematurely, that the Beatles no longer existed. It was an unhappy and totally pointless remark. It was far too late to cancel the show. The way audiences were reacting and the way ticket sales were going, it could run forever!

Classical music, grand opera, jazz and Broadway – all have their spiritual claims on people and their devoted following. No music on the planet, however, has transcended the barriers of age, culture, race and class like that of the Beatles. Their music has defied the passage of time as much as it has defined and influenced rock and popular music since the 1960s. In a dumbfounding way, it has now become part of a global culture that succeeding generations identify with the music of the Beatles. For this reason I deem myself foolish not to have taken a closer, more temperate, adult look at the man-god, Lennon, that New Year's night.

CHAPTER 52

THE DEMISE OF NELLIE THOMAS

It was July 1962 and Frank Ifield's top ten hit travelled with me down the corridor of Newsham General Hospital:

I've got a feelin' called the blues

Since I saw my Nan today

I'll swear that's what the yodelling swagman was singing, as I pushed through the exit doors and into the far from fresh, but restorative air flowing down Oakfield Road from the holy citadel of the Anfield Kop.

Playing a lead role in the surgical drama of an operating theatre has never bothered me. I have always trusted in the surgeon's skill to cut me up, stitch me together again and have me sitting up in bed, chatting away to a queue of relatives and friends before I could count to ten. No. It's the rigor mortis lurking in the unbending, institutional environment of a hospital, which I have difficulty in coping with. You feel it most keenly as a visitor; the constant awareness of just how many of your fellow human beings get seriously ill. The vast majority who, thankfully, recover have a heavy price to pay. For days, perhaps weeks on end, they are forced to live in the highly regimented world of neatly aligned beds, where a monotony of idleness is broken only by the excitement of listening to yourself pee, after an agonisingly familiar walk to the toilet at the end of the ward.

My Nan's ward was a particularly depressing one. It was small and full of mentally ill females, whose condition ranged from geriatrics with advanced senile dementia, to the even more distressing sight of an eighteen-year-old girl with a terminal brain tumour.

I had come on one of my dutiful, twice-weekly visits to see the unrecognisable, anorexic remnant of the woman who, for more than sixty years, had been the human dynamo powering the life of the Thomas family. The fragile bag of old bones, who sat staring from her chair at the side of a neatly made bed, was the same woman who, until a few months ago, could do the work of several housewives, half her age. It was hard for me to accept the sudden decline of Nellie Edith Thomas and see her mind unravelling ahead of an alarming physical collapse. There was no longer any look of recognition in her eyes, nor did she seem to care if you were there or not.

Nellie Edith Mansell Dawkin was my Nan's rather posh maiden name. She came from respectable stock and enjoyed a comfortable childhood out at Seaforth, in a lovely home provided by Edward Dawkin's top-drawer job, as a chief steward on a Cunard liner. In spite of this promising beginning, my Nan was a peasant by nature; someone instinctively programmed for a lifetime of taxing every muscle and sinew. She could not, therefore, have been given a longer-term guarantee of endless, grinding toil, than by falling for the flaxen-headed, Golden Vision called Teddy Thomas. My acquiescent, uncomplaining Nan could not have found anyone better qualified to preserve her low level of expectation from life than Pop, who was so richly blessed with an abundance of talent for underutilising God's gifts of high intelligence and exceptional sporting prowess.

Of all the places for a Scouser to be born, my grandmother picked the port of London, in May 1881. Nan's mother had surprised everyone by becoming pregnant while travelling with her husband, as his ship called at various ports in the Middle East. There was something visibly un-Liverpudlian — something distinctly Mediterranean and, more particularly, Jewish about her Semitic features, tanned skin, and black hair — to encourage the persistent family rumour that Mrs Dawkin had strayed too far from ship, when it docked at Haifa. Nan's brother and sister both believed that their mother had dallied a little too long among the juicy, Jaffa groves of a kibbutz! Nellie Thomas had more than a trickle of Jewish blood in her!

My Nan's lack of polish and sophistication was feudal. From the time she rose at 6.30am to going to bed at 11pm she was a prisoner to a routine of hard labour. Uncle Stan made a point of buying his mother enough clothes to make her smart and respectable, including a Sunday best which she was forced to wear only at a couple of weddings. Instead of decorating herself with coats, she threw them on the bed like a Cossack tribeswoman laying down some extra warmth against the freezing winters of the Steppes. Nan had lost all her teeth by the time she was sixty; the false set of dentures, especially commissioned to bestow a smile more befitting the mother of an Oxford man, remained locked away in a kitchen drawer.

Having taken the place of my mum, following her death in 1951, Nellie Thomas was a slave to my every need. This was partly out of a loving instinct, but also in memory of her daughter, for whom she had never stopped grieving. I had become the surrogate son; a stand-in for doted-upon Uncle Stan who, approaching the ripe age of thirty-six, had startled the family by getting married.

For someone who would be eighty on her next birthday, Nellie Edith Thomas was in remarkable physical and mental condition when we got the notice to quit Borrowdale Road in the spring of 1960. The council transfer happened so quickly that I did not get the chance to dwell on the fact that I was being uprooted from the only home I had ever known. I was seventeen and in my last year at Toxteth Tech, having been accepted to study for an Honours degree in Geography at Liverpool University. All I now required was to get a top set of A Level passes. It was the last bout of studying I would ever do at No.52 Borrowdale and my good results were delivered to our new address out at Gateacre, in August 1960.

Moving to a brand-new council housing estate near Lee Park, on the outskirts of Liverpool, was the death sentence on my childhood and the rich family life I had known. All my friends, the Smithdown Road community of shops, schools, churches, cinemas and the wondrous Sefton Park were, suddenly, gone with absolutely nothing put in their place.

Lee Park was a sprawling, featureless landscape of assembly line, identikit houses and streets. Mud tracks and bare, rubble-strewn gardens awaited a decade of good husbandry to soften the harsh contours of a council estate still smelling of cement and paint. It needed human activity; the planting of a few trees, along with some hedging, shrubs and flowers, to turn it into a more welcoming place to live.

"I was down in Gateacre and took a look at your new house, son… It's a far cry from the old home."

"Don't I know it… It's not in the same league as No.52 Borrowdale."

"Of all the bloody locations they could have picked to re-house people used to living in a thriving community like Smithdown Road… Your move is about as unsympathetic as you can get." My dad was spot on. However, it was an unfortunate stroke of bad luck to find myself living only a few hundred yards from the very prefab across Childwall Valley Road, where Hilda had set up her wartime love nest with my father.

A few streets away, behind our new home on the estate, lived my Nan's niece whose husband, Bert, had spied for the Thomases during my mother's abortive divorce proceedings against Arthur Williams in 1948-49. I used to hear the Harry Lime zither-theme playing its ghostly rhythm in the hall every time Bert came and went like some furtive, B-movie secret agent. He helped make life far too conspiratorial for the young seven-year-old who, from all the whisperings behind the kitchen door, was able to decipher that his father was up to no good. Bert was a decorated war hero, so he was bound to be believed. Honourable or not, he was part of the amateur – as well as professional – detective work in the protracted legal drama. The ongoing acrimonious business not only damaged my mother's health, but so disrupted Uncle Stan's studies in his final two terms at Oxford that it ruined his chances of the First Class degree expected of him by his tutors.

Studying for my A Levels in the, seemingly, endless summer term of 1960, took my mind off the move down into the mists of Childwall Valley and our new home at No.11 Mildenhall Way. Uncle Stan had never encouraged me to apply for a place at Liverpool University, but was clearly pleased with my decision to stay at home. John P, who had won a place to study Physics, also chose to live at home, where he would be waited on hand and foot.

"Yea... I'm going to stay at home. It'll make sure the grant provides me with all the ale I'll be getting through."

In those halcyon days, our tuition fees were paid and grants were so generous they would send today's students into the paroxysms of joy only reserved for the "Quote Me Happy" brigade. With the two household drudges, Nan and John's mum, continuing to slave for us on a pittance, our money would help us lead the life of Riley – a man my father often referred to when describing how I was getting on at university.

By not applying for Halls of Residence I helped Uncle Stan keep half an eye on his doting, ageing mother. It also meant that he could protect his new family from a possessive woman, who felt that she was being marginalised and had begun to apply all the cunning she could muster into snaring his help and attention. Recently married with three young daughters, my uncle had his hands so full that he lost the power of reason and stalled for time.

Dad was present at Borrowdale Road, one Sunday in 1952, when Uncle Stan brought Margaret to dinner, so that we could all meet the future Mrs Thomas for the first time. "Did you see Nanny's eyes following Margaret around the house last Sunday? It was like one of those paintings of Jesus, where the gaze seems to follow you wherever you go in the room... If looks could kill, then Margaret would have been dead and buried half-way through her first spoonful of soup. Nanny is going to find it hard having her son taken from her." I understood my uncle's need for space and privacy with his new family. I did not want to burden him and, therefore, did not tell him how desperate my situation had become.

"Come on Nan... Please take your pills. You have got to take them. If you don't, you'll be back in hospital."

"No... no... I don't want to take them. I don't like them. I don't like the taste... I can't swallow them..." Shades of *Little Britain's* dear Lou, creating havoc from his wheelchair.

Had I gone to study geography at Aberystwyth or Durham, as contemplated, I would have escaped the disaster of Nan's collapse at No.11 Mildenhall Way, in the flu-plagued winter of 1960-61.When a bad bout of gastro-enteritis struck my grandmother down at the beginning of the second term, my chances of getting a good degree went down with all hands on the supposedly unsinkable, SS Nellie Thomas. It was the same agony, night after bloody night, between the hours of midnight and early morning and it lasted for months. My grandmother's moaning and walking the floor began to overwhelm me. I was not too sure what had happened to her since the hysterectomy in December 1960. The operation could well have been carried out by a couple of extras from *The Invasion of the Body Snatchers*.

Nellie Thomas was expected to outlive us all. "That woman will live until she's a hundred," Dad remarked. We were passing the door of Evans sweet shop, at the bottom of Borrowdale Road, when we happened to glance in on her, scrubbing away at the tongue-and-groove wooden floor, which had been worn into hollows by the ceaseless tread of countless, craving, sweet-tooths. Mrs Evans was well into her sixties and should have been ashamed to employ a woman nearly twenty years older than herself to do the dirty work. My dad and Uncle Stan were mortified by Nan's refusal to give up her addiction to the servile sideline of cleaning half a dozen shops on Smithdown Road.

"What must the street think of your Uncle Stan... and me for that matter? They must wonder how we can allow your Nan to stoop so low for a few extra pennies. She loves getting down on her knees to scrub those shops. We've all tried, but no one can stop her."

The severe bout of gastric flu, which finished her in the winter of 1960 was, perhaps, payback time for her body's lifetime of selfless soldiering to the needs of her family. An apparent immunity to all known ailments and illnesses had, at long last, been breached. She had lost three stone. Worse still, her mind had been left behind in the operating theatre at Newsham General.

"She won't take her medicine. You'd never believe it. She pulls me around the bedroom like a cart-horse in her determination not to swallow the pills. Where she gets the bloody strength from, I don't know?" John P's antidote for the curse of Nellie Edith was, for my sake, to make light of it.

"Pills... You should try blowing them down her throat when she's asleep."

"Sleep? She never seems to sleep. Anyway, it's too fucking dangerous. Did you see the Norman Wisdom film *Trouble in Store*? There's a scene where a crook tries to blow a sleeping pill down Norman's throat and then has it blown back down his own... It's not worth the bloody risk, mate! My grandmother's still got the lung power to inflate all the tyres in the Garston Depot's fleet of double-decker buses."

It became impossible to study. I attended most lectures and pretended to work at the International Library, next to St John's Gardens, near the Mersey Tunnel entrance. There I was anonymous amongst hundreds of speechless automatons and could pretend to be busy seeking out listed references and making notes when, in fact, my mind was everywhere but on geomorphology and the geography of towns. I transcribed page after page without interest or understanding.

The best part of my day was the balmy indulgence of eating a three-course meal every dinner time. Better by far than the dummy of the pram, the threadbare Teddy of the infant cot, the comforting blanket or frayed-to-doll-rags handkerchief of the distressed, little child was the sight of the fingers of the library clock, gleefully ticking on past noon. At one o'clock, a little man in long coat and wearing a tall hat, would pop out of my brain and shout down to my stomach "It's Showtime!" Emile Zola later informed me that before sex, drugs and Rock'n'Roll, all that mattered to the peasants and the miners was sex, food and drink – though not necessarily in that order.

I chose to let my day rotate around the lunch-time visit to a Chinese restaurant, or the cafeteria of one of the big city-centre stores like Woolworth, John Lewis or the Kardomah on Church Street. Here, I relied on the maternal instincts of the serving ladies to respond to my Oliver Twist look of longing and supply me with mountainous platefuls of food.

I would ignore the grim looks of exasperated shoppers searching for an empty space to park their loaded trays and amuse myself with the behaviour of others. I could identify with the self-conscious people eating on their own who, denied the comfort of a newspaper to hide behind, would pull out a bus or cinema ticket and give it all the attention of a best-seller. Then there was the small group of elderly ladies, who regularly met up for a pot of tea and the chance to fill their faces with a couple of plates of cream cakes. Musing upon how they all managed to continue a conversation whilst shifting their facial features, as if they had a mouthful of gerbils chasing around after a chocolate éclair, was an entertainment Picasso would willingly have paid a cup of tasteless, instant coffee for. "Look at that woman over there, son… Trying to eat that huge cake with lips as tight as a threepenny piece… If her fanny is the same size as her mouth then its no wonder she's never married." Occasionally meeting my father for lunch at the Kardomah was an education. I began to understand why he had gravitated away from my gentle, refined mother towards the hungrier sexual appetite of the bus clippie, Hilda.

The best and cheapest three-course lunches were served up in any one of the many Chinese restaurants in the city. My arteries have never recovered from the countless plates of mushroom, chicken and tomato soup I consumed, all bearing the same trademark taste of the deadly monosodium glutamate. The Chinese are a delightful people, blessed with a self-effacing calm and graciousness. They needed both, in full measure, if they were to think of opening a restaurant where pig ignorance could walk in, off the street, and order pork chow mein without being charged under a Race Relations Act, which was still more than a decade away.

"Confucius say, 'Many men eat, but Fu Manchu'... Chinky, chinky! Chop, chop! Come here my little oriental fellow, we wish to order."

No... I wasn't listening to the *Goon Show*, but about to begin my 3/6d, lunch-time special, in a Chinese restaurant in Dale Street. Four students had strutted past me and sat down at a nearby table. The gaggle of assertively posh, middle-class accents straight away put my back up, and helped misdirect a forkful of egg foo yung on to my chin.

"Please Sirs... Please not be so rude, or I will not be able to serve you... Please."

They continued to put on a conspicuous drama, making loud and offensive comments about the menu. The dish of the day was racial abuse.

"Did you feel rain, Andrew? I'm sure I felt the first drops. Better safe than sorry, eh."

With that, one of the ignorant twits opened a large, black umbrella over the table.

"Please to take down umbrella in restaurant, Sir, or you will have to leave."

The bunch of arrogant middle-class tossers had been knocking back too many cheap glasses of Australian white wine. I had once seen a guy come out of a Yates' Wine Lodge at the bottom of William Brown Street − where you could get a glass of Australian white for sixpence − and try to lift up a bus, as it moved out from its stop at the pavement. I did not stay to see the well-rolled and neatly cut gingerbread man scraped up, placed on a large baking tray, and then slid into a pre-heated ambulance for a put-on-the-gas dash to the Royal Infirmary. After a couple of hours in a wine bar, these silly twats had taken the idea of a little sharp satire well beyond the script of last weekend's *That Was The Week That Was*. The umbrella stayed up, as the fool holding it went into a routine later to be copied by Benny Hill.

"Ah!... I rike to order a prate of your rubbery chicken flied lice... prease."

378

That was it! Three other white-coated waiters, plus two suited members of the management, appeared from nowhere and surrounded the table. It was the days before we had become acquainted with what happens to people who are unspeakably and persistently rude to inscrutable types like Bruce Lee, Jackie Chan, David Carradine and Monkey. There were no sudden cries of "Ah..So!" No one spoke, but the stance of each of the Chinamen made me suspect that the lowest kung fu ranking in the family group was a Sixth Dan of a young man in a natty Burton's off-the-peg. As the umbrella came down and the students paraded out of the door it crossed my mind that, in my isolation and loneliness at university, I could be in much worse company than my own.

I once sat marvelling at a transsexual, who was sitting in all his/her splendour at a table in the Lewis's cafeteria. At one point, he took out a lipstick and a small compact to freshen up his face so that he could step back on to Ranelagh Street having perceptibly brightened up his ring of confidence. I thought to myself, "I could do with some of that!"

"And just who are you today, Stanley?" I might well have been Walt Disney's Alice, standing in front of the giant toadstool, listening to the caterpillar sounding out "O... R... U?" with every puff of smoke from his hubbabubba.

Arthur Williams had his own ideas about character building. "If you had lived with me as a child you would have learned how to cope without women looking after you and protecting you all the time. You would have learned to stand on your own two feet."

"OK... but who would have looked after Nan?"

Dad laughed. "Do you call living with your Nan looking after her? For the last five years you've been a thoughtless, bloody teenager... Looking after her?... She's been wiping your arse all your life, old son. When Uncle Stan left Borrowdale Road to get married your eyes lit up, I'll bet. Since you were thirteen, you've been able to have the bloody time of your life with no one to put a curb on your antics. I wouldn't care to know what unearthly hours you were getting home. And once you got to university... Well, that's just a licence to stay open all hours. We all know what students are like!"

My father was now suffering from angina. In spite of a catalogue of recent operations, including appendicitis, haemorrhoids, mastoids, varicose veins, and a double hernia, he was happy to know nothing about the fake disorders of anxiety and depression. He neither recognised the symptoms of such counterfeit illnesses, nor did he have any sympathy for those who malingered through the day with petty excuses for things getting on top of them. He never wanted to know how I was getting on, and I never felt inclined to tell him that the arse was falling out of my world.

By the end of the Christmas term, my personality had begun to unravel. My daily routine became patterned with disordered, irrational behaviour, as I slowly lost all desire to study and withdrew into a world of my own. John P was as socially confident as I was insecure. When not personally supervising the cracking open of a barrel of Worthington E, he seemed to know where the beer and music were flowing. I suppose there was always somewhere to go, but most times I never went anywhere, feeling that I was not part of the social scene. I was a lost soul, wandering through student life without purpose; untouched by a single, edifying or beneficial experience, and certainly not one important relationship.

As all confidence ebbed away, I stopped going into common rooms and to the Students' Union where friendships may have helped me navigate my way through the work and social life. Whenever I was forced to be with people, the actor in me − the sixth former who wanted to go to RADA − took over; the natural impersonator and comic stepped into the breach. I struggled on in Honours Geography, amazingly failing nothing, but achieving bugger all, while the real Stan Williams travelled on ahead to wait for his release, as a teacher in Scotland.

Had I mixed properly and found a few friends, I might have had more of a clue about what to study without wasting my energies to no clear purpose. I would have a better idea about what day it was. Hopefully, I would not have fouled up on critically important dates and times, such as the interview which determined who was being taken into Second Year Honours.

"Why are you sitting there? Williams, isn't it?"

Dr Mansell-Prothero, a senior lecturer and one of the decision takers in the Geography Department, had stopped in front of me outside Professor Steel's office. This Welshman had an accent so phoney in its display of anglicised sophistication, that he made me wonder whether all those honest, black-faced coal miners, bursting their lungs down the dark pits of South Wales were from the BBC's *Black and White Minstrel Show*.

"Are you waiting for someone, or something?" He knew the true nature of my predicament, all right. He was just being a nasty bastard.

"I'm waiting for my interview." I looked at the clock on the wall which told me that, unbelievably, I had managed to get here on time... "It's at ten fifteen," I said with a rare confidence. I was referring to the viva voce, the oral exam, which in my case would probably have secured me a place in Second Year Honours. The man gave me a disdainful look.

"You may well have got the time right, Williams, but do you know what day it is?"

"Oh-oh," I thought to myself, but like Dr Who, stuck to my own perception of the time and space continuum.

"Yes. It's Wednesday the twenty-sixth of May."

"Well... You are a day late. The First Year interviews were yesterday!" With that he went into the Prof's room and had a brief discussion about my total unsuitability to be seated in one of his fiercely dreary lectures next session. Mansell-Prothero was the last person to put in a good word for anyone like me. He had been with the First Year students on the recent field week trip to the Mendips.

After our last lecture of the week, we played a game of football against the local Shipham village team, and then returned to the nearest pub to get pissed on draught cider. The last time I can remember seeing Mansell-Prothero was at the farewell dance, when he appeared to have three or four heads. There were about 120 of us in the hall, but I could see enough faces to fill the bullring in Valencia. If only I had been sensible enough to stick with the majority of the students, who were accommodated in two dormitories, my subsequent behaviour would have been well-camouflaged amongst the dozens of other drunken sods who, on that last night, proved to be equally unsuitable ambassadors for Liverpool University. One of the girls had squatted in the middle of the street for a piss, but no one except herself turned a hair. Not for me the luxury of getting off with such shameless impropriety. Socially a loner, and the author of the best-selling *Gullible's Travels*, I had to be one of the few students farmed out to local guest-houses.

What sealed my fate was Mansell-Prothero's vivid memory of me being reported to him by a landlady in the village. The sensible and extremely sober woman had to live for years with the sordid memory of pulling me off her toilet at four in the morning, trousers around my boots and sick as a dog from both ends on too many pints of scrumpy.

"I thought you were a nice lad."... I can still hear the woman's rolling, rustic Somerset accent every time I find myself sitting on the toilet with a bad case of the shits. I have never been able to stomach cider since.

"You see, Williams... It's simply not just intellectual ability we are measuring here when we award Honours degrees. There is also the matter of..."

He paused, and let out an exasperated sigh. Unable to find words to describe how pathetic he found me, the man turned and went back into the Professor's office.

My personal tutor – a fine man who sensed what I was capable of – gave me the bad news that I was out of Honours. I was humiliated, of course, but secretly relieved that the struggle to do well was over.

Nellie Thomas was never going to come back to No.11 Mildenhall Way, but I stayed there for the rest of my four years at university. Senile dementia and anorexia could not kill her off. Time and time again, she responded to the efforts of doctors and nurses, who resuscitated her from bouts of starvation. Finally, she settled into a semi-conscious, twilight state of existence and was transferred to Lismore, a nursing home on Aigburth Drive, near my uncle's house in Mossley Hill.

Twenty years later, and some four hundred miles plus a new identity away from the most depressing time of my life, I was watching *Boys From The Black Stuff*, Alan Bleasdale's definitive, television drama statement on the human consequences of the political philosophy of Margaret Thatcher.

"Surely not?... Yes, there it is! It's Nan's nursing home!"

I had caught a glimpse of the impressive, converted Victorian mansion house as the police car, taking Yosser to a night in the cells, sped past its entrance opposite the Big Lake in Sefton Park. To stop Yosser throwing up in the car, the two coppers had let him out for a breath of fresh air. "Everything I've ever wanted and all the things that I thought I had... they've all been taken way."

I thought of Nellie Edith Thomas sitting motionless at the window of her upstairs room, her mind turning into a blank page; the memories – so many of them dark and unpleasant – no longer able to plague her as, each day, a million more brain cells were switched off forever. Her mind had moved into the shadowlands, where images of people and places shifted and flickered, with no clear connection. She had become a stranger to herself, something not quite human. This was a wicked twin of the Nellie Thomas I knew as a child; a mischievous being, carrying a destructive will in her transformed nature. Like Yosser, she may have drawn from the depths of her spirit a sense of all the great injustices in her life. Had this once passive and obedient woman acquired a capacity for revenge on those for whom she had slaved all her life? Pop was dead, but her son was an even better target.

I sometimes collected Nanny, as my little cousins chose to call her, from the nursing home and took her to my uncle's house to see the grandchildren and have tea. She was interested in neither. "Would you like some ice cream Nanny?" Aunt Margaret was acting her socks off, trying to keep the atmosphere in the dining room as sweet as the dessert now being served up. Nellie Thomas sat, staring impassively from her deep-set, doleful brown eyes.

"No!... No!" She no longer said 'please' or 'thank you'... "I don't like ice cream any more."

"What a pity. The girls are all having some with their strawberries. Are you sure that you wouldn't like some, with beautiful, fresh strawberries?... I'll put sugar on the strawberries for you, if you want?" My aunt's broad smile was as programmed as the switched-on grin of Tony Blair.

"No. Strawberries give me a sore stomach." Nan intensified the sorrowful expression, and held her stomach in a brief moment of melodramatic poise.

Margaret left the room and returned with plates of strawberries for everyone, except Nanny Thomas. "Yummy, yummy!" said the girls as they tucked in. Nanny's wonky circuitry experienced another brief burst of static, created by the noise of the girls enjoying their ice cream.

"No one has brought me my strawberries and ice cream."

Now call me unsympathetic if you want, but I thought there was more to this abrupt change of heart than a few brain cells going pop. I looked across at Margaret. The pupils of her eyes had taken the escalator to the roof of her head. She rose, deliberately, and left the table.

"It's all right Nanny... I'll go and get you some, but you were offered, you know."

A few moments later Margaret returned with a dish of delicious strawberries, which she placed down on my grandmother's lap.

"No... No... I don't want any!" There was another buzz of neuron-activity. "I said I did not want any... Take it away! Take it away!"

The three little girls sat watching, silently spooning their vanilla scoops and waiting for daddy to, once again, mediate between his crazy old mother and a wife who was now back in the kitchen throwing plates around in the sink.

Nellie Thomas seemed to be heading for a birthday card from the Queen, when she slipped and cracked her skull a couple of days short of her ninetieth birthday. Mercifully, the fall precipitated a fatal stroke, which the remnant of her worn out spirit craved. She had lived for nearly ten years beyond her usefulness, to present her son and his family with the burden of loving the unlovable.

The real Nellie Thomas was not the obstinate old devil, who tormented the peace of my uncle's home and placed such a tremendous strain on his family and marriage. She was the resilient silent, put-upon woman, who had held up the sky so that Pop Thomas could walk beneath it with such a swagger. She was the person who made the world of difference to my life when I was a child. The woman was immense. It was my Nan who made sure that I went to sleep in a clean warm bed, and provided the Florence Nightingale care and attention when I was ill. She sent me to school each morning fired up with a good breakfast and turned out as smart as a new pin. Nan cooked, baked, scrubbed the house out, knitted, darned and mended me into shape for nearly eighteen years. Not once did she query — or report upon — any of my many indulgences, which were a part of the unrestricted social life I led as a free-wheeling teenager. Unsophisticated and partially educated, her devotion was worth more to me than all the intelligence which came flooding out of the front door at No.52 Borrowdale Road.

All the unworthiness of those final years of her life does little to diminish the memory of the Nellie Thomas of my childhood. For me, more so than her other much younger grandchildren, the good does not lie buried with Nellie's mischievous old bones. Nan's virtue triumphed in the successful struggle to support her son. Her unconditional sacrifice allowed him the best schooling any age could provide, at a time when children from the slums of Liverpool had no chance to shine like the uncut diamonds many of them were. Stan loved his mother to the point of indulgence because, by a ceaseless toil, she had lifted him out if the mire. It was Nellie Thomas, alone, who made it possible for my uniquely gifted uncle to lay the foundations for the family's resurgence, and provide us all with prosperity and happiness in fulfilled lives for generations to come.

CHAPTER 53

NO.11 MILDENHALL WAY: THE UNINVITED GUEST

I stayed on at No.11 Mildenhall Way for another three years after Nan succumbed to the illness which put her in hospital and then into care. However grateful I was to Uncle Stan for continuing to pay the rent and give me a roof over my head, I never felt comfortable in the place. There was something unsettling – even a little spooky – about the newly built council house. Until our arrival it was a house without a history. Despite its freshly plastered walls, the lingering smell of newly applied emulsion and the faint waft of pine from the floor and skirting boards, there was something decidedly odd in the atmosphere of the pristine, three-apartment semi. The ambience was ambivalent, you might say.

"It's not bad, Stan. It's got a nice big living room. Hey, Marley tiles on the floor… great for wiping up the spilt beer after parties." I said nothing, but thought "There'll be little chance of that going on." John P looked out of the window at the far end of the room. "Bloody hell… What a mess the back garden is in. I can't see you getting around to tidying that pile of boulders and weeds." He was prophetically right about the garden being in no better shape when I left, three years later. John laughed and went into the small kitchen. "Modern units, eh… Formica tops." Not quite the designer, showcase kitchen of a suburban bungalow out in Hunt's Cross. A stark contrast, nevertheless, to the starring roles played by the deep, white enamel sinks and tin draining boards in the homes we came from. He ran a finger along the fresh, new technology of laminated work-surfaces and cupboards. "Oh, yes… Very posh, mate!" Not too posh for a poltergeist, perhaps.

We had been given the keys to No.11 Mildenhall Way and Nellie Thomas was due to arrive from her son's home in a few days' time. Meanwhile, late one Friday night, on the spur of the moment, I had asked John to come out with me to Lee Park and try the place out. Uncle Stan had supervised the delivery of all the furniture and carpets. Curtains and cushions, pots and pans; cups and saucers, knives, forks and spoons had all been put in place.

"I'll sleep down in the living room, on the studio couch, if you can give me a couple of blankets. You've got curtains up, and it's warm enough down here. I'll get a good night's sleep, don't worry." To show me that he felt at home, John made a pot of tea, while I grilled a few pieces of toast to test the new oven out. We sat until after midnight, talking about the end of life at Toxteth Tech, and what might lie ahead at university, should we both pass to get there. Without the company of television and a few cans of beer there was no incentive to lose too much sleep, so I said goodnight and went upstairs to sample my new bedroom for the first time.

I did not sleep well, being continually wakened by John moving about below. At one point, I heard him come up the stairs to the toilet, but there was no waterfall of pee or the forceful flush which only a brand-new ballcock can produce. I put my restlessness down to a combination of strange surroundings and the sad reflection on never going back to No.52 Borrowdale Road again.

I was wide-awake at 7am and crept down the stairs, careful not to disturb John lying flat out on the studio couch. Very quietly, I opened the living room door.

"For fuck's sake man! What a bloody scare!" My pal was standing behind the door as if he had been waiting for me to come down since the first light of dawn. He was fully dressed, with a cup of tea in one hand and a lit cigarette in the other. John seemed highly alert and more than ready to be off.

"What's wrong?… Are you OK?" The big bear of a fella had given me a real start. Like his timberland cousins, he usually went into mini-hibernation once he put his head down for the night.

"It's a funny place this, Stan. I've not had any sleep all night." John had been up for some time. I noticed that the pillow, sheets and blankets had all been neatly folded and put in a pile on a chair.

"What do you mean… a funny place?"

"I can't quite say. I'm not easily kept awake but, to be honest, I did not like sleeping down here at all."

"I couldn't sleep either. I heard you moving about downstairs and when you came upstairs to the toilet." The conversation needed a little humour. "Did you see anything that looked like it would run from Peter Cushing?"

"No. Nothing I could hold a crucifix up to. I just had an uncomfortable feeling that someone else was in the place. It wasn't upstairs. It was down here… I didn't get out of bed and I certainly did not go up the stairs to the toilet, by the way, so what you thought you heard, I don't know." John never came back to the house again.

For the next three years, whilst at university, I continued to live at Nan's house, on my own. Often, I would wake up thinking that I heard her in the next bedroom or in the kitchen below. Once, I thought that someone was trying to get in from the garden. I would get up and check the place out, but there was nothing.

I put the feeling down to never getting used to staying in an empty house on my own.

Two days before I was due to lock the front door of No.11 Mildenhall Way for the last time, something very odd occurred. All the furniture, save the single bed and a chair in my bedroom, had been taken away. My uncle had arranged for a second-hand furniture dealer to remove these remaining items, together with the cooker, the next morning. I also had a television in the living room, which was being collected by Radio Rentals on the same day.

On a night of pissing rain I came home, late, on the last bus. The house echoed to the tread of my shoes as I trailed wet footprints through the hall and across the tiles of the living room. I looked back and thought, "What a welcome... I seem to be following myself into the house." There were no curtains on the windows in any of the downstairs rooms, so I did not bother with supper – not even a drink of water – and went straight up to my bedroom. I pulled the only pair of curtains in the house shut against the night and got undressed. Before getting into bed I stood listening, for God knows what, before taking the odd precaution of wedging the bedside chair under the handle of the door.

Nothing had given me the creeps since my childhood fear of the attic above my bedroom at No.52 Borrowdale Road. Tales of terror, the dead and the undead, now tended to fascinate or amuse, rather than frighten. If I had ever come face-to-face with some vampire or demon from the pit, I would have knee-jerked into Van Helsing mode and done mankind a favour with the quickly sharpened leg off an old chair.

Hello darkness my old friend

I've come to talk with you again

I understand these lyrics. As a profoundly noisy person by day, I luxuriate in the sound of silence, which only the dead of night can impose upon our manic, helter-skelter society.

I am not easily spooked or intimidated by the stillness of an empty house in the early hours of the morning, when the slightest noise sends the wrong signals to the frail-minded or nervously disposed. Things that go bump in the night don't bother me one bit. As a teenager and then a student, I spent a good few nights stretched out under the stars, on one of Sefton Park's long slatted benches. Once, I was stopped by a police patrol car, on my way to sleep it off in one of the shelters at Otterspool Prom. "OK lad... It's far too late for you to get a bus back from here to Lee Park tonight, but if you don't want to get your throat cut and have your body dragged up from the Mersey tomorrow, then go back to one of your comfy benches in Sefton Park."

It was, therefore, a totally unexpected reaction for me to barricade myself in my bedroom against unwelcome intrusion. Eventually, I got a few hours' sleep before waking, early, to get a wash in the bathroom where, intent on having a quick shave, I noticed nothing unusual. I came down stairs to daylight streaming in from the window at the front door, and thought how bloody foolish I had been to want to place a chair behind the bedroom door.

Before catching the bus to Old Swan, I knocked at my neighbour's house to hand them the key, so that they could let Radio Rentals in to collect the television.

"Thanks very much for doing this for me. I'll get the key back from you tonight. I won't be too late as this will be my last night before I leave for good tomorrow."

"That's OK, Stan… Well then, if I don't see you later, good luck with your new job. I hope that you will be happy up in…"

The conversation was interrupted by the woman's husband, who had come through from the living room to speak to me.

"What on earth were you up to in the middle of the night?"

My neighbour gestured to her husband to drop what might lead to an embarrassing conversation. I got on reasonably well with the middle-aged couple, but detected a dislike of the behaviour of students in general, and particularly those lazy bastards who couldn't keep their back garden tidy. The man did sound as if he were a little pissed off with me.

"What are you talking about? What happened, like?"

"It's a strange time to take a bath at three in the morning. You woke both of us up with the racket. It's a bloody good job I'm not working today."

"Hang on… Me… having a bath at three in the morning? No way. You're hearing things. Once I got into bed at about eleven-thirty I did not get up until about eight-thirty this morning." I glanced down at my wrist-watch. "That's a little over an hour ago Scout's honour!" I refrained from telling them that something had persuaded me to jam a chair under the handle of the bedroom door and that it was still firmly in place the next morning.

My neighbour seemed irritated by me not wanting to own up to the after-hours ablutions. The least I could do was admit to inconsiderate, anti-social behaviour and apologise for ruining the man's sleep.

"Well then, who ran the bleedin' bath taps for a good ten-to-fifteen minutes? The walls of these houses are paper thin especially when, in the dead of bloody night, you're lying there listening to a hot water tank filling up for fifteen minutes."

The woman tried to end the conversation, which was beginning to take a metaphysical turn. "Now, come on Jim. It doesn't matter if the lad did take a bath." She turned to me... "We know that you've got a lot to do at the moment."

"But, I'm really serious about this. I did not stay up late. I definitely did not take a bath... Tell me that you're winding me up... Please."

Exasperation had replaced the look of annoyance on Jim's face. "Well, Stan, someone... something... was a splishin' and a splashin' like Charlie Drake. It went on for about fifteen minutes because I looked at the alarm twice. If it wasn't you, then it must have been Casper the Ghost." With that, he gave up on getting the truth out of me. He smiled and flapped a hand in dismay, as he turned back into the living room. I never saw my neighbours again.

I went back inside No.11 and shot straight upstairs to the bathroom. The bath was bone dry. That was enough. I claimed a few remaining items and decided to let Uncle Stan pick up the rest of my belongings. I was finished with the place. For the last three weeks of my remaining time in Liverpool I stayed at my uncle's home. In August 1964 I left for Scotland, the land of misty mountains and the Loch Ness monster, with a ghostly tale of my own to tell.

"It's a strange business, Stan... However, it no longer matters as you are out of the place for good." It was the evening after my speedy exit from No.11and I was back at my uncle's home in Mossley Hill, where he sat listening intently to my story without making any dismissive comment.

"I never wanted to let you know how uncomfortable that house made me feel. I am very cautious in any conversation about such things but... " My uncle paused and stared straight ahead as if he were questioning the wisdom of what he was about to say. Margaret, his wife, began to laugh, "Go on, Stan. You've got us all on the edge of our seats here... What is it you're so cautious about?"

"From the very first time I stepped into that house and whenever I visited you, I got a most unpleasant feeling. There was something which made me very uneasy... something I did not like about the atmosphere in the house."

"Is that right dear?" Margaret realised her husband was in a deadly serious mood. "You never said anything to me... Why didn't you tell me, love?"

"Well, my mother was in a new home and Stan had just begun university. I did not want to create more problems and could not dismiss the effect, which the move from No.52 Borrowdale Road had on us all. However, there was something more sinister than just a feeling of unfriendliness... I sensed a hostility as you moved about the rooms."

"Did you ever see anything?"

"Drifting spectres you mean? No... But once, out in the back garden, I got the shivers down my spine. It was a warm evening and not yet dark... that is why I found the sudden draught so chilling. In the fading light of an autumn evening something of the dead of winter had brushed past me... In all my war years of flying I never had a feeling like that... It was one of those occasions you remember forever." Uncle Stan paused and looked across at his wife. "It took me back to when we were in Ullapool in 1953."

"Perhaps the place has got too many bad memories for us all," I replied.

"That's true enough, but there's something extremely odd about a new council house... a house without a past, if you like, which gives you such an unsettling feeling. Unless..."

Uncle Stan went out of the room and came back with an ordnance survey map of Liverpool, which he opened up on his lap.

"Do you know what sort of land the houses on that part of the Lee Park estate were built on?"

"It was all farmland and countryside beyond the city boundary, I guess... Why? What are you looking for?"

"This map is not old enough. I was wondering about the existence of, say, an old cemetery... something like that." I got goose pimples at the thought of Mildenhall Way being built on the site of some ancient graveyard.

For years I wondered about the superstitious numbering of the small row of houses named Mildenhall Way. The people next door lived in No.15... No.13 was missing! Perhaps, the uninvited guest who roamed the place for years and decided to take a bath in the early hours is still living there, in limbo, between Nos.11 and 15.

CHAPTER 54

LIFE AND DEATH AT WINGATE TOWERS

It was characteristic of the essential goodness of Uncle Stan that he should come up to Liverpool from Somerset to be with me for my father's funeral. On a Tuesday morning in early November 1977, the janitor of the tower block of flats had called around for his routine, mid-morning smoke and cup of coffee to find his friend lying dead on the floor in the kitchen. My dad and Elvis, both delivered from the stresses of this world by massive heart attacks within weeks of one another; very heavy stuff for the son of Arthur Williams and a child of Rock'n'Roll!

I did not need to rush down to Liverpool from my home in Aberdeenshire. A post-mortem was required, as a result of my father's body being found alone in the seventh-floor flat at Huyton's bleak Wingate Towers. This delay gave me a little time to think. I was more than grateful that my grandfather's niece was married to an undertaker, so I travelled down to stay with Vera and Bernard free from much of the stress which goes with having to make funeral arrangements. Apart, that is, from waking up with the feeling of being choked to death as the train pulled in to the fug of Preston Station; my nose and throat once again bunged up with the pollution of industrial Lancashire.

On my last journey down to my home city for Nan's funeral in 1971, Dad's advice had been for me to lighten-up on such inevitable occasions. "You're too much like your Uncle Stan. Don't carry the world on your shoulders, son. Death is part of life… It's got to happen to us all, sooner or later." We were on a bus taking me to catch the train from Lime Street Station back to Scotland, leaving Arthur Williams to his unhappy lot with the unstable, unpredictable Hilda. "Don't get concerned for me living down here, mate. I must be next on the family list, but I'm not worried about shaking off this mortal coil, as the bard would put it. In fact, I'll be well out of it… I bloody well mean it!" I thought this jaundiced view of life might be a reflection on the state of his marriage to Hilda, but my dad was painting on a much broader canvass. "This city… this society… has had it, as far as I'm concerned. I could go in my sleep tonight and have no regrets about not staying a single day longer."

When my father legalised his twenty-year-old relationship with Hilda in 1957, the marriage contract seemed to end all hope of him finding a little domestic happiness in his years of retirement. It also conditioned him to more darkly fashion an already dim view of the world he was forced to live in. It was clear that the formalisation of their long liaison had acted like the breaking of a magic spell. Don't tell me it was just the menopause that had got to work on Hilda. Troubled spirits, locked up in the mind and personality of the unstable woman, were now released to attack the man who had saddled her with unwelcome misgivings, following the death of my mum. After, finally, getting Arthur Williams to herself she now realised that it was not just the passion but also the allure of their scandalous adultery, all those faded years ago, which had been the buzz she wanted from him. Did the desire to have what was not hers prove, in the end, to be the thing that really mattered?

Although he would not care to admit it, my mother's death shook my father to the core. It was clear he had a conscience and, perhaps, it persuaded him never again to surrender to Hilda's every whim and gesture. Instead of freeing the two of them to openly enjoy each other, my mum's death seemed to cast a sinister shadow over their ill-fated life together. As their relationship soured into a mutual contempt, Hilda descended to a new level of abuse towards her husband. For his part, Dad could not give up on what he had committed himself to so long ago and both seemed determined to go down together on a sinking ship.

Hilda's increasingly psychotic bouts of cruel and vicious behaviour were not my father's only punishment. Outside the deterioration of his domestic life, he felt more and more threatened by the sudden decline in the social values which had once helped people maintain a dignity in coping with life. He lost all optimism for the future and began to express views which placed him well to the right of Attila the Hun, as played by Jack Palance in my 1954 trip with him to see *Sign of the Pagan* at the Allerton Plaza.

He knew exactly what to do with the post-war politicians and planners who were pleased to preside over the destruction of the life of our cities. Wingate Towers was the name given to a group of multi-storey flats, out in Huyton with Roby, where he and Hilda had moved to in the mid-1960s. Wingate Towers: the name could sit so nicely on the pages of a Catherine Cookson novel. A less romantic place, however, you would not wish to visit. The three, sentinel tower blocks had been constructed as the focal point of low-minded, architectural ugliness on a new council estate which was the negation of the old-fashioned idea of a neighbourhood. My dad and Hilda had been made prisoners in the sky. The sharing of a one-bedroomed, high-rise apartment with someone as unsympathetic as the soulless streets of council houses below weakened my father's spirit as much as it aggravated his recently diagnosed angina. Sadly, they were but two of thousands of re-housed citizens denied access to any community life; people with no sense of identity, or belonging.

"When I go, son," he once remarked whilst up on holiday with me in the Scottish Borders, "come down and do the needful, OK? But don't shed any tears on my behalf. If there's a few quid left in my bank account, then have a drink on me. Rise to your feet and toast the fact that I'll be well out of what is coming." He did not need Saruman's crystal ball to show him a vision of Thatcher, Hatton and the Toxteth riots. He had seen enough already and wanted out! The man who taught me, as a child, to fight back was now expressing a much more resigned and negative perspective on a less-than-fruitful, sixty-year journey through the twentieth century.

All in all, I felt as comfortable as any disengaged son could be at the prospect of burying his capricious, misunderstood father. I travelled from Vera's house into town and then boarded one of the claustrophobic, new-style single-decker buses to take me out to my dad's flat in Huyton. It was many years since I had travelled on this route. For twenty minutes or so, I sat staring blankly out of the window as street after street and one set of traffic lights after another passed by, giving me not a clue about where I was going. "Excuse me… this bus… It does go to Huyton, doesn't it?" I had disturbed the trance of a raw-boned woman in her mid-fifties who was wearing a headscarf, which she would later pass on to Dot Cotton. In making her considered reply she did not move a muscle; there was not even the goodwill gesture of a sideways glance. "Dis bus goes all around the world." That is all she wished to say on the matter. I could only live in the hope that, during the next half an hour, I might see a sign for Prescott Road, or Dovecot, which I knew from childhood.

"Excuse me again… I seem to have been on this bus for ages. How much longer is it until we get to Wingate Towers?" Dot Cotton turned her head to give me the implacable look my Pop had once hoped Neville Chamberlain would fix on Herr Hitler, across the negotiating table at Munich. "How old are you, son?" I was struck by the woman's hollow-eyed and desolate countenance. This was a person who had spent a diminishing, fifty-five-year existence in an increasingly hostile environment. "Me?… I'm, er, thirty-seven." The woman stared ahead, her deadpan expression set to deliver the withering punch line. "Well, you'll be forty-one when you geroff dis bus!" All Liverpudlians think they are comedians. This droll wife was up there with the best and she did not know it.

Rummaging about in my father's flat for a few, small keepsakes to take back home to Scotland with me, I was saddened at the loss in the quality of the man's life since his inevitable marriage to Hilda in the mid-1950s. My mind rolled back to a very different set of circumstances in the late 1940s, when he and Hilda enjoyed the well-furnished comfort of their Garmoyle Road flat, from where the pair of them ghosted around our neighbourhood in the haunting of my mother. I was only taken to Hilda's flat once, but that was enough for me to be able to

393

report back to the family about the moquette three-piece suite, quality carpeting, the big, American-style fridge and radiogram; luxuries my mum could only dream about.

My father's flat at Wingate Towers now had the appearance of a well-kept, second-hand furniture shop. One Wednesday less than eighteen months previously, while her husband was away on a day's fishing trip to North Wales, Hilda decided to flit with all their possessions save the bed, a rented television and an electric toaster. Perhaps she thought the quick purchase of a sliced loaf, a tub of margarine and a packet of his favourite Cracker Barrel cheese would restore the man's equilibrium! Arthur Williams was far from amused and only a close friendship with the janitor of the tower block enabled him to cobble together a temporary replacement of essential items until he could think of trying to build things up again.

Long before her sudden departure, Hilda made sure that my father's married life had deteriorated into a hell on earth. A well-documented pattern of cruelty and vindictiveness had escalated into guerrilla-style attacks, which replicated the mercurial Kito's startling leaps from nowhere onto his bumbling master, Inspector Clouseau. There were Oscar winning performances by Hilda, from scripts old Hollywood might have seen fit to lay in front of Joan Crawford or Bette Davis:

"You're not going to hit me again like that, Arthur. Aaagh!... Ohh! Ohh! You cruel, evil man. If only your friends could see you hitting your wife like that. If they knew just what you were like behind the closed door of this flat. Oh, no... Not again. Please, please, stop it! You're breaking my arm... Aaagh!"

What was Joe to make of all the shrieks and shouts coming from the open window of the Williams' flat, as he stepped out of the lift and onto the gusty, open landing of the seventh floor? "I could not credit your dad with being a wife-beater, Stan, but the ranting and raving coming from No.83 was enough to summon a squad of police cars." Joe thought hard about knocking on the door, but didn't have a good enough excuse for making his call look genuine. He took the lift back down to the ground floor and had decided to tell his wife she must revise her high opinion of Arthur Williams, because he was about to report him to the police!

It was lucky for Arthur that his good friend decided to have a last cigarette before turning in to watch *Coronation Street*. Leaning against a wall outside the main entrance to the tower block and taking a long, exasperated drag on a Capstan Full Strength was the very fellow who only seconds earlier could be heard beating the living daylights out of his missus. "Hang on! Wasn't that Hilda's voice I was picking up, squawking away from the apartment window back up there?" Hilda still believed that she was under the studio lights of director Billy Wilder and continued with her performance not knowing she had been sussed by the most reliable of witnesses. "You horrible, violent bastard, Arthur. Ahh!... Stop it!... You're going to kill me one day." Joe was too stupefied to speak, but my father's facial expression said it all. It was, perhaps, not the police Joe should be ringing, but a GP with a sectioning order. My dad made light of the fact that he was the victim of a dangerous, put-up job. As much as he tried to make a joke of Hilda's histrionics, what had become a regular performance in their domestic life was beyond any comic fabrication. Her erratic, violent behaviour had now been flavoured with a madness and cunning capable of putting a husband behind bars.

Where the woman had gone to, following her vanishing act with all the furniture, no one knew. Both police and undertaker had worked hard to try and locate her. A notice had been placed in the obituary column of the *Liverpool Echo*, but a week had passed and no one could trace her. She was either dead or disinterested and I did not care to find out which was the case.

On the day before my dad's funeral, I returned to Wingate Towers to finalise the removal of his furniture and pick up a few personal effects of sentimental value. I had decided to take back with me his best fishing rod and a box of the fly feathers he liked to select from to adorn the band on his trilby hat. I also wanted to keep his wrist-watch, wedding ring and a few photos of my mum, taken in 1931, the year of their marriage. Uncle Stan had now joined me and finding the lift vandalised, together we climbed the prison-like cement staircase to the seventh floor.

Suddenly, we were accosted by the looming presence of a very large, angry woman whose manner suggested a preposterously out-of-place Hattie Jacques look-alike, from the nearby Broadgreen Hospital. It turned out that she was, indeed, a retired matron who had never subscribed to the idea of a bedside-manner. The woman was blocking our progress, as well as most of the sunlight on the narrow stairs and we could do nothing but brace ourselves for the outrageous attack on our propriety; an attack made so much worse by the sober, cheerless nature of our visit.

"Are you two responsible for this?" We were smartly enough dressed in an alien landscape to look like extra-terrestrials from the twin planets of Burton and Hepworth, mistakenly beamed down to a punk world of Mohican hair-do's, skinheads, bovver boots and bomber jackets. Matron had clearly identified us as local low-life, capable of the most obnoxious behaviour known to man. She might have taken us for a pair of snazzy hoods, but one look at my uncle should have made her ask, "How often do you see a Jewish gangster?" Shysters, yes; men who can make the cash till sound like a Steinway piano, yes... but gangsters? One thing was for certain, the woman did not have a clue as to who her real neighbours might be. "Do you know who is then? Look at the disgraceful state of the staircase. People have been urinating down the steps. There is a sewer of human excrement at the bottom of the stairs behind you. They are even bringing in women to have sex up against the walls... Look, you can see used contraceptives lying on the floor down there."

In her excitement at being able to collar someone for all the pernicious, anti-social behaviour piling up on her own doorstep, the besieged woman had made a monumental error of judgement in attempting to blacken the name of Stanley Herbert Thomas. She had chosen to give nil points for presentation and style to a man with the appearance of an Emeritus Professor of Moral Philosophy, the cultural aura of the Keeper of the Queen's Art Collection and the graciousness of one of the Twelve Apostles. When I told Stan's daughters how he had been so gloriously slandered, the thought of their father getting a knee-trembling shag from some old tart, against a brick wall, had them all laughing themselves to sleep for months!

Uncle Stan's generous and measured reaction was to explain our solemn reason for being on the staircase and calm the woman with a sympathetic hearing of her many woes. She did not know my father. In fact, she knew no one in the tower block, even though she had lived there for many years. One thing she did know was how to graphically articulate life for the inmates of Wingate Towers.

"My generation grew up well-acquainted with poverty... But then we lived in streets with a community of neighbours and a common decency to fall back on. I don't know what life is like for you, up in Scotland or down in Somerset, but here we are forced to run a daily gauntlet of intimidation." A two-year-old ran past on the landing above. "There are mothers with small children trapped in this building all day long. These places are death traps as well as prisons. Where do you let the toddlers play? There are no parks, no play areas, no community centres nearby." I had noticed the lack of shops. "Shops... They belong to the old idea of streets with corners. If you want the shops you have to take a bus journey to Old Swan." I mentioned the lift not working. "No one repairs things. No one does a thing about the vandalism. Look at the graffiti on the walls. Look above you... Look, there's no lights!... As soon as they are put in they are smashed. The teenagers hang around these tower blocks in wolf packs. There's absolutely nothing for them to do at night."

That was it. She had exhausted herself in a five-minute litany of protest. The angry woman had got a lot off her 46 double-D chest. After apologising once more for the unprovoked attack on our decency, she was gone into one of the characterless front doors on the landing of the third floor.

Before we left Wingate Towers for the last time, Uncle Stan and I stood on the small, balcony leading out from my father's living room. He was right about the panoramic view he said he had of South Liverpool, looking out to Bowring Park and further south, to the golf courses surrounding the green field suburbs of Gateacre and Woolton. Unfortunately, Wingate Towers was unsafely anchored in a sea of unimaginatively laid-out council houses stretching out to junction five on the M62. Dad told me that the view was one of the few pleasant things about life on the estate. He must have been having a good day with Hilda; his mind prejudiced by blue skies, a summer sun and the occasional sip from his favourite glass of Teachers.

I looked across at my uncle. He was lost to the world; gazing out at the light drizzle which had just begun to fall. What deep and serious thoughts were stirring in that discerning mind of his? Were they travelling back to happier times before the war when Arthur and his sister, despite their poverty and fears for the future, had a marriage blessed with a lot more hope and laughter than this blighted landscape could offer his doomed and afflicted relationship with Hilda.

"Where in all of this sad ending is Hilda, Stan? Do you know?" I told him of the efforts made to contact my father's wife and said that, for all I knew, she might be dead. Hilda, however, was far from dead. Weeks after the funeral she phoned my home in Scotland, claiming that I had deliberately sidelined her from her husband's cremation and accused me of making off with my father's money. If she meant the £300 left in his TSB account, after all the expenses were met, then she was as welcome to it as she was as legally entitled. Far from letting Hilda out of his life, artful Arthur had kept secret the fact that for the past six months he had been treating his estranged wife to coffee and cakes, once a week, in town. The man was bewitched as well as bedevilled and took his obsession with him to the grave.

Standing on the balcony of the small flat at Wingate Towers, a sense of the depressing emptiness of my father's life over these last few years bore down on me. The feeling of neglect and abandonment must have been very difficult for him to have come to terms with. In 1969, five years after I had left Liverpool to teach in Scotland, he decided to make a re-appearance in my life. From that point he came regularly to see his two grandchildren while I was teaching in the Scottish Borders. Living with Hilda, in that flat in the sky, must have been like having to share a small pond with a female anaconda. Every so often the grip would become unbearable; somehow he managed to struggle out of the water and take a few quick breaths before throwing himself back in again. When he stayed with us, we could get little out of him about the past, and even less about his life, back in Liverpool with Hilda.

Uncle Stan was leaning over the balcony as the wind rose, spitting rain into his face to bring him out of his trance. He turned, visibly upset... "Oh, Stanley. What a sad end to a life... It need not have come to this." My uncle had collected his thoughts and turned to speak. "Your dad's problems went back to his own childhood and the death of his mother. She was replaced by a hard-bitten stepmother, who made it painfully obvious that her own children mattered most and were to be placed at the front of the queue for any crumbs of loving care."

"My father seemed to have a problem showing and responding to warmth and tenderness... Remember in 1976, when you, Margaret and the children arrived up in Fraserburgh, with the girls showing all that affection on seeing us again?" Uncle Stan nodded and smiled sadly. Arthur Williams had been unable to handle all the kisses and cuddles of our reunion. He brushed passed me in the kitchen with the immortal put-me-down, "I'm getting out into the garden, son... All this loving gets on my tits!"

"Your dad's tragedy was to be drawn away from the undemanding attention of a gentle, soft-hearted, caring person like your mum, by someone who replicated his childhood experience with an Ice Queen of a woman."

"My mum obviously, but also you, Nan, even Pop... You all cared for him and treated him with real affection."

"He had all the attention and understanding he desired from Nell, but he wanted pain. Well he certainly gave himself plenty of that, Stanley... We all loved your father and he knew that. In fact, Arthur played on it to torment your mother."

I asked the million pound question, "And why Hilda, do you think?"

"What did your dad see in Hilda?... Heaven only knows. At one time we thought she must have some terrible hold on him. A secret he did not want the world to know about. An illegitimate child. Something criminal, even... But no, he simply had an addiction and could not come off it."

"It must have been sex?" I put the question to my uncle in rhetorical fashion, for throughout all the years of childhood I had never been able to talk to him about such a subject. "By that, I mean a type of sex he felt he could not get from my mother."

"Despite the deaths of her two babies your mother was never a frigid person, Stan. She was a loving and affectionate woman. She was upset enough, once, to confide in me that the sex your father demanded was instant and over with in a

398

flash. He would come home and throw her down on the bed without any consideration for her deeper feelings and quiet, sensitive nature... But yes, sex was part of it and paradoxically, I think the coldness of Hilda attracted him. Perhaps there was the chill echo of his attempt to squeeze some love and attention from his stepmother... Who knows? The one thing I do know is that when the lust was gone and the passion had died down, the two of them had nothing else to offer one another."

"And look where it has ended up," I said. "In this high-rise hell. This place which would dehumanise a saint."

Uncle Stan took one, final look down at the sprawling estate below. "Your father had plenty of unwanted company in his loneliness and isolation out here, Stanley. There should be Nuremberg Trials for the architects, planners and politicians who built these high-rise ghettos. Ordinary people have enough problems to cope with in life without imposing this struggle upon them... A person should be able to live and die with a little more dignity than this in a modern, so-called civilised society."

With the funeral over, my uncle's deep sense of moral responsibility for the family and his spiritual guardianship over my life was, finally, at an end. This good and generous-hearted man, who had such a profound understanding of the strengths and weaknesses of human nature, was aware that the behaviour of individuals within the web of family life can damage or, worse still, break the tenuous threads which bind us together. Weaken just one important strand and the whole structure is threatened.

The family I belonged to survived the punishing tests of pre-war poverty and post-war betrayal because, at its heart, there were two people strong enough to draw us all together and make good the damage done when relationships failed. My Nan's contribution was her immense, peasant-like physical strength. She showed great courage and endurance in the face of the destitution brought about by a clever, but often drunken and unsupportive husband. She was the family's powerhouse that never once ran out of steam. In Uncle Stan, her doted-upon son, we had someone whose spiritual strength and moral authority, utter kindness and compassion, kept us all believing that it is the good, rather than bad within us, which must be encouraged and allowed to triumph.